INTERPERSONAL COMMUNICATION:
Evolving Interpersonal Relationships

WITHDRAWN

COMMUNICATION

A series of volumes edited by
Dolf Zillmann and Jennings Bryant

INTERPERSONAL COMMUNICATION:
Evolving Interpersonal Relationships

Edited by

Pamela J. Kalbfleisch
University of Kentucky

LEA LAWRENCE ERLBAUM ASSOCIATES, PUBLISHERS
1993 Hillsdale, New Jersey   Hove and London

Lawrence Erlbaum Associates, Inc., Publishers
365 Broadway
Hillsdale, New Jersey 07642

Library of Congress Cataloging-in-Publication Data

Interpersonal communication : evolving interpersonal relationships /
edited by Pamela J. Kalbfleisch.
    p.   cm.
Includes bibliographical references and index.
ISBN 0-8058-1260-1. — ISBN 0-8058-1297-0 (pbk.)
1. Man-woman relationships. 2. Dating (Social customs) 3. Sex
role. 4. Interpersonal communication. I. Kalbfleisch, Pamela J.
HQ801.I68 1993
305.3—dc20   92-18167
                                                        CIP

Printed in the United States of America
10 9 8 7 6 5 4 3 2

This book is dedicated to
Paul and *Marian*
and the love they share

Contents

Contributors

PETER A. ANDERSEN, Department of Speech Communication, San Diego State University, San Diego, CA 92182

LESLIE A. BAXTER, Department of Rhetoric and Communication, University of California, Davis, CA 95616

LYN BENDTSCHNEIDER, Department of Communication Studies, Miami University, Oxford, OH 45056

CONNIE BULLIS, Department of Communication, University of Utah, Salt Lake City, UT 84112

DANIEL J. CANARY, School of Interpersonal Communication, Ohio University, Athens, OH 45701

CAROLYN CLARK, Department of Communication, University of Utah, Salt Lake City, UT 84112

MICHAEL J. CODY, Department of Communication Arts and Sciences, University of Southern California, Los Angeles, CA 90089-1694

STEVE DUCK, Department of Communication Studies, University of Iowa, Iowa City, IA 52242

WILLIAM C. DONAGHY, Department of Communication and Mass Media, University of Wyoming, P.O. Box 3904, Laramie, WY 82071

SYLVIE V. ELOY, Department of Communication, University of Arizona, Tucson, AZ 85721

MARY ANNE FITZPATRICK, Department of Communication Arts, University of Wisconsin, Madison, WI 53706

LAURA K. GUERRERO, Department of Communication, University of Arizona, Tucson, AZ 85721

JEROLD L. HALE, Department of Speech Communication, University of Georgia, Athens, GA 30602

JACQUELINE D. HILLIS, Delta Airlines, Cincinnati/Northern Kentucky International Airport, P.O. Box 75027, Cincinnati, OH 45275

KRISTEN L. JOHNSON, Department of Communication Studies, Northwestern University, Evanston, IL 60208-2260

PETER F. JORGENSEN, Department of Communication, University of Arizona, Tucson, AZ 85721

PAMELA J. KALBFLEISCH, Department of Communication, University of Kentucky, Lexington, KY 40506; Center for Communication Research, P.O. Box 23440, Lexington, KY 40523

LIANA B. KOEPPEL, Department of Speech Communication, Cypress College, Cypress, CA 90630

DELL HASTINGS McKINNEY, Department of Communication and Mass Media, University of Wyoming, P.O. Box 3904, Laramie, WY 82071

PAUL A. MONGEAU, Department of Communication, Miami University, Oxford, OH 45056

YVETTE MONTAGNE-MILLER, Department of Communication Arts and Sciences, University of Southern California, Los Angeles, CA 90089-1694

DAN O'HAIR, Department of Communication Studies, Texas Tech University, Lubbock, TX 79409

WILLIAM FOSTER OWEN, Department of Communication Studies, California State University, Sacramento, 6000 J. Street, Sacramento, CA 95819

JAMES F. ROIGER, Department of Communication, University of Arizona, Tucson, AZ 85721

WILLIAM F. SHARKEY, Department of Speech, University of Hawaii at Manoa, 2560 Campus Road, George Hall 326, Honolulu, Hawaii 96822

CHRISTOPHER A. SIMMONS, Department of Rhetoric and Communication, University of California, Davis, CA 95616

RICK SLINE, Department of Communication, University of Utah, Salt Lake City, UT 84112

LAURA STAFFORD, Communication Department, Ohio State University, Columbus, OH 43210

ANDREA SWARTZ, Department of Rhetoric and Communication, University of California, Davis, CA 95616

WILLIAM W. WILMOT, Department of Interpersonal Communication, University of Montana, Missoula, MT 59812

RANDY WOOD, Department of Communication, University of Kentucky, Lexington, KY 40506

Preface

Interpersonal relationships are the core of our societal system and have been since before the dawn of civilization. Our ancestors formed associations and alliances to insure survival in a hostile environment, and passed on this need for human companionship as an integral part of our physical and emotional composition. In today's world, friends, lovers, companions, and confidants make valuable contributions to our everyday lives. Yet, there is still much that is not known about how these relationships are formed, how partners communicate in on-going relationships, how people keep their relationships together, and how they cope when they fall apart. These are the central issues addressed in this book. Primary to the focus of this work is the underlying theme of evolving interpersonal relationships from the initial encounter to the mature alliance.

Contributions in the introductory chapters of this book tackle issues such as: (a) How do people make contact for the first time? (b) What do people say or do when they are trying to begin a relationship? (c) Does it matter if a woman makes the first move? (d) Does it matter if she doesn't? (e) Is the affable smile in an initial encounter just plain friendliness, or something more? and (f) What sorts of schemata are used when sizing someone up for the first time? This research breaks new ground and appraises the ultimate question of what impact initial interactions have on further relational development.

Once people have become part of a relationship, how do they deal with life's ups and downs? The midsection of this volume concerns communication issues that confront the members of a relationship in process. The contributors for this intermediate segment analyze: (a) What sorts of events spur conflict in a relationship? (b) How do married and single people experience jealousy? (c) How is jealousy communicated when a threat is perceived? (d) How do friends use relational power to achieve influence? (e) Do friends and lovers intentionally embarrass their partners? and (f) How do members of a romantic relationship communicate with both their individual and mutual friends? Research on conflict and jealousy has been a popular area of consideration for scholars studying personal relationships. However, the chapters in this volume examine these issues from an interpersonal communication perspective. The focus here is on how conflict and jealousy are communicated to a relational partner. Other forms of communication are also considered, such as attempts by a partner to influence or embarrass, as well as investigating how friendships exist concurrently with romantic relationships. This research considers relational development as well as obstacles and barriers to evolving relationships.

Ultimately, do all good things have to come to an end? The concluding chapters probe this question. The contributors in this section consider: (a) Why some friendships are able to flourish for a lifetime while others fail, (b) turning points that lead romantic partners from passion to commitment, (c) how partners maintain their interpersonal relationships, and (d) how people use metaphors to describe the pain of relationships that are lost. The pain that is metaphorically expressed by communicators in the last of these studies helps explain the efforts by relational partners to nurture long-term commitments. Research presented in these final chapters employs innovative techniques to examine maturing and disengaging relationships. The focus of these studies is on how interpersonal relationships become committed and mature. The emphasis in this section is long-term relational maintenance, rather than prediction of eventual and unavoidable disengagement. Metaphors from terminated relationships provide an antipode to the communication of intensifying and maintaining relationships. This research provides a fresh perspective for evaluating the final status of interpersonal relationships.

The contributions in this volume should be of interest to those who study interpersonal relationships. Given the burgeoning attention close relationships have received from the fields of communication, psychology, sociology, and family studies, scholars working in these disciplines may find the treatment of communication in these relationships to be a useful heuristic for future research. Contributors present original research that uses a variety of research methods to study evolving relationships. These diverse approaches to investigating interpersonal relationships should provide a multilevel understanding of interpersonal comunication in the context of relational evolution.

ACKNOWLEDGMENTS

Summer is here as I write these acknowledgments. It's a time when we can sit outside soaking up the sun and be thankful for life itself. The sun and relaxation are even more sweet when we think of the hours spent in darkened, grubby academic offices or corners put aside in our homes, toiling to come to a better understanding of human behavior and, on the way, perhaps coming to a better understanding of ourselves. With that thought in mind, the first people I want to thank are the contributors who worked to make this book possible. It is their combined work that brings us closer to understanding interpersonal communication and human relationships. All of the contributors worked hard to make their chapters the best possible representations of their work. They kept tight deadlines and made necessary revisions without complaint. I am thankful for having gotten to know so many dedicated scholars in the process of completing this book. I would also like to thank Hollis Heimbouch and Dave Salierno for their advice during this project, Sally Vogl for helping proofread manuscripts, and Ramona Rush for her collegial support and good cheer. A special thank you goes to Jan Gierman who worked tireless hours helping me convert computer files, set up tables, draw figures, and prepare indices. In addition, I would like to thank my family for always being there for me. I appreciate their love and kindness. Finally, I would like to thank the Center for Communication Research for providing financial support for this project. Stationery, paper, photocopies, laser cartridges, and postage all add up, and this project would not have been possible without this support. Thank you all.

Pamela J. Kalbfleisch

I

INTRODUCTION AND OVERVIEW

1

Looking For a Friend and a Lover: Perspectives on Evolving Interpersonal Relationships

Pamela J. Kalbfleisch
University of Kentucky

Interpersonal relationships are the cherished ingredients of our everyday social milieu. Our friends, lovers, and those who are dear to us are irreplaceable. As Duck, Lock, McCall, Fitzpatrick, and Cayne (1984) delineated, replacing a member of a personal relationship changes the very nature of this relationship itself. These are the people for whom there are no substitutes. They are the ones we turn to in times of need, look to for comfort and companionship, and laugh, cry, and share our lives with throughout the cycle of our existence.

These unique relationships have received extensive attention recently by researchers in the combined fields of communication, psychology, sociology, and family studies. This research focus is an atypical setting, in which scholars from several sister disciplines in the social sciences are working together to understand the nature of these close relationships.

It is this very backdrop of the human relationship that is the nucleus of this book. Specifically, this book considers the fundamentally voluntary or self-selected interpersonal relationships of friends, companions, and romantic partners. These are the relationships whose members are not automatically participants as a result of their birth and kin affiliations. They are relationships that must be forged from the sometimes indifferent, and sometimes hostile social milieu. The contributors to this book consider (a) how these relationships evolve from initial interactions, (b) how they flourish and fade in the process of ongoing relationships, and (c) whether these relationships can eventually become mature affiliations that will withstand the test of time.

The underlying assumption of the work presented in the following chapters is that interpersonal communication is an essential ingredient for relational evolution. Each of these studies considers interpersonal communication in the context of the relational characteristics that they examine. This systematic investigation should contribute to a better understanding of how people accomplish the formation and development of their interpersonal relationships.

The overall theme of interpersonal communication and the evolution of interpersonal relationships is explicated in further detail in this chapter. In accomplishing this objective, individual chapters are previewed in terms of their contributions to the study of relational evolution.

Initial Interactions: Beyond Attraction

There has been substantial debate regarding the ingredients affecting our attractiveness to others and what types of people make preferable partners. Research has identified innumerable factors related to attraction and attractiveness; however, the subject that is receiving the most attention by interpersonal scholars has been the relationship between attitude similarity and attraction (cf. Bochner, 1991; Cappella & Palmer, 1990; Duck, 1976; Sunnafrank, 1991).

The debates regarding the attraction–similarity hypothesis culminated recently in a national communication journal. The basic rudiments of these arguments are presented herein. In brief, Cappella and Palmer (1992) argued that an enormous body of research in the social sciences indicates that attitude similarity is directly related to interpersonal attraction in the formation of initial relationships. Sunnafrank (1992), however, called this body of research into question. Referencing his prior research (e.g., Sunnafrank, 1983; Sunnafrank & Miller, 1981), Sunnafrank contended that once people have a chance to interact, perceived similar and dissimilar attitudes do not play an important role in interaction. Conversely, Duck and Barnes (1992) charged that similarity, and recognition of this similarity in others, is a primary component in interpersonal relationships. Additionally, Hatfield and Rapson (1992) suggested that similarity between relational partners becomes more critical when relationships mature. In this debate, these scholars were responding to a long line of research concerning similarity in attitudes or perspectives and ensuing relationship initiation and development.

Although interesting and popular, these debates regarding similarity and consequent relationship initiation leave major questions unanswered. Specifically, questions remain concerning: (a) how communicators attempt to initiate relationships in initial encounters, (b) attributions that are made during these initial interactions, and (c) resultant relational development following these initial interactions. The centrality of how attractive two people are to one another becomes lost if the interactants develop the wrong impression in an initial encounter, or if they perceive their partner to be attractive, but untrustworthy. Further, the very method by which these potential relational partners initiate initial encounters could have long-term consequences on the evolution of these interpersonal relationships. It is not argued here that the similarity and attraction research is not worthwhile or useful; what is being said is that a wide array of things can happen in initial interactions that should be considered. Mutual attraction may not be enough to form a relationship. In addition, perceptions of mutual attraction may actually create problems for future relational evolution.

The first set of chapters in this volume considers these initial interactions. These chapters suggest in part that initial interactions could be the beginning of a beautiful relationship, an exercise in frustration, or the emergence of a horrible nightmare.

The first of these chapters, by Koeppel, Montagne-Miller, O'Hair, and Cody (chapter 2), examines perceptions of sexual interest in initial interactions. They found, among several other things, that by merely initiating a conversation a female communicator could be perceived as being seductive. Meanwhile, Koeppel and her associates found that a male communicator initiating a similar conversation was more likely to be perceived as just being friendly.

McKinney and Donaghy (chapter 3) follow the Koeppel et al. study with their examination of self-disclosure and uncertainty reduction in initial interactions. They found the interactants studied used minimal verbal strategies to reduce uncertainty, and self-disclosed to their partners at only superficial levels. There were gender differences in the levels of self-disclosure and in uncertainty reduction, but overall, neither gender actively tried to obtain anything other than superficial information about their partners.

Mongeau, Hale, Johnson, and Hillis (chapter 4) accelerate the study of initial interactions to the next logical step in relational development. These researchers consider female initiation of dating. Of specific interest are Mongeau et al.'s findings concerning male perceptions of females who initiate dates, who hint about going out on dates, and who wait for the male to ask them out. As with the Koeppel et. al. study (chapter 2), the females who initiated contact were perceived as more sexually interested than those who did not. Specifically, the females who initiated dating in the Mongeau et. al. study were perceived as more promiscuous and likely to have sex on the date they initiated. These researchers draw some disturbing conclusions about the perceptions of females who initiate dates that result in tragedy, such as date rape. In light of the Koeppel et al. findings regarding simple initiation of conversations, the Mongeau et al. conclusions are particularly troubling.

Finally, Wood (chapter 5) considers the schemata used in forming initial impressions of others. By examining reactions to two different types of communicators, Wood found that observers do seem to form differing schemata for making attributions of a communicator's truthfulness. These perceptions of deceitfulness and honesty, in combination with possible perceptions of seductiveness and a failure to ask initial interactants anything more than superficial questions, lead to some interesting considerations in terms of the development of initial interactions. It is easy to see how initial interactions can go astray from the very beginning. There is obviously much more going on in initial encounters than simple attraction and attitude similarity. The chapters examining these initial contexts provide some insight regarding the initiation of relationships and the attributions inherent when only stereotypical information guides the interactants (cf. Miller, 1978).

The barriers to forming relationships that meaningfully evolve past superficial levels are considerable. However, people do get past these challenges and form interpersonal relationships. Sadly, challenges for friends and lovers do not end with the formation of a relationship. For most, the challenge of pulling a relationship together is only the first in a series of challenges confronting them as their relationships evolve.

Relationships in Process: Communication as Relational Lifeblood

Relationships in process are those relationships that have gotten past the initial stages of development and have taken root, but have not matured into longstanding relationships. The majority of research on interpersonal relationships has focused on this stage of relational evolution. This midpoint is a broad classification of relationship development. As is evident from the previous section, relationships do not always develop in a linear fashion. Simply because communicators begin an interaction does not necessarily mean that they will become friends. Accordingly, simply because a man and a woman marry does not mean their intimacy will intensify. We all know that the opposite may occur at any point along this relationship's development. Some interpersonal researchers have examined opposing forces or "dialectics" in relational development in an effort to understand how interactants deal with the "balancing act" of being part of a relationship (cf. Baxter, 1990; Rawlins, 1992).

In any event, relationships in process are the type of relationships that researchers have examined the most extensively. In addition, interpersonal communication scholars have begun adding their perspective to this dynamic stage of relational evolution. This research perspective contributes a concern for the actual communication between the members of a personal relationship. The chapters in the intermediate section of this book exemplify this approach to research by addressing several communication issues in ongoing relationships. These studies give us a perspective on how relational partners communicate about possible threats to their relationships (such as conflict and jealousy). They also examine the communication of influence, intentional embarrassment, and friendship.

The first of this set of studies is Baxter, Wilmot, Simmons, and Swartz's (chapter 6) examination of conflict events that are identified in ongoing relationships and the semantic features that distinguish them. These researchers found that relational partners do not perceive conflict "as a single, monolithic phenomenon." Instead they found 12 different types of conflict that platonic and romantic partners could identify in their relationships.

The communication of jealousy is considered in the following chapter by Guerrero, Eloy, Jorgensen, and Andersen (chapter 7). Guerrero and her associates found that females both felt and communicated more jealousy than males. Interestingly, dating couples experienced and communicated more jealousy than married couples. In discussing these findings and others, these researchers speculated that jealousy may actually decrease as the longevity and intimacy of a relationship increases.

In the chapter by Roiger (chapter 8), the extensive research tradition of influence and compliance gaining is brought to the realm of interpersonal relationships. Previously, relational scholars have overlooked the role of power and influence in these relationships; Roiger brings this research tradition to the context of friendship. Roiger found that friends, who have an imbalance in relational power, will use more verbally aggressive influence strategies than friends who are in more egalitarian relationships. Roiger suggests that inequity of relational resources may bring about more aggressive communication patterns in ongoing relationships.

In a somewhat fanciful study, Sharkey (chapter 9) considers the relational phenomena of intentional embarrassment. Among other results, Sharkey finds that relational partners embarrass each other for reasons such as to show solidarity, spice up a relationship, and save a partners "face" (get them out of a bad spot). He refutes the concept that people embarrass each other for malevolent reasons and conjectures that embarrassment may be a method relational partners use to intensify their relationship.

Finally, Bendtschneider and Duck (chapter 10) consider how couples communicate with their joint and their individual friends. The relational partners in their study reported that the move from single life to a coupled life was accompanied by the loss or reduction of intimacy with their individual friends. Furthermore, the marital partners found that they did not experience as much intimacy with their joint friends as they did with their single friends. Bendtschneider and Duck suggest that relational partners may want to make it a point to discuss the continuance of their individual friendships as they enter together into a deeper stage of relational development.

As a group, these chapters illustrate the breadth of the interaction dynamics that occur in relationships in process. The choices made by relational partners to confront relational equity, conflict, and jealousy may ultimately evolve relationships toward a deeper level of intimacy and adjustment. Displays of relational solidarity, such as the lighthearted solidarity underlying intentional embarrassment, and proactive decisions to be an active part of more than one interpersonal relationship (e.g., relational closeness with a romantic partner and with friends), may allow the relationships in process to reach some stability. Although nothing in life is guaranteed, the chapters in the following section will primarily consider relationships that have reached or are in stages of moving toward an apex of relational evolution. Specifically, these chapters examine the maturing relationship.

Maturing and Disengaging Relationships: Do All Good Things Come to an End?

Often, the final sections of books on relational communication conclude with a chapter(s) on relational termination. The chapters in these books march steadily toward their eventual destruction as the relationships built throughout the volume fall victim to the final stage of "relationship development." Fortunately, this book offers some hope to the relational traveler.

The perspective of relational evolution set forward in this volume provides an alternative to the destruction of the relationship. The final set of research chapters in this book offers a peek at the advanced stages of relational evolution. These are the maturing and long-term relationships. Many of the relationships examined in this section have withstood the test of time. They have moved from passion to commitment and embody relational maintenance and unspoken understanding.

In deference to the longstanding tradition of the books written about interpersonal relationships, the final research chapter does address the termination of relationships. However, the chapter's placement at this location does not serve as a reminder of the ultimate state of our evolving relationships. Instead it serves as the antithesis to the maturing interpersonal relationship. The pain and anguish that are clear from the metaphors describing relationships that have ended are in contrast to the joy and challenge of the relationships that endure. In reality, the final chapter on metaphors describing disengaging relationships could be placed in any of the sections of this book because relationships can always shatter.

In general, the relationships considered in the concluding chapters offer alternatives to relational destruction and alternatives to relationships stuck in the purgatory of forever being "in process" states of relationships. The first chapter in this final set considers public portrayals of enduring relationships (Kalbfleisch, chapter 11). In this chapter, Kalbfleisch examines essays written to a local newspaper by members of the community. These essays describe long-term friendships and attempt to account for why the friends have been able to stay in these special relationships for so many years. Excerpts from these essays show extraordinary intimacy and care in these relationships. One excerpt from a person, who was writing about a best friend who had died, still described this relationship as being "alive" and a relationship that would be continued later on a higher plane.

Bullis, Clark, and Sline (chapter 12) chart the progression of romantic relationships as they move from passion to commitment. In their study, Bullis and her associates had respondents indicate the turning point or points where they perceived their interpersonal relationships had undergone a change. They found, among other things, that the more turning points relational partners reported, the less satisfied they were with their relationships. It seemed that the more relational change that was perceived, the more erratic the relational evolution. These researchers speculated that the relationships with the fewer perceived turning points were those that experienced the most steady and predicable progression toward commitment.

Canary and Stafford (chapter 13) analyze the techniques relational partners use to maintain their relationships. One of the more interesting findings these researchers discovered was that the strategy of being positive about the relationship and the relational partners was strongly predictive of maintaining the characteristics of mature interpersonal relationships. Specifically, "positivity" was related to increased relational trust and promotion of mutual control in relationships. Canary and Stafford found that simple little things, like acting cheerful and avoiding criticism of the relational partner, promoted relational trust and consensus on relational control.

Finally, as promised, the chapter by Owen (chapter 14) examines the metaphors used to describe the termination of romantic relationships. Owen grouped these metaphors into three major themes of relationship termination: (a) up/down ("We were both on cloud nine, then things went bad and started going downhill"), (b) organic growth/deterioration ("I was torn to shreds"), and (c) presence/absence ("There's just a blank space where she used to be before"). These metaphors constitute the ways former romantic partners communicate about their relationships lost.

Ultimately, do all good things have to come to an end? Of course, partners die and friends and lovers are sometimes separated. So in a sense yes, good things do end. However, relationships do not have to come undone at the hands of the relational partners themselves. These concluding chapters offer the maturing long-term relationship as an alternative to a steady progression toward relational death. These mature relationships may well be the final stages of an evolving interpersonal relationship. The uniqueness of these special relationships is easily understood when considering the difficulty in maintaining increasingly more intimate relationships over time.

Summary

The research described in this chapter offers a contemporary perspective for the study of interpersonal relationships. These contributors combine the research on interpersonal communication with the study of relationships to add to our understanding of these unique human relationships. The contributions in this volume are placed in the context of the evolving interpersonal relationship. The chapters chart this evolution from the bumpy initial interactions, through relationships in process, to the potential for longstanding maturing interpersonal relationships. It is acknowledged that relational partners may not progress from one stage to another and that a relationship may stay in one stage indefinitely. However, the perspective illustrated by the body of work presented suggests it is possible for relational partners to maintain their relationships over time with increasing uniqueness and intimacy.

REFERENCES

Bochner, A. P. (1991). On the paradigm that would not die. In J. A. Anderson (Ed.), *Communication yearbook* (Vol. 14, pp. 484–491). Newbury Park, CA: Sage.

Baxter, L. A. (1990). Dialectical contradictions in relational development. *Journal of Social and Personal Relationships, 7,* 69–88.

Cappella, J. N., & Palmer, M. T. (1990). Attitude similarity, relational history, and attraction: The mediating effects of kinesic and vocal behaviors. *Communication Monographs, 57,* 161–183.

Cappella, J. N., & Palmer, M. T. (1992). The effect of partners' conversation on the association between attitude similarity and attraction. *Communication Monographs, 59,* 180–189.

Duck, S. (1976). Interpersonal communication in developing acquaintance. In G. R. Miller (Ed.), *Explorations in interpersonal communication* (pp. 127–148). Beverly Hills, CA: Sage.

Duck, S., & Barnes, M. K. (1992). Disagreeing about agreement: Reconciling differences about similarity. *Communication Monographs, 59,* 199–208.

Duck, S., Lock, A., McCall, G., Fitzpatrick, M. A., & Cayne, J. C. (1984). Social and personal relationships: A joint editorial. *Journal of Social and Personal Relationships, 1,* 1–10.

Hatfield, E., & Rapson, R. L. (1992). Similarity and attraction in close relationships. *Communication Monographs, 59,* 209–212.

Miller, G. R. (1978). The current status of theory and research in interpersonal communication. *Human Communication Research, 4,* 164–178.

Rawlins, W. K. (1992). *Friendship Matters: Communication, dialectics, and the life course.* New York: Aldine De Gruyter.

Sunnafrank, M. (1983). Attitude similarity and interpersonal attraction in communication processes: In pursuit of an ephemeral influence. *Communication Monographs, 50,* 273–284.

Sunnafrank, M. (1991). Interpersonal attraction and attitude similarity: A communication-based assessment. In J. A. Anderson (Ed.), *Communication yearbook 14* (pp. 451–483). Newbury Park, CA: Sage.

Sunnafrank, M. (1992). On debunking the attitude similarity myth. *Communication Monographs, 59,* 164–179.

Sunnafrank, M., & Miller, G. R. (1981). The role of initial conversations in determining attraction to similar and dissimilar strangers. *Human Communication Research, 8,* 16–25.

II

INITIAL INTERACTION

2

Friendly? Flirting? Wrong?

Liana B. Koeppel
Cypress College

Yvette Montagne-Miller
University of Southern California

Dan O'Hair
Texas Tech University

Michael J. Cody[1]
University of Southern California

Ten years ago, the topic of flirting would produce smiles, laughter, and even sneers from audience members in communication and psychology. The pop books on "body language" had done little more than confirm in the minds of the public that nonverbal communication is a trivial area; also, the pop books of the 1980s fueled simplistic and unsubstantiated beliefs about flirting. Indeed, only months before the Clarence Thomas–Anita Hill hearings (and the rape trials of William Kennedy Smith and Mike Tyson) forced most Americans to grapple with issues of sexual harassment, male–female relations, and date-rape, Louise Lague (1990) published an article, "Flirting For the Fun of It" in *Glamour* that likened flirting to a sport: Flirting can be as satisfying as a workout for the mind, and a boost for the ego. Some of the advice included: "If you don't mean anything by it, people know you don't mean anything by it" (p. 243), and, "Flirting is pure pleasure, like eating ice cream, but unlike most indulgences, it's a pleasure that gives pleasure" (p. 300). Simplistic? Yes. Also potentially dangerous.

Ten years ago, the publication of Antonia Abbey's (1982) work raised the awareness that males generally construe the world in more sexual terms than do females, and indicated that, as a group, men were much more likely than females to judge "friendly" behavior as "seductive" or "promiscuous" behavior. Further, work by Charlene Muehlenhard (Muehlenhard, Koralewski, Andrews,

---

[1]Inquiries regarding additional information on this chapter should be directed to Michael J. Cody.

& Burdick, 1986; Muehlenhard & McFall, 1981; Muehlenhard, Miller, & Burdick, 1983) was, in part, predicated on the view that some women may not be very competent in flirting effectively, and women would benefit both from training and from understanding why certain cues were misperceived (see especially, Muehlenhard et al., 1986). The literature on flirting is no longer a laughing matter: Flirting effectiveness, flirting error, flirting misperceptions, and consequences deserve systematic study.

CHAPTER OUTLINE AND OVERVIEW

There are three sections to this chapter. The first section introduces the reader to the published literature on flirting and identifies the nonverbal behaviors that should differentiate between different types of interactions: control ("normal"), friendly, flirtatious, and seductive. A brief description of our main study is provided. The second section presents results of the study, and the third section details implications concerning long-term relational maintenance, and outlines further research.

In our main study, college students viewed one of eight interactions of a male and a female conversing outside a professor's office. Half of the interactions were initiated by the male; the other half were initiated by the female. Three basic hypotheses (H) were examined, given (a) the sex of the initiator, (b) the level of intimacy of the interaction, and (c) the sex of the observer (see Section I for rationale):

H_1: Both male and female interactants will be rated significantly more "seductive" in the "seductive" interactions than in the "control, "friendly," or "flirting" interactions;

H_2: Females who initiate the interaction will be perceived as more "seductive" than males who initiate the conversation;

H_3: Male observers will rate both the male and the female interactants significantly more "seductive" than female observers (i.e., males naturally and instinctively construe the world in more sexual terms than do females).

However, it is also clear that not *all* males might react so quickly in judging the behavior of others in sexual terms. Also, it would probably be simplistic to believe that all female observers are equally innocent in *not* judging the behaviors of others in sexual terms. But, what individual difference variables are closely aligned to misperceiving sexual intent? One common belief on college campuses (indeed it is taught by some staff at the University of Southern California to the sorority houses) is that competitive, intense, muscular men ("mesomorphs") are more likely to misperceive flirtatious intent and engage in date rape. Without stereotyping all mesomorph males as potential rapists, we argue that we need to look directly at the role of traditional personality constructs that might account in some way for misperceptions directly related to flirting; beliefs that predictably affect how observers process information and react to communication encounters.

Beliefs concerning flirting represent central aspects of a person's "mental model" concerning male–female relations and sexual encounters. Although little previous literature on this matter is available, we believe that there are three commonly held cultural beliefs concerning flirting: *Flirting as Common Fun* (as reflected in popular articles in *Glamour* and the like); *Flirting as Reflecting Uncontrollable Sexual Urges* (as reflected [we presume] in a good deal of pornography); and *Flirting as Invitation* (as reflected in sexist beliefs that men should take action when they believe others are flirting with them, that women want men to sweep them off their feet, and so on). Obviously, people who endorse these beliefs concerning flirting are likely to make certain inferences concerning seductiveness and promiscuity than people who do not endorse these beliefs.

Indeed, two obvious models relating beliefs to judgments of seductiveness and promiscuity can be offered. First, and more simplistic, is the model that posits that cognitive scripts concerning sexual encounters and "the come on" can be activated by very rudimentary cues. The mere fact that a male and a female are alone together and the female initiates the conversation might be sufficient evidence for a person who believes that flirting reflects uncontrollable sexual urges, or flirting reflects invitation, to characterize the event in sexual terms. Once a "come-on" script is activated, such an observer may scan the interaction searching for cues supporting the interpretation of a "seductive" encounter. If this general model is true, such observers may pay little attention to the variables manipulated in our videotapes of friendly, flirting, and seductive encounters, and they may perceive a good deal of seductiveness (coyness, tension, etc.), in order to create an image of female seductiveness.

On the other hand, observers who adopt certain beliefs concerning flirting may be more strongly affected as they process the nonverbal cues indicative of friendliness and seductiveness (see Section I for literature review). That is, when a conversation between a male and a female is normal, observers might rate perceived seductiveness low regardless of beliefs about flirting, and regardless of who initiated the conversation. However, when interactants are portrayed in a friendly interaction (smiling, nodding, leaning forward, etc.), certain observers might take evidence of friendliness to also suggest seductiveness and promiscuity (as implied in Abbey's [1982] earlier research). Evidence in support of this model would stem from the fact that certain beliefs (sexual urges, invitation) would be related to elevated ratings of female seductiveness for several (but not all) of the videotaped conversations (i.e., significant interaction effects between levels of intimacy [characterized in the tapes] with beliefs concerning flirting).

The following section reviews the literature concerning gender differences in friendly and flirting behaviors. After reviewing this literature, we describe our main study and then present results concerning how both the male and female interactants were perceived in regard to seductiveness, as well as in regard to ratings of intimacy/liking and immediacy (in order to provide a general framework for reactions to the videotaped presentations). A summary, complete with implications and directions for future research, follows.

GENDER DIFFERENCES IN PERCEPTIONS OF SEXUAL INTEREST

Previous Research

The examination of perceptions and misperceptions of friendly versus flirting behavior has been increasing over the last several years. Abbey's (1982, 1987) research in particular suggests that misinterpretations of a female's friendly behavior seems to be fairly common. As we have seen in recent news headlines, these misperceptions of behavior can be extremely problematic for both males and females. In addition to the legal and moral implications of sexual harassment and date rape, the examination of misperceptions in this area has important implications for such applied and theoretical areas as attraction, sex-role socialization, and relational development.

In her seminal work, Abbey (1982) examined whether males were more likely than females to misperceive females' friendliness as sexual interest. She had participants talk in a male–female dyad while other participants unobtrusively observed the interaction. Findings indicated that males were more likely to rate females as being more promiscuous and seductive. Later works by Abbey and her colleagues (Abbey, 1987; Abbey, Cozzarelli, McLaughlin, & Harnish, 1987; Abbey & Melby, 1986) further examined the role of various nonverbal cues in the perceptions and attributions of seductiveness including: distance, eye contact, touch, and clothing. Much of this research confirmed that males were more likely to perceive the interaction in more sexual terms than females. Additionally, this research indicated that females' behavior was viewed as more sexual or promiscuous than male behavior. For instance, Abbey and Melby (1986) found that female initiated touch was perceived to be a stronger indicator of the relationship than male touch, and females' revealing clothing were rated as more seductive than males' revealing clothing (Abbey et al., 1987).

Other research further examines the differences in perceptions between male and female behavior. Shotland and Craig (1988) examined whether males and females could distinguish between friendly versus sexual behavior, as well as whether males were more likely to attribute sexual intent than females. Their results found that, not only could males and females differentiate between the two types of behaviors, but also concurred with Abbey's research regarding males perceptions of sexual intent. Saal, Johnson, and Weber (1989) also examined perceptions of gender differences in behaviors and found, in three separate studies, that men perceive less friendliness and more seductiveness.

Sigal, Gibbs, Adams, and Derfler (1988) also examined gender differences in the perception of friendly/seductive behavior specifically in terms of the nonverbal cues: eye contact, distance, tone of voice, touching and smiling. Although this study confirmed Shotland and Craig's (1988) findings that individuals could distinguish between friendly and seductive behavior, they found no differences between male and female ratings of seductiveness that contradicts previous research. The authors suggest that methodological differences may account for the contradictions in their results. They argue that Abbey's studies did not have actors engage in typical sexual or friendly behavior, which may have resulted in cues being unclear. Additionally, Abbey and Melby (1986) and Abbey et al. (1987) utilized photographs as opposed to actual interactions.

A potential problem with much of this previous research may be the lack of standardized interaction between the actors viewed by respondents. It is unclear how variations in both verbal and nonverbal channels of the actors may have influenced the results, particularly in the findings that indicate higher seductiveness ratings for female actors. Especially troublesome is the fact that the one study, which contradicts the previous findings regarding gender differences, is the only one to standardize conditions.

Our main study used a standardized script across all treatment conditions in order to focus the study on manipulated nonverbal cues and gender differences. Additionally, we manipulated multiple nonverbal cues in order to utilize a more gestalt approach. A multichannel approach to studying nonverbal cues can overcome methodological problems of single nonverbal channels (Schwartz, Foa, & Foa, 1983; Siegman & Feldstein, 1987). Schwartz et al. (1983) suggested that using one nonverbal cue can cause ambiguity and that it often takes a combination of channels together to clarify meanings. Additionally, it is more likely to correspond with behavior that individuals are likely to use naturally in real situations.

Nonverbal Behaviors Associated with Friendly, Flirtatious, and Seductive Interactions

Given the discrepancies in some of the previous research and the lack of standardization of manipulations of treatments, our main study was designed to examine the perceptions of nonverbal behaviors associated with friendly, flirtatious, and seductive interactions. We first surveyed nonverbal research to determine which cues were associated with friendly, flirtatious, and seductive behaviors. We decided to focus on the nonverbal areas of kinesics (movement), haptics (touch), proxemics (distance), oculesics (eye movement), and vocalics (voice). Appropriate nonverbal cues were assigned to one of four treatments: control (or normal), friendly, flirting, or seductive interactions.

Kinesics. Body movements, particularly smiling and body posture, are seen as indicants of friendly, flirting, and seductive behaviors. Research indicates that the amount of smiling varies along a continuum: (a) a small amount of smiling for friendly behavior (Andersen, 1985; Muehlenhard et al., 1986; Sigal et al., 1988; Walsh & Hewitt, 1985), (b) medium to large amounts of smiling for flirting behavior (Coker & Burgoon, 1987; Muehlenhard et al., 1986), and (c) constant smiling in seductive interactions (Andersen, 1985; Coker & Burgoon, 1987; Muehlenhard et al., 1986; Sigal et al., 1988; Walsh & Hewitt, 1985). Friendly versus seductive behavior is also characterized by differing degrees of body relaxation—the more relaxed, the more seductive (Schwartz et al., 1983). Finally, flirting behavior is characterized by the use of childlike expressions, open mouth (pouting) and head tilting (Burgoon, Buller, & Woodall, 1989).

Haptics. The use of touch is a common form of communication, particularly in terms of indicating the nature of a relationship. Friendly behaviors are characterized by very little to no touch (Abbey & Melby, 1986; Andersen, 1985; Muehlenhard et al., 1986; Perper & Weis, 1987; Sigal et al., 1988). On the other hand, moderate amounts of touch indicate a flirtatious interaction (Abbey & Melby, 1986; Muehlenhard et al., 1986), whereas touching the hand or leg represents seductive behavior (Abbey & Melby, 1986; Andersen, 1985; Burgoon et al., 1989; Muehlenhard et al., 1986; Perper & Weis, 1987; Sigal et al., 1988). Another sign of seductive behavior is the use of clothing adjustments (i.e., playing with buttons, smoothing skirt, adjusting pants) and self-touch (Burgoon et al., 1989).

Proxemics. The amount of personal distance between interactants also varies depending on the type of interaction. The greater the amount of distance between interactants, the less seductive the interaction (Abbey & Melby, 1986; Coker & Burgoon, 1987; Muehlenhard et al., 1986; Patterson & Edinger, 1987; Perper & Weis, 1987; Schwartz et al., 1983; Sigal et al., 1988). Body orientation and physical planes have also been shown to indicate different degrees of friendliness/seductiveness. Individuals who lean toward one another and who are at the same body angle are perceived as being more seductive than those individuals who lean away from each other (Andersen, 1985). Finally, flirtatious behavior is further characterized by crossing legs toward one another (Burgoon et al., 1989; Muehlenhard et al., 1986), and more face to face interaction (Burgoon et al., 1989).

Oculesics. The amount and type of eye contact/movements are also indicants of the type of interaction. Friendly behavior exhibits little to moderate eye contact, flirtatious behavior uses moderate degrees of eye contact, and seductive behaviors are characterized by constant eye contact (Abbey & Melby, 1986; Andersen, 1985; Burgoon et al., 1989; Coker & Burgoon, 1987; Muehlenhard et al., 1986; Perper & Weis, 1987; Schwartz et al., 1983; Sigal et al., 1988; Walsh & Hewitt, 1985). In addition, flirtatious behavior includes demure glances downward (Burgoon et al., 1989).

Vocalics. The use of the voice is one of the most telling indicators of the type of interaction. General friendly interactions utilize a neutral tone of voice (Muehlenhard et al., 1986; Perper & Weis, 1987; Sigal et al., 1988), are less fluent (Andersen, 1985), exhibit decreased amounts of laughter, and more silences and less warmth (Coker & Burgoon, 1987). Flirtatious behaviors utilize animated speech (Muehlenhard et al., 1986), moderate amounts of laughter (Coker & Burgoon, 1987; Perper & Weis, 1987), decreased silences/latencies, and increased warmth and interest (Coker & Burgoon, 1987). Finally, seductive interaction is characterized by an intimate tone of voice (Coker & Burgoon, 1987; Muehlenhard et al., 1986; Perper & Weis, 1987; Sigal et al., 1988), increased laughter (Coker & Burgoon, 1987; Muehlenhard et al., 1986), greater fluency, less silence, and greater warmth (Andersen, 1985; Coker & Burgoon, 1987). See Table 2.1 for a complete array of these nonverbal behaviors across friendly, flirting, and seductive interactions.

METHOD

Subjects. Three hundred thirty-nine undergraduate college students (144 male, 195 female) from various southwestern colleges and universities were shown one of eight different videotapes depicting a conversation between a male and female student waiting outside a professor's office. Subjects were chosen from randomly selected classes and divided into different groups.

Procedure. Eight videotapes of a scripted interaction were made, utilizing two volunteer actors. The interaction involved a male and a female student who meet outside a professor's office and strike up a conversation. In each of the interactions, the dialogue was standardized and no references made to specific gender. Efforts were made to avoid either interactant engaging in "typically male" or "typically female" language use.

The interactions varied in two ways: nonverbal behavior and gender of initiator. There were four levels of relationships exhibited through nonverbal cues: (a) Control-which was void of any type of behavior previously characterized, (b) Friendly, (c) Flirting, and (d) Seductive. The interaction at each

TABLE 2.1.
Nonverbal Dimensions of Friendly, Flirting, and Seductive Behavior

DIMENSION	FRIENDLY DYAD	FLIRTING DYAD	SEDUCTIVE DYAD
KINESICS	*Small Amount of Smiling* - Andersen (1985) - Muehlenhard et al. (1986) - Sigal et al. (1988) - Walsh & Hewitt (1985)	*Med/Large Smiling* - Coker & Burgoon (1987) - Muehlenhard et al. (1986)	*Constant Smiling* - Andersen (1985) - Coker & Burgoon (1987) - Muehlenhard et al. (1986) - Schwartz et al. (1983) - Sigal et al. (1988) - Walsh & Hewitt (1985)
	Body Relaxation - Schwartz et al. (1983)	*Open Mouth/Pout* - Burgoon et al. (1989) *Childlike Expression* - Burgoon et al. (1989) *Head Tilt* - Burgoon et al. (1989)	*Body Relaxation* - Schwartz et al. (1983) *Expose Skin/Protrude Chest* - Burgoon et al. (1989)
HAPTICS	*No Touch* - Abbey & Melby (1986) - Anderson (1985) - Muehlenhard et al. (1986) - Perper & Weis (1987) - Sigal et al. (1988)	*Moderate Touch* - Abbey & Melby (1986) - Muehlenhard et al. (1986)	*Touch on Hand/Leg* - Abbey & Melby (1986) - Andersen (1985) - Burgoon et al. (1989) - Muehlenhard et al. (1986) - Perper & Weis (1987) - Sigal et al. (1988) *Adjust Clothing/Self-touch* - Burgoon et al. (1989)
PROXEMICS	*Farther Away* - Abbey & Melby (1986) - Coker & Burgoon (1987) - Muehlenhard et al. (1986) - Patterson & Edinger (1987) - Perper & Weis (1987)	*Moderately Close* - Abbey & Melby (1986) - Burgoon et al. (1989) - Coker & Burgoon (1987) - Muehlenhard et al. (1986)	*Very Close* - Abbey & Melby (1986) - Coker & Burgoon (1987) - Muehlenhard et al. (1986) - Patterson & Edinger (1987) - Perper & Weis (1987)

Body Orientation/Physical Planes
- Andersen (1985)

Constant Eye Contact
- Abbey & Melby (1987)
- Andersen (1985)
- Burgoon et al. (1989)
- Coker & Burgoon (1987)
- Muehlenhard et al. (1986)
- Perper & Weis (1987)
- Schwartz et al. (1983)
- Sigal et al. (1988)
- Walsh & Hewitt (1985)

Intimate Tone of Voice
- Coker & Burgoon (1987)
- Muehlenhard (1986)
- Perper & Weis (1987)
- Sigal et al. (1988)

Greater Fluency/Little Silence
- Andersen (1985)
- Coker & Burgoon (1987)

Increased Laughter
- Coker & Burgoon (1987)
- Muehlenhard et al. (1986)

Face to Face Positions
- Burgoon et al. (1989)

Body Orientation/Physical Planes
- Burgoon et al. (1989)

Cross Legs Toward Each Other
- Burgoon et al. (1989)
- Muehlenhard et al. (1986)

Moderate Eye Contact
- Coker & Burgoon (1987)
- Muehlenhard et al. (1986)

Glance Down/Demure
- Burgoon et al. (1989)

Animated Speech
- Muehlenhard et al. (1986)

Decreased Silences/Latencies
- Coker & Burgoon (1987)

Moderate Laughter
- Coker & Burgoon (1987)
- Perper & Weis (1987)

Increased Warmth/Interest
- Coker & Burgoon (1987)

- Schwartz et al. (1983)
- Sigal et al. (1988)

Body Orientation/Physical Planes
- Andersen (1985)

OCULESICS

Little to Moderate Eye Contact
- Abbey & Melby (1986)
- Andersen (1985)
- Coker & Burgoon (1987)
- Muehlenhard et al. (1986)
- Patterson & Edinger (1987)
- Perper & Weis (1987)
- Schwartz et al. (1983)
- Sigal et al. (1988)

VOCALICS

Neutral Tone of Voice
- Muehlenhard et al. (1986)
- Perper & Weis (1987)
- Sigal et al. (1988)

Less Fluency
- Andersen (1985)

Decreased Laughter
- Coker & Burgoon (1987)

More Silences/Less Warmth
- Coker & Burgoon (1987)

of these levels was initiated by both the male and female actor. Thus, eight different variations of the same conversation were created.

After viewing the interaction, observers completed a questionnaire containing several sections. First, they completed items that measured Burgoon's relational dimensions for both the male and female interactant (Burgoon, Buller, Hale, & deTurck, 1984; Burgoon et al., 1989); we focus attention on two of these dimensions in the present analyses: Intimacy/liking (alpha = .838, for female; .848 for male), and Immediacy (alpha = .850, for female; .872 for male). The five Burgoon et al. (1984) intimacy/liking items (which included references to both the male and female actors) were:

1. The woman didn't care if the man liked her.
2. The woman was attracted to the man.
3. The woman wanted the discussion to be intimate.
4. The woman wanted the man to trust her.
5. The woman was interested in talking to the man.

The five immediacy items (Burgoon et al., 1984) were:

1. The woman was bored by the conversation.
2. The woman was intensely involved in the conversation.
3. The woman was very unemotional.
4. The woman made the conversation seem distant.
5. The woman communicated coldness rather than warmth.

Embedded randomly among the Burgoon items were seven items measuring levels of "seductiveness" (alpha = .911, for female; and .909 for male):

1. The woman was sexually interested in the man.
2. The woman was trying to "pick-up" the man.
3. The woman was being promiscuous.
4. The woman was being very seductive.
5. The woman was being flirtatious.
6. The woman was aroused by the man.
7. The woman wanted to appear sexy.

The last section of the questionnaire included the items used for measuring beliefs about flirting. The latter items appear in Table 2.2. The belief items are self-explanatory. The *sexual urges* belief includes the idea that people cannot control their emotions, and that true sexual desires "leak out." The *common fun* belief includes the idea that flirting is common fun, harmless, and that

TABLE 2.2.
Flirting Beliefs Scale

Flirting as Uncontrollable Sexual Urges (alpha = .705)

1. Most people are not aware of how their true sexual desires nonverbally "leak out" of their bodies.
2. People don't realize the amount of sexual cues they send off.
3. People do not realize how strong the sexual motive influences their behavior everyday.
4. In today's society, people have to be careful about flirting.
5. Many people give off mixed signals; first they flirt, and then try to deny it.
6. I ignore some flirting I see because people are not often in control of their emotions.
7. Most TV shows I watch (situation comedies, soap operas, and so forth) involve people who are flirting.
8. Flirting always has sexual meanings.

Flirting as Common Fun (alpha = .711)

1. Most women I know flirt frequently.
2. When men and women get together for social gatherings, there will always be flirting.
3. Most men I know flirt frequently.
4. I like to meet exciting, sexy people (of the opposite gender).
5. I have to admit that I like to flirt.
6. People of the opposite sex flirt with me at nearly every party I attend.
7. I have to admit that I flirt whenever the opportunity presents itself.
8. I think I am a good flirter.
9. Flirting is harmless fun.
10. I frequently attend parties or social gatherings where people flirt.

Flirting as Invitation (alpha = .797)

1. Once a person flirts with you, you should take strong confident action before their feelings change and you miss an opportunity.
2. Flirting is a public way of expressing a commitment to another person.
3. You should reciprocate flirting (flirt back when someone flirts with you) when you are certain that s/he is definitely flirting with you.
4. Serious flirting is a nonverbal way of saying "yes" to a conversation or a date.
5. The best way for a male to impress a female in a flirting situation is to show confidence and strong action.
6. Most females would be disappointed if a male didn't take charge of a flirting situation.
7. Despite how our society is changing, it is still up to the male to take control in initiating relationships.
8. In flirting situations, it is the role of the male to take the initiative.

everyone engages in the behavior. The *invitation* orientation includes the idea that people (especially males) should take action when they perceive others are flirting. This last section of the questionnaire also included questions concerning previous mistakes in flirting ("I have been in situations where someone thought I was flirting, but I wasn't," and "I have been in situations where I thought someone was flirting with me but they weren't"), and dating frequency ("How many dates have you had during the average month for the last year?")

Table 2.3 presents the correlations between the three beliefs with date fre-

TABLE 2.3.
Correlations Between Beliefs, Dating Frequency,
and Self-Reported Mistakes in Flirting

	Sexual Urges	Common Fun	Invitation	Date Frequency	Previous Mistakes
Sexual Urges	1.000				
Common Fun	.378**	1.000			
Invitation	.335*	.177**	1.000		
Date Frequency	−.096	.026	−.036	1.000	
Previous Mistakes	.303**	.292**	.109*	−.073	1.000

*$p < .05$. **$p < .001$.

quency and the self-report on previous mistakes. Although none of the beliefs were correlated with frequency of dating, the self-report of mistakes in flirting were significantly associated with each belief, especially the belief that flirting reflects *sexual urges* ($r = .303$) and *common fun* ($r = .292$). Not surprisingly, the belief that flirting reflects *sexual urges* is correlated with both other beliefs, but the belief that flirting is *invitation* is only weakly associated with the belief that flirting is *common fun* (see Table 2.3). The gender of the observer was not related to either the belief that flirting reflects *sexual urges* ($M = 5.07$ for males; $M = 5.09$, for females [$p = .761$]) or the belief that flirting is *common fun* ($M = 5.04$ for males; $M = 4.98$ for females [$p = .565$]). Males, however, were more likely to adopt the belief that flirting is *invitation* ($M = 4.05$), relative to women ($M = 3.58$) ($t(337) = 4.43, p = .001$).

RESULTS

First, we present results bearing on the basic expectations concerning how both the female interactant and the male interactant were perceived in regard to seductiveness, intimacy/likability, and immediacy as a function of sex of initiator, sex of observer, and level of intimacy reflected in the interaction. The impact of individual difference variables on the observers is presented in the subsequent section.

Basic Expectations: Perceptions of the Female Interactant

Seductiveness. Ratings of the woman's "seductiveness" were significantly affected by levels of intimacy $F(3, 326) = 41.61, p = .001$), sex of initiator $F(1, 326) = 138.57, p = .001$), sex of observer $F(1, 326) = 5.58$,

TABLE 2.4.
Perceptions of Seductiveness, Intimacy/Liking and Immediacy
of the Female Interactant as a Function of Level of Intimacy
in the Interaction and Sex of Initiator

| | | Type of Interaction | | | |
		Control	Friendly	Flirtatious	Seductive
Seductive	FI	3.82	3.49	4.19	5.01
	MI	1.97	1.59	2.60	4.25
Intimate	FI	5.07	4.69	5.40	5.54
	MI	2.30	2.08	3.80	4.84
Immediate	FI	5.22	5.17	5.91	5.80
	MI	2.33	2.51	4.35	5.06

$p = .019$), the interaction of levels of intimacy and sex of initiator $F(3, 326)$ = 3.92, $p = .009$), and the interaction of sex of initiator and sex of observers $F(3, 326) = 6.24, p = .013$). Table 2.4 presents the general ratings for each variable for female interactant both when the male is the initiator (MI) and when the female is the initiator (FI).

When the male was the initiator of the conversation, the female interactant was rated extremely low in seductiveness during the control interaction ($M = 1.97$), the friendly interaction ($M = 1.59$), and the flirting interaction ($M = 2.60$), and received relatively high ratings of seductiveness when the male initiator behaved in a seductive fashion ($M = 4.25$) (see Table 2.4). The female initiator was rated as somewhat seductive even when engaged in the control encounter ($M = 3.82$) and the friendly encounter ($M = 3.49$). When initiating a flirtatious encounter, she was rated as more seductive ($M = 4.19$), and she was rated as significantly higher when actually engaging in the seductive encounter ($M = 5.01$).

Male observers rated the woman significantly higher in seductiveness ($M = 3.53$) than did female observers ($M = 3.34$); however, the sex of initiator × sex of observer interaction revealed that male observers were significantly more likely to rate the female as seductive when she was the initiator ($M = 4.45$) than when the male was the initiator ($M = 2.60$). Female observers did not rate the female quite as seductive when she was the initiator ($M = 3.89$), or when the male was the initiator ($M = 2.48$).

Intimacy/Liking. Ratings of female's level of intimacy/liking were significantly related to levels of intimacy $F(3, 326) = 57.57, p = .001$, sex of initiator $F(3, 326) = 386.30, p = .001$, the interaction of levels of intimacy and sex of initiator $F(3, 326) = 22.44, p = .001$), and sex of initiator and sex of observer $F(3, 326) = 4.34, p = .038$). As in the case with seductiveness, the female interactant was perceived equally low in intimacy/liking during the less intimate interactions (Ms = 2.30, 2.08), when the male was the initiator. When the male flirted, the female was rated slightly higher in intimacy/liking (M = 3.80), and was rated as fairly high on intimacy/liking when the male initiated a seductive encounter (M = 4.84). The female was rated relatively high on intimacy/liking merely by the fact that she initiated the conversation (see Table 2.4). The female initiator was rated equally high on intimacy/liking when she either initiated the flirtatious encounter (M = 5.40) or when she was seductive (M = 5.54).

When the male was the initiator, there was no difference between the female interactant's ratings of intimacy/liking by male (M = 3.22) or female (M = 3.11); however, male observers rated the female higher in intimacy/liking when the female was the initiator (M = 5.28) than did the female observer (M = 5.09).

Immediacy. There was a significant effect due to levels of intimacy $F(3, 326) = 54.28, p = .001)$, sex of initiator $F(3, 326) = 346.34, p = .001)$, and significant levels of intimacy $F(3, 326) = 21.38, p = .001)$. The female initiator was rated higher in immediacy, especially during either the flirtatious interaction (M = 5.91) and the seductive interaction (M = 5.80). When the male was the initiator, the female was rated low in immediacy when the interaction was less intimate, but she was rated higher after both the flirtatious interaction (M = 4.35) and the seductive interaction (M = 5.06).

Basic Expectations: Perceptions of Male Interactants

Seductiveness. There was a significant effect for levels of intimacy $F(3, 326) = 71.92, p = .001)$, sex of initiator $F(1, 326) = 148.30, p = .001)$, sex of observer $F(1, 326) = 7.55, p = .006)$, and significant interaction effects for levels of intimacy $\times$ sex of initiator $F(3, 326) = 7.90, p = .001)$, and levels of intimacy $\times$ sex of observer $F(1, 326) = 2.60, p = .052)$. Table 2.5 presents the breakdown for the levels $\times$ sex of initiator breakdown. When the male was the initiator, the male was perceived as somewhat seductive (Ms = 3.89, 4.33, 4.46) at low levels of intimacy in the interaction, and was rated fairly high in seductiveness when he was, in fact, engaged in the seductive encounter (M = 5.37). When the female was the initiator, the male received very low ratings of seductiveness at the less intimate levels of interaction (Ms = 2.09, 2.34 [see table 5]), but ratings of male seductiveness increased when the female initiator was flirtatious (M = 3.42), and when the female initiated a seductive interaction (M = 4.78).

Interpretation of the sex of observer $\times$ levels of intimacy interaction revealed that at the highest level of intimacy, the "seductive" interaction, the male interactant was rated highly seductive by both male (M = 5.00) and female

TABLE 2.5.
Perceptions of Seductiveness, Intimacy/Liking and Immediacy
of the Male Interactant as a Function of Level of Intimacy
in the Interaction and Sex of Initiator

| | | Type of Interaction | | | |
		Control	Friendly	Flirtatious	Seductive
Seductive	FI	2.09	2.34	3.42	4.78
	MI	3.89	4.33	4.46	5.37
Intimate	FI	2.41	2.77	4.29	5.02
	MI	5.55	5.75	5.47	5.73
Immediate	FI	2.46	2.98	4.89	5.24
	MI	5.20	5.90	5.68	5.83

($M = 5.07$) observers. However, at all other levels of intimacy, males rated the male interactant as more seductive than female observers: after the control interaction ($M = 3.36$ [male observers], $M = 2.71$ [female observers]), after the friendly interaction ($M = 3.57$ [male observers], $M = 2.88$ [female observers]), and after the flirtatious interaction ($M = 4.13$ [male observers], $M = 3.63$ [female observers]).

Intimacy/Liking. There was a significant effect for levels of intimacy $F(93, 326) = 52.35, p = .001$), sex of initiator $F(1, 326) = 449.30, p = .001$), and significant interactions for levels of intimacy × sex of initiator $F(3, 326) = 35.67, p = .001$) and levels of intimacy × sex of observer $F(3, 326) = 3.05, p = .029$). The male interactant received high ratings of intimacy/liking merely by being the initiator (see Table 2.5; Ms 5.55 to 5.75). When the female initiated the interaction, the male was rated low in intimacy/liking in the less intimate interactions, and received higher ratings of intimacy as the level of intimacy in the interaction increased.

Interpretation of the sex of observer × level of interaction effect indicated that at the highest level of intimacy, the seductive encounter, the male interactant was rated equally high in intimacy/liking by both male ($M = 5.25$) and female ($M = 5.38$) observers. However, in all other interactions, male observers rated the male interactant higher in intimacy/liking than did female observers: after the control conversations ($M = 4.30$ [male observers], $M = 3.71$ [female observers]), after the friendly conversation ($M = 4.24$ [male observers], $M = 3.82$ [female observers]), and after flirtatious conversation ($M = 4.94$ [male observers], $M = 4.65$ [female observers]).

Immediacy. There was a significant effect for levels of intimacy $F(3, 326) = 55.69, p = .001$), sex of initiator $F(1, 326) = 254.92, p = .001$), sex of observer $F(1, 326) = 13.61, p = .001$), and a significant interaction for levels of intimacy × sex of initiator $F(3, 326) = 23.30, p = .001$). When the male was the initiator, the male received high levels of immediacy nearly across the four conditions (Ms 5.20 to 5.90; see Table 2.5). When the female was the initiator, the male received low ratings when the interaction was low in intimacy, and he received high ratings only when the interaction was an intimate one (see Table 2.5). Female observers rated the male interactant more immediate ($M = 4.81$) than did male observers ($M = 4.38$).

Individual Differences in Judgments of Seductiveness/Promiscuity

One model of the relationship between observers' beliefs about flirting and judgments of the interactants implied that certain observers would react quite differently than others to several of the videotaped presentations; that some observers would judge interactants as "seductive" when in fact they are merely portraying friendliness. MANOVA analyses, however, revealed no significant interaction effects between any of the three beliefs, levels of intimacy (or interaction effects with either sex of observer or sex of initiator). Only significant main effects were obtained. Given direct, linear, relationships between beliefs and judgments of seductiveness, the relationships between beliefs and judgments of seductiveness can be parsimoniously presented as correlations. Furthermore, because gender of the observer was significantly associated with ratings of flirting as invitation, we present partial correlations, statistically controlling for gender of observers.

Table 2.6 presents correlations between beliefs and judgments both when the male is the initiator and when the female is the initiator. When the male initiated the conversation, the belief that flirting reflects sexual urges significantly affected the ratings of the male—in regards to seductiveness, intimacy, and immediacy. However, ratings of the females were hardly phased. Quite a different pattern of results was obtained when the female was the initiator. Observers who adopted the belief that flirting is "invitation" rated both the male and female interactants higher in seductiveness, intimacy, and immediacy. On the other hand, observers who adopted the belief that flirting reflects sexual urges attributed significant, although modest, increases in ratings of seductiveness (for both the male and female), intimacy/liking, and immediacy.

Clearly the mere fact that the male and female were alone and the woman initiated the conversation was sufficient for those observers who adopted the "man should initiate" belief to characterize the encounter in more sexual and intimate terms. For these observers, a sexual "come on" script is activated quite easily, and they are apparently not affected by what we had manipulated in the videotapes as different levels of intimacy in the exchange.

TABLE 2.6.
Correlations Between Beliefs About Flirting and Perceptions of Seductiveness,
Intimacy/Liking and Immediacy as a Function of Sex of Initiator

	Male Initiator			Female Initiator		
	Sexual Urges	Common Fun	Invitation	Sexual Urges	Common Fun	Invitation
Female Seductiveness	.040	.092	.161	.147*	.214**	.318**
Male Seductiveness	.139*	.184*	.110	.133**	.130*	.350**
Female Intimacy	−.020	.103	.137*	.129**	.169**	.311**
Male Intimacy	.291**	.086	−.280	.038	.049	.217**
Female Immediacy	−.132	.026	−.044	.134	−.033	.167*
Male Immediacy	.304**	.206**	.015	.071	.034	.276**

Note: These are partial correlations, statistically controlling for the sex of the observer.
*p < .05.
** p < .01.

DISCUSSION

The results on this research on flirting and perceived seductiveness highlights several important aspects of communication and dating behavior. First, the obvious and mundane: Certain nonverbal behaviors are perceived as indicative of a seductive motive on the part of the communicator, and both male and female observers are able to discern these different levels and interpret them accordingly. However, it is also clear that males and females interpret the meanings of the behaviors differently, and that certain observers more easily and readily infer seductive intent than other observers.

The sex of the initiator played a much stronger role in perceptions than we originally thought, greatly overshadowing the impact of low versus high levels of intimacy in nonverbal behaviors (touching, extended eye contact, forward leans, etc.). The sex of the initiator was important for three interrelated observers. First, despite the alleged progress made in male-female relationships, it still appears that when a male initiates the conversation, such initiation is apparently considered normal, and the male is not quickly judged as seductive. When the male was the initiator, he was rated low in seductiveness by both male ($M = 2.60$) and female ($M = 2.48$) observers. However, the mere act of initiating the conversation prompted female observers ($M = 3.89$) and (especially) male observers ($M = 4.45$) to rate the woman as somewhat seductive—regardless of the level of intimacy of the nonverbal display!

Secondly, it appears that male observers placed greater emphasis on who initiated the conversation, whereas females placed greater emphasis on the nonverbal displays. For example, even when the male was the initiator, male observers rated the actor as more seductive than female observers—discriminating only modestly from the control interaction ($M = 3.36$), and from the truly seductive interaction ($M = 5.00$). Female observers, however, rated (realistically, in our opinion) the male substantially less seductive in the two non-intimate interactions ($Ms = 2.71, 2.88$) than in the flirting ($M = 3.63$) and seductive ($M = 5.07$) interactions—thus discriminating on the basis of the interactant's behavior. Third, the mere fact that the female initiated the conversation was sufficient to prompt certain observers (regardless of gender) to perceive both males and females as pursuing promiscuous and seductive motives. We conclude that both male observers and observers who believe that flirting reflects sexual invitation to characterize encounters as sexual merely on the basis of who initiates the conversation; probably they then search out nonverbal behaviors that could be used to justify the (mis)perception. The fact that results are so strong given the context at hand (waiting idly outside a professor's office for him to arrive), is also a significant point. Judgments of promiscuity and seductiveness would be undoubtedly higher if similar interactions occurred at the "marketplace" (spas, beaches, bars, and the like).

If such individuals perceive a woman's initiation of an interaction as seductive, the entire meaning assigned to an interaction will be altered, and how the interaction (beyond the few minutes we videotaped) and relationship progresses will be intractably changed. Women, who perceive themselves to be "friendly" will act accordingly to that mindset. On the other hand, (some) men will view the same interaction from a "seductive/sexual" mindset and also act accordingly (presumably attempting to fulfill a "self-fulfilling prophecy"). This misperception of the intent of the interactants is likely to lead to misunderstandings about expectations of future outcomes. It may well be that men and women misinterpret initiation as interest and respond based on that misinterpretation; with outcomes varying, from harmless embarrassment to serious problems, such as date or acquaintance rape.

There are also implications for relational development as well. Certainly, the more closely aligned interpretations of behavior are, the more likely effective communication will occur. And certainly, appropriate interpretation of mutual flirting behavior can eventually lead to the initiation of a relationship. Flirting is, after all, an indication of some type of interest and can be the first step in a long-term relationship. However, the fact that the initiation of an interaction is perceived to be seductive (particularly for females) suggests the potential problems of jealousy and distrust. For example, if the male in a relationship perceives interaction initiation to be an expression of sexual interest, and the female initiates interaction with other males, the male may develop distrust and jealousy ultimately resulting in some form of conflict. In terms of future relational development and maintenance, it is important to effectively respond to these misinterpretations and misunderstandings.

Another important aspect of this research lies in an individual's predisposition to view interaction in seductive terms. Those individuals who adopt the "man should initiate" belief, or those who see flirting as sexual urges or invitation need to examine how these predispositions are affecting their interpretations of interaction and, ultimately, their interpretations of sex roles and relationships in general. Clearly, this "mental model" creates a psychological context that influences the way individuals see communication, relationships, and the world at large. For example, how such observers would process evidence if they were jurors in rape cases is a fascinating area for future investigation. Indeed, much research must be in understanding the dynamics concerning how observers make decisions concerning who is seductive and who is merely being friendly, and how a coherent (complete, thorough, detailed) decision concerning seductiveness judgments are made (see Miller, Bettencourt, DeBro, and Hoffman, in press; Miller and Read, 1991; Read and Collins, 1992). Clearly, more than just *who* initiates the conversation, and more than a few nonverbal behaviors should be studied to fully account for seductiveness evaluations.

Men and women will continue to be in situations in which they are alone together and women will continue to initiate conversations with men. It is unrealistic to expect otherwise. On the other hand, we are bombarded daily by magazines, television shows (most soap operas, "Cheers," "Northern Exposure"), movies (i.e., *Top Gun*), and music that perpetuates various beliefs that women want to be swept off their feet, that flirting is common fun, and/or that flirting reflects true sexual urges. It is unrealistic to expect any fundamental change in such beliefs being advocated and adopted. As responsible researchers, however, we can play a role in advancing a more detailed understanding of the mistakes individuals make (and why), and, it is hoped, make communicators aware of how to avoid potentially serious mistakes in social relations.

REFERENCES

Abbey, A. (1982). Sex differences in attributions for friendly behavior: Do males misperceive females' friendliness. *Journal of Personality and Social Psychology*, *42*, 830–838.

Abbey, A. (1987). Misperceptions of friendly behavior as sexual interest: A survey of naturally occurring incidents. *Psychology of Women Quarterly*, *11*, 173–194.

Abbey, A., Cozzarelli, C., McLaughlin, K., & Harnish, J. (1987). The effect of clothing and dyad sex composition on perceptions of sexual intent: Do women evaluate these cues differently. *Journal of Applied Social Psychology*, *17*, 108–126.

Abbey, A., & Melby, C. (1986). The effects of nonverbal cues on gender differences in perceptions of sexual intent. *Sex Roles*, *15*, 283–298.

Andersen, P. A. (1985). Nonverbal immediacy in interpersonal communication. In A.W. Siegman & S. Feldstein (Eds.), *Multichannel integrations of nonverbal behavior* (pp. 1–36). Hillsdale, NJ: Lawrence Erlbaum Associates.

Burgoon, J. K. , Buller, D. B., Hale, J. L., & deTurck, M. A., (1984). Relational messages associated with nonverbal behaviors. *Human Communication Research*, *10*, 351–378.

Burgoon, J. K., Buller, D. B., & Woodall, W. G., (1989). *Nonverbal communication: The unspoken dialogue*. New York: Harper & Row.

Coker, D. A., & Burgoon, J. K. (1987). The nature of conversational involvement and nonverbal encoding patterns. *Human Communication Research*, *13*, 463–494.

Lague, L. (1990, March). Flirting for the fun of it. *Glamour*, pp. 242, 243, 300.

Miller, L. C., Bettencourt, B. A., DeBro, S., & Hoffman, V. (in press). Negotiating safer sex: Interpersonal dynamics. In J. Pryor & G. Reeder (Eds.), *The social psychology of HIV infection*. Hillsdale, NJ: Lawrence Erlbaum Associates.

Miller, L. C., & Read, S. J. (1991). On the coherence of mental models of persons and relationships: A knowledge structure approach. In G. J. O. Gletcher & F. D. Fincham (Eds.), *Cognition in close relationships* (pp. 69–99). Hillsdale, NJ: Lawrence Erlbaum Associates.

Muehlenhard, C. L., Koralewski, M. A., Andrews, S. L., & Burdick, C. A. (1986). Verbal and nonverbal cues that convey interest in dating: Two studies. *Behavior Therapy*, *17*, 404–419.

Muehlenhard, C. L., & McFall, R. M. (1981). Dating initiation from a woman's perspective. *Behavior Therapy*, *12*, 682–691.

Muehlenhard, C. L., Miller, C. L., & Burdick, C. A. (1983). Are high-frequency daters better cue readers? Men's interpretations of women's cues as a function of dating frequency and CHI scores. *Behavior Therapy*, *14*, 626–636.

Patterson, M. L., & Edinger, J. A. (1987). A functional analysis of space in social interaction. In A. W. Siegman & S. Feldstein (Eds.), *Nonverbal behavior and communication* (2nd ed., pp. 523–562). Hillsdale, NJ: Lawrence Erlbaum Associates.

Perper, T., & Weis, D. L. (1987). Projective and rejective strategies of U. S. and Canadian college women. *Journal of Sex Research*, *23*, 455–480.

Read, S. J., & Collins, N. L. (1992). Accounting for relationships: A knowledge structure approach. In J. H. Harvey, T. L. Orbuch, & A. L. Weber (Eds.), *Attributions, accounts and close relationships* (pp. 116–143). New York: Springer-Verlag.

Saal, F. E. , Johnson, C. B., & Weber, N. (1989). Friendly or sexy? It may depend on who you ask. *Psychology of Women Quarterly*, *13*, 263–276.

Schwartz, L. M., Foa, U. G., & Foa, E. B. (1983). Perceived structure of nonverbal behavior. *Journal of Personality and Social Psychology*, *45*, 274–281.

Shotland, R. L., & Craig, J. M. (1988). Can men and women differentiate between friendly and sexually interested behavior? *Social Psychology Quarterly*, *51*, 66–73.

Siegman, A. W., & Feldstein, S. (1987). (Eds.) *Nonverbal behavior and communication* (2nd ed.). Hillsdale, NJ: Lawrence Erlbaum Associates.

Sigal, J., Gibbs, M., Adams, B., & Derfler, R. (1988). The effect of romantic and nonromantic films on perceptions of female friendly and seductive behavior. *Sex Roles*, *19*, 545–554.

Walsh, D. G., & Hewitt, J. (1985). Giving men the come-on: Effect of eye-contact and smiling in a bar environment. *Perceptual and Motor Skills*, *61*, 873–874.

3

Dyad Gender Structure, Uncertainty Reduction, and Self-Disclosure During Initial Interaction

Dell Hastings McKinney[1]
University of Wyoming

William C. Donaghy
University of Wyoming

Conversational development in initial interaction has long been of interest to communication scholars. Initial interactions are one of the best available examples of highly scripted communication situations ("Hi, how are you?" "What's your name?" "Where do you come from?" "What do you do for a living?" etc.). Uncertainty reduction theory (URT) posits the goal of initial interaction partners to be the reduction of uncertainty in an attempt to determine the future of the relationship (Berger & Calabrese, 1975). As uncertainty declines, URT predicts that information-seeking behavior will also decrease (Axiom 3). Further, the theory suggests (Axiom 4) that "low levels of uncertainty produce high levels of intimacy" (Berger & Calabrese, 1975, p. 54). Self-disclosure theory (SDT; Berg & Derlega, 1987; Derlega, Harris, & Chaikin, 1973; Jourard, 1968) rests on the assumption that strangers self-disclose in an attempt to establish an appropriate intimacy level and that recipients respond by disclosing information about themselves at the same or comparable intimacy level (reciprocity; Cozby, 1973; Gouldner, 1960); hence as uncertainty declines and intimacy increases, self-disclosure should increase. The relationship between dyad gender structure (same and mixed gender), uncertainty reduction, and self-disclosure during initial interaction has received some investigation but with very mixed results. The importance of same and opposite gender dyad structures has been substantiated in many other communication

---

[1]Request for further information on this chapter should be directed to Dell Hastings McKinney.

contexts (Andrews, 1987; Archer, 1979; Aries, 1977; Dindia, 1987; Eakins & Eakins, 1978; West & Zimmerman, 1983).

The present analysis examines the nature of information seeking and self-disclosive behavior in same and opposite gender dyads. Specifically, this investigation sought to (a) test the URT prediction that as the uncertainty level declines in an initial interaction, information seeking behavior will also decrease, (b) examine the SDT prediction that self-disclosure will increase as the level of certainty and intimacy increases in the relationship, (c) evaluate the impact of dyad gender structure on information seeking behavior, and (d) assess the effect of dyad gender structure on self-disclosive behavior.

UNCERTAINTY REDUCTION THEORY AND GENDER

Uncertainty refers to one's inability to predict and explain events that will occur in the future. *Uncertainty reduction*, the increase in capacity to predict and explain events, is seen as one of the driving forces between actors in an initial interaction (Berger & Calabrese, 1975). Central to URT is the assumption that, when strangers meet, their primary concern is one of reducing uncertainty and increasing predictability about self and other behavior during the interaction (Berger, 1973, 1975; Berger & Bradac, 1982; Berger & Calabrese, 1975). Hence, a high level of initial uncertainty should be accompanied by high levels of information seeking and decline over time as uncertainty is reduced.

Both Gudykunst (Gudykunst, 1985; Gudykunst & Nishida, 1984; Gudykunst, Sodetani, & Sonoda, 1987) and Douglas (1987, 1990a, 1990b, 1991) attempted to empirically test these URT predictions. Research examining the relationship between uncertainty and information seeking has had mixed results. Gudykunst and Nishida (1984) found no relationship between certainty (called attributional confidence) and information seeking; whereas Gudykunst's later studies (Gudykunst, 1985; Gudykunst et al., 1987) found that as attributional confidence increased, information seeking also increased. These findings are contrary to the axiomatic prediction of URT. Douglas found "use of interrogation decayed across interaction segments" (1990a, p. 75), providing broad confirmation for Axiom 3. Later Douglas' findings, however, suggest "that high uncertainty is not sufficient to induce high levels of information seeking" (1990a, p. 22).

The concept of uncertainty as originally developed in information theory (Shannon & Weaver, 1949) refers to the number of alternatives (choices) that could occur in a given situation and the likelihood of their occurrence (Berger & Bradac, 1982). In other words, the interaction context may contribute to either high uncertainty or relatively low uncertainty, depending upon the interlocutors' familiarity with the socially appropriate contextual behavior rules (Berger, 1973; Berger & Bradac, 1982; Rubin, 1977, 1979). A critically important part of the dyad interaction context is gender structure; that is, one's own gender and that of one's partner.

Berger and Calabrese (1975) posited that the conversational goal underlying initial interaction is to reduce uncertainty and assess the value of continued relationship development. In order to accomplish their relational goals, interactants begin by gathering information concerning their partner and progress from demographic or biographic information requests (low risk) to discussing opinions and attitudes (higher risk). Because behavior in initial interactions is constrained by rules of socially appropriate behavior (Berger & Calabrese, 1975), there may be a trade off between seeking information and behaving appropriately in a social situation (Berger & Kellermann, 1983). Relational goals as well as the rules of socially appropriate behavior in mixed and same gender dyads, however, may be different.

Most of the literature on URT does not directly test behavioral differences in an initial encounter due to gender. The main study which examined the effect of gender structure on uncertainty reduction (Douglas, 1987) found that questions were asked more often in same gender dyads than in opposite gender dyads. Same gender dyads also contained more questions about the partner's goals in second encounter and negotiated future interaction conditions than in a mixed gender dyad structure. Douglas, however, did not follow-up these findings, but instead used same gender dyads in later research (Douglas, 1990a, 1990b, 1991).

SELF-DISCLOSURE THEORY AND GENDER

After over 1400 self-disclosure studies (Hill & Stull, 1987), self-disclosure research continues to be plagued with inconsistent results. The most consistent finding regarding the interpersonal effects of self-disclosure is reciprocity. Reciprocity predicts that self-disclosure recipients will respond by disclosing about themselves at the same or comparable intimacy level (Derlega et al., 1973; Gouldner, 1960; Jourard, 1968). Preconditions for self-disclosure include trust and/or liking (Derlega, et al., 1973: Gilbert, 1976; Gilbert & Whiteneck, 1976; Steel, 1991) and positive attributions toward other (Derlega, Winstead, Wong, & Greenspan, 1987; Gilbert & Horenstein, 1975; Wortman, Adesman, Herman, & Greenberg, 1976).

Although self-disclosure may arise out of various frameworks, the main purpose again seems to be meeting relational goals (Gilbert, 1976). The partner who discloses least, determines the intimacy level of the relationship (Altman & Taylor, 1973). As relationships develop, both the intimacy and disclosure level should increase. Douglas (1990b) found that "disclosive statements were significantly more frequent during minutes 5 and 6 of conversation than during minutes 1 and 2" (p. 75).

Whereas relatively little research has been done on URT and gender, a fairly substantial number of studies have examined SDT and gender. Early research found females to be more self-disclosing that males (Archer, 1979; Derlega, et al., 1973; Jourard & Laskow, 1958). Jourard (1971) explained this finding in terms of the "tough, objective, striving, achieving, unsentimental, and emotionally unexpressive" (p. 35) male sex role. Archer (1979) described high self-disclosers as "likely to be women or at least persons who possess feminine psychological characteristics" (p. 37). Berg and Derlega (1987) predicted that factors such as gender, gender-role, and awareness of inner thoughts and feelings may lead to differences in disclosing behavior. Cozby (1973) reported in his review of the self-disclosure literature that results were found indicating that either females disclose more than males or that there is no difference in self-disclosure levels, but in no instance did men disclose more than women. The rationale underlying these predictions appears to be that females find self-disclosure to be more socially appropriate behavior than do males. Other studies found no gender difference in self-disclosure (Cozby, 1973; Goodstein & Reinecker, 1974). Finally, during initial interactions in the mixed gender dyad structure men have been found to be more self-disclosive than women (Davis, 1978; Derlega, Winstead, Wong, & Hunter, 1985; Stokes, Childs, & Fuehrer, 1981).

Hill and Stull (1987) suggested that factors such as topic, target sex, and target relationship may mediate gender differences. It appears that women disclose more than men on intimate topics (Morgan, 1976; Rubin, 1974; Rubin & Shenker, 1978; Stull, 1981). Dyad gender structure studies have demonstrated differences in opposite and same gender disclosure (Annicchiarico, 1973; Brooks, 1974; Certner, 1970; Hyink, 1975; Inman, 1978; Jourard, 1971). Cash (1975) found that both men and women disclose more to a woman than to a man. "Often female–female disclosure is highest, male-male disclosure is lowest, and opposite-sex disclosure is in between" (Hill & Stull, 1987, p. 83). They attribute this phenomena to reciprocity; that is, because females encourage males to disclose more and males encourage females to disclose less, individuals in mixed-gender dyad structures end up disclosing at intermediate levels and less than same-gender dyad structures.

Finally, target relationship studies reveal that people disclose more to friends than to strangers (Chaikin & Derlega, 1974; Jourard, 1971; Jourard & Lasakow, 1958; Morgan, 1978). Again, these results are qualified by gender differences. Stokes et al. (1981) found that women disclosed more to best friends, but men disclosed more than women to strangers. The latter finding has been substantiated by Rosenfeld, Civikly, and Herron (1979) as well as Colwill and Perlman (1977). Lombardo, Franco, Wolf, and Fantasia (1976), however, did not support this result. All of these factors need to be taken into account when examining self-disclosure and gender.

GENDER RESEARCH

After more than a decade of gender-oriented studies, researchers have begun to talk in terms of gender similarities and differences. "Very few gender differences have been firmly substantiated by empirical studies" (Thorne, Kramarae, & Henley, 1983, p. 13). Thorne et al. (1983) maintained that, in a few cases, research findings actually revealed inverted stereotypes. For example, women, stereotypically, are said to be more talkative than men, but studies of mixed-gender structures tend to find the reverse—that men talk more than women (Kramer, 1977). These findings are fairly consistent with regard to same-gender dyad structures; males consistently talk more than females (Hall, 1984). Hall (1984) attributed this to differences in what is considered socially appropriate behavior in the various dyad structures. The same-gender male dyad structure encourages what she calls "dominance matching" (p. 138); that is, men react to actual or perceived dominance on the part of their male partner by increasing their own dominance behavior, creating escalation.

> Female–female vocal communication could reflect norms that bar the expression of dominance, competition, or ego-oriented motives in female–female communication. Such norms would, at the same time, encourage the expression of trusting, prosocial, or other-oriented attitudes in female–female conversation. (Hall, 1984, p. 138)

McMillan, Clifton, McGrath, and Gale (1977) reported finding gender-based differences in the dyadic setting. Females tend to accommodate for the gender of a male partner by behaving in a more male-oriented fashion. Males, on the other hand, did not change their conversational style to accommodate female partners. Studies conducted by Mulac, Wiemann, Widenmann, and Gibson (1988) showed two main factors that contributed to language use: gender and gender of partner (same or opposite; i.e., context).

> This supports a dynamic view of language use, one that changes with context. Even more important theoretically is the fact that male/female language differences were smaller in mixed-sex than in same-sex dyads. It appears that persons in the mixed sex context reduce their gender indicative language use. This contradicts the notion that persons act in a more sex-role stereotypical fashion when with discussion partners of the opposite sex. (Mulac et al., 1988, pp. 329–330)

Smith (1985) believed that gender behaviors are inherently understood by individuals in our society. However we learn behaviors, most individuals know what socially appropriate behaviors are expected in particular situations according to the norms of feminine and masculine behavior. Research shows that femininity and masculinity norms encourage both males and females to interpret communication situations and the goals of interaction somewhat differently (Smith, 1985).

METHOD

Subjects

The subjects were selected from volunteers in introductory communication courses at a western university. The data for this study was part of a larger study on humor and the media. One hundred five dyads, randomly generated, were videotaped, with consent, completing a series of tasks. Subjects were seated in a room equipped with two video cameras, two microphones, and one-way glass. The first interactional task required of the subjects was to "get to know one another." They were instructed to converse for six minutes.

Upon completion of the conversation, subjects were directed to separate rooms where they were asked to complete a two-part, 7-point bipolar questionnaire requesting specific information concerning their perceptions of the conversation and their partner. The first question on the questionnaire was a measure of how well, if at all, subjects knew their assigned partner prior to the videotaped conversation. Only those dyads who answered *1* on the question *"Before* the discussion, how well did you know the other person?" were used in the study; this response represented *not at all*. Thirty dyads met the criteria for inclusion in the analysis: 10 male–male dyads, 10 female–female dyads, and 10 male–female dyads.

Procedure

Berger and Kellermann (1983) developed a coding scheme that included three question types: (a) about partner, (b) about third parties, and (c) general information. Douglas (1990b) modified their scheme to include (a) questions about partner, (b) questions not about partner, (c) statements about self, and (d) statements not about self. His modified coding scheme was used for this study. All conversations were transcribed in their entirety. Each was checked for content and time accuracy from the videotape with an on-screen timer.

The initial coding was done by the researchers who read each corrected transcript and divided it into utterances. Because *utterances* are discreet speech acts, they often coincided with conversational turns (Douglas, 1990b). An example of an utterance, "What is your major?" (Utterance 1), followed by the response "Elementary Education" (Utterance 2) represents a single conversational turn. However, a single conversational turn may include more than one utterance: "I'm an Elementary Education major." (Utterance 1); "I really like young children." (Utterance 2); and "What is your major?" (Utterance 3). Now the floor goes to the partner as the conversational turn is completed (Douglas, 1990b). If an utterance ended after a time period, it was coded in the next time period. A second coder also read a set of the transcripts ($n = 10$) and divided the conversation into utterances using the same criteria as the researchers. Coder reliability for this division was calculated using Cohen's kappa (Cohen, 1960). The number of decisions for the division of utterances was 1,235, Cohen's kappa $= .97$. This justified using the divisions made by the first coder for the remainder of the transcripts.

After dividing the conversation into utterances, the coder assigned each utterance to one of the following categories: questions, answers, statements, and verbal prompts. Questions were defined as information requests or requests for confirmation, which distinguished them from other utterances that were worded as questions but were not intended to elicit particular information (e.g., Oh really?). These latter utterances were coded as verbal prompts along with verbal backchannels such as "Uh huh." Because this study focuses on question asking about partner and disclosure about self, the question utterances were further divided into two categories: questions about partner and questions not about partner. The same approach was used with utterances coded as statements. These were divided into two categories, statements about self and statements not about self.

A question about partner represented an attempt to elicit information concerning the person which required an answer of a more intimate nature. An example would be "Are you married?" Questions that did not specifically address the other in a personal (high risk) way were coded as questions not about partner. An example would be "Who do you have as an instructor?" Utterances were defined as answers if they satisfied questions (minimally). If a subject was asked, "How do you like your math class?" (question) and responded, "It's okay, I like the instructor." "It's okay" was coded as an answer, and "I like the instructor" was coded as a separate statement (Douglas, 1990b).

Statements about self were those statements that revealed personal (high risk) information about the individual. Examples would include statements such as "I am married with two children" or "I lost my scholarship because I had such poor grades." Statements not about self were defined as those statements that concern topics other than self, even though they may include "I" statements. For example, "I think the weather is about normal for this time of year." Even though an opinion was given in the form of an "I" statement, the information was superficial.

In order to establish coder reliability, a second coder examined the conversations. Coder A and Coder B each coded the 30 transcripts into the five categories: (a) questions about partner, (b) questions not about partner, (c) answers, (d) statements about self, and (e) statements not about self. Verbal prompts and answers were not used for further analysis because of their minimal information value (Douglas, 1984, 1987, 1990a, 1990b). Intercoder reliability was calculated using Cohen's kappa. The question category contained 794 decisions, Cohen's $K = .99$. The statement categories involved 3,032 decisions, Cohen's $K = .97$. Coding sheets were then tabulated for data entry. The number of responses for each category during each one minute segment were counted and placed on a matrix. Internal checks were made mathematically by adding the columns and rows for each category by speaker and category. The two totals matched when the matrix contained no errors.

Development of minutes as the within subjects variable was pretty straightforward. The independent variable of dyad gender structure, however, needs some explanation. There has been much controversy concerning the best way to measure gender effects in dyadic interaction. The problem is that the person with whom a subject interacts influences that subject's behavior and certain statistical procedures do not allow such interdependence (Kraemer & Jacklin, 1979). Several approaches have been used to overcome this difficulty, depending upon the specific research question under examination. These procedures include using confederates, eliminating one subject from the analysis, using a generalization of the matched-pair *t*-test, testing for nesting effects, using pair-average scores, and developing scores that apply only to the interacting pair. All of these approaches have strengths and limitations.

Since the interdependence problem is particularly difficult in initial interactions and the primary focus of this study was the effect of dyad gender structure rather than subject and/or partner differences, the dyad score approach was used. For questions about partner, for example, the total number of such questions per minute was divided by the total conversational utterances. The result provided not only the proportion of questions about partner in each minute but also how that proportion compared to the proportion of other coded utterance types in the same minute.

Design

Because of the number of dependent variables and their possible relationship, a multivariate repeated measures factorial design was employed to test for interdependence between the dependent variables: (a) questions about partner, (b) questions not about partner, (c) statements about self, and (d) statements not about self. The independent variables were dyad structure as a between-subjects measure (male–male, male–female, and female–female) and conversational minute as a within subjects measure (one through six). Analyses were performed on both the raw and proportional data (Douglas, 1991). Only the statistical results for proportional data are reported. Proportional data is normally considered a more conservative and a better measure of behavioral difference (Douglas, 1987, 1990a, 1990b, 1991). The results for both analyses were essentially the same. Where significant multivariate results were noted, univariate analyses were performed.

RESULTS

Box's test showed a lack of homogeneity of dispersion matrices [$F(170, 15,709)$ = 1.30, p < .006]. This does not present a problem according to Barker and Barker (1984) who conclude that "MANOVA is robust with respect to lack of homogeneity of dispersion matrices and there should be little concern — especially when each treatment group has an equal number of individuals" (p. 26). Mauchley's sphericity test was significant for the four dependent variable analyses (X^2 = 56.51, W = .53, p < .001), indicating that the dependent variables met the interdependence assumption of MANOVA.

Multivariate Effects

A nonsignificant two-way interaction was found for the MANOVA analysis of subject dyad gender structure by minute, based on Wilks's lambda [$F(40, 604)$ = .74, p = .89, eta^2 = .16, Power = .78]. Significant multivariate main effects, however, were found for both dyad gender structure [$F(8, 318)$ = 3.01, p = .003, eta^2 = .14, Power = .96] and minute [$F(20, 258)$ = 4.65, p < .001, eta^2 = .42, Power = 1.00].

Univariate Analyses

The univariate analyses for dyad gender structure showed significant differences for questions not about partner [$F(2, 162)$ = 4.22, p = .016, eta^2 = .05, Power = .73] and statements about self [$F(2, 162)$ = 6.80, p = .001, eta^2 = .08, Power = .92], but nonsignificant results for questions about partner [$F(2, 162)$ = 1.25, p = .29, eta^2 = .02, Power = .27] and statements not about self [$F(2, 162)$ = .16, p = .85, eta^2 = .002, Power = .08].

Just the opposite dependent measures were found to be significant for the univariate analyses by minute. Significant differences were found for questions about partner [$F(5, 162)$ = 14.14, p < .001, eta^2 = .30, Power = 1.00] and statements not about self [$F(5, 162)$ = 8.71, p < .001, eta^2 = .21, Power = .99], but nonsignificant results for questions not about partner [$F(5, 162)$ = .67, p = .65, eta^2 = .02, Power = .24] and statements about self [$F(5, 162)$ = 1.15, p = .34, eta^2 = .03, Power = .40].

An examination of Table 3.1 shows the direction and magnitude of the differences for both dyad gender structure and minute.

TABLE 3.1.
Dyad Structure by Minute for Each Dependent Variable:
Means and Standard Deviations

Dependent Variable	Minute	Dyad Gender Structure Means		
		M/M Dyad	M/F Dyad	F/F Dyad
Questions About Partner	First	.19 (.08)	.18 (.08)	.17 (.06)
	Second	.08 (.05)	.17 (.09)	.12 (.05)
	Third	.09 (.07)	.08 (.07)	.06 (.04)
	Fourth	.10 (.12)	.09 (.08)	.06 (.05)
	Fifth	.09 (.04)	.05 (.06)	.06 (.05)
	Sixth	.06 (.05)	.07 (.06)	.05 (.06)
Questions Not About Partner	First	.11 (.08)	.10 (.08)	.07 (.03)
	Second	.10 (.07)	.08 (.07)	.05 (.02)
	Third	.10 (.07)	.05 (.04)	.06 (.05)
	Fourth	.09 (.08)	.09 (.07)	.06 (.05)
	Fifth	.09 (.09)	.05 (.05)	.08 (.07)
	Sixth	.08 (.05)	.05 (.06)	.07 (.05)
Statements About Self	First	.19 (.08)	.26 (.09)	.35 (.11)
	Second	.33 (.14)	.23 (.10)	.36 (.15)
	Third	.31 (.12)	.28 (.17)	.38 (.17)
	Fourth	.27 (.13)	.32 (.13)	.43 (.24)
	Fifth	.30 (.20)	.32 (.11)	.33 (.12)
	Sixth	.22 (.13)	.27 (.17)	.34 (.21)
Statement Not About Self	First	.29 (.13)	.24 (.12)	.24 (.11)
	Second	.34 (.14)	.31 (.14)	.33 (.16)
	Third	.35 (.22)	.49 (.19)	.43 (.18)
	Fourth	.39 (.19)	.35 (.13)	.35 (.19)
	Fifth	.39 (.18)	.47 (.18)	.44 (.18)
	Sixth	.54 (.11)	.51 (.16)	.47 (.22)

The male–male dyads had a higher mean percentage of questions not about partner ($M = .10$, $SD = .07$) than those dyads with a female present (M–F: $M = .07$, $SD = .06$; F–F: $M = .07$, $SD = .05$). Scheffe F-tests revealed differences when male–male dyads were compared to the female–female dyad structure [$Fs(118) = 2.90, p < .05$] and nearly significant results when compared to the male–female dyad structure [$Fs(118) = 1.90, p < .06$]. On the other hand, the female–female dyads had a higher mean percentage of statements about self ($M = .36$, $SD = .17$) than those dyads with a male present (M–M: $M = .27$, $SD = .14$; M–F: $M = .28$, $SD = .13$). These differences were significant when the female–female dyads were compared to the other dyad structures [F–F vs. M–M: $Fs(118) = -3.23$, $p = .01$; F–F vs. M–F: $Fs(118) = -2.90$, $p = .01$] but not when the same gender male and mixed gender dyad structures comparison was made.

The results for the main effect of minute showed the mean questions about partner dropping fairly steadily from the first through the sixth minute (Min. 1: $M = .18$, $SD = .07$; Min. 2: $M = .12$, $SD = .07$; Min. 3: $M = .07$, $SD = .06$; Min. 4: $M = .08$, $SD = .09$; Min. 5: $M = .07$, $SD = .05$; Min. 6: $M = .06$, $SD = .06$). Scheffe F-tests revealed that the first minute was significantly different from every other minute for questions about partner [1-2: $Fs(58) = 3.01$, $p < .01$; 1-3: $Fs(58) = 6.22$, $p < .001$; 1-4: $Fs(58) = 4.69$, $p < .001$; 1-5: $Fs(58) = 7.03$, $p < .001$; 1-6: $Fs(58) = 7.15$, $p < .001$]. Minute 2 was also significantly different from Minute 3 [$Fs(58) = 2.90$, $p < .01$], Minute 5 [$Fs(58) = 3.51$, $p < .001$], and Minute 6 [$Fs(58) = 3.77$, $p < .001$]. Other minute combinations were not significantly different.

Conversely, the mean percentage of statements not about self increased fairly steadily as the conversation progressed (Min. 1: $M = .26$, $SD = .12$; Min. 2: $M = .33$, $SD = .14$; Min. 3: $M = .42$, $SD = .20$; Min. 4: $M = .36$, $SD = .16$; Min. 5: $M = .44$, $SD = .18$; Min. 6: $M = .51$, $SD = .16$). Scheffe F-tests revealed that the proportion of statements not about self in the first minute was significantly lower than those in all other minutes [1-2: $Fs(58) = -2.11$, $p = .05$; 1-3: $Fs(58) = -4.05$, $p = .001$; 1-4: $Fs(58) = -2.90$, $p = .01$; 1-5: $Fs(58) = -4.61$, $p = .001$; 1-6: $Fs(58) = -6.69$, $p < .001$]. Minute 2 was significantly lower than Minute 3 [$Fs(58) = -2.22$, $p < .05$], 5 [$Fs(58) = -2.66$, $p < .01$] and 6 [$Fs(58) = -4.48$, $p < .001$]. Minute 4 was significantly different from Minute 6 [$Fs(58) = -3.34$, $p < .001$]. All other minute combinations were nonsignificant.

Depending on how you look at it, the perfectly linear trend was broken in either Minute 3 or 4. Either Minute 3 was abnormally high for these subjects or Minute 4 was abnormally low. Since the standard deviation for Minute 3 was fairly high compared to the others, we assume that may account for the odd counter linear result. The trend for the male–male dyads was perfectly linear, whereas a similar increase occurred in Minute 4 for both the male–female and female–female dyad gender structures.

DISCUSSION

This study examined both URT and SDT predications regarding conversational behavior in initial interactions as well as the effect of dyad structure on uncertainty reduction and self-disclosure. This discussion is organized around the research questions in the order in which they were presented.

Research Question 1

The first research question tested URT axiom three that "high levels of uncertainty cause increases in information seeking behavior. As uncertainty levels decline, information seeking behavior decreases" (Berger & Calabrese, 1975,

p. 103). The significant finding of questions about partner decreasing over time supports this URT axiom. There was significantly more personal information seeking in the first and second minutes than in almost every other time period. This result is in line with that found by Douglas (1987) and contrary to those of Gudykunst and his associates (Gudykunst, 1985; Gudykunst & Nishida, 1984; Gudykunst et al., 1987).

What tends to lend even more support for the claim that uncertainty and personal information seeking are closely related is the fact that a similar linear pattern occurred in all dyad gender structures. In the male–male dyad structure, high levels of personal information seeking dropped rapidly after the first minute whereas individuals in the other two structures continued to ask a fairly large number of questions about their partner on into the second minute. What is also interesting is that no significant difference was found for information seeking of a less personal nature. The mean number of questions not about partner was fairly consistent throughout the conversations for all dyad structures. It appears, therefore, one cannot say that information seeking in general is related to uncertainty, but only the seeking of certain types of information (i.e., more intimate or personal information). The findings of this study suggest that URT Axiom 3 is overly general and needs to be redrafted to take into account the type of information seeking that occurs under high levels of uncertainty.

Research Question 2

The second research question, derived from self-disclosure theory, proposed that, as communication intimacy increases, self-disclosure will increase. This study did not support that SDT prediction. Statements about self did not increase over time. An examination of Table 3.1 shows a rather random distribution of mean percentages of statements about self for all dyad gender structures. One explanation would be that the intimacy level did not increase in these initial interactions. It is more likely, however, that because this finding is similar to that of Douglas (1990b), his conclusion that "it is probably not useful to treat disclosure as an information-seeking strategy" (p. 77) is partially accurate. It may be that self-disclosure serves more than one function. It may serve the function of reducing uncertainty (early in a conversation) as well as an expression of attributional confidence and intimacy (later in the conversation).

On the other hand, a significant difference was found for statements not about self over time. This result also parallels that of Douglas (1990b). Disclosive statements *not* about self did appear to indicate attributional confidence, decreased uncertainty, or increased intimacy. The consistently linear pattern of these results across all dyad gender structures provides strong support for this conclusion. Whereas, URT appears to be too broad, the findings of this study suggest that SDT may be too narrow. It may simply be that disclosure of all types is related to increased intimacy and attributional confidence. When one finds a compatible partner in an initial interaction, he or she responds by disclosing, not only personal information, but all types of information. It may even be that general information disclosure is a better indicator of intimacy level in initial interactions than personal information. Highly personal disclosure may, in fact, be socially inappropriate behavior during the opening minutes of an initial interaction.

Research Question 3

Research Question 3 addressed the effect of dyad gender structure on information seeking strategies. No significant difference was found for questions about partner between the various dyad gender structures. It appears that personal information seeking of this nature may be socially inappropriate regardless of dyad gender structure. On the other hand, a significant difference was found in the way questions not about partner were handled in the various dyad structures. Same gender male dyads asked significantly more questions not about partner than subjects in the other dyad structures. This is in line with earlier findings that greater quantities of interaction take place in male–male dyads, but is contrary to the literature that suggests that (a) females ask "overwhelmingly more questions than males" (Fishman, 1978), and (b) females tend to accommodate (i.e., match) the conversational behavior of males (Martin & Craig, 1983). Not only did the subjects in same gender male dyads seek more general information from their partner, males appeared to change their behavior to accommodate the females in a mixed-gender dyad. Once again it appears that the stereotypes of male and female communication behavior are inaccurate. This finding also suggests that future research on uncertainty reduction in initial interactions should pay closer attention to such contextual features as subject gender and dyad structure. Those who have suggested that males and females have differing perceptions of socially appropriate behavior may be right.

Research Question 4

Research question four addressed the effect of dyad gender structure on self-disclosure. The results support the conclusion that female–female dyads use significantly more self-disclosure statements than dyads containing at least one male. This result was not surprising. Most of the literature (Archer, 1979; Berg & Derlega, 1987; Cash, 1975; Cozby, 1973; Derlega, et al., 1973; Jourard, 1971; Jourard & Laskow, 1958) suggests that females disclose more than males.

In early childhood, males learn what behaviors are associated with masculinity and females learn what behaviors are associated with femininity. These learned behaviors are reflected in the communicative patterns for each gender. For example, in one female–female dyad, a subject commented "I'm divorced with two kids, so it makes it hard, going to school." Another subject commented, "I just got married two weeks ago, so. . . ." These examples point out that self-disclosure in the female–female dyad went past low-risk or low-involvement disclosure strategies. This appears to confirm the findings of Archer (1979), Morgan (1976), Rubin (1974), Rubin & Shenker (1978), and Stull (1981). In the same-gender female dyad structure, intimate disclosure appears to be appropriate behavior.

On the other hand, appropriate behavior in the mixed-gender and same-gender male dyad structures seemed to be low-risk or low-involvement disclosive statements. For example, a female subject said to her male partner "I don't like the dorms. I'd much rather have my own place; next year I'm going to get an apartment." He responded, "My roommates and I are moving out of our dive into a better one, hopefully." The male subject doesn't tell his partner where he and his roommates are moving. He doesn't offer much in the way of intimate information for his partner. The number of low risk, nonpersonal statements made in the three dyad gender structures was approximately the same (M–M: $M = .38$, $SD = .18$; M–F: $M = .39$, $SD = .18$; F–F: $M = .38$, $SD = .19$). This would appear to indicate that the norms of socially appropriate behavior are similar for the various dyad gender structures with regard to the disclosing of nonintimate information.

SUMMARY AND IMPLICATIONS

The results of this study provide some empirical support for Axiom 3 of Berger and Calabrese's (1975) Uncertainty Reduction Theory; however, they also suggest that URT needs to become more specific as to the type of information seeking that occurs under uncertainty conditions in initial interactions. In this study, uncertainty level was related to personal or intimate information seeking, but not general information seeking. This finding tends to support Douglas' (1987, 1990a, 1990b) conclusions rather than those of Gudykunst and associates (Gudykunst, 1985; Gudykunst & Nishida, 1984; Gudykunst et al., 1987); that is, information seeking *is* related to uncertainty but in more subtle ways than the original URT predicted. Little support was found for Self-Disclosure Theory. Personal (high risk) self-disclosure was unrelated to increased intimacy. Low risk, nonintimate information sharing appeared to be more socially appropriate and a better indicator of intimacy level in these initial interactions.

Dyad gender structure does appear to have an effect on both uncertainty reduction and self-disclosure. Significantly more general questions were found in the same gender male dyads while significantly more self-disclosure statements were found in the same gender female dyads. The former result is fairly unique; although the latter result has been well documented in the literature (Archer, 1979; Berg & Derlega, 1987; Cozby, 1973; Derlega, et al., 1973). Contrary to the female accommodation predictions (Martin & Craig, 1983; McMillan, et al., 1977), the behavior pattern in mixed gender dyads was more in line with those found in all female dyads than in all male dyads; that is, the males appeared to accommodate the females. The gender results also confirm previous findings that more total talk takes place in all male dyads (Hall, 1984; Kramer, 1977) but contradicts other findings (Fishman, 1978) regarding greater female question asking.

The implications of this study for understanding and conducting future research on initial interactions are obvious, but what may not be quite so apparent is how these findings might also help us understand relationships in other stages of development as well. In an established relationship, the level of uncertainty and intimacy constantly fluctuates; whereas reduced intimacy and increased uncertainty is likely when a relationship is disengaging (just the opposite of an initial interaction). The implication is that information seeking (personal vs. impersonal) and self-disclosure (high vs. low risk) might provide worthwhile information for our understanding of communication behavior in these relationship stages as well. As in this study, it is possible that such research might reveal that personal information seeking and general statement frequency are reliable measures of uncertainty level and/or intimacy. For example, as the intimacy level in a disengaging relationship declines, it seems reasonable to expect that personal information seeking and self-disclosure of all types will decline as well.

A second, but related, implication of this project is the importance of considering gender context as it relates to interpersonal communication in other relationship stages. This and other studies (Annicchiarico, 1973; Brooks, 1974; Certner, 1970; Davis, 1978; Derlega, et al., 1985; Hyink, 1975; Inman, 1978; Jourard, 1971; Stokes, et al., 1981) demonstrated that dyad gender structure is an important contextual element when studying the way in which people self-disclose in an initial interaction. Simplistic observations such as "women disclose more than men" are of little value when unconnected to a dyad gender structure and relationship context. More studies should be done comparing various types of communication behavior in developing, established, and disengaging female–female, male–male, and female–male dyads. It seems reasonable that different rules of socially appropriate behavior might apply to each of these conditions. Now that multivariate methods are available to explore subtle contextual differences, such as target gender, target relationship, and topic (Hill & Stull, 1987), interpersonal communication scholars should no longer be satisfied with generic studies that neglect these and other potentially relevant variables.

REFERENCES

Altman, I., & Taylor, D. (1973). *Social penetration: The development of interpersonal relationships.* NY: Holt, Rinehart & Winston.

Andrews, P. (1987). Gender differences in persuasive communication and attribution of success and failure. *Human Communication Research, 13,* 372–385.

Annicchiarico, L. K. B. (1973). Sex differences in self-disclosure as related to sex and status of the interviewer (Doctoral dissertation, University of Texas at Austin, 1973). *Dissertation Abstracts International, 34,* 2296B.

Archer, R. L. (1979). The role of personality and the social situation. In C. J. Chelune (Ed.), *Self-disclosure* (pp. 1–27). San Francisco: Josey-Bass.

Aries, E. (1977). Male–female interpersonal styles in all male, all female, and mixed groups. In A. Sargent (Ed.), *Beyond sex roles* (pp. 292–298). St. Paul: West.

Barker, H., & Barker, B. (1984), *Multivariate analysis of variance (MANOVA): A practical guide to its use in scientific decision making.* Alabama: University of Alabama Press.

Berg, J., & Derlega, V. (1987). Themes in the study of self-disclosure. In V. J. Derlega & J. H. Berg, (Eds.), Self-disclosure: Theory, research, and therapy (pp. 117–130). New York: Plenum.

Berger, C. (1973, November). *The acquaintance process revisited: Explorations in initial interaction.* Paper presented at the meeting convention of the Speech Communication Association, New York.

Berger, C. (1975). Proactive and retroactive attribution processes in interpersonal communication. *Human Communication Research, 2,* 33–50.

Berger, C., & Bradac, J. (1982). *Language and social knowledge: Uncertainty in interpersonal relations.* London: Arnold.

Berger, C., & Calabrese, R. (1975). Some explorations in initial interactions and beyond: Toward a developmental theory of interpersonal communication. *Human Communication Research, 1,* 99–112.

Berger, C., & Kellermann, K. (1983). To ask or not to ask: Is that a question? In R. Bostrom (Ed.), *Communication yearbook* (Vol. 7, pp. 342–368). Beverly Hills, CA: Sage.

Brooks, L. (1974). Interactive effects of sex and status in self-disclosure. *Journal of Counseling Psychology, 21,* 469–474.

Cash, T. F. (1975). Self-disclosure in the acquaintance process: Effects of sex, physical attractiveness, and approval motivation (Doctoral dissertation, George Peabody College for Teachers, 1975). *Dissertation Abstracts International, 35,* 3572B.

Certner, B. C. (1970). *The exchange of self-disclosures in same-sexed and heterosexual groups of strangers.* (Doctoral dissertation, University of Cincinnati, 1970). *Dissertation Abstracts International, 31*(9), 4885.

Chaikin, A. L., & Derlega, V. J. (1974). *Self-disclosure.* Morristown, NJ: General Learning.

Cohen, J. (1960). A coefficient of agreement for nominal scales. *Educational and Psychological Measurement, 20,* 37–46.

Colwill, N. L., & Perlman, D. (1977). Effects of sex and relationship on self-disclosure. *JSAS Catalog of Selected Documents in Psychology, 7,* 40.

Cozby, P. (1973). Self-disclosure: A literature review. *Psychological Bulletin, 79,* 73–91.

Davis, J. D. (1978). When boy meets girl: Sex roles and the negotiation of intimacy in an acquaintance exercise. *Journal of Personality and Social Psychology, 36,* 684–692.

Derlega, V., Harris, M., & Chaikin, A. (1973). Self-disclosure and reciprocity, liking, and the deviant. *Journal of Experimental Social Psychology, 9*, 227–284.

Derlega, V., Winstead, B., Wong, P., & Hunter, S. (1985). Gender effects in an initial encounter: A case where men exceeded women in disclosure. *Journal of Social and Personal Relationships, 2*, 25–44.

Derlega, V., Winstead, B., Wong, P. & Greenspan, M. (1987). Self-disclosure and relationship development: An attributional analysis. In M. E. Roloff & G. R. Miller (Eds.), *Interpersonal processes: New directions in communication research* (pp. 172–187). Newbury Park: Sage.

Dindia, K. (1987). The effects of sex of subject and sex of partner on interruptions. *Human Communication Research, 13*, 345–371.

Douglas, W. (1984). Initial interaction scripts: When knowing is behaving. *Human Communication Research, 11*, 203–220.

Douglas, W. (1987). Question asking in same- and opposite-sex initial interactions: The effects of anticipated future interaction. *Human Communication Research, 14*, 230–245.

Douglas, W. (1990a, November). *Uncertainty reduction during initial interactions: The effects of anticipated future interaction.* Paper presented at the annual meeting of the Speech Communication Association, Chicago.

Douglas, W. (1990b). Uncertainty, information-seeking and liking during initial interaction. *Western Journal of Speech Communication, 54*, 66–81.

Douglas, W. (1991). Expectations about initial interactions: An examination of the effects of global uncertainty. *Human Communication Research, 17*, 355–384.

Eakins, B., & Eakins, R. (1978). *Sex differences in human communication.* Boston: Houghton Mifflin.

Fishman, P. (1978). Interaction: The work women do. *Social Problems, 25*, 397–406.

Gilbert, S. (1976). Empirical and theoretical extensions of self-disclosure. In G. Miller (Ed.), *Explorations in interpersonal communication* (pp. 197–216). Beverly Hills, CA: Sage.

Gilbert, S., & Horenstein, D. (1975). A study of self-disclosure: Level versus valence. *Human Communication Research, 1*, 316–322.

Gilbert, S., & Whiteneck, G. (1976). Toward a multidimensional approach to the study of self-disclosure. *Human Communication Research, 2*, 347–355.

Goodstein, L. D., & Reinecker, V. M. (1974). Factors affecting self-disclosure: A review of the literature. In B. A. Maher (Ed.), *Progress in experimental personality research, 7* (pp. 49–77). NY: Academic.

Gouldner, A. (1960). The norm of reciprocity: A preliminary statement. *American Sociological Review, 25*, 161–178.

Gudykunst, W. (1985). The influence of cultural similarity, type of relationship, and self-monitoring on uncertainty. *Communication Monographs, 52*, 203–217.

Gudykunst, W., & Nishida, T. (1984). Individual and cultural influences on uncertainty reduction. *Communication Monographs, 51*, 23–36.

Gudykunst, W., Sodetani, L., & Sonoda, K. (1987). Uncertainty reduction in Japanese-American/Caucasian relationships in Hawaii. *Western Journal of Speech Communication, 51*, 256–278.

Hall, J. A. (1984). *Nonverbal sex differences: Expression accuracy and expression style.* Baltimore: John Hopkins University Press.

Hill, C. T., & Stull, D. E. (1987). Gender and self-disclosure: Strategies for exploring the issues. In V. J. Derlega & J. H. Berg (Eds.), *Self-disclosure: Theory, research, and therapy* (pp. 81–101). NY: Plenum.

Hyink, P. W. (1975). The influence of client ego strength, client sex, and therapist sex on the frequency, depth, and focus of client self-disclosure (Doctoral dissertation, Michigan State University, 1975). *Dissertation Abstracts International, 35*, 4652B.

Inman, D. J. (1978). Self-disclosure and interview reciprocity (Doctoral dissertation, Louisiana State University, 1978). *Dissertation Abstracts International, 38*, 3398B.

Jourard, S. (1968). *Disclosing man to himself.* New York: Van Nostrand Reinhold.

Jourard, S. M. (1971). Some lethal aspects of the male role. In S. M. Jourard (Ed.), *The transparent self* (rev. ed., pp. 34–44). NY: Van Nostrand.

Jourard, S. M., & Lasakow, P. (1958). Some factors in self-disclosure. *Journal of Abnormal and Social Psychology, 56*, 91–98.

Kramer, C. (1977). Perceptions of female and male speech. *Language and Speech, 20*, 151–161.

Kramer, C. H., & Jacklin, C. N. (1979). Statistical analysis of dyadic behavior. *Psychological Bulletin, 86*, 217–224.

Lombardo, J. P., Franco, R., Wolf, T. M., & Fantasia, S. C. (1976). Interest in helping activities and self-disclosure to three targets on the Jourard Self-Disclosure Scale. *Perceptual and Motor Skills, 42*, 299–302.

Martin, J., & Craig, R. (1983). Selected linguistic sex differences during initial social interactions of same-sex and mixed sex dyads. *Western Journal of Speech Communication, 47*, 137–141.

McMillan, J., Clifton, A., McGrath, D., & Gale, W. (1977). Women's language: Uncertainty or interpersonal sensitivity and emotionality? *Sex Roles, 3*, 545–559.

Morgan, B. S. (1976). Intimacy of disclosure topics and sex differences in self-disclosure. *Sex Roles, 2*, 161–166.

Morgan, T. L. (1978). Intimacy and reciprocity of exchange: A comparison of spouses and strangers. *Journal of Personality and Social Psychology, 36*, 72–81.

Mulac, A., Wiemann, J., Widenmann, S., & Gibson, T. (1988). Male/female language differences and effects in same-sex and mixed-sex dyads: The gender-linked language effect. *Communication Monographs, 55*, 315–335.

Rosenfeld, L. B., Civikly, J. M., & Herron, J. R. (1979). Anatomical and psychological sex differences. In G. J. Chelune (Ed.), *Self-disclosure* (pp. 80–109). San Francisco: Jossey-Bass.

Rubin, R. (1977). The role of context in information seeking and impression formation. *Communication Monographs, 44*, 81–90.

Rubin, R. (1979). The effect of context on information seeking across the span of initial interactions. *Communication Quarterly, 27*, 13–20.

Rubin, Z. (1974). Lovers and other strangers: The development of intimacy in encounters and relationships. *American Scientist, 62*, 182–190.

Rubin, Z., & Shenker, S. (1978). Friendships, proximity, and self-disclosure. *Journal of Personality, 46*, 1–11.

Shannon, C., & Weaver, W. (1949). *The mathematical theory of communication*. Urbana, IL: University of Illinois Press.

Smith, P. (1985). *Language, the sexes, and society*. NY: Basil Blackwell.

Stokes, J., Childs, L., & Fuehrer, A. (1981). Gender and sex roles as predictors of self-disclosure. *Journal of Counseling Psychology, 28*, 510–514.

Steel, J. (1991). Interpersonal correlates of trust and self-disclosure. *Psychological Reports, 68*, 1319–1320.

Stull, D. E. (1981). *Sex differences in self-disclosure: A comparison of men's and women's same-sex relationships.* (Unpublished master's thesis, University of Washington).

Thorne, B., Kramarae, C., & Henley, N. (Eds.) (1983). *Language, gender, and society: Opening a second decade of research*. Rowley, MA: Newbury House.

West, C., & Zimmerman, D. (1983). Small insults: A study of interruptions in cross-sex conversations between unacquainted persons. In B. Thorne, C. Kramarae, & N. Henley (Eds.), *Language, gender, and society* (pp. 102–117). Rowley, MA: Newbury House.

Wortman, C., Adesman, P, Herman, E., & Greenberg, R. (1976). Self-disclosure: An attributional perspective. *Journal of Personality and Social Psychology, 33*, 184–191.

4

Who's Wooing Whom?
An Investigation of
Female Initiated Dating

Paul A. Mongeau
Miami University

Jerold L. Hale
University of Georgia

Kristen L. Johnson
Northwestern University

Jacqueline D. Hillis
Delta Airlines

At the turn of the 20th century, courtship centered upon the "call." Calling generally consisted of a male visiting a female at her home and at her invitation. The call allowed the female to display domestic abilities under the watchful eye of her parents (Koller, 1951). During the first two decades of the century, however, calling was replaced by a new courtship ritual: the "date." Dates were generally held outside the home, centered around some specific activities (e.g., dancing, a movie), and were paid for by the male. With the transition from the "call" to the "date," Black (1924) asserted that:

> Home and its arts went out of date. The domestic phonograph gave a certain impetus to impromptus in dancing, but the motor horn furnished a more potent music. Doing anything without a car became equivalent to doing nothing at all. (p. 342)

This transition from the call to the date created considerable confusion. One popular anecdote of the time described a male arriving at a woman's home. Expecting an evening of domestic entertainment, the man was surprised to find that "she had her hat on" (Black, 1924, p. 342). The punch line implies that, whereas the man expected to stay in on a call, the woman expected to go out on a date.

This transition also influenced *who* initiated courtship. In calling, the female "could bestow an invitation to call upon any unmarried man to whom she had been properly introduced" (Bailey, 1988, p. 15), whereas the male was relegated to waiting for such an invitation. The initiation of the date, on the other hand, has traditionally been the privilege of the male, in part because they generally paid for the date and arranged for transportation. In a few decades, the tables had turned. Now it was the female who was relegated to waiting for a male's invitation.

The male-dominated domain of date initiation remained for more than half a century. The past two decades, however, have seen many social changes that have created greater equality between the sexes. This greater equality has been manifested, among other areas of life, in females' ability to initiate dating relationships. This shift in norms regarding female initiation, however, has not been universally accepted, as reflected in conflicting advice found in etiquette books and advice columns designed for daters.

A denunciation of female initiation of dating was advanced by etiquette guru Emily Post (1984) who asserts that an initiating female:

> . . . may find that she is alienating the very person she wants to impress. A girl who knows how to use her femininity and her charm to get the man she wants, instead of displaying her independence and "strength" to bowl him over has a far better chance of success. (pp. 313–314)

A more moderate position is taken by those who assert that females may ask males out on a date, but only to certain types of activities (while no restrictions are generally placed on males). Craig (1969), for example, asserted that females should ask males to ". . . group affairs—party or dance—not a date alone together" (p. 196). Finally, the impossibly correct Miss Manners avoids the issue of female initiation entirely. When asked what is the best way for a girl to ask a boy out on a date, she responds "What is the best way for a *boy* to ask a *girl* on a date?" (Martin, 1984; italics added). Only recently have etiquette books suggested that the rules for male and female initiation of dating are the same (Stewart, 1987; see Bailey, 1988 for a historical review of advice given to daters).

Although advice and etiquette books reflect a change in norms, recent script research indicates that there is still an expectation that, in heterosexual relationships, males will initiate the first date. Rose and Frieze (1989) asked college students to indicate the typical actions enacted on a first date. They report that the first act in the male's script tended to be "ask for a date," whereas the first act in the female's script tended to be "tell friends and family." These data indicate that college students' expectations are for males to initiate the first date and that females are to wait. Pryor and Merluzzi (1985) reporting similar results, however, instructed respondents to list typical behaviors when a male asks a female out on a date.

Against the backdrop of shifting cultural norms and traditional expectations is the finding that female initiation of a date is a relatively common experience.

Kelley, Pilchowicz, & Byrne (1981) reported that 87% of males surveyed had been asked out on a date by a female. Males' reaction to female initiation was overwhelmingly positive. Of those men who had been asked out by females, 86% accepted. Moreover, of those men who participated in the first date, 75% were subsequently asked out again by the same female. On the other hand, Kelley and associates report that 87% of those relationships ended by the third date. Therefore, this study's first goal is to determine what proportion of the sample has experienced a female-initiated date. The second goal is to examine the longevity of female-initiated dating relationships. Thus the following research (R) questions are proposed:

R_1: What proportion of individuals have experienced a female-initiated date?

R_2: How long do female-initiated relationships last?

Perceptions of Female Initiators

Because so many female-initiated relationships were quite short, Kelley et al. (1981) concluded that, although female initiation creates a positive verbal response, it may, at the same time "elicit some degree of negative affect in males" (1981, p. 196), which could be directed toward the relationship, the self, or the female initiator. If the latter route is taken, males may draw negative dispositional attributions about women who initiate dates.

In a similar vein, Muehlenhard and Scardino (1985) argued that female initiators are likely to be perceived as being more sexually active (i.e., wanting to have sex more) than females who do not initiate dates. Muehlenhard and her associates found that date rape was considered somewhat more justifiable when the female initiated the date than when the male initiated the date (Muehlenhard, 1988; Muehlenhard, Friedman, & Thomas, 1985). It deserves note that date rape was considered unjustifiable in all conditions; however, the gender of the person who initiated the date did significantly influence these perceptions.

To test this hypothesis, Muehlenhard and Scardino (1985) developed four videotapes of a heterosexual interaction where both the intelligence of a female and whether or not the female initiated a date were varied. Following exposure to one of the four videotapes, males indicated their perceptions of the female initiator on a number of dimensions. Results indicate that female initiators were evaluated as being more flexible and agreeable (a single dimension), more of a casual dater, and more sexually active than noninitiators. Moreover, the intelligent initiator was evaluated as more of a feminist and more likable than the intelligent noninitiator and the unintelligent female. In sum, Muehlenhard and Scardino's (1985) results suggested that female initiation of dating seems to produce a variety of attributions in males. They concluded that "more research is needed on how a woman can ask a man out without him falsely concluding that she wants to have sex with him" (p. 566).

Females may be able to avoid incorrect sexual attributions or expectations by varying their initiation strategy. For example, Muehlenhard and McFall (1981) described three date-initiation strategies that a female might take; asking, hinting, and waiting. Muehlenhard and Scardino (1985) investigated only the "asking" strategy (other conditions contained no initiation). It is possible that varying one's approach in initiating a date may generate differing interpretations of the act and the initiator. Therefore, a third research question is posited.

R_3:   Do the various forms of initiating a date (i.e., waiting, hinting, asking) create differing perceptions of female initiators?

Individual Differences and Relational Interpretations

It is likely that individual differences will moderate the perceptions of female initiators. Two variables that may moderate these perceptions are sex differences and the traditional nature of one's social attitudes.

Sex Differences.   There are data to indicate that males and females vary in their evaluations of the same interactive behaviors. Several studies by Montgomery (1989, 1990) indicated that males and females encode and decode flirtatious behavior differently. Montgomery (1989) found that males flirt in order to communicate sexual interest whereas females flirt to communicate friendship or liking. Similarly, Montgomery (1990) reported that males interpret female's flirting as communicating sexual interest whereas females interpret male's flirting as communicating friendship.

Abbey (1982) reported a similar pattern in an initial interaction study. Abbey had males and females interact with a stranger (or observe such an interaction) on the positive qualities of their university. Male raters perceived both male's and female's behavior as more seductive and promiscuous than did females. Males also reported greater attraction toward opposite-sex interactors than did females.

These data point toward males and females interpreting the same behavior in quite different ways. Specifically, males are more likely to generate greater perceptions of sexual interest and intent from a variety of interactions than are females. It is possible that female initiation of dating is another of those areas where differences in interpretations might occur. As a consequence, a fourth research question is posited.

R_4:   Do males and females evaluate female initiators differently?

Traditionality of Social Attitudes.   Traditionality of social attitudes (particularly attitudes toward feminism and the place of women in society) is another variable that may moderate perceptions of female initiators. Both Muehlenhard and McFall (1981) and Muehlenhard and Miller (1988) found that men's attitudes toward the women's liberation movement significantly influenced their preference for female initiation. Men with positive attitudes toward the women's liberation movement preferred women to ask them out on a date, whereas men with negative attitudes preferred that women hint. In addition, Muehlenhard and Scardino (1985) found that these attitudes traditionality influenced perceptions of female initiators of a first date. Traditional males (when compared to nontraditional males) rated female date initiators as significantly more sexually active, less interesting, less extroverted, and less of a feminist.

R_5:   Does traditionality of social attitudes influence perceptions of female initiators?

METHODS

Respondents

Four hundred forty-four male ($n = 202$; 45.5%) and female ($n = 242$; 54.5%) undergraduates at a moderate-size midwestern university participated in this research in partial fulfillment of a research requirement.

Design

This study utilized a one-way factorial design with four levels of the independent variable: directness of the female's initiation. Respondents read one of four scenarios describing a social interaction (see Table 4.1). Scenarios described a male and female student talking before their English class was to begin. The students in the scenarios are discussing current events and movies. The scenarios conclude with a description of the date initiation. The degree of the female's directness in making the date was varied by having the female: (a) wait, that is, the male asks the female to the movie; (b) hint, that is, the male asks the female to the movie after the female hints that she would like to go; (c) asks, but following the male's hint; or (d) asks (with no hint).

Instrumentation

Experience with Female Initiated Dating.   Experience with female initiated dates was measured with a series of four questions. These questions were worded differently for male and female respondents and varied across

TABLE 4.1.
Dating Initiation Scenarios

Female Asks

Ron and Janet are sitting in a classroom waiting for their English class to start. As it is several minutes before class is to begin, they are alone. They strike up a conversation about various current events on and off campus. They end up discussing movies. After discussing a new movie for a few minutes Janet asks "I don't know if you're interested – maybe you're dating someone else or something – but that movie is at the Princess. If you are not busy, would you like to go with me?"

Female Asks (following male's hint)

Ron and Janet are sitting in a classroom waiting for their English class to start. As it is several minutes before class is to begin, they are alone. They strike up a conversation about various current events on and off campus. They end up discussing movies. After discussing a new movie for a few minutes Ron says "Gee, I'd really like to see that movie." Janet then replies, "I don't know if you're interested – maybe you're dating someone else or something – but that movie is at the Princess. If you are not busy, would you like to go with me?"

Female Hints

Ron and Janet are sitting in a classroom waiting for their English class to start. As it is several minutes before class is to begin, they are alone. They strike up a conversation about various current events on and off campus. They end up discussing movies. After discussing a new movie for a few minutes Janet says "Gee, I'd really like to see that movie." Ron asks, "I don't know if you're interested – maybe you're dating someone else or something – but that movie is at the Princess. If you are not busy, would you like to go with me?"

Female Waits

Ron and Janet are sitting in a classroom waiting for their English class to start. As it is several minutes before class is to begin, they are alone. They strike up a conversation about various current events on and off campus. They end up discussing movies. After discussing a new movie for a few minutes Ron asks "I don't know if you're interested – maybe you're dating someone else or something – but that movie is at the Princess. If you are not busy, would you like to go with me?"

two waves of data collection. In the first wave, males were asked "Has a female ever asked you out on a date"; females were asked "Have you ever asked a male out on a date." If the respondent responded *yes* to that question, they were asked if the request was accepted. If they answered affirmatively to the second question, males were then asked if they had been asked out again by the same person (and, if so, if they had accepted). Females were asked if they had asked the same male out again (and if so, if he accepted). In the second data collection wave, the words "first date" replaced the word "date" in the initial question. Longevity of the relationship was measured by asking respondents how many times they had dated.

Perceptions of the Female Initiation. After reading the scenario describing the date initiation, respondents were asked to rate the female on 11 dimensions reported by Muehlenhard and Scardino (1985). Items reported by Muehlenhard and Scardino were supplemented with items created for this investigation. Likability (alpha = .90) was measured with twelve items. Truthfulness (alpha = .86) was measured with seven items. Flexibility (alpha = .83) was measured with six items. Intelligence (alpha = .64) and extroversion (alpha = .76) were both measured with five items. Religious (alpha = .86) was measured with four items. Sexual activity (alpha = .69) and casual dater (alpha = .53) were both measured with three items. Feminism (alpha = .82) and attractiveness (alpha = .63) were each measured with two items. Finally, tactful was measured by a single item. In addition, three dimensions of the female's role in making the date, that is, expected (three items, alpha = .81), appropriate (two items, alpha = .61), and open (two items, alpha = .81) were measured using seven-interval, semantic differential-type items. Finally, the female's activity–passivity in making the date (i.e., a manipulation check measure) was measured with a single item.

Traditionality of Social Attitudes. Traditionality of social attitudes was measured in two ways. First, attitudes toward feminism were measured, using Smith, Ferree, and Miller's (1975) FEM scale. This scale consists of 20, five-interval, Likert-type items. The scale was designed to measure individual's agreement with various aspects of the feminist movement (alpha = .87).

Traditional social attitudes were also measured by asking respondents their attitudes toward female initiation of dating. This scale was composed of nine, seven-interval, semantic differential scales to determine respondents' evaluation of female initiation of dating to be (alpha = .95).

Procedures

Upon arriving at the laboratory, participants were asked to read and sign an informed consent form and then given an experimental packet. The packet included experimental instructions, a scenario depicting a heterosexual interaction where one person (either male or female) asks the other person out on a first date. After reading the scenario, participants were asked to indicate their perceptions of the female and her role in making the date. Participants were then asked to provide demographic information, report on their own dating history, and personality characteristics. Upon completing the experimental packet, participants were fully debriefed, thanked for their participation, and excused.

RESULTS

Research Question 1: Experience with Female-Initiated (First) Dates

In the first wave (*n* = 172), nearly all (90.8%) males indicated that they had been asked out on a date by a female. Of those males who were asked, an overwhelming majority accepted (97.5%). Of those males who accepted the first request, three in four (75.6%) were asked out again by the same female and, again, an overwhelming majority accepted (98.8%).

Responses from females were quite similar. Overall, 84.5% of women indicated that they had asked a male out on a date. Of those women that had asked, nearly all (92.3%) reported that their request had been accepted. Of those women whose first request was accepted, just less than two-thirds (64.8%) asked the same male out on a date again. All women reported that their second request was accepted.

Data from the first wave are quite similar to those presented by Kelley et al. (1981). In inspecting the data from the first wave, however, an interesting pattern was noted. Thirty (17.4%) respondents indicated that the female had asked a male out on a date, that the male had accepted, that the female had *not* asked the male out again, yet they had dated more than once. This sequence of responses could be indicative of one of two processes. First, females may be asking males out on a first date, after which the initiating role returns to the male (or is mutual). Second, this pattern could occur if the female is reporting on a date that falls within a string of male-initiated (or mutually initiated) dates (i.e., *not* their first date). This is important because initiating a first date may have different consequences than will initiating a subsequent date.

To test between these possibilities, questions investigating experience with female initiation were modified in a second wave of questionnaires ($n = 272$). Males were asked to indicate whether they had ever been asked out by a female on a first date. Over four in five (83.5%) had. Of those males who had been asked out by a female on a first date, nearly all (95.8%) accepted. Of those males who had accepted the first request, 71.2% were asked out again by the same female. Of those males asked out again by the same female, nearly all (97.1%) accepted.

When asked if they had ever asked a male out on a first date, 63.1% of females answered affirmatively. Of those women who asked, 87.9% reported that the male had accepted. Of those females whose first request was accepted, less than half asked the same male out again (44.4%). Of those women who asked the male the second time, 95.5% report the request being accepted.

Comparing female's responses across the two waves indicates that substantially fewer women reported initiating first dates in Wave 2 than initiated dates in Wave 1 (63% vs. 84%). Moreover, fewer females in Wave 2 (when compared to women in Wave 1) asked males on a date a second time (65% vs. 44%).

Research Question 2: Longevity
of Female-Initiated Relationships

It is unclear whether the dates reported in the first wave represent female initiated first dates. Because this research question was designed to investigate the longevity of female initiated dating relationships, only those data from

Wave 2 (which asked specifically about female initiated first dates) will be reported here. Of the 272 respondents in the second wave, 169 indicated that they had been involved in a female initiated first date and provided a valid response to the longevity question. These data indicate that female initiated relationships may be more successful than suggested by Kelley et al. (1981). On average, respondents reported dating an average of 27.2 times.[1] Only 41.3% of the relationships had ended by the third date (as compared to 87% of the relationships reported by Kelley et al., 1981). On the other end of the spectrum, 12 respondents (7.5%) were reported having engaged in 100 or more dates with their partner.

Perceptions of Female Initiators/Initiation

Analyzing the Measurement Model. A total of 77 items were either taken from Muehlenhard and Scardino (1985) or developed for this investigation to measure 15 dimensions of participants' perceptions of the initiator or the initiation. For the most part, the factor structure reported by Muehlenhard and Scardino emerged from these analyses. The factor structure was changed dramatically in only two ways. First, several items were removed from the intelligence and likability factors to improve reliability and face validity. The other change in the factor structure was to combine the casual dater and sexually active dimensions. Once corrected for attenuation due to measurement error, these factors were very strongly correlated ($r > .90$). The new, combined, six-item measure is labeled *socially liberal* (alpha = .75).

Manipulation Check. The four scenarios were designed to present varying levels of the female's directness or activity in making the date. The impact of the female's role in making the date on participants' perceptions of her level of activity–passivity is depicted in Table 4.2. These data indicate that the manipulation was successful. As the female's role in making the date became more active (i.e., direct), participants perceived the female as acting in an increasingly active manner; $F(3, 439) = 112.28 \, p < .001$. Moreover, this effect is linear; $F_{lin}(1, 439) = 316.94; p < .001; r = .64$. Duncan's multiple range tests indicates that all four means differ significantly.

Research Question 3: Perceptions of Female Initiators

Participants' perceptions of the female in the scenario were subjected to one-way analysis of variance (ANOVA). The impact of the female's activity in

---

[1]The distribution of number of dates, however, is strongly positively skewed. Although the mean is 27.2, the median number of dates is 5.

TABLE 4.2.
The Impact of the Female's Directness in Making the Date on Perceptions
of the Female and of Her Behavior.

	Female's Request Strategy				
Perception	Wait	Hint	Ask After Hint	Ask	F(3, 440)
Active	3.86_a	5.21_b	6.22_c	6.56_d	109.91*
Intelligent	5.02	4.86	4.92	5.00	1.31
Likeable	5.16	5.33	5.33	5.42	3.09
Interesting	5.25	5.17	5.05	5.39	2.86
Flexible	5.07_a	5.25_{ab}	5.41_b	5.63_c	11.70*
Truthful	4.75_a	4.93_{ab}	5.11_{bc}	5.17_c	7.75*
Extrovert	5.48_a	5.59_a	5.64_a	5.92_b	5.30*
Feminist	4.06_a	4.23_a	4.92_b	5.21_b	25.64**
Tactful	4.94	5.00	5.13	4.98	<1.00
Attractive	4.89_a	4.67_{ab}	4.44_c	4.61_{bc}	5.32*
Religious	4.12	4.16	4.20	4.21	<1.00
Socially Liberal	4.58_a	4.80_{bc}	4.63_{ab}	4.84_c	3.80*
Open	4.89_a	4.97_a	6.06_b	6.20_b	49.93*
Expected	5.13_a	5.22_a	3.85_b	3.54_b	61.88*
Appropriate	4.71_a	5.35_b	5.55_{bc}	5.73_c	24.42*

Means without common subscript differ significantly ($p < .05$).
*$p < .01$. **$p < .001$.

making the date on participants' perceptions is presented in Table 4.2. The female's activity in making the date significantly influenced perceptions of the female's flexibility, truthfulness, feminism, extroversion, and social liberalism.[2]

First, the female's role in making the date significantly influenced participants' perceptions of her attitudes toward feminism; $F(3, 438) = 26.51$; $p < .001$. Multiple range results indicate that when a female initiates a date (asks with or without a hint), she is perceived as being more of a feminist than when she uses a more passive initiation strategy (i.e., waiting or hinting).

Second, the female's activity in making the date significantly influenced perceptions of her flexibility; $F(3, 440) = 12.17$; $p < .001$. As the female's role in making the date became more active, she was perceived as being increasingly flexible. Multiple range tests indicate that waiting resulted in the lowest ratings of flexibility, whereas asking without a hint resulted in the highest ratings of flexibility.

Third, the female's role in making the date significantly influenced perceptions of her truthfulness; $F(3, 440) = 8.03$; $p = .001$. As the female's role

---

[2]With a sample size of 444, relatively small and unimportant differences in means will be statistically significant. As a consequence, a more stringent level of significance ($p < .01$) will be used as the criteria in these analyses.

became more direct, respondents perceived her as being more truthful. Multiple range tests indicate that waiting resulted in the lowest ratings, whereas asking without a hint resulted in the highest ratings of truthfulness.

Fourth, the female's role in making the date significantly influenced perceptions of her extroversion; $F(3, 440) = 7.43; p = .001$. Multiple range tests indicate that the female initiator was perceived as being more extroverted when she asked without a hint, than in any of the other three conditions (which did not differ from one another).

Fifth, as the female's initiation became more direct, she was perceived as less physically attractive; $F(3, 440) = 5.32; p < .01$. Multiple range tests indicate that the female initiator was perceived as most attractive when she waited and least physically attractive when she asked following the male's hint.

Finally, the female's role in making the date had a significant impact of perceptions of the extent to which she is socially liberal; $F(3, 440) = 3.76; p = .01$. Ratings of social liberalness were highest when the female hinted and when she asked without a hint. Ratings of social liberalness were lowest when she waited and when she asked following the male's hint. Multiple-range tests, however, indicate that the only significant mean difference was between waiting and asking without a hint.

Because considerable data indicate that males perceive female's behavior in more sexual ways than do females, post hoc tests were performed to see if the impact of directness on perceptions of social liberalness were more pronounced for male than female respondents. The interaction between respondent sex and directness of initiation approached, but did not reach, significance; $F(3, 436) = 2.50; p = .06$. Interestingly, female respondents' perceptions of the female initiator varied across directness conditions (ranging from 4.44 in the "wait" condition to 4.91 in the "ask without hint" condition). Males' ratings of the female's social liberalness, on the other hand, were nearly constant across conditions (ranging only from 4.73 in the "wait" condition to 4.78 in the "hint" condition).

Perceptions of Behavior. Perceptions of the female's behavior were also subjected to one-way ANOVAs. Results indicate that the female's level of directness in making the date significantly and substantially influenced how open, $F(3, 439) = 49.26; p < .001$; expected, $F(4, 439) = 61.92; p < .001$; and appropriate, $F(3, 439) = 25.82; p < .001$; her behavior was perceived (see Table 4.2).

The impact of initiation strategy on perceptions of openness and appropriateness were similar. More direct approaches (i.e., asking with or without a hint) lead to perceptions of greater openness and appropriateness than indirect or passive tactics (waiting or hinting). Interestingly, however, the direct tactics are perceived as being less expected than the indirect tactics.

Predicting Perceptions of Female Initiators/Initiations. Perceptions of female initiations and initiators were also analyzed using multiple regression procedures. In order to determine the predictors of perceptions of female initiators and/or initiations, only the two conditions where the female asked the male for the first date were included in these analyses. Sex and traditionality measures were included as predictors of each of the perceptions separately for each multiple regression procedure.

Research Question 4: Sex Differences in Perceptions

Sex of respondent emerged as a significant predictor of several perceptions. In these analyses, a negative regression coefficient indicates that means for females were higher than means for males for that particular dimension. Analyses indicated that females rated the female initiator as more likable, $B = -.12$; $p = .09$; and more tactful, $B = -.17$; $p < .05$; than did males. Moreover, females rated the initiation (i.e., the act itself) as more open, $B = -.13$; $p = .053$; more expected, $B = -.28$; $p < .05$; and more appropriate, $B = -.12$; $p = .09$; than did males. Overall, it appears clear that males make slightly less positive attributions about female initiations and initiators than do females.

Research Question 5: Traditionality of Social Attitudes

Traditionality of respondents' social attitudes were measured with two scales; attitude toward feminism and attitude toward female initiation of dating. Attitude toward feminism emerged as a significant predictor of ratings of the female initiator's truthfulness, $B = .18$; $p < .05$. As respondents' attitudes toward feminism became more positive, perceptions of the female initiator's truthfulness increased.

Attitude toward female initiation of dating emerged as a significant predictor of several perceptions. Conversely, as attitudes toward female initiation of dating become more positive, perceptions of the female initiator's intelligence, $B = .27$; $p < .05$; likability, $B = .32$; $p < .05$; interestingness, $B = .17$; $p < .05$; religiosity, $B = .21$; $p < .05$; truthfulness, $B = .20$; $p < .05$; and tactfulness, $B = .23$; $p < .05$; all increased. Conversely, as attitudes toward female initiation of dating increased, perceptions of the female initiator's social liberalness decreased, $B = -.12$; $p = .09$.

Attitude toward female initiation of dating emerged as a significant predictor of perceptions of the female's behavior in making the date. As attitudes toward female initiation of dating become more positive, perceptions of the openness, $B = .28$; $p < .05$; and appropriateness, $B = .23$; $p < .05$; of the initiation increased as well.

In sum, these data present a consistent picture. Females, respondents with positive attitudes toward feminism, and respondents with positive attitudes toward female initiation of dating tended to report more positive perceptions of the female initiator and initiation. Because attitudes toward female initiation of dating emerged as the most important predictor of perceptions of the female initiator and initiation, post-hoc analyses investigating predictors of these attitudes seems warranted.

Predicting Attitudes Toward Female Initiation of Dating. Post-hoc analyses investigated the impact of sex, traditionality of social attitudes, and experience with female initiated dates on attitudes toward female initiation of dating. Three variables emerged as significant predictors of attitudes toward female initiation of dating. The strongest predictor of attitude toward female initiation of dating was attitudes toward feminism, $B = .41; p < .0001$. As attitudes toward feminism became more positive, so did attitudes toward female initiation of dating. Sex of respondent also emerged as a significant predictor of attitude toward female initiation of dating, $B = .32; p < .0001$. Males reported significantly more positive attitudes than did females. Finally, whether a male had accepted the female's invitation on a first date also significantly influenced attitudes toward female initiation of dating, $B = .15; p < .001$.

DISCUSSION

For the better part of the 20th century, the power to initiate a date has been within the male's domain (Bailey, 1988; Korman, 1983). During this time, men have been expected to initiate, plan, and pay for dates as well as be the sexual aggressor, whereas females have been expected to wait for the male's invitation, be alluring, facilitate conversation, and limit sexual activity (Rose & Frieze, 1989). The female taking the initiative, either sexually or socially, has been thought to turn a man off rather than to arouse his interest (cf., Ginsberg, Frosch, & Shapiro, 1972; Jesser, 1978; Post, 1984). Recent social changes, however, have created conditions where it is increasingly acceptable for female's to initiate dates with males.

Experience with Female Initiated Dates

The first goal of this investigating was to determine college students' experiences with female initiated dates. Data collected in two waves indicate, first, that a vast majority of college students have experienced a heterosexual, female initiated date. Data from the first wave were consistent with Kelley et al. (1981)

in that nearly 90% of respondents had experienced a female initiated date. In the second wave of data, less than three in four respondents had experience with a female initiated first date. Some of the female initiated dates in Wave 1 were very likely not first dates. That is, women may be more likely to ask for a date when the males have already initiated the dating relationship. Because females may have less experience in initiating dates (Berger, 1988), they may fear rejection if they were to ask for the first date. Females may use the male's earlier invitation (or invitations) as an indication that their initiation is less likely to be turned down.

Data from Wave 2, on the other hand, ask specifically about female initiation of first dates. Although nearly two-thirds of respondents in Wave 2 had been on a female initiated first date, less than half of the females initiated a second date with the same male, despite the fact that over 90% of the couples went on subsequent dates. An interesting question then is to consider how subsequent dates are initiated after a female initiated first date. Does the responsibility of initiation return to the male or are subsequent dates negotiated mutually by the dating parties (S. Duck, personal communication, September 27, 1990)? In addition, it would be interesting to compare subsequent date initiation following male and female initiated first dates.

Moreover, there are considerable data to indicate that these initiations were quite successful. Across the two waves, over 90% of the initiations were accepted. The female's subsequent requests were even more successful. If the initial request was accepted, only 2% of second requests were turned down. The relationship generated by these initiations were also quite successful, lasting an average of 27 dates. Together, these data are inconsistent with both Kelley et al.'s (1981) conclusion that "[w]omen have apparently developed relatively little skill in discerning the most likely candidates for their dating requests" (p. 196) and the perception that female initiation may act as a "turn off" for males (Jesser, 1978; Sirkin & Mosher, 1985).

In summary, these data indicate that female initiation is a very effective means of developing a dating relationship. Future research should investigate what factors influence how successful subsequent relationships might be. Berger and Bell's (1988) research on planning is quite relevant here. Clearly, females are able to develop date initiation plans that are quire successful. One interesting question would be to ask if there is a difference in the strategic presentation of successful and unsuccessful initiators.

Perceptions of Female Initiators

Directness in female initiation, for the most part, creates a number of positive perceptions. As directness increases, the female initiator is perceived as more flexible, truthful, extroverted, and more of a feminist; yet at the same time, perceptions of her physical attractiveness decrease. Increasing the directness of the female's initiation strategy, however, also influenced perceptions of the female's social liberalness (i.e., a casual dater and sexually active). Socially liberal ratings were lowest when the female waited and when she asked after the male hinted. Socially liberal ratings were higher when the female hinted or asked without a hint from the male.

It is interesting that the female initiator was rated as less socially liberal when she asked for a date following the male's hint than when she asked without that hint. The male's hint may create the idea that the male likes the female and wants to participate in a future social interaction and/or a relationship with her. In other words, the "hint" provides subjects with some cue regarding the nature of the relationship between the male and female in the scenario.

The impact of directness of initiation on perceptions of the female initiator has implications for a male's expectations of date activities. Pryor and Merluzzi (1985) and Rose and Frieze (1989) both found that there was considerable agreement for "the content and sequence of actions that hypothetically would occur on a first date" (Rose & Frieze, 1989, p. 158). At the same time, however, female initiators are perceived as more feminist, extroverted, truthful, and flexible than those females who wait. It is possible that these differences in perceptions may change the nature of the script males develop prior to the date. Put another way, a male's expectations for a specific date may differ, depending on whether he is dating an extroverted feminist or an introverted nonfeminist.

Thus, it is possible that sequences of expected behaviors may differ, depending on whether the male or the female initiated the first date. If this is the case, then, differing perceptions and expectations may very well influence actual behavior enacted on first dates. If directness of initiation has an impact on both perceptions of the initiator and the expected sequences of behavior on that date, it is possible that the different sets of relational themes (Burgoon & Hale, 1984, 1987) are presented under different initiation conditions.

Female Initiation and Perceptions of Sexual Interest

Sex differences were expected to play a strong part in the perceptions of female initiators. In previous research, males seem to consistently perceive their heterosexual interactions in more sexual ways than do females (Abbey, 1982; Montgomery, 1989, 1990; Shotland, 1989). In the present data, however, male's perception of the female's social liberalness did not vary as a function of the directness of the female's approach.

The important implication of these results is that males tend not to equate a direct date initiation as a direct sexual invitation. Muehlenhard and her associates (i.e., Muehlenhard, 1988; Muehlenhard et al., 1985; Muehlenhard & Scardino, 1985) found that female date initiation consistently influences perceptions of the initiator's sexual interest or in the perceived justifiability of date rape.

Two important questions remain regarding the relationship between directness of initiation and perceived sexual interest. First, the way the initiation was described (i.e., the initiator says, in part, "I don't know if you are dating anyone") may indicate that the male and female did not know one another well (Muehlenhard & Scardino, 1985). Therefore, it is unclear whether the social liberalness findings are a result of the female's initiation or the fact that partners don't know each other well, or both.

Along the same line is the finding that, as the female's initiation becomes more direct, her behavior is perceived as increasingly unexpected. It remains an open question whether it is the female initiation itself or whether it is the female initiation in the unfamiliar context that is unexpected.

The second question involves the measurement of perceived sexual activity. An important question is whether either the present investigation or Muehlenhard and Scardino (1985) asked the correct question to tap perceived sexual interest. Both studies asked subjects to report their general perception of the female's sexual activity. A more relevant question is whether the perception of whether the female wants to engage in sexual activity *on that date*.

Sex Differences in Perceptions

Sex differences in perceptions reached statistical significance only for the perception of the female's tactfulness and in how expected the initiation was. In both cases, males made slightly less positive evaluations than did females. On the other hand, males did espouse substantially more positive attitudes toward female initiation of dating than did females. The question of why males tend to make more negative attributions of female initiators, yet at the same time profess to more positive attitudes toward female initiation, is an interesting question deserving of future research.

Several potential explanations for this inconsistency are possible. The first explanation could come from a reciprocity and/or exchange perspective. Korman (1983), for example, asserted: "Viewed from an exchange perspective the traditional practices of male-initiation . . . might imply a power arrangement that works to require females to reciprocate for valued benefits" (pp. 575–576). Therefore, the traditional date initiation system provides the male with a degree of power that is upset when it is the female who initiates. The lack of power may upset males, leading to less positive perceptions.

Similarly, when the male initiates, he may be quite confident in his relational goals, plans (Berger & Bell, 1988), and desired relational trajectory (Jensen & Trenholm, 1988). On the other hand, if the female initiates, goals and trajectories may be more ambiguous to the male.

In summary, the resulting development of relationships reflecting these early initiation patterns is likely to be influenced by the perceptions and confidence of the individuals in the initial pairing. Ultimately the foundation of a relationship may well be determined by its very initiation.

REFERENCES

Abbey, A. (1982). Sex differences in attributions for friendly behavior. Do males misperceive females' friendliness? *Journal of Personality and Social Psychology, 42,* 830–838.

Bailey, B. L. (1988). *From front porch to back seat: Courtship in twentieth century America.* Baltimore, MD: Johns Hopkins University Press.

Berger, C. R. (1988). Planning, affect, and social action generation. In R. L. Donohew, H. Sypher, & E. T. Higgins (Eds.), *Communication, social cognition, and affect* (pp. 93–116). Hillsdale, NJ: Lawrence Erlbaum Associates.

Berger, C. R., & Bell, R. A. (1988). Plans and the initiation of social relationships. *Human Communication Research, 15,* 217–235.

Black, A. (1924). Is the young person coming back? *Harper's, 149,* 337–346.

Burgoon, J. K., & Hale, J. L. (1984). The fundamental topoi of relational communication. *Communication Monographs, 51,* 193–214.

Burgoon, J. K., & Hale, J. L. (1987). Validation and measurement of the fundamental themes of relational communication. *Communication Monographs, 54,* 19–41.

Craig, H. L. (1969). *Thresholds to adult living* (2nd ed.). Peoria, IL: Chas. A. Bennet Co.

Ginsberg, G. L., Frosch, W. A., & Shapiro, J. (1972). The new impotence. *Archives of General Psychology, 5,* 218–220.

Jensen, A., & Trenholm, S. (1988, November). *Beyond intimacy: An alternative trajectories model of relational development.* Paper presented to Annual Meeting of the Speech Communication Association, New Orleans.

Jesser, C. J. (1978). Male responses to direct verbal sexual initiatives of females. *The Journal of Sex Research, 14,* 118–128.

Kelley, K., Pilchowicz, E., & Byrne, D. (1981). Responses of males to female-initiated dates. *Bulletin of the Psychonomic Society, 17,* 195–196.

Koller, M. R. (1951). Some changes in courtship behavior in three generations of Ohio women. *American Sociological Review, 16,* 366–370.

Korman, S. K. (1983). Nontraditional dating behavior: Date-initiation and date expense-sharing among feminists and nonfeminists. *Family Relations, 32,* 557–581.

Martin, J. (1984). *Miss Manners' guide to rearing perfect children.* New York: Athenaeum.

Montgomery, B. M. (1989). *Understanding flirtatious communication from the participants' perspective.* Unpublished manuscript, University of New Hampshire.

Montgomery, B. M. (1990). *Sociable versus sexual flirting: The influence of gender.* Unpublished manuscript, University of New Hampshire.

Muehlenhard, C. L. (1988). Misinterpreted dating behaviors and the risk of date rape. *Journal of Social and Clinical Psychology, 6,* 20–37.

Muehlenhard, C. L., Friedman, D. E., & Thomas, C. M. (1985). Is date rape justifiable? The effects of dating activity, who initiated, who paid, and men's attitudes toward women. *Psychology of Women Quarterly, 9,* 297–310.

Muehlenhard, C. L., & McFall, R. M. (1981). Dating initiation from a woman's perspective. *Behavior Therapy, 12,* 682–691.

Muehlenhard, C. L., & Miller, E. N. (1988). Traditional and nontraditional men's responses to women's dating initiation. *Behavior Modification, 12,* 385–403.

Muehlenhard, C. L., & Scardino, T. J. (1985). What will he think? Men's impressions of women who initiate dates and achieve academically. *Journal of Counseling Psychology, 32,* 560–569.

Post, E. L. (1984). *The new Emily Post's etiquette.* New York: Harper & Row.

Pryor, J. B., & Merluzzi, T. V. (1985). The role of expertise in processing social interaction scripts. *Journal of Experimental Social Psychology, 21,* 362–379.

Rose, S., & Frieze, I. H. (1989). Young singles' scripts for a first date. *Gender and Society, 3,* 258–268.

Shotland, R. L. (1989). A model of the causes of date rape in developing and close relationships. In C. Hendrick (Ed.), *Close relationships* (pp. 247–270). Newbury Park, CA: Sage.

Sirkin, M. I., & Mosher, D. L. (1985). Guided imagery of female sexual assertiveness: Turn on or turn off? *Journal of Sex and Marital Therapy, 11,* 41–50.

Smith, E., Ferree, M., & Miller, F. A. (1975). A short scale of attitudes toward feminism. *Representative Research in Social Psychology, 6,* 51–56.

Stewart, M. Y. (1987). *The new etiquette: Real manners for real people in real situations an A-to-Z guide.* New York: St. Martin's Press.

5

Deceptive Schemata: Initial Impressions of Others

Randy Wood[1]
University of Kentucky

Immediately upon encountering another person, people begin forming impressions. Judgments of this person's personality traits are made by observing their behavior and drawing inferences from these observations. Observers may decide that an individual is friendly, intelligent, witty, honest, or possess any number of other dispositional characteristics. By integrating information about the situation and the behaviors of the target individual, perceivers use what has been termed *implicit personality theory* to form overall judgments of the personality of others (Brown, 1986; Jones, 1990). These judgments are quite often made on the basis of limited information, but this does not deter elaborate assessments of character.

One reason observers readily make these judgments is that they do not come to an encounter with a blank slate. In fact, research has suggested that many people bring with them preconceived associations of traits and behaviors to their initial interactions with others (Brown, 1986; Dion, Berscheid, & Walster, 1972; Fiske & Taylor, 1991). At the most primitive level, positive characteristics are associated with each other and, accordingly, negative characteristics imply other negative characteristics (Asch, 1946; Brown, 1986; Bruner, Shapiro, Taguiri, 1958; Dion et al., 1972). For example, the classic study by Dion and associates (1972) found that subjects given photos of more physi-

[1]The Author would like to thank Pamela Kalbfleisch and Norm Van Tubergen for their assistance with this project.

cally attractive individuals were more likely to think they would make happier mates, be happier people, and have higher status occupations than less physically attractive individuals. In other words, once we assign positive traits to someone, we are more likely to assign other positive traits to them and fill in any gaps in our knowledge for a complete impression.

This is not to suggest that we do not integrate traits that do not fit easily with previous impressions (Asch, 1946; Asch & Zukier, 1984; Brown, 1986; Jones, 1990). One way attributes are integrated results from the primacy effect. The first attributes we assign to someone provide information used to interpret other attributes that may be subject to various subtleties of meaning. Asch and Zukier (1984) showed that we can integrate traits that do not seem to fit together in a variety of ways, such as segregating each trait to a particular domain of the individual's life, assigning a common source to create unity, and interpolating. Clearly, the more we interact with a person, the more opportunity we have to refine and develop our impressions of them (Brown, 1986).

Initial impressions of another person can lead to changes in the behavior of the observer and corresponding changes in the person being observed (Jones, 1990). Thus, the phenomenon of self-fulfilling prophecies is well supported (Snyder, Tanke, & Berscheid, 1977). Conversely, expectations about an individual's behavior can be disconfirmed by that person's behavior (Miller & Turnbull, 1986). In other words, the observer, in expecting a certain behavior, may act in such a way that the person being observed does not conform to the observer's expectations. For example, if an observer expects someone to be nervous, they may act very calmly in anticipation of this person's nervousness, which would lead consequently to calm behavior by the person being observed (Miller & Turnbull, 1986).

A different line of inquiry on impression formation involves social schema research (Fiske & Taylor, 1991). In contrast to the accumulation of traits in a "bottom up" fashion, schema research focuses on the effects of previously developed mental pictures of associations of traits into social types and their implications for "top down" processing in forming initial judgments (Fiske & Neuberg, 1990; Fiske & Taylor, 1991).

The beginning of schema research is generally attributed to Bartlett (1932), but the concept was little utilized until the last couple of decades (Fiske & Taylor, 1991; Rumelhart & Ortony, 1977). A *schema* is a cognitive framework used to interpret life experiences (Rumelhart & Ortony, 1977; Taylor & Crocker, 1981). There are two general types of schemata: process and content (Fiske & Taylor, 1991). *Process schemata* are mental structures that process content and may be illustrated by Heider's balance theory (Taylor & Crocker, 1981). *Content schemata* are mental structures that represent some stimulus including attributes about the stimulus and knowledge about the associations between the attributes (Fiske & Dyer, 1985; Taylor & Crocker, 1981).

The content schemata are particularly relevant for the study presented in this chapter. Individuals may have any number of content social schemata representing types of people and the roles they fill. For example, most individuals would have schemata for "singles," "divorcees," "playboys," the "marrying type," "jocks," "politicians," and "car salesmen." Schema research suggests that categories such as these are represented by mental networks of attributes and their interrelationships. Schema for categories can overlap, vary in abstractness, and can be "fuzzy categories" or specific prototypes (Cantor & Mischel, 1979; Fiske & Taylor, 1991).

In social interaction, schemata come into play when they are activated by some physically relevant attribute (sex, clothing, location of the encounter, etc.); by an assigned label (the individual is known to be an athlete, or divorced, etc.); by the degree of salience of the schema; or, because of repeated usage, the schema is more easily accessible (Fiske & Taylor, 1991). Once a category or schema is activated, the individual is likely to expect a number of relevant traits in the target based on the schema, and if information is incomplete for forming an impression, the individual is likely to attribute the traits to fill in the knowledge gaps about the person (Fiske & Taylor, 1991; Jones, 1990).

Fiske and Neuberg (1990) integrated the two general streams of research on impression formation. They provide a model of impression formation that posits a continuum from category-based (top down) to piece-meal based (bottom up) impressions. They suggest that, initially, observers attempt to categorize others according to some schema, and as long as the behavior of an individual is consistent with the schema, this satisfies the observer. However, if the individual's behavior calls the schema into question, the observer will attempt to recategorize and ultimately use piecemeal processing to build an impression if relevant categories are not deemed appropriate for this particular individual.

Although schemata may be formed according to social roles, events, person types, or scripts (Taylor & Crocker, 1981), Planalp (1985) called attention to relational schemata, which provide expectations about communicative interaction in various types of relationships. Planalp found that people use behavior-specific knowledge about appropriate relational communication and that this knowledge (*relational schema*) influenced memory of communication in such a way that consistent communication was remembered; but inconsistent communication for the relationship was more likely not to be remembered.

Because individuals use various types of schemata in forming impressions of others, and the communicative behavior of others often forms an important element in these schemata, these initial impressions will have a tremendous impact on relationship development. Perhaps one of the more important personality traits people desire in others is honesty. It is important for most people to know that they can trust another individual. The question, "Can I trust him or her? is paramount when considering whether to begin a relationship with another person.

Schemata can function to provide individuals with information about the honesty of others by the extent to which the relevant schema being applied to the target incorporates honesty as a part of the schema. For example, if an individual has a schema for a person type such as "womanizer" or "sweet talker," and the schema consists of connected traits of being a flatterer, being deceitful, self-centered, and manipulative, the individual (when categorizing another with such a schema) will likely judge the target person to be dishonest and untrustworthy, even with little personal knowledge on which to base such an impression.

Fiske and Taylor (1991) suggested that schemata are overlapping and interrelated. Therefore it is likely that various schemata for deceptive people are connected by their common traits of dishonesty or deceitfulness. Fiske and Taylor (1991), following the research on nonsocial schemata (cf. Cantor & Mischel, 1981; Rosch, Mervis, Gray, Johnson, & Boyes-Braem, 1976), suggested that people find a certain level of schemata more practical than others. This implies that, rather than use a broad schema for deceptiveness, people should rely on a less generalized category.

In other words, it may be that individuals have a general category for deceptive people that contains certain behavioral attributes. In this schema, there may be a number of other subschemata, each with its own subset of behaviors and attributes. Each of these subschemata could then, in turn, have subschemata. Fiske and Taylor (1991) suggested that it is not clear which level of schemata people use, but it appears that they do *not* use either the most general level of schemata or the most specific level.

Past research on deception detection has operated under the general assumption that people have one general conception about how deceptive people behave. The purpose of the study presented in this chapter is to examine the possibility that individuals may have more than one schema for deceptive individuals and that these schemata may have overlapping communication-relevant behaviors. It should be kept in mind that this study examines people's schemata or cognitive representations of deceptive individuals, and not how these individuals actually behave or actual deceptive types of behavior. There is a difference in perceptions of deceptive behavior and actual deceptive behavior (Kalbfleisch, 1992; Zuckerman, DePaulo, & Rosenthal, 1981). The study presented examines the cognitive schemata used in forming initial impressions of deceptiveness for two different types of communicators. This study is presented after a review of relevant deception literature on cue usage. The results of this investigation are followed by a discussion of the implications of deceptive schemata for the formation of initial impressions and the possible development of relationships.

MICROLEVEL AND MACROLEVEL CUES
TO DECEPTION

Research on perceptions of deceptiveness has typically involved some attempt by an observer to detect a communicator's deception or rate perceptions of a communicator on an honesty scale (cf. Kalbfleisch, 1990, 1992). These studies have either focused on more macro assessments of behavior (O'Hair, Cody, Goss, & Krayer, 1988; Riggio, Salinas, & Tucker, 1988; Riggio, Tucker, & Throckmorton, 1988) or more micro level cues (Hocking, Bauchner, Kaminski, & Miller, 1979; Krauss, Apple, Morency, Wenzel, & Winton, 1981; Zuckerman, DeFrank, Hall, Larrance, & Rosenthal, 1979).

Knapp, Cody, and Reardon (1987) suggested that, unless people suspect deceit, they will likely use macro level assessments of personality in forming impressions. O'Hair et al. (1988) adopted Norton's (1978) communicator style measure to determine subjects' impressions of both honest and dishonest communicators. When subjects believed the actor was honest, they associated communication behaviors of friendliness, attentiveness, preciseness, along with communication styles that were dramatic and low in animation.

In their study, O'Hair et al. (1988) found complex relationships in perceptions of honesty when the gender of the subject and that of the target were entered into the analysis. Males were more likely to judge other males honest when they also judged them as attentive, but they were more likely to judge females honest when they were also judged friendly. Females were more likely to judge both males and females as honest when they were attentive.

On the other hand, deception research focusing on microlevel cues associated specific nonverbal behaviors with perceptions of deceptive behavior or with actual deceptive behavior. In their meta-analysis of studies using microlevel cues, Zuckerman et al. (1981) found eight nonverbal behaviors significantly associated with perceptions of deceptiveness. The behaviors they found with a negative relationship to perceptions of deceptiveness were gaze, smiling, and speech rate. Behaviors positively associated with perceptions of deceit were postural shifts, response latency, speech errors, speech hesitations, and pitch. However, as Kalbfleisch (1992) indicates, observer perceptions of deceptive behavior and actual deceptive behavior may not often be the same.

DECEPTIVE SCHEMATA: INTEGRATION
OF MICROLEVEL AND MACROLEVEL CUES

Because prior research indicates that people appear to use both microlevel and macrolevel cues in forming impressions of deceptiveness, a natural area of inquiry centers around the relationship between these two types of cues in making judgments of honesty or deceit. Given the nature of our cognitive representations of types of people reviewed in the aforementioned schema literature, it would seem a natural conclusion to assume that these microlevel and macrolevel deception cues are somehow interrelated in various schemata. More specifically, a likely integration would relate differing microlevel cues with various macrolevel attributes to form schemata for deceptive types of people. For example, gaze or eye contact would likely be related to attentiveness, and smiling could be related to perceptions of friendliness. Because nonverbal cues are subject to many interpretations given various contexts, it is the overall fit with a given set of behaviors and attributes that determines their meaning. In other words, although a lack of smiling could indicate a case of depression or boredom, when considered in conjunction with other nonverbal cues and more macrolevel attributes, a schematic fit for a deceptive type emerges and provides the perceiver a basis for interpreting the behavior of an individual and forming an impression.

In keeping with the research on social schemata, another likely assumption is that people have more than one schemata for deceptive behavior. That is, people are likely to have different subschemata for various deceptive types. Thus, the current study proposes the following hypotheses (H):

H_1: Individual research participants will have different schemata for deceptive behavior.

H_2: Each schemata for deceptive behavior will have overlapping microlevel and macrolevel cues but will also have distinct microlevel and macrolevel cues.

Because schemata are often overlapping and have differing levels of abstractness, schemata for various social roles or person types can be viewed as subcategories of deceptive types or vice versa. For example, the deceptive "fast-talker" could have several subschemata such as "politician," "used car salesman," or "lady killer." When deception is not salient for the situation, these schemata could form subcategories for other more abstract schemata such as "public servants," "salespeople," or "romantic types."

Schemata are individual cognitive frameworks, and although they are likely to be shared by others (i.e., in the case of broadly recognized social roles), it cannot be assumed that everyone shares the same schemata or that individuals will apply the same schemata in the same situation. Thus, an additional hypothesis is as follows:

H₃: Research participants will vary in their schemata for deceptive types.

METHOD

Research Participants

Research participants for this study were 64 students enrolled in the spring semester at a large southeastern university. Subjects were 38 females and 26 males.[2]

Analysis

The analysis for this study used Q methodology (Stephenson, 1953). *Q technique*, which implements Q methodology, is designed to assess the relative influence of items within a research participant as opposed to across research participants (Nunnally, 1978). Its advantage is that it allows the research participant to provide his or her own frame of reference (Brooks, 1970). Developed by William Stephenson in the 1930s, it was intended to measure what Stephenson referred to as the subjectivity of individuals (Stephenson, 1953). Rather than compare how items relate across research participants, Q technique measures how items relate to each other within each research participant.

Q technique involves a rank ordering task (Kerlinger, 1986) of relevant items representative of a given "statistical universe" of items (Stephenson, 1953). The number of items varies with the purpose of the study, but Kerlinger (1986) suggested they should range somewhere between 40 and 120 items. Items are numbered for analysis purposes. Each research participant ranks the items in what is called a Q sort. The correlation of research participant responses are then factored to discover whether research participants can be similarly grouped into types according to the similarity of their ranking of items.

For determining the cognitive structure of individuals and how they can be grouped into types, Q methodology and technique is especially appropriate. Although some schema research uses more hidden methods for detecting subject use of given schemata (cf. Planalp, 1985), the conscious use of schemata

---

[2]McKeown and Thomas (1988), and Brown and Ungs (1970), indicated that a sample size of 40 to 50 research participants is sufficient for a Q analysis. These authors suggest that major associations stabilize after only a few cases and additional cases typically do not result in further clarification of these relationships.

implied in impression formation discussed (cf. Fiske & Neuberg, 1990) indicated that such procedures are not necessary for discovering research participants' cognitive frameworks, and given that they typically compare items across research participants rather than within research participants as in Q technique, they may not be as helpful in deciphering any given individual or group of individuals schemata.

Again, it should be remembered that the study is designed to explore types of schemata and not types of actual behavior. The Q technique will allow research participants to rank both microlevel and macrolevel cues that they associate with deceptive behavior. Additionally, it will allow research participants to provide different combinations of microlevel and macrolevel cues for deceptive behavior depending on the schema utilized in the prescribed sort. For example, research participants could sort microlevel items and rank items of excessive smiling, long verbal responses, and increased eye contact as expected behavior for a "lady killer" or "smooth-talker" schema but rank items of fidgeting, shorter response length, and speech hesitations as expected behavior for a "naive" or "self-conscious" liar.

Procedure

For this study of deceptive schemata, a deck of microlevel and macrolevel cues associated with deception was prepared. The microlevel cues selected in this study were derived from cues typically associated with perceptions of deception in previous research and focus group discussions. Each cue, such as eye contact, was placed into three cards representing three levels of intensity. This means, for example, that eye contact was represented on three cards with one card for each of the following: (a) looks away, (b) normal eye contact, and (c) stares. The macrolevel cues were derived from Norton's communicator style measure and items derived from focus group discussions of deceptive behavior. As with the microlevel cues, these cues were employed according to the relative intensity of the cue expected. For example, *attentiveness* was placed onto three cards: *not attentive at all*, *attentive*, and *overly attentive*. There were 72 macrolevel and microlevel cue items in the deck. These cue items are listed in Table 5.1.

Subjects were told the purpose of the study was to learn about people's perceptions of how others behave while lying. Each research participant sorted the deck for two situations. The two situations were designed to tap different deceptive schemata. The situations were derived from focus group discussions of deceptive types. The first situation involved a "smooth-talker" and incorporated a social role of used car salesperson. To avoid intentionally confounding the study with sex bias, the used car salesperson was described as a salesperson and not a salesman. The research participants were told to im-

TABLE 5.1.
Microlevel and Macrolevel Sort Items

Macro Items	Micro Items
overly attentive	excessive smiling
attentive	smiling
not attentive at all	forced smile
overly apprehensive	drop in smiling behavior
apprehensive	no change in smiling behavior
not apprehensive at all	increase in physical contact
overly relaxed	physical contact unchanged
relaxed	physical contact drops
tense	excessive fidgeting
overly tense	no change in fidgeting
overly dramatic	drop in fidgeting
dramatic	pitch increases
not dramatic at all	pitch unchanged
overly animated	pitch decreases
animated	speech hesitations increase
not animated at all	speech hesitations unchanged
overly friendly	speech hesitations decrease
friendly	stares
not friendly at all	normal eye contact
overly open	looks away
open	verbal response longer
not open at all	amount of talk is same
communicates exceptionally well	verbal response shorter
communicates well	talks faster
does not communicate well	no change in rate of speech
overly contentious	talks slower
contentious	talks louder
not contentious at all	volume does not change
definitely leaves an impression	talks softer
leaves an impression	quick to respond verbally
does not leave an impression	amount of time before responding
overly dominant in conversation	unchanged
dominates conversation	takes long time to respond verbally
overly passive in conversation	increase in body shifts
overly precise	no change in body movement
precise	fewer body shifts
vague	

agine they were observing a used car salesperson on a used car lot, selling a car (known to the salesperson) to be "a lemon." The research participant is to assume the salesperson has lied in the past, and in order to make the sale, lies about the condition of the car. Given this scenario, research participants sorted the deck of cards in the order of the behaviors they would least likely expect to the behaviors they would most likely expect. The sort was a forced "quasi normal" distribution.

The second situation was designed to tap the more stereotypical picture of a "naive" or self-conscious deceiver. To tap this schema, research participants were told to imagine they are observing a new college student who desires to become a member of a college social club. The student knows of improprieties in the club's activities and is being interrogated about those activities by an investigating board. Rather than jeopardize his or her chances of becoming a member of the club because of "ratting," the student, unaccustomed to lying in the past, lies about any knowledge of the group's activities. Given this scenario, subjects sorted the deck of items in the order in which they would expect to observe the behaviors from the *least likely to observe* to the *most likely to observe*. Again, a forced quasi normal curve was used for the distribution.

Quanal Program

The quanal computer program, developed by Van Tubergen (1980), was used to factor the research participants by similarity of ranked items. This program will provide factors, which are types of research participants based on similarity of ranking of items. The number of factors can be manually requested and eigenvalues used to ascertain the validity of the factors represented as well as other criteria typically used to judge the representativeness of factors such as the Skree Test. The program provides the average z scores for items within factors, differences in z scores across factors, and consensus items across factors. One can assess the items that distinguish the types, both from the items most likely expected (positive z scores), as well as items least likely expected (negative z scores), and those items that were relatively unimportant or neutral for expected behavior in the deceptive schema.

RESULTS

This section presents the results of the Q analysis first for Situation 1, which was designed to tap the "smooth-talker" schema. As predicted, there were different schemata for the first situation.

After the first situation results are given, Situation 2 schema results are presented. This situation was designed to tap the "self-conscious" deceiver schema. Again, more than one schema was found for within this situation.

Table 5.2 depicts the schemata for Situation 1, and Table 5.3 shows the schemata for Situation 2. Taken together the results from the two situations confirm that subjects combine both microlevel and macrolevel cues differently across situations and thus represent distinct schemata for deceptive types.

TABLE 5.2.
Macro and Micro Items and Corresponding z Scores for Schema Types
in Situation 1

Type 1		Type 2	
N = 16	z	N = 17	z
overly dominant	2.0	excessive fidgeting	1.9
excessive smiling	1.8	increased body shifts	1.7
quick to respond	1.7	looks away	1.6
overly friendly	1.7	overly dominant	1.6
overly attentive	1.7	excessive smiling	1.5
overly dramatic	1.5	hesitations increase	1.4
talks faster	1.5	talks faster	1.4
longer response	1.5	quick response	1.4
definitely leaves an impression	1.5	long time to respond	1.3
dominates	1.5	vague	1.2
increased physical contact	1.5	overly tense	1.2
talks louder	1.2	increased physical contact	1.1
attentive	1.2	overly dramatic	1.1
dramatic	1.1	longer response	1.1
smiles	1.0	overly friendly	1.0
overly animated	1.0		

Type 3		Type 4	
N = 22	z	N = 9	z
overly dominant	2.1	smiles	2.6
overly friendly	1.9	friendly	1.8
excessive smiling	1.9	communicates exceptionally well	1.8
dominates	1.7	leaves an impression	1.8
vague	1.7	relaxed	1.7
forced smile	1.6	definitely leaves an impression	1.5
smiles	1.4	communicates well	1.4
overly animated	1.3	normal eye contact	1.3
overly dramatic	1.3	attentive	1.2
dramatic	1.2	precise	1.0
excessive fidgeting	1.1	response time unchanged	1.0
tense	1.1		
animated	1.0		
looks away	1.0		

Situation 1

For the sort in Situation 1, 52% of the variance is explained by a three factor solution. The Factor 1 eigenvalue is 22.47. For Factor 2, the eigenvalue is 8.63, whereas the Factor 3 eigenvalue is 2.5. Factor 1 accounts for 35% of the variance; Factor 2 accounts for 13%; Factor 3 accounts for 4%. Factors were obtained with an orthogonal solution in oblimax rotation (Harman, 1967).

TABLE 5.3.
Macro and Micro Items and Corresponding z Scores for Schema Types
in Situation 2

Type 1		Type 2	
N = 48	z	N = 15	z
overly tense	2.0	looks away	2.1
looks away	1.9	overly tense	1.9
excessive fidgeting	1.9	tense	1.9
vague	1.6	excessive fidgeting	1.8
tense	1.6	apprehensive	1.6
overly apprehensive	1.5	increase body shifts	1.5
hesitations increase	1.5	vague	1.4
increase body shifts	1.5	long time to respond	1.4
apprehensive	1.5	talks faster	1.3
not open at all	1.4	overly dramatic	1.2
forced smile	1.3	overly apprehensive	1.2
long time to respond	1.3	hesitations increase	1.1
shorter response length	1.3	talks softer	1.1
overly passive	1.2	quick to respond	1.0

Factor 2 was 39% negative. Negative items were extracted and formed into Type 4. Thus, the factor analysis yielded 4 types: Type 1 ($N = 16$); Type 2 ($N = 17$); Type 3 ($N = 22$); and Type 4 ($N = 9$). With a sample population 58% female, Type 1 research participants were 69% female, Type 2 participants were 65% female, Type 3 were 48% female, and Type 4 were 66% female. Table 5.2 gives all items expected for the types with a z score of 1.0 and above.[3] Key items for Type 1 research participants' schema of the used car salesperson were *overly dominant, excessive smiling, quick verbal response, overly friendly, overly attentive, overly dramatic, talks faster, verbal response length longer, leaves an impression,* and *dominates the conversation* ($z = 1.5$ and above). Type 1 mixes both microlevel and macrolevel cues and generally expects high-intensity cues. This Type is a strong indicator of the social stereotype of the used car salesman and fits the schema for the "smooth-talker," which this situation was designed to tap.

Type 2 research participants focused on microlevel cues including *excessive fidgeting, increase in body shifts,* and *looks away*. The only macrolevel cue above $z = 1.5$ was *overly dominant*. Type 2 differs from Type 1 in that they expect overly tense behavior ($z = 1.2$) and the microlevel cues are strongly expected reflect this macrolevel assessment. Oddly, this type was just as likely to expect very quick responses as they were to expect a very long time to

---

[3]Norm Van Tubergen, creator of the Quanal program, suggests the use of 1.00 z as a normalizing standard for selecting item loading on particular factors (personal communication, May 21, 1992).

respond. Perhaps, the simple explanation is that research participants expected something out of the ordinary in the kind of response given and either of these would have fit the schema. Although this type (Type 2) does not as clearly represent the social schema for the smooth-talker as Type 1 does, this type does incorporate some key elements of this social schema such as *fast talking, excessive smiling, dominance, longer verbal responses,* and *overly friendly.*

The schema of Type 3 is close to Type 1 at the macrolevel, but focuses more on smiling behavior and vagueness of the communication. Type 3 does not have any microlevel vocal cues above $z = 1.0$. The only microlevel body cue above $z = 1.0$ is *excessive fidgeting* at $z = 1.1$.

Type 4 research participants did not expect the high intensity behavioral cues (See Table 5.2). Instead they expected a normal, pleasant and skilled communicator. Key items are *smiles, friendly, communicates exceptionally well, leaves an impression,* and *relaxed* ($z = 1.5$ and above).

Situation 2

In Situation 2, the two-factor solution explains 47% of the variance in the sort. Eigenvalues were Factor 1 = 26.71; Factor 2 = 3.66. Factor 1 accounted for 41% of the variance, and Factor 2 accounted for 6%. Factors were obtained with an orthogonal solution in varimax rotation. $N = 48$ and $N = 15$ respectively for the two types. Both types had approximately 60% female subjects, which was proportional to the overall sample population.

Table 5.3 indicates the z scores (1.0 and above) for the types in Situation 2. This situation was designed to tap the naive, self-conscious liar with more stereotypical deception cues expected. The two types are very similar with the exception that Type 1 research participants ranked *not open at all* as very central to their schema, whereas Type 2 did not. In addition, Type 2 research participants ranked *talking faster* and *quick to respond verbally* at 1.0 or above whereas Type 1 did not. Type 1 more closely represents the anticipated schema of the self-conscious liar with cues of *overly tense, looking away, excessive fidgeting, vague, tense, overly apprehensive,* and *increased speech hesitations* as predominant ($z = 1.5$ or above).

Both types integrate microlevel and macrolevel cues but lean heavily toward microlevel cues in this situation. There were some strong agreements across types on cues. At $z = 1.5$ or above across types of research participants are the macrolevel cues *looks away, overly tense, excessive fidgeting, tense, vague,* and *apprehensive.* At $z = 1.0$ or above across types research participants also expected an increase in *body shifts, a long time to respond, overly apprehensive, an increase in speech hesitations,* and a *forced smile.*

DISCUSSION

The Q analysis confirmed that people have different schemata for deceptive people. In contrast to previous research, which focused either on microlevel or macrolevel cues this study incorporated both microlevel and macrolevel cues of perceptions of deceptive behavior and has demonstrated that, at both levels, the expected cues vary with the schema employed by the perceiver. Previous cues associated with perceptions of deception can be found in the various schemata in this study. Whether the cues are perceived as relevant depends on the situation and the schema perceivers' use of these elements in judging someone in an initial interaction. Microlevel cues found in the current study are *looking away, smiling, shorter response length*, and *faster speech rate*. In addition to cues previously associated with perceptions of deceit, a number of other microlevel cues were found scattered in the schemata such as *speech hesitations* and *volume*. Interestingly, *pitch* was not a major element in the schemata.

Macrolevel cues in the schemata are generally counter to previous findings. For example, *attentiveness* was associated with perceptions of honesty in the O'Hair et al. (1988) study, but here *overly attentive* becomes an expected behavior for the deceptive smooth-talker schema. Both microlevel and macrolevel cues can be found to be reversed and still be incorporated into a deceptive schemata. For example, a communicator could be *quick to respond* as in the Type 1 schema in Situation 1 or *slow to respond* as in both schema types in Situation 2. At the macrolevel *overly dominant* is found in Type 1, 2, and 3 schemata in Situation 1, but *overly passive* is found Type 1 schema in Situation 2.

This analysis indicates that quite a number of macrolevel cues can be perceived as associated with deceptive behavior and are dependent on the schema invoked in the impression formation process. Situation 1, which attempted to invoke the smooth-talker schema actually produced four distinct schemata even though three of those contained similar macrolevel cues and all three of these included excessive smiling at the microlevel.

When tense or overly tense macrolevel cues are not expected, the associated microlevel cues (such as *fidgeting, looking away*, and *body shifts*) disappear. People can envision deceptive people who are either over compensating for the deception by talking faster and smiling a lot (Type 1, Situation 1), or just doing a good job and have very little deceptive cue "leakage" (Type 3, Situation 1).

Some schemata are heavily cued with microlevel cues (Type 2, Situation 1), whereas others are mixed. At least one schema, Type 3 in Situation 1, was heavily focused on facial as opposed to body or vocal microlevel cues. At least one schema was heavily cued with macrolevel cues (Type 4, Situation 1).

The results indicate that certain microlevel cues are more typically associated with specific macrolevel communicator style attributes. Just as the fidgeting and body shifts seem to be associated with tenseness, a communicator's smiling or excessive smiling appears to be associated with friendliness and overly friendliness. *Talking faster* is found in conjunction with *dominance* and *overly dominant* as is *longer response length* and *quicker responses*. Thus, different microlevel cues are more strongly associated with certain macrolevel cues in the various schemata.

The results of this study imply that trying to isolate a given set of characteristics at either the microlevel or macrolevel that people use across situations to make judgments of deceit in another are inappropriate. Because there is an indication that research participants have schemata that vary in their microlevel and macrolevel cues, a better route for determining how people make such assessments of honesty or deception would be to consider various possible combinations of cues to form types that correspond to people's cognitive framework. Any given microlevel or macrolevel cue can be interpreted in a number of different ways; it is the particular combination of cues forming a deceptive type of person that is more likely to influence beliefs about another's deceptive character on initial contact.

Planalp (1985) demonstrated that knowledge about appropriate communication behaviors in given relationships is an integral part of relational schemata. The present study gives additional weight to the role of expected communicative behavior by demonstrating that people differentiated deceptive types on the basis of nonverbal (microlevel) cues and communicator style dimensions (macrolevel cues).

The effects of deceptive schemata on initial impressions of others are as yet unexamined, but, given the current study, some implications can be suggested. First, Berger (1987) suggested that schemata can serve to reduce uncertainty. Through use of a schema, individuals have knowledge about how they should respond to specific individuals. Reduction in uncertainty would lead to a decrease in information seeking (McKinney & Donaghy, this volume). However, because the schema utilized in this case is one of a deceptive individual, information seeking could increase in an attempt to confirm or disconfirm the schema or to make sure of the truth of the information being provided in the initial interaction. Planalp and Honeycutt (1985) noted that deception typically increases uncertainty, which would lead to increases in information seeking.

A second implication is that, if people have a variety of schemata for deceptive types, they may respond differently to different types of people. Intuitively, it would seem that the level of confidence one has in interacting with the self-conscious deceiver would be much greater than when interacting with the smooth talker. Accordingly, the potential for relationship development and the interactions pursuant to that relationship would appear to be different if one sees an individual as an average "Don Juan" or "Mata Hari" than if they are viewed as a "Ted Bundy" or "Fatal Attraction."

Although not investigated in this study, the schemata for deceptive types would likely include a number of additional attributes beyond the dimensions of the communicator style measure. A part of this schema material could include the types of things a person would lie about. If a potential relational partner concludes that the other would lie about anything, the level of trust would be much lower than if he or she believed they would only lie to protect someone important to them.

A third implication is that, if physical attributes are particularly relevant for activating schema (Fiske & Taylor, 1991), targets of impression formation who share similar physical qualities to deceptive individuals encountered in the past will be likely to evoke the same emotional responses as those individuals. For example, if a previous relational partner was found to be particularly deceptive and one meets another person who has strong similarities to the relational partner, then this new person may not even be given the benefit of the doubt in an initial interaction. It is possible that sufficient trust may never be built to carry this meeting beyond an initial interaction.

REFERENCES

Asch, S. E. (1946). Forming impressions of personality. *Journal of Abnormal and Social Psychology, 41*, 258–290.

Asch, S. E., & Zukier, H. (1984). Thinking about persons. *Journal of Personality and Social Psychology, 46*, 1230–1240.

Bartlett, F. (1932). *Remembering: A study in experimental and social psychology.* Cambridge, England: Cambridge University Press.

Berger, C. R. (1987). Communicating under uncertainty. In M. E. Roloff & G. R. Miller (Eds.), *Interpersonal processes: New directions in communication research* (pp. 39–62). Newbury Park, CA: Sage.

Brooks, W. D. (1970). Q-sort technique. In P. Emmert & W. D. Brooks (Eds.), *Methods of research in communication* (pp. 165–180). Boston: Houghton Mifflin.

Brown, R. (1986). *Social cognition* (2nd. ed.). New York: Free Press.

Brown, S. R., & Ungs, T. D. (1970). Representativeness and the study of political behavior: An application of Q technique to reactions to the Kent State incident. *Social Science Quarterly, 51*, 514–526.

Bruner, J. S., Shapiro, D., & Taguiri, R. (1958). The meaning of traits in isolation and in combination. In R. Taguiri & L. Petrullo (Eds.), *Person perception and interpersonal behavior* (pp. 277–288). Stanford, CA: Stanford University Press.

Cantor, N., & Mischel, W. (1979). Prototypes in person perception. In L. Berkowitz (Ed.), *Advances in experimental social psychology* (Vol. 12, pp. 4–52). New York: Academic Press.

Dion, K., Berscheid, E., & Walster, E. (1972). What is beautiful is good. *Journal of Personality and Social Psychology, 24*, 285–290.

Fiske, S. T., & Dyer, L. M. (1985). Structure and development of social schemata: Evidence from positive and negative transfer effects. *Journal of Personality and Social Psychology, 48*, 839–852.

Fiske, S. T., & Neuberg, S. L. (1990). A continuum of impression formation, from category-based to individuating processes: Influences of information and motivation on attention and interpretation. In M. P. Zanna (Ed.), *Advances in experimental social psychology* (Vol. 23, pp. 1–74). San Diego, CA: Academic Press.

Fiske, S. T., & Taylor, S. E. (1991). *Social cognition* (2nd ed.). New York: McGraw-Hill.

Harman, H. H. (1969). *Modern factor analysis* (2nd ed. rev.). Chicago: University of Chicago Press.

Hocking, J. E., Bauchner, J., Kaminski, E. P., & Miller, G. R. (1979). Detecting deceptive communication from verbal, visual, and paralinguistic cues. *Human Communication Research*, 6, 33–46.

Jones, E. E. (1990). *Interpersonal perception*. New York: W. H. Freeman.

Kalbfleisch, P. J. (1990). Listening for deception: The effects of medium on accuracy of detection. In R. N. Bostrom (Ed.), *Listening Behavior: Measurement and Application* (pp. 155–176). New York: Guilford Press.

Kalbfleisch, P. J. (1992). Deceit, distrust and the social milieu: Application of deception research in a troubled world. *Journal of Applied Communication Research, 20,* 308–334.

Kerlinger, F. N. (1986). *Foundations of behavioral research* (3rd ed.). New York: Holt, Rinehart & Winston.

Knapp, M. L., Cody, M. J., & Reardon, K. K. (1987). Viewing nonverbal signals from multilevel perspectives. In C. Berger & S. Chaffee (Eds.), *Handbook of communication science* (pp. 385–418). Beverly Hills, CA: Sage.

Krauss, R. M., Apple, W., Morency, N., Wenzel, C., & Winton, W. (1981). Verbal, vocal, and visible factors in judgments of another's affect. *Journal of Personality and Social Psychology, 40,* 312–320.

McKeown, B., & Thomas, D. (1988). Q methodology. *Sage University Paper Series on Quantitative Applications in the Social Sciences* (Series No. 07-001). Beverly Hills: Sage.

Miller, D. T., & Turnbull, W. (1986). Expectancies and interpersonal processes. *Annual Review of Psychology, 37,* 233–256.

Norton, R., (1978). Foundations of a communicator style construct. *Human Communication Research, 4,* 99–112.

Nunnally, J. C., Jr. (1978). *Psychometric theory* (2nd ed.). New York: McGraw Hill.

O'Hair, H. D., Cody, M. J., Goss, B., & Krayer, K. K. (1988). The effect of gender, deceit orientation and communicator style on macro-level-assessments of honesty. *Communication Quarterly, 36,* 77–93.

Planalp, S. (1985). Relational schemata: A test of alternative forms of relational knowledge as guides to communication. *Human Communication Research, 12,* 3–29.

Planalp, S., & Honeycutt, J. M. (1985). Events that increase uncertainty in personal relationships. *Human Communication Research, 11,* 593–604.

Riggio, R. E., Salinas, C., & Tucker, J. (1988). Personality and deception ability. *Personality and Individual Differences, 9,* 189–191.

Riggio, R. E., Tucker, J., & Throckmorton, B. (1988). Social skills and deception ability. *Personality and Social Psychology Bulletin, 13,* 568–577.

Rosch, E., Mervis, C. B., Gray, W. D., Johnson, D. M., & Boyes-Braem, P. (1976). Basic objects in natural categories. *Cognitive Psychology, 8,* 382–439.

Rumelhart, D. E., & Ortony, A. (1977). The representation of knowledge in memory. In R. Anderson, R. Spiro, & W. Montague, (Eds.), *Schooling and the acquisition of knowledge* (pp. 99–136). Hillsdale, NJ: Lawrence Erlbaum Associates.

Snyder, M., Tanke, E. D., & Berscheid, E. (1977). Social perception and interpersonal behavior: On the self-fulfilling nature of social stereotypes. *Journal of Personality and Social Psychology, 35,* 656–666.

Stephenson, W. (1953). *The study of behavior: Q-technique and its methodology*. Chicago: University of Chicago Press.

Taylor, S. E., & Crocker, J. (1981). Schematic bases of social information processing. In E. T. Higgins, C. P. Herman, & M. P. Zanna (Eds.), *Social cognition: The Ontario symposium* (pp. 89–134). Hillsdale, NJ: Lawrence Erlbaum Associates.

Van Tubergen, N. (1980). *Quanal* [Computer program]. Lexington, KY: N. Van Tubergen, University of Kentucky.

Zuckerman, M., DePaulo, B., & Rosenthal, R. (1981). Verbal and nonverbal communication of deception. In L. Berkowitz (Ed.), *Advances in experimental social psychology* (Vol. 14, pp. 1–59). New York: Academic Press.

Zuckerman, M., DeFrank, R. S., Hall, J. A., Larrance, D. T., & Rosenthal, R. (1979). Facial and vocal cues of deception and honesty. *Journal of Experimental Social Psychology, 15*, 378–396.

III

RELATIONSHIPS IN PROCESS

6

Ways of Doing Conflict: A Folk Taxonomy of Conflict Events in Personal Relationships

Leslie A. Baxter
University of California, Davis

William W. Wilmot
University of Montana

Christopher A. Simmons
University of California, Davis

Andrea Swartz
University of California, Davis

Our understanding of the role of conflict in personal relationships has increased dramatically in recent years (for recent reviews see Cahn, 1990; Hocker & Wilmot, 1991). We have seen research detailing the interaction behaviors of relational partners (e.g., Gottman, 1979; Newton & Burgoon, 1990; Zeitlow & Sillars, 1988), studies illustrating the importance of dispositional, personal styles of conflict management (e.g., Canary & Spitzberg, 1989; Metts & Cupach, 1990), and research that examines the content issues of conflict disputes (e.g., Argyle & Furnham, 1983; Braiker & Kelley, 1979; Sillars, Weisberg, Burggraf, & Wilson, 1987). Although this research collectively has advanced our thinking about the role of conflict in relationships, certain limitations can be noted. First, conflict has been studied almost exclusively at the individual level of analysis (Knapp, Putnam, & Davis, 1988). Second, extant approaches are dominated by the researcher point of view rather than the view of the "native" participants (Grimshaw, 1990). Each of these perspectives limits our understanding of the complexity and richness of conflict events as they are experienced in everyday relational life by the participants. The goal of the current study is to develop a folk taxonomy of the kinds of conflict events that participants distinguish in their friendships and romantic relationships.

Although conflict is most often defined as an interpersonal or system event, data collected on conflict tactics and styles typically are limited to individual behavioral actions coded by researchers or self-reports of generalized individual actions. Although it has been noted that "we cannot understand conflict dynamics by examining the individuals in isolation" (Hocker & Wilmot, 1991, p. 129), extant research has only begun to specify the communicative patterns that correlate with style preferences (Conrad, 1991).

Some researchers and theorists have attempted to address conflict at the event level, particularly in the articulation of taxonomies or typologies of types of conflict. Grimshaw (1990), for instance, distinguished conflicts based on (a) differences in the substantive issues that precipitate conflict talk; (b) the opportunity for, or inevitability of, conflict; (c) the "stakes" of the conflict; (d) the identities of the participants; and (e) the emotional tone of the conflict. Cahn (1990) reviewed several of the conflict typologies advanced by others, noting that a number of these appear to be organized by the scope or magnitude of the issue at stake. Although researchers who take a typological approach to interpersonal conflict are recognizing the complexity of interpersonal conflict events, they are ignoring the participant perspective in favor of outsider sense making. To date, there is limited insight into whether participants distinguish different kinds of conflict events from one another and the basis of such distinctions. When participants are asked to evaluate dyadic-level conflicts, they are generally asked to give globalized judgments about the overall frequency of conflict as if conflict were a single, monolithic phenomenon (Lloyd, 1990).

Substantial research from the ethnography of communication tradition has examined conflict events as part of the broader ethnographic research agenda to describe the full range of communication events enacted in speech communities. The communication event is the central analytic unit in the ethnography of communication perspective and is conceptualized as a unified constellation of features that is distinguishable from other events by members of a given speech community (Philipsen & Carbaugh, 1986; Saville-Troike, 1989). Hymes' (1972) classic essay introduced a useful acronym by which to summarize the possible features that could meaningfully distinguish one event from another: S-P-E-A-K-I-N-G. According to Hymes, communication events could vary in their

Settings of enactment, the

Participant actors in the event, the

Ends or purposes of the interaction event, the sequencing of

Acts from the beginning to the end of the event, the

Key or emotional tone of the event, the verbal and nonverbal

Instrumentalities of enactment, the broader cultural knowledge or

Norms that the participants need to know in order to make the event intelligible, and the alternative

Genres or interaction gestalts recognized in the speech community.

Although this framework is a useful synthesis of possible sources of variation in communication events, Hymes emphasized that the insider perspective, not that of the researcher, is crucial in determining which events are meaningfully distinguishable from one another.

Unfortunately, the ethnographic work on conflict events focuses largely on formalized and ritualized conflict in non-American speech communities and thus affords limited insight into informal interpersonal conflict events enacted in the U.S. society (for a review see Brenneis, 1988). Some ethnographic research considers conflict-related enactments in a variety of demographic enclaves in U.S. society, including black urban adolescents (Goodwin, 1990; Kochman, 1981); male residents in the working-class Chicago neighborhood of Teamsterville (Philipsen, 1975); residents of an affluent suburb of New York City (Baumgartner, 1988); dorm residents on the Rutgers campus (Moffatt, 1989); and college-bound high school adolescents (Baxter & Goldsmith, 1990). In general, however, this work fails to situate conflict enactment in the personal relationships of the participants.

We were able to identify only a few studies in which dyadic-level conflict events in personal relationships have been studied from the "native's" point of view. In a naturalistic study, Lloyd (1990) asked parties from romantic relationships to keep diary records for a 2-week period on the conflicts that were enacted in their relationship. Although this study emphasized dyadic-level conflict events as they were perceived by the participants, Lloyd provided the parties with a researcher-determined definition of the conflict domain and researcher-defined scales upon which to record information about the conflict. In defining conflict as interaction that displayed disagreement or which concerned any issues or problems in the relationship, Lloyd may have systematically eliminated conflicts that were enacted in ways other than through verbal expression or disagreement. Further, her instructions may have biased participants to report on conflicts that involved relationship-relevant issues to the relative neglect of conflicts over other issues. Lloyd also elicited static information in the diary records of conflict events, including when and where the conflicts took place, how long they lasted, how intense they were, and whether they were resolved. Participant insights were not elicited on the process dynamics by which conflicts unfolded, nor were participants asked to identify in their own terms how the episodes were similar or different from one another.

In contrast to Lloyd's (1990) naturalistic study of how often disagreements are enacted in romantic relationships, other studies have focused in detail on particular kinds of conflict-related episodes. Harris, Gergen, and Lannamann (1986), for example, explored the cultural logic of a single kind of conflict event, the aggression ritual as enacted in the male acquaintance dyad and in the marital couple. Harris and her colleagues found that escalating, verbalized aggression has a distinct internal logic that is systematically perceived by members of the broader speech community. Although the Harris et al. study is insightful with respect to one kind of conflict event, it does not inform us about other possible kinds of interpersonal conflict events that might be similar to or different from the aggression ritual.

In a number of studies, Newell and Stutman (1988) examined the social confrontation episode, a patterned interaction event in which one party perceives that the other has behaved inappropriately. Newell and Stutman have suggested that the social confrontation episode involves disagreement over behavior in contrast to a different kind of confrontation that involves disagreement over issues. Newell and Stutman (1988, p. 284) argued that the social confrontation episode is "congruent with popular definitions of conflict," yet this congruence has not been established from the native point of view.

Because of the paucity of empirical work devoted to participant perspectives on the kinds of conflict events enacted in their personal relationships, the primary purpose of the current study is the description of a folk taxonomy of conflict events. Grimshaw (1990, p. 282) has noted that taxonomic organization is a "necessary first step" in any research domain and urges conflict researchers to devote more attention to the descriptive adequacy of research on conflict phenemena as a foundation for explanatory efforts. Thus, the first research (R) question is simply:

R_1:   What are the kinds of interpersonal conflict events identified by relationship parties, and what are the semantic features by which those conflict events are distinguished?

As Healey and Bell (1990) recently observed, the friendship relationship has received very limited attention with respect to conflict management. Instead, personal relationships have tended to concentrate on romantic or marital relationships in the study of conflict tactics and styles. However, as Hays (1988) noted, close platonic friendships are subject to the same emotional aggravation and conflict as romantic relationships. Whether the forms of conflict enactment are similar for platonic friendships and romantic relationships has yet to be determined. Existing work suggests that friendships and romantic relationships are characterized to some extent by different relational expectations; basic relational differences might result in different forms of dyadic conflict enactment. For example, romantic relationships more so than platonic friendships are characterized by an expectation of exclusivity and an expectation of emotional expressiveness (Davis & Todd, 1985; Wright, 1985). The expressiveness expectation might result in more direct conflict enactments for romantic partners, whereas platonic friends might engage in conflict less openly. Further, the direct conflict enactments of romantic partners might be characterized by greater emotional intensity than those of platonic friends because of the expectation of exclusivity and its possible correlates of jealousy and perceived loss of independence. The second research question is thus:

R$_2$:   To what extent are the conflict events identified by platonic friends similar to those identified by romantic partners?

The third research question examines possible gender differences in the identification of conflict-event types. Although substantial research has examined male and female differences in reported individual-level tactics and styles of conflict management, results in general are mixed (for reviews see Burggraf & Sillars, 1987; Hocker & Wilmot, 1991). Further, individual-level data on tactics and styles do not address dyad-level conflict events. Some research suggests that male friendships differ from female friendships, particularly with respect to the role of talk, but male and female friendships also have many qualities in common (for a review see Sapadin, 1988). Because prediction is difficult with respect to systematic gender differences in the identification of dyadic-level conflict events, the following research question is advanced:

R$_3$:   Do females and males distinguish different types of conflict events in their personal relationships?

METHODS

Pilot Study

Before undertaking the study reported in this chapter a pilot investigation was conducted to determine whether participants could distinguish different kinds of conflict events in their interpersonal lives. Thirty-four informants in an undergraduate course in the ethnography of communication provided data for the pilot study in exchange for extra credit. After class discussion and reading on the concept of a *communication event*, informants were given 1 week to reflect on all of the different kinds of conflicts they experienced in a personal relationship of their selection. At the end of a week, informants were asked to turn in a written summary of all of the kinds of conflict events that occurred in their relationship. Informants were clearly capable of differentiating conflict events from one another, identifying a total of 146 kinds of conflict events with a range of 2–10.

Actual Study

Participants.   Participants in the actual study were 101 undergraduates who volunteered to be interviewed in exchange for extra credit in their lower division communication courses. In order to be eligible for participation, respondents had to have a close same-sex friend with whom they interacted often and an opposite-sex romantic partner with whom they interacted often and with whom they had been involved romantically for at least 3 months. Prior to the establishment of contact by the interviewer, each participant was randomly assigned to be interviewed about either his/her same-sex friendship or his/her opposite-sex relationship. The distribution of interviews by gender and relationship type included 22 male participants who were interviewed about their friendships, 23 male participants who were interviewed about their romantic relationships, 27 female participants who discussed their friendships, and 29 female participants who were interviewed about their romantic relationships. The average relationship length was 22.2 months.

Ethnographic Interviewing Procedures. An interviewing team consisting of eight advanced undergraduates and two of the authors conducted all of the hour-long interviews. Interviewers underwent a month-long training period, including pretesting of the interview protocol. In the initial telephone contact with an informant, the interviewer indicated that the purpose of the interview was to hear about "all of the different ways you and your friend/romantic partner enact conflict between you." Informants were asked to think about this topic before coming to the scheduled interview, usually scheduled from 5 to 7 days after the initial telephone contact. All interviews were audio taped for purposes of subsequent analysis.

The interview protocol was based on Spradley's (1979) "grand tour" method.[1] That is, informants were first asked to provide a detailed description of their most recent conflict with their friend/romantic partner. Interviewers probed, with respect to the issue or topic of the conflict, (a) how the conflict began, (b) how the conflict unfolded, (c) how the conflict ended, and (d) what the informant liked and disliked about the conflict enactment. After completing a detailed description of their most recent conflict enactment, each informant was asked to take the interviewer on a grand tour of all of the other ways the pair enacted conflict that were different from the most recent enactment. The interview proceeded in a compare–contrast mode, with the interviewer asking the informant to identify, for each identified way of enacting conflict, how that enactment process compared and contrasted with the forms of enactment already identified. The "final product" of each interview was a verbalized list of all of the different ways the pair enacted conflict from the perspective of the informant. After completing the grand tour of all of the ways of enacting conflict, informants filled out Wheeless' 20-item Solidarity Scale (1976, 1978). The Solidarity Scale was selected as a measure of relationship closeness because of its suitability for both platonic friendships and romantic relationships (Baxter, 1988).

---

[1]A copy of the complete interview protocol is available from the first author upon request.

Data Analysis Procedures. In order to reduce the corpus of identified conflict enactment processes to a smaller number, three of the researchers independently employed Bulmer's (1979) method of analytic induction and Spradley's (1979) method of componential analysis. *Analytic induction* involved the derivation of categories by selecting a subsample of the data, forming a category set that fit the selected data, and then modifying the category set in an iterative back-and-forth manner, as needed, in response to additional data instances. The *componential analysis* involved the identification of underlying semantic themes or dimensions that were salient in informant talk in differentiating conflict events from one another. After independently analyzing the data using these two related procedures, the three researchers met to establish the final set of conflict-event categories and the semantic dimensions that served to differentiate the categories from one another. The final set of 12 conflict-event categories is presented in the "Results" section. The three researchers independently had agreed on 9 of the 12 categories and their salient semantic dimensions. After developing the final category set, two of the researchers independently used the category scheme to code all of the enactment types that had been identified by informants in the interview process. Absolute coding agreement was 77.3% with a kappa coefficient (Cohen, 1960) of .75 ($z = 44.9$, p < .0001). The independent coding decisions of a third coder were used to resolve discrepancies in the judgments of the two initial coders.

RESULTS

Preliminary Analyses

Prior to undertaking the analyses relevant to the research questions, a number of preliminary analyses were performed. A two-way ANOVA of relationship type X gender on relationship length indicated that same-sex friendships were not significantly longer than opposite-sex romantic relationships [$F(1, 97) = .60, p > .05$]. Males and females did not differ in the lengths of their relationships [$F(1, 97) = .016, p > .05$], nor was there a significant interaction between relationship type and gender [$F(1, 97) = .003, p > .05$].

A principal-components analysis with varimax rotation was performed on the Solidarity Scale, confirming Wheeless' (1976, 1978) suggestion that the instrument is unidimensional. The reliability of the Solidary Scale for the present data set was a Cronbach's alpha value of .92. A two-way ANOVA of relationship type X gender revealed that romantic relationships were closer ($M = 6.20$) than platonic friendships ($M = 5.53$) [$F(1, 97) = 11.28, p < .001$]; however, no significant main effect emerged for gender [$F(1,97) = 1.28, p > .05$], and no significant interaction effect was found [$F(1, 97) = .13, p > .05$].

Relationship length was modestly correlated with closeness for both friendships [$r (47) = .17$] and romantic relationships [$r (50) = .15$], although neither
correlation reached significance at the .05 level.

Substantive Analyses

Research Question 1.   The first research question addressed the different
types of conflict events that were identified from the native point of view. Consistent with Spradley's (1979) semantic componential analysis procedures, the
conflict-event types were differentiated from one another based on binary
semantic pairs evident in informant talk. Table 6.1 presents a summary of the
kinds of conflict events and their semantic dimensions which are organized
through a series of binary Yes–No questions. *Mock Conflict* is differentiated
from all other kinds of conflict events by its playful intent. In contrast to other

TABLE 6.1.
The Kinds of Conflict Events and Their Semantic Dimensions

	Semantic Dimensions*									
	1	*2*	*3*	*4*	*5*	*6*	*7*	*8*	*9*	*10*
Mock Conflict	Yes									
Déjà Vu	No	Yes								
Third-Party Intervention	No	No	Yes							
Indirect	No	No	No	Yes						
Silent-Treatment Conflict	No	No	No	No	Yes					
Time-Out Conflict	No	No	No	No	No	Yes				
Escalatory Conflict	No	No	No	No	No	No	Yes			
One-Sided Conflict	No	No	No	No	No	No	No	Yes		
Blowup Conflict	No	No	No	No	No	No	No	No	Yes	Yes
Sarcastic Sniping	No	No	No	No	No	No	No	No	Yes	No
Civil Discussion	No	No	No	No	No	No	No	No	No	Yes
Tacit Conflict	No	No	No	No	No	No	No	No	No	No

*Column numbers correspond to the following binary questions:
 1. Is the conflict event playful in its intent?
 2. Is the conflict enactment recurring for the parties, as if it were a 'broken record'?
 3. Do third-party outsiders get involved in the enactment of the conflict?
 4. Does the conflict enactment occur without the parties ever expressing it verbally?
 5. Does the enactment occur over multiple interaction episodes marked by silence or with-
    drawal at the outset?
 6. Does the enactment occur over multiple interaction episodes punctuated by withdrawal
    from interaction after verbal expression of the conflict issue?
 7. Does the conflict escalate in intensity or scope over the course of the enactment?
 8. Does one party fail to engage the conflict?
 9. Is the tone of enactment uncooperative and hostile?
10. Are sentiments expressed directly?

kinds of conflict enactments, informants identified a form of conflict event that could display any of the surface features of serious conflict but which was enacted "just for the fun of it." One male informant described this kind of conflict event as a "ripping battle" that he and his male friend enacted when they were making fun of each other. "Ripping battles" were over "small" matters and involved "no anger, grudges, or hatred." Rather, ripping battles involved "smart-ass remarks" said in fun in which each friend tried to enact a "better rip" than the other. To an outsider, ripping battles might appear as serious arguments, but the friends were playing an entertaining verbal game for the pleasure of its enactment.

Déjà Vu Conflicts are serious conflicts characterized by predictable repetition. The parties enact the same conflict over and over again, as if they are the proverbial "broken record." A female respondent who discussed conflict enactments in her romantic relationship identified this form by labeling it their "predictable conflict." The informant indicated that she and her partner "know in advance" that they will (a) enact the conflict on a certain topic or issue, (b) know how the conflict enactment will play itself out, and (c) know that the enactment will never end in genuine resolution. The parties have the sensation of enacting something they have enacted before in exactly the same way.

The third kind of conflict enactment, *Third-Party Intervention*, involves outside third parties in the expression of the conflict. One female informant illustrated this kind of conflict enactment in her platonic friendship by describing a conflict she labeled "adding a boyfriend." The informant's friend/roommate had engaged in some behavior that had "bugged" her, so she left the apartment in order to escape from the offensive behavior. The informant's boyfriend stayed behind and tried to talk to the friend/roommate, "ending up in a big fight between the two of them," but an apology from the friend/roommate was forthcoming to the informant by the next day. Third-Party Interventions could involve the taking of sides, as in this informant's account, or they could involve neutral intervention by outsiders in an attempt to achieve resolution without bias toward either party.

Indirect Conflict involves the presence of conflict without a word ever being exchanged between the parties. A male friend referred to this type of conflict enactment as the "don't talk about it" conflict and elaborated by saying that he and his friend enacted this form of conflict over serious issues that could rupture the relationship if discussed. Both "just understood" that the issue was serious from the tension they felt. When the tension was "close to being talked about, we would change the subject because we didn't want the other to be hurt by what was said." The conflict issue generally dissipated with time or when one of the parties changed his behavior.

Two kinds of conflict events, *Silent-Treatment Conflict* and *Time-Out Conflict*, are protracted in length and extend across two or more interaction episodes. The two types differ from one another in the placement of silence or withdrawal in punctuating the episodes. Silence or withdrawal, typically by one party, marks the beginning of the Silent-Treatment Conflict, signaling that something is wrong and that the offender needs to take remedial action. A female in a romantic relationship illustrates this type of enactment:

> This typically begins with some challenge to authority or knowledge or something like that. The person challenged gets kind of defensive and reacts with "the silent treatment." A period of time passes with none or minimal conversation between us. The challenger finally tries to get the other one to talk until the problem gets discussed openly.

By contrast, silence or withdrawal in the Time-Out Conflict does not signal the beginning of a conflict event; rather, the absence of interaction is used by the parties to allow them to gain distance from the conflict in order to resolve it more productively. A female described this type of enactment in her romantic relationship in what she labeled a "taking-time-apart" kind of conflict:

> Everything is laid out or put on the table. It's putting everything on the table and then separating from it and thinking about it on our own. This ends in a coming together. We're able to reflect, sleep on it, and come up with more ideas, rather than whatever comes to mind at first.

Escalatory Conflicts take place within a single interaction episode, but the enactment goes through multiple stages in which the scope of the conflict or the intensity of the conflict increases over time. Some Escalatory Conflicts initially began as Mock Conflicts that "got out of hand" or were "taken the wrong way." Other Escalatory Conflicts involved increasing emotional intensity as the conflict was enacted. One female respondent provided this example for her romantic relationship: "I might bring up a topic. Then he will get mad that I brought up this particular topic. Then I will lose my patience and get frustrated. He, in turn, will get more mad." Other Escalatory Conflicts involved increasing the scope or domain of issues under dispute. A female respondent described in detail her "build up conflict" type in her romantic relationship:

> My boyfriend will do something that bothers me. I will say that I don't like it. But then I will typically bring up similar things that he has done in the past. You know, "And another thing . . . I didn't like it when you rolled your eyes."

One-Sided Conflicts are enactments in which one party expresses a complaint or attempts to start a serious fight, but the partner fails to engage. The failure to engage the other in a two-sided conflict could be motivated by many factors, but informants frequently expressed futility or lack of opportunity as reasons. A female friend captured the futility motive in describing the "one is wrong and knows it" kind of conflict that she and her girlfriend enact:

This starts when one person does something that is sure to cause a conflict. When the other person calls her on it, the conflict officially begins. There is anger by the person who is in the right, and the other just apologizes.

One male informant captured the lack of opportunity associated with some One-Sided Conflicts in the following description of the "hit and run" kind of conflict that he and his girlfriend enact:

This conflict is a very short one in which somebody makes confrontational statements or criticisms of the other person. It's a sort of drive-by shooting conflict in which there is no time or opportunity for response.

Blowup Conflicts and *Sarcastic Sniping Conflicts* are both characterized by a spirit of uncooperativeness between the parties that is typically hostile in nature. Sniping employs indirect sarcasm to accomplish the expression of hostility, whereas Blowup typically involves the heated or intense expression of emotions to the point of yelling. Sarcastic Sniping is illustrated by a male informant's account of the following conflict enactment form in his platonic friendship:

It's the "I'm right, you're wrong" conflict because that's what's really going on. When a touchy issue like drugs or drinking comes up in conversation, we will make our positions known to each other through sarcastic remarks back and forth. Neither one of us is really listening to the other, because we're both set in our ways on the topic and think the other one is wrong. We get really frustrated and then we forget it once it's over.

The labels that informants provided of the Blow Up Conflict reveal its basic characteristics, for example, the "can't hold it in scream and yell" conflict, the "explosion" conflict, the "angry exchange" conflict, the "blowout" conflict, the "yelling match" conflict, the "yelling outburst" conflict, and the "confrontation" conflict. In enacting the Blowup Conflict, relationship parties engage in reciprocal venting of negative emotions with little regard for cooperative solutions.

Civil Discussion and *Tacit Conflict*, by contrast, are characterized by a spirit of cooperation between the parties. In enacting Civil Discussions, informants described calm and rational discussions in which both parties stated their positions clearly and in nonaccusatory ways. Tacit Conflict is "cautious" expression of conflict motivated by a desire to prevent escalation of the situation or hurt to the other party. A male informant illustrates Tacit Conflict in the following example of what he labeled the "dance-around-it conflict" in his romantic relationship:

Conflict is perceived by both partners but it isn't directly addressed but said in a softer, more joking way. Both of us see the conflict and dance around it, do ing something to make it easy so emotions won't get high or so nobody will actually be hurt.

Unlike the joking that may occur in Mock Conflict, this informant's joking was not said in fun but for strategic purpose in seeking a cooperative solution to a serious conflict issue.

Table 6.2 provides information on the frequency and proportion of informants who reported at least one instance of each conflict-event type. Overall, Civil Discussion was the most frequently identified form of conflict enactment; 47.5% of all informants identified this form of conflict enactment. Escalatory Conflict, Silent-Treatment Conflict, and One-Sided Conflict were each identified by over one-third of the informants. Approximately one-fourth of the informants identified each of the following conflict-event types: Mock Conflict, Time-Out Conflict, Indirect Conflict, Blowup Conflict, Tacit Conflict, and Déjà Vu Conflict. Sarcastic Sniping and Third-Party Intervention were each identified by about 12% of the sample. About 8% of the identified kinds of conflict events could not be categorized into the twelve types summarized above, comprising the other category.

Research Questions 2 and 3.   The second and third research questions addressed possible differences in the reported kinds of conflict events as a function of relationship type and informant gender, respectively. Table 6.2 provides information on the frequencies and proportions of males and females in friendships and romantic relationships who reported each type of conflict event. Statistical analyses involved loglinear logit model-fitting (Knoke &

TABLE 6.2.
The Frequencies and Proportions of Informants Who Identified the Types
of Conflict Events by Gender and Relationship Type

	Friendship		Romantic		
Conflict Event Type	Male	Female	Male	Female	Overall
Mock Conflict	12(.55)	6(.22)	3(.13)	9(.31)	30(.30)
Déjà Vu	3(.14)	1(.04)	3(.13)	15(.52)	22(.22)
Third-Party Intervention	2(.09)	4(.15)	1(.04)	2(.07)	9(.09)
Indirect	6(.27)	12(.44)	5(.22)	3(.10)	26(.26)
Silent-Treatment Conflict	4(.18)	10(.37)	8(.35)	15(.52)	37(.37)
Time-Out Conflict	4(.18)	6(.22)	8(.35)	9(.31)	27(.27)
Escalatory Conflict	10(.46)	4(.15)	12(.52)	12(.41)	38(.38)
One-Sided Conflict	7(.32)	8(.30)	12(.52)	9(.31)	36(.36)
Blowup Conflict	6(.27)	6(.22)	5(.22)	9(.31)	26(.26)
Sarcastic Sniping	2(.09)	4(.15)	2(.09)	5(.17)	13(.13)
Civil Discussion	9(.41)	14(.52)	11(.48)	14(.48)	48(.48)
Tacit Conflict	8(.14)	16(.59)	3(.13)	3(.10)	25(.25)

Burke, 1980; Norusis, 1988), with relationship type and informant gender as the classification variables, relational closeness as a covariate, and the presence/absence of a given conflict-event type as the dependent variable. A separate logit analysis was performed for each of the twelve conflict-event types.

The model of independence, that is, the absence of relationship between conflict type and the classification variables, could not be rejected for eight of the twelve conflict-event types: Third-Party Intervention [$L^2(2) = .55$, $p = .76$]; Silent-Treatment Conflict [$L^2(2) = 5.89$, $p = .06$]; Time-Out Conflict [$L^2(2) = 1.96$, $p = .38$]; Escalatory Conflict [$L^2(2) = 3.87$, $p = .14$]; One-Sided Conflict [$L^2(2) = 2.41$, $p = .30$]; Blowup Conflict [$L^2(2) = .74$, $p = .69$]; Sarcastic Sniping [$L^2(2) = .90$, $p = .64$]; and Civil Discussion [$L^2(2) = .17$, $p = .92$].[2] However, the model of independence was rejected for the remaining four kinds of conflict events.

The model of independence was rejected for Mock Conflict [$L^2(2) = 8.14$, $p = .02$]. The best-fitting logit model [$L^2(1) = .25$, $p = .62$; concentration $= .10$] was (conflict, conflict × relationship, conflict × relationship × gender). The z-value of -2.68 associated with the relationship type X gender parameter indicated that males were more likely to report Mock Conflict in their friendships, whereas females were more likely to report this conflict type in their romantic relationships. Largely because of the high proportion of males who reported Mock Conflict in their friendships, a tendency existed for Mock Conflict to be present in friendships more so than in romantic relationships ($z = 1.91$).

The model of independence was rejected for Déjà Vu Conflict [$L^2(2) = 19.16$, $p < .0001$]. The best-fitting logit model [$L^2(1) = .09$, $p = .768$; concentration $= .22$] was (conflict, conflict × relationship, conflict × relationship × gender). The z-value of -2.84 associated with the relationship type X gender parameter indicated that females were more likely to report Déjà Vu Conflict in their romantic relationships as opposed to their friendships. Largely because of the high proportion of females who reported Déjà Vu Conflict in their romantic relationships, the odds for this conflict event were greater in romantic relationships than in friendships ($z = 2.73$).

Independence was also rejected as the best-fitting model for Indirect Con-

---

[2]The process of analysis followed the logic of backward elimination for all logit model fitting. That is, a comparison was initially made between the fully saturated model and the model of independence; if the independence model fit the saturated model, its expected cell entries did not differ at $p < .05$ from the saturated model. If the independence model differed significantly from the fully saturated model, that is, its p level was $< .05$, a search was undertaken to locate the most parsimonious model that fit the saturated model. Terms were backed out of the fully saturated model one at a time and a check was made at each elimination point to determine whether the resulting model fit the saturated model. Unlike traditional chi square analysis, where one is searching for a small significance value to indicate major discrepancies between observed and expected cells, loglinear logit analysis involves the search for the smallest likelihood chi square values and the largest p levels.

flict [$L^2(2)$ = 7.74, p = .02]. Logit analysis revealed that the best-fitting model [$L^2(1)$ = .0002, p = .996, concentration = .09] consisted of (conflict, conflict × relationship, conflict × relationship × gender). The odds for the presence of Indirect Conflict were greater in friendships than in romantic relationships (z = −2.21). The relationship type difference tended to be greater among females than among males (z = 1.59).

Last, independence was rejected as the best-fitting model for Tacit Conflict [$L^2(2)$ = 17.40, p < .0001]. The best-fitting model [$L^2(1)$ = 3.65, p = .06, concentration = .18] was (conflict, conflict × relationship, conflict × relationship × gender). The odds of Tacit Conflict being reported were greater for females than for males in friendships (z = 2.66). Largely because of the high proportion of females who reported Tacit Conflict in their friendships, the odds in favor of the presence of Tacit Conflict were greater in friendships than in romantic relationships (z = −2.83).

DISCUSSION

The results of this study strongly indicate that interpersonal conflict is not perceived as a single, monolithic phenomenon to relationship parties. Not all conflict is alike, and this study's informants distinguished twelve types of conflict events from one another. Similar to the findings from other ethnographic work in communication events (e.g., Baxter & Goldsmith, 1990), a variety of Hymes' S-P-E-A-K-I-N-G features are used to organize differences in conflict-event types. In particular, the P, E, A, K, and I elements collectively differentiated the twelve conflict-event types. The P feature (Participants) is evident in the distinction between conflicts that involve third parties and those that are dyadic. The E feature (Ends) is evident in the playful versus serious intent of the conflict. The A feature (Act Sequencing) is the most salient element, involving five of the semantic features: (a) multiple episodes versus single episode, (b) beginning versus ending punctuation through withdrawal, (c) single-stage versus multiple-stage within a single episode, (d) one-sided versus two-sided engagement in conflict behavior, and (e) repeating versus nonrepeating. The K feature (Key) is evident in the semantic feature of hostility. The I feature (Instrumentalities) is apparent in two semantic features: (a) whether or not the conflict is ever expressed verbally, and (b) whether language is used directly or indirectly. Of course, whether the same semantic features would be salient in distinguishing conflict types for relationships other than friendships, or romantic relationships, or for a population other than university students remains for future researchers to determine.

Some of the types of conflict events appear to involve competitive, collaborative, and avoidance-based, individual-level styles of conflict management (Hocker & Wilmot, 1991). Blowup Conflict, Sarcastic Sniping, and Escalatory Conflict, for example, display competitive behavior from both parties. Civil Discussion and Tacit Conflict are characterized by reciprocal collaboration. Indirect Conflict, Silent-Treatment Conflict, Time-Out Conflict, and One-Sided Conflict involve avoidance behavior at one point or another during the enactment. Yet, individual-level styles do not suffice in distinguishing these conflict events from one another, nor do they assist us in identifying the three conflict events in which competition, collaboration, and avoidance are not readily apparent (i.e., Mock Conflict, Déjà Vu Conflict, Third-Party Intervention). In short, the findings of this study appear to underscore the claim that knowledge about the separate individuals in a dyad does not inform us fully about dyadic-level interaction.

Some of the types of conflict events identified by our informants appear similar to those identified in existing research. The Escalatory Conflict event appears similar to the Aggression Ritual identified by Harris and her colleagues (1986). Our informants joined those of Harris et al. in identifying a kind of conflict that appears to take on a deterministic quality of increasing verbal aggression. The One-Sided Conflict event appears similar to the social confrontation episode identified by Newell and Stutman (1988), in that one party attempts to initiate an argument by complaining about the partner. The Déjà Vu Conflict reinforces Lloyd's (1990) distinction between conflicts that are resolved versus those that are ongoing. Mock Conflict appears similar to playful verbal dueling, a communication event identified by several ethnographic researchers (Saville-Troike, 1989). Indirect Conflict appears remarkably similar to Fitzpatrick's (1988) discussion of meshed avoidance conflict enactment between marital partners.

Given the pervasive finding in existing ethnographic research that verbal dueling is largely a male event enacted between friends, it is not surprising that we found males more likely than females to report Mock Conflict in their friendships. However, females were more likely than males to report Mock Conflict in romantic relationships. Because females are relatively less likely than males to experience verbal dueling in their same-sex friendships, Mock Conflict may be more salient to females in romantic relationships because of a contrast effect.

Much Mock Conflict involves sarcastic exchange between the parties, yet the playful sarcasm of Mock Conflict differs from the hostile sarcasm of Sarcastic Sniping. Sarcastic Sniping was mentioned relatively infrequently, and no differences were apparent by relationship type and gender. How relationship parties distinguish playful from serious sarcasm is an interesting issue for future research. The fact that several Escalatory Conflicts began as playful sarcasm that was taken the wrong way suggests that Mock Conflict, Sarcastic Sniping, and Escalatory Conflicts are interrelated in complex ways.

Déjà Vu Conflict was more likely in romantic relationships than in friendships, largely attributable to a high proportion of females who reported the conflict type in their romantic relationships. The Déjà Vu Conflicts identified in this study were not limited to unresolved issues of relationship definition, unlike prior work on repetitive conflicts. Some Déjà Vu Conflicts, for example, involved repeating arguments about which the parties had already established a norm of "agreeing to disagree." The particular issue that is unresolved may be the critical factor determining how recurring conflict impacts a relationship.

The greater likelihood of Indirect Conflict and Tacit Conflict among friends as opposed to romantic partners is fully consistent with the expectation of expressiveness that accompanies romantic relationships (Davis & Todd, 1985; Wright, 1985). Further, the prevalence of Tacit Conflict and Indirect Conflict among female same-sex friendships is fully consistent with gender socialization norms in which females more so than males are socialized to employ indirect, face-saving behavior (Brown & Levinson, 1987). Because Indirect Conflict never gets expressed through words, the interesting question for subsequent research is how the parties know when such conflicts begin and end.

Future research needs to examine the extent to which the various types of conflict events emerge for relationships at different developmental stages. Such conflict types as Déjà Vu Conflict or Indirect Conflict appear to require a tacit code between the two parties in order for successful enactment. Such a tacit code is likely to be developed only over time as a pair develops their own unique relationship "culture" (Baxter, 1987). Other conflict types, such as Mock Conflict and Sarcastic Sniping, require sophisticated skills of interpretation by the relationship parties if they are to be enacted successfully. Such interpretation skill is likely to develop only gradually over time as the parties come to know one another better. By contrast, other conflict types, such as Civil Discussion, could be enacted successfully by any relationship pair without benefit of a well-developed dyadic code of interpretation.

This study examined the various conflict types in isolation of one another. Subsequent research could benefit from an examination of how these conflict events are patterned sequentially in relationships. Of particular interest is the Third-Party Intervention type of conflict event. Because it is important for relationship parties to establish and sustain a boundary of privacy which outsiders cannot permeate, special circumstances are probably necessary to legitimate third-party interventions. Certain types of conflict events, for example, Blowup Conflicts, might qualify as special circumstances that legitimate, if not require, third-party assistance, whereas other conflict events, such as Time-Out Conflicts, might not legitimate the involvement of third parties. Also of interest is the Blowup Conflict, which these respondents regarded as a particularly negative form of conflict. Blowups might result from protracted conflicts over time, which are initially expressed through such event episodes as Silent-Treatment or One-Sided Conflict. Longitudinal research will clearly be necessary in identifying possible sequential patterns in the various conflict event types.

Subsequent research also needs to address the implications of the various conflict types for relationship satisfaction. Some types of conflict are likely to correlate differently with satisfaction depending on the relationship's developmental stage. For example, Mock Conflict is likely to correlate positively with satisfaction in well-established relationships based on extant research in the forms and functions of play in personal relationships (for a review see Baxter, 1992). However, as noted earlier, Mock Conflict might be risky in newly formed relationships because of the likelihood of misinterpretation. Other types of conflict are likely to vary from one relationship to another in their implications for satisfaction. As Fitzpatrick (1988) suggested for different marital types, some relationship cultures value the direct expression of conflict whereas other relationship cultures value the avoidance of conflict expression. For conflict-expressive pairs, events such as Indirect Conflict or Silent-Treatment Conflict are likely to correlate negatively with relationship satisfaction; by contrast, conflict-avoidance pairs are likely to react more positively to these two types of conflict events. Still other types of conflict events are likely to impact satisfaction differently depending on the sequence of events in which they are embedded. For example, Time-Out Conflicts might be viewed as dysfunctional by the relationship parties if they repeatedly evolve into protracted enactments punctuated by other conflict events; however, a particular instance of a Time-Out Conflict might be productive for the parties if the time-out positions them to manage their conflict in ways they find constructive. In short, the conflict types are likely to relate to satisfaction in complex ways.

This study described a folk taxonomy of conflict conceived not as an individual-level phenomenon but as a jointly enacted interaction event. However, as Grimshaw (1990) observed, taxonomy development is but a first step in understanding the joint enactment of conflict. Subsequent work needs to explore the conflict landscape of personal relationships in order to map more precisely how the twelve types of conflict events function in evolving friendships and romantic relationships.

REFERENCES

Argyle, M., & Furnham, A. (1983). Sources of satisfaction and conflict in long-term relationships. *Journal of Marriage and the Family, 45*, 481–493.

Baumgartner, M. P. (1988). *The moral order of a suburb.* New York: Oxford University Press.

Baxter, L. A. (1987). Symbols of relationship identity in relationship cultures. *Journal of Social and Personal Relationships, 4*, 261–280.

Baxter, L. A. (1988). Dyadic personal relationships: Measurement options. In C. H. Tardy (Ed.), *A handbook for the study of human communication: Methods and instruments for observing, measuring, and assessing communication processes* (pp. 193–228). Norwood, NJ: Ablex Publishing Corporation.

Baxter, L. A. (1992). Forms and functions of intimate play in personal relationships. *Human Communication Research, 18,* 336–363.

Baxter, L. A., & Goldsmith, D. (1990). Cultural terms for communication events among some American high school adolescents. *Western Journal of Speech Communication, 54,* 377–394.

Braiker, H. B., & Kelley, H. H. (1979). Conflict in the development of close relationships. In R. L. Burgess & T. L. Huston (Eds.), *Social exchange in developing relationships* (pp. 135–168). New York: Academic Press.

Brenneis, D. (1988). Language and disputing. *Annual Review of Anthropology, 17,* 221–237.

Brown, P., & Levinson, S. (1987). *Politeness: Some universals in language usage.* New York: Cambridge University Press.

Bulmer, M. (1979). Concepts in the analysis of qualitative data. *Sociological Review, 27,* 651–677.

Burggraf, C. S., & Sillars, A. (1987). A critical examination of sex differences in marital communication. *Communication Monographs, 54,* 276–294.

Cahn, D. D. (1990). Intimates in conflict: A research review. In D.D. Cahn (Ed.), *Intimates in conflict: A communication perspective* (pp. 1–24). Hillsdale, NJ: Lawrence Erlbaum Associates.

Canary, D. J., & Spitzberg, B. H. (1989). A model of the perceived competence of conflict strategies. *Human Communication Research, 15,* 630–649.

Cohen, J. (1960). A coefficient of agreement for nominal scales. *Educational and Psychological Measurement, 20,* 37–48.

Conrad, C. (1991). Communication in conflict: Style-strategy relationships. *Communication Monographs, 58,* 135–155.

Davis, K. E., & Todd, M. J. (1985). Assessing friendship: Prototypes, paradigm cases, and relationship description. In S. Duck & D. Perlman (Eds.), *Understanding Personal Relationships: An Interdisciplinary Approach* (pp. 17–38). Beverly Hills: Sage Publications.

Fitzpatrick, M. A. (1988). *Between husbands and wives.* Newbury Park: Sage Publications.

Goodwin, M. (1990). *He-said-she-said: Talk as social organization among black children.* Bloomington: Indiana University Press.

Gottman, J. M. (1979). *Marital interaction: Experimental investigations.* New York: Academic Press.

Grimshaw, A. D. (1990). Research on conflict talk: Antecedents, resources, findings, directions. In A. D. Grimshaw (Ed.), *Conflict talk: Sociolinguistic investigations of arguments in conversations* (pp. 281–324). New York: Cambridge University Press.

Harris, L. M., Gergen, K. J., & Lannamann, J.W. (1986). Aggression rituals. *Communication Monographs, 53,* 252–265.

Hays, R. B. (1988). Friendship. In S.W. Duck (Ed.), *Handbook of personal relationships: Theory, research and interventions* (pp. 391–408). New York: Wiley.

Healey, J. G., & Bell, R. A. (1990). Assessing alternative responses to conflicts in friendships. In D. D. Cahn (Ed.), *Intimates in conflict: A communication perspective* (pp. 25–48). Hillsdale, NJ: Lawrence Erlbaum Associates.

Hocker, J. L., & Wilmot, W. W. (1991). *Interpersonal conflict* (3rd ed.). Dubuque, IA: Wm. C. Brown, Publishers.

Hymes, D. (1972). Models of the interaction of language and social life. In J. J. Gumperz & D. Hymes (Eds.), *Directions in sociolinguistics* (pp. 35–71). New York: Holt, Rinehart, & Winston.

Knapp, M. L., Putnam, L. L., & Davis, L. J. (1988). Measuring interpersonal conflict in organizations. *Management Communication Quarterly, 1,* 414–429.

Knoke, D., & Burke, P. J. (1980). *Log-linear models.* Beverly Hills: Sage Publications.

Kochman, T. (1981). *Black and white styles in conflict.* Chicago: University of Chicago Press.

Lloyd, S. (1990). A behavioral self-report technique for assessing conflict in close relationships. *Journal of Social and Personal Relationships, 7,* 265–272.

Metts, S., & Cupach, W. R. (1990). The influence of relationship beliefs and problem-solving responses on satisfaction in romantic relationships. *Human Communication Research, 17,* 170–185.

Moffatt, M. (1989). *Coming of age in New Jersey: College and American culture.* New Brunswick: Rutgers University Press.

Newell, S. E., & Stutman, R. K. (1988). The social confrontation episode. *Communication Monographs, 55,* 266–284.

Newton, D. A., & Burgoon, J. K. (1990). The use and consequences of verbal influence strategies during interpersonal disagreements. *Human Communication Research, 16,* 477–518.

Norusis, M. J. (1988). *SPSS/PC+ V3.0 Update Manual.* Chicago: SPSS, Inc.

Philipsen, G. (1975). Speaking 'like a man' in Teamsterville: Culture patterns of role enactment in an urban neighborhood. *Quarterly Journal of Speech, 61,* 13–22.

Philipsen, G., & Carbaugh, D. (1986). A bibliography of fieldwork in the ethnography of communication. *Language in Society, 15,* 387–398.

Sapadin, L. A. (1988). Friendship and gender: Perspectives of professional men and women. *Journal of Social and Personal Relationships, 5,* 387–404.

Saville-Troike, M. (1989). *The ethnography of communication* (2nd ed.). New York: Basil Blackwell, Inc.

Sillars, A. L., Weisberg, J., Burggraf, C. S., & Wilson, E. A. (1987). Content themes in marital conversations. *Human Communication Research, 13,* 495–528.

Spradley, J. P. (1979). *The ethnographic interview.* New York: Holt, Rinehart, & Winston.

Wheeless, L. R. (1976). Self-disclosure and interpersonal solidarity: Measurement, validation, and relationships. *Human Communication Research, 3,* 47–61.

Wheeless, L. R. (1978). A follow-up study of the relationships among trust, disclosure, and interpersonal solidarity. *Human Communication Research, 4,* 143–157.

Wright, P. H. (1985). The acquaintance description form. In S. Duck & D. Perlman (Eds.), *Understanding personal relationships: An interdisciplinary approach* (pp. 39–62). Beverly Hills: Sage Publications.

Zeitlow, P. H., & Sillars, A. L. (1988). Life-stage differences in communication during marital conflicts. *Journal of Social and Personal Relationships, 5,* 223–245.

7

Hers or His? Sex Differences in the Experience and Communication of Jealousy in Close Relationships

Laura K. Guerrero[1]
University of Arizona

Sylvie V. Eloy
University of Arizona

Peter F. Jorgensen
University of Arizona

Peter A. Andersen
San Diego State University

Jealousy is one of a wide array of relational feelings that are commonly experienced by men and women alike. Yet only in the past 15 years have social scientists begun to empirically examine the role jealousy plays in intimate male/female relationships (Pfeiffer & Wong, 1989; White & Mullen, 1989). Moreover, studies on sex differences in the experience, expression, and communication of jealousy have yielded inconsistent and confusing results. In an effort to begin resolving this confusion, this chapter reports two studies. Study 1 examines sex differences in jealousy experienced by married individuals at the cognitive, emotional, and behavioral levels. Study 2 investigates how both sex and relationship status (dating versus married) affect the emotional experience and communicative reactions associated with jealousy. Because both of these studies focus upon romantic jealousy in particular, an overview of jealousy as a relational construct is provided first in order to set this framework.

Jealousy is an intrinsic part of many relationships in process. In particular, jealousy is likely to be experienced by romantic partners who value their relationships and want to preserve them (Bringle, Renner, Terry, & Davis, 1983; Salovey & Rodin, 1989; White, 1981a, 1981b). Salovey and Rodin (1989) defined jealousy as occurring when an individual feels that something he or she possesses (such as a relationship) can be taken away. Thus, threats to rela-

---

[1]The authors thank Dale Brashers, Jeff Bryson, Judee Burgoon, Pamela Kalbfleisch, Michael Payne, and Brian Spitzberg for their helpful comments on various sections of this chapter.

tionship stability can lead to jealousy. Using the concept of possession, Salovey and Rodin distinguished jealousy from the related constructs of envy and rivalry. Envy occurs when an individual wants something that another person has, but that he or she does not possess. For instance, Paul might be envious of Sandra's new computer. Paul would like to have a new computer, but cannot afford one. Hence, Paul might feel envy toward Sandra. On the other hand, rivalry exists when neither of two individuals possess a desired commodity, and both actively compete for it. Siblings are often rivals who compete for the attention of their parents.

Some researchers have considered jealousy to be a general concept encompassing both envy and rivalry (Salovey & Rodin, 1989; Shettel-Neuber, Bryson, & Young, 1978). For example, imagine a husband who is jealous and fears losing his wife to another man. If the husband feels his rival is more worldly and sophisticated, he may envy those qualities that he lacks. Similarly, he may feel that he needs to compete with the rival in order to win back his wife's affection. In such cases, jealousy can lead to envy and rivalry.

Whether or not the experience of jealousy leads to envy or rivalry, jealousy appears to be multifaceted. Often, jealousy has been conceptualized as a primarily emotional reaction (Bringle & Boebinger, 1990; Bringle & Buunk, 1985; Teismann & Mosher, 1978). Yet, White (1981a, 1981b, 1981c) conceived of jealousy as a complex of thoughts and actions, as well as feelings, which are activated when one's relationship is threatened by a third party. Similarly, Pfeiffer and Wong (1989) maintained that jealousy is multidimensional, consisting of cognition, emotion, and behavior. Cognitive jealousy involves the possession of suspicious thoughts and worries. Emotional jealousy involves feelings such as anger, fear, loss, insecurity, and depression. Finally, behavioral jealousy constitutes actions such as probing the partner for information, confronting the partner, and looking through the partner's possessions (Pfeiffer & Wong, 1989).

This three-dimensional approach to studying jealousy appears promising. For example, Pfeiffer and Wong (1989) found that the relationship between jealousy and love may differ depending on the jealousy dimension tapped. Cognitive jealousy was found to be negatively related to love within dating relationships, whereas emotional jealousy was found to be positively related to love. Additionally, two studies focusing on married couples found particular dimensions of jealousy related to different relational variables. Guerrero and Jorgensen (1991) reported that length of marriage predicts behavioral jealousy (with long marriages displaying less jealousy behavior), whereas frequency of discussion about relational termination is predictive of cognitive jealousy. A related study by Guerrero and Eloy (1992) found that marital satisfaction, though negatively associated with all three dimensions of jealousy, was most strongly related to cognitive jealousy. Together, these findings indicate that each jealousy dimension is uniquely associated with a variety of relational qualities.

There is at least one more jealousy dimension that may have predictive power—communication. Duck (1982) argued that jealousy researchers tend to treat behavior as a noninteractive action that involves a single person doing something to the external world, often alone, such as looking through a relational partner's purse or pockets for evidence of a love affair. What is often missing, then, is a focus on dyadic interaction. As Duck (1992) stated, behavior "is not just an individual action that happens in the head or in the heart or to the external world but is most often an interpersonal dyadic activity with communication consequences and interactive implications" (p. 51). Self-disclosing feelings of jealousy, confronting a partner with evidence of a love affair, or questioning a partner about his or her whereabouts are all examples of communicative reactions to jealousy involving dyadic exchange. Thus, under such a system, dyadic communication is a subset of behavior. The present set of studies will investigate sex differences for each of these four dimensions—emotion, cognition, behavior, and communication.

STUDY 1

Despite considerable literature on sex differences in close relationships, little research has examined sex differences in jealousy. Limited comparisons on general jealousy measures have yielded inconsistent results. For example, two Dutch studies reported by Bringle and Buunk (1986) found that women were more jealous than men. In contrast, Mathes and Severa (1981) found that men were more jealous than women. Other studies have failed to find sex differences in the amount of displayed jealousy (Strzyzewski & Comstock, 1990; White, 1981b). Examining multiple dimensions of jealousy may prove to be a more successful and reliable approach for gauging sex differences in the possession of jealousy. As White and Mullen (1989) noted, more reliable gender differences are observed when elements of the jealousy complex are studied individually.

Several studies have focused on sex differences in the manifestation of jealousy. Shettel-Neuber et al. (1978) reported that jealous men were likely to display anger and to verbally threaten others whereas jealous women were likely to cry alone, feign indifference, and bolster their attractiveness. In sharp contrast, other studies have found that women express jealousy whereas men repress it (Clanton & Smith, 1977). Still other studies report that jealous men work on repairing their individual self-esteem after a bout of jealousy whereas women work on repairing the relationship (Knapp, 1984).

While the pattern of sex differences in jealousy is not yet clear, empirical findings in the areas of emotional reaction and communication style have posited some general sex differences that may have some applicability to jealousy.

Buck (1979), for example, found that women tend to display their emotions outwardly and to share their feelings more often than men, who typically hold their emotions inside. Several researchers have argued that men tend to exert more control over their emotions due to their task orientations, whereas women tend to be more emotional and expressive due to their social orientations (Balswick & Avertt, 1977; Hatfield, 1984; LaFrance & Mayo, 1978). Balswick and Avertt found that wives are often dissatisfied with the low intensity of emotion expressed by their husbands. Hatfield (1984) noted that women are socialized to be more comfortable with intimate, intense feelings. Indeed, Hatfield argues that "the ideal woman is supposed to be expressive and warm. She is comfortable expressing a rainbow of 'feminine' feelings—love, anxiety, joy, and depression" (p. 211). Bringle and Buunk (1986) reviewed past research, which looked more specifically at the emotional dimension of jealousy, and reported that women experience more intense emotional responses to jealousy than men. Clanton and Smith (1977) argued that men deny jealous emotions yet feel competitive toward third-party rivals. Women, conversely, tend to acknowledge their feelings, blame themselves rather than third parties, and attempt to recapture romance. These findings indicate that emotional expressions of jealousy, with the exception of angry responses, are seen as more appropriate for women than for men.

Related to the idea that women are more emotionally expressive than men is the notion that women generally display more open, spontaneous behavior, and engage in more communication. Research on self-disclosure shows that wives tend to disclose more than their husbands. In fact, an early review by Cozby (1973) failed to find even a single study where men reported greater disclosure than women. A more recent study by Rubin, Hill, Peplau, & Dunke-Schetter (1980) found that in intimate relationships men and women may engage in similar amounts of open, intimate communication, yet the topics of such communication tend to be different. Specifically, Rubin et al. found that men tend to disclose more about accomplishments, politics, and career goals, whereas women disclose more about their hopes, dreams, fears, and feelings. This finding is particularly relevant to the display and communication of jealousy because jealousy is an intense feeling based partially on the fear stemming from threat.

Some jealousy research suggests that behavioral responses to jealousy are more likely for women. Bringle and Buunk (1986) reviewed empirical findings connecting behavioral response in the form of open, honest discussions to coping with jealousy. Specifically, three strategies for coping with jealousy were found: avoidance, reappraisal, and communication. Of these three, communication was found to be used most frequently. Bell and Buerkel-Rothfuss (1990) found that jealous women reported a greater likelihood of using behavioral strategies, such as entrapment, than jealous men. Additionally, Strzyzewski and Comstock (1990) found that, in opposite-sex relationships, women were more likely than men to want to discuss jealousy. Finally, Salovey and Rodin's (1985) findings from a large survey led to the conclusion that "women tended to display certain kinds of jealous behavior more often than men did, such as searching through a lover's personal belongings" (p. 28). In sum, these findings support Bowers, Metts, and Duncanson's (1985) assertion that "the American cultural stereotype of the nonemotional male and the emotional female is reflected to some extent in actual behavior" (p. 501). Thus, the following hypotheses (H) are advanced:

H_1: Wives experience more emotional jealousy than husbands.

H_2: Wives display more behavioral jealousy than husbands.

The role sex plays in determining levels of cognitive jealousy is less clear. On the one hand, males may harbor jealous thoughts for longer periods of time than females due to their tendency to internalize affect. On the other hand, males might dismiss jealous thoughts more readily due to smaller levels of accompanying emotions. Whether or not the expression and communication of jealousy is reciprocal within marital relationships is also unclear. Thus, the following research (R) questions are asked:

R_1: Are there sex differences in the amount of cognitive jealousy experienced by husbands and wives?

R_2: Are individual experiences of jealousy correlated within a marital dyad?

METHOD

Subjects

A sample consisting of 132 subjects (66 married couples) living primarily in California participated in this study. The subjects ranged in age from teenagers to senior citizens, with the average couple in their mid- to late thirties. The length of these couples' marriages ranged from a single year to 51 years, with a mean of 11.4 years. The number of children per marriage varied from no children to eight, with an average of 1.5 children per couple.

Procedure

Self-report questionnaires were utilized to collect both data related to the hypotheses and demographics. Two questionnaires were set in an envelope and given to each couple. In order to capture a diverse sample population, envelopes were distributed through three channels: (a) graduate teaching assistants in a speech communication department, (b) senior undergraduates in a relational communication course, and (c) an apartment complex manager. The sources administered the questionnaires to couples they knew. To insure that the subjects answered the questionnaires independently, the administrators were instructed to observe the actual completion of the questionnaires. The questionnaires were then placed into an envelope, sealed, and signed by the administrator in front of the couple to insure confidentiality.

Instrumentation

Sex, which served as the independent variable, was reported by participants on the questionnaire. Jealousy was measured using Pfeiffer and Wong's (1989) Multidimensional Jealousy Scale (MJS). This scale consists of three eight-item subscales that measure the three dimensions of jealousy—cognition, emotion, and behavior—separately. The cognitive, emotional, and behavioral jealousy subscales were originally reported with reliabilities of .92, .85, and .89, respectively (Pfeiffer & Wong, 1989). The current study found alpha reliabilities of .89 for the cognitive subscale, .81 for the emotional subscale, and .80 for the behavioral subscale.

Analyses

The two hypotheses and first research question were analyzed using correlated t-tests. Alpha was set at .05. Power for all three t-tests was in excess of .99 for large effects, .88 for medium effects, and .31 for small effects (Cohen, 1977). The second research question was analyzed using Pearson product moment correlations.

RESULTS

Table 7.1 reflects the following findings. The first hypothesis predicted that wives would possess more emotional jealousy than their husbands. This hypothesis was not confirmed, $t(65) = .13$; $p = .45$; female $M = 29.4$; male $M = 29.3$. The second hypothesis, which posited that wives would display more behavioral jealousy than their husbands, was confirmed, $t(65) = 1.84$; $p = .035$; eta$^2 = .09$; female $M = 13.35$; male $M = 12.42$. The first research question, which sought to ascertain whether or not there were sex differences in cognitive jealousy, was nonsignificant, $t(65) = 1.44$; $p = .16$; female $M = 12.6$; male $M = 11.6$. In answer to the second research question,

TABLE 7.1.
Summary of Results: Study 1

	Wives M	Husbands M	t	r	r²
Emotional Jealousy	29.4	29.5	.13	.57***	.32
Behavioral Jealousy	13.4	12.4	1.84	.52***	.27
Cognitive Jealousy	12.6	11.6	1.44	.30**	.09

*Significant at an alpha of .05. ** Significant at an alpha of .01. *** Significant at an alpha of .001.

jealousy was correlated between spouses at each dimension ($r = .57$ for emotional, $p < .001$; $r = .52$ for behavioral, $p < .001$; and .30 for cognitive jealousy, $p = .01$).

DISCUSSION

The present study provides some support for the conceptualization of jealousy as consisting of multidimensional properties of cognition, emotion, and behavior. Findings indicate that sex differences in jealousy do exist, but not on all dimensions. First, the strong dyadic effect will be discussed, followed by a discussion of sex differences and the multidimensional approach to jealousy.

The Dyadic Effect

Fairly strong correlations were observed within marital dyads for all three dimensions of jealousy. Thirty-three percent of variance in emotional jealousy, 27% of variance in behavioral jealousy, and 9% of variance in cognitive jealousy is shared within the marital relationship. One likely explanation is that feelings and actions produce reciprocal behavior from one's partner. A partner's displays of jealousy make jealousy a salient issue to the other and promotes a reciprocal response. Indeed, the correlations between husbands and wives on behavioral and emotional jealousy were both higher than the correlations between husbands' and wives' levels of cognitive jealousy, although all three correlations proved to be significant. It may be that emotional and behavioral jealousy are more overt manifestations of jealousy, and hence are likely to be reciprocated. Cognitive jealousy, on the other hand, is covert, and so may be less reciprocal. A second explanation, of course, is that similarity in possessiveness or jealousy proneness of individuals promotes attraction and increases the likelihood of marriage.

Sex Differences

The present findings indicate that the individual dimensions of jealousy are an important factor to consider when examining sex differences in jealousy. Although wives scored higher on each of the dimensional subscales, only the difference on the behavioral subscale was statistically significant. Because behavioral jealousy was correlated among spouses, it is possible that certain amounts of behavioral jealousy are normative within a marriage, but wives have the prerogative to exceed their husbands' level of behavioral jealousy. As Buck (1979) suggested, men may be socialized to keep jealous feelings internal and opt not to display them behaviorally. Conversely, wives may be likely to confront their husbands in order to communicate about jealous feelings. This interpretation coincides with the plethora of literature that asserts that women are more self-disclosive, expressive, and communication oriented than men (e.g., Cozby, 1973; Hatfield, 1984; Noller, 1980). Furthermore, the present finding, along with the past finding that women in opposite-sex relationships tend to discuss jealousy more often than men (Strzyzewski & Comstock, 1990), lends credence to the contention that women communicate about jealousy more frequently than men. The fact that no sex differences were observed for either emotional or cognitive jealousy suggests that the primary sex difference may be in the communication of jealousy. Frequency and style of communicating is likely to impact marital happiness, equality, and a host of other relational qualities. Study 2 provides an initial examination of how women and men communicatively react to jealousy.

Finally, there are at least three possible reasons why the hypothesis predicting wives to be more emotionally jealous than husbands was not confirmed. First, the feelings connected to jealousy may be different for men and women but equally intense. For example, in the presence of jealousy, men may tend to react with anger, whereas women may tend to associate their feelings with fear and vulnerability. In an effort to examine such possibilities, Study 2 concentrates on sex differences in the *type* of emotional expression rather than just the *amount* of emotional jealousy. Second, the low statistical power to detect small effects may have affected the results. Finally, a failure to find significant sex differences in emotional jealousy may be due in part to a flaw in the measurement device for that subscale.

Strengths and Weaknesses
of the Multidimensional Jealousy Scale

The aforementioned findings suggest that the multidimensional approach to jealousy has predictive value. However, the predictive value of the MJS could be enhanced by modifying the emotional subscale. Although all three subscales were found to be highly reliable in this study, there is reason to suspect that the emotional subscale is substantially different from the other two. This can easily be seen when comparing the means for each scale. Means were as follows: 12.1 for cognitive, 12.9 for behavioral, and 29.3 for emotional. The inflated mean for the emotional subscale appears to be a product of the items which ask respondents to rate how they would feel in a hypothetical jealousy-evoking situation. Possible responses to these situations range from (1) *very pleased* to (5) *very upset*. However, the *very pleased* and *somewhat pleased* options to the given scenarios may be inappropriate. For example, one of the situations calls for the respondent to envision their relational partner "hugging and kissing" a member of the opposite sex. It seems extremely unlikely that one would consider this scenario pleasing. Indeed, even among the least jealous individuals, only a single participant responded that such a situation was pleasurable. Thus, the emotional subscale suffers from a restricted range.

Besides the wording of these items, another fundamental difference in the emotional scale deals with temporal orientation. The cognitive and behavioral scales ask participants to rate how much they actually experience jealous thoughts and behaviors. The emotional subscale, on the other hand, deals with how subjects would feel in the given scenarios. It is therefore plausible that the situations posed in the emotional scale elicit generally normative responses from married couples. The frequency and intensity of actual feelings, however, may vary considerably. Therefore, an improved version of Pfeiffer and Wong's (1989) emotional subscale is used in Study 2.

These results answer preliminary questions about jealousy in close relationships and provide a basis from which to ask new questions. Study 1 focuses exclusively on marriage, yet many other types of relationships are bound to be marked by some degree of jealousy. A comparison of how jealousy is experienced and communicated differently in married and dating relationships could increase understanding about the role jealousy plays during various phases of in-process relationships. Additionally, results from Study 1 indicate that more detailed information on the communicative and affective aspects of jealousy is necessary. These ideas for extending the first study's findings paved the way for the second research project.

STUDY 2

The second study's purpose is threefold. First, the effects of relationship status (dating versus married) are explored across different aspects of jealousy. Second, a modified version of Pfeiffer and Wong's (1989) emotional subscale is used to examine various emotions and thus, to provide a more thorough test of sex differences in emotional jealousy. Finally, because Study 1 found wives to report more behavioral jealousy than their husbands, sex differences in communicative reactions to jealousy are investigated.

Relationship Status and Jealousy

Consistent with the results of the first study, researchers have found relationship variables to account for more variance in jealousy scores than personality variables (Bringle & Buunk, 1985). These authors also noted that "most theorists agree that characteristics of the relationship influence the intensity, frequency, and management of jealousy" (p. 254). Relationship status is one such characteristic. Unfortunately, however, the majority of prior research has been conducted on daters. As Bringle and Buunk (1986) suggested:

> Most research on jealousy has been conducted on relationships of college students that are either relatively uncommitted or, even when there is a clear commitment, has been of rather short duration. . . . There is sufficient reason to suppose that in long-term, committed marriages jealousy plays quite a different role and has different courses and consequences than in relationships that are in their early phases of development. (p. 227)

Thus, according to Bringle and Buunk, dating and married individuals are likely to experience jealousy in different ways.

The few studies that have focused on differences in cognitive and emotional jealousy based upon relationship type have yielded rather consistent findings. For example, several authors have found that couples who are seriously dating or cohabiting tend to be more jealous than other types of romantic couples (Bringle & Boebinger, 1990; Salovey & Rodin, 1985; White, 1985). Salovey and Rodin (1985) found that divorced, separated, and cohabiting couples were more prone to jealousy than their married counterparts. Not surprisingly, a study by Strzyzewski and Comstock (1990) found that jealousy is more appropriate and intense in romantic relationships than in friendships. Together, the results seem to indicate that romantic love and attraction are positively related to jealousy, but that security is negatively related. Thus, the commitment afforded by marriage may aid in combating jealousy. This is consistent with White's (1980) finding that individuals who feel more insecure about their relationships are more likely to be jealous. Despite such speculation, at least two studies (Bush, Bush, & Jennings, 1988; White, 1981c) failed to find differences in jealousy based on relationship status.

Although security and romantic love are likely to change based on relationship status, so are the related concepts of *permanence* and *emotional dependency*. *Permanence*, or longevity of the relationship, has been studied in connection with jealousy. White (1981c) failed to find an association between relationship length and jealousy. However, results from a study by Guerrero and Jorgensen (1991) indicated that the longevity of a marriage predicts behavioral jealousy but does not predict emotional or cognitive jealousy. Specifically, length of marriage was inversely related to behavioral jealousy, with those in new marriages displaying the most jealous behavior. Thus, it appears important to examine the various aspects of jealousy, rather than jealousy in general, when investigating the effects of relationship status.

A second factor that may vary depending on relationship status is emotional dependency. Several scholars have found that emotional dependency, which is related to love, cohesion, attachment, and comparison levels, is positively correlated with jealousy (Bringle & Buunk, 1985; Buunk, 1982; Mathes & Severa, 1981; White & Mullen, 1989). In addition, when a partner's need for emotional dependency is not reciprocated within a relationship, insecurity may develop. White (1980) found that in such instances, individuals feeling insecure about their relationships are more likely to induce jealousy. Buunk (1982) found that emotional dependency is associated with three additional components. First, couples with mutual friends may fear losing their friends as well as their partners. Second, individuals may worry that, after relationship termination, it would be difficult to find new partners, and thus, they may fear being alone. Finally, emotionally dependent partners are likely to share old memories that are hard to relinquish. Relationship status may reflect these components of emotional dependency. For instance, dating partners may not always share a balance of emotional dependency and thus, they may fear relationship termination and being alone. Spouses, on the other hand, are more likely to have intertwined social networks and memories.

Finally, sex and relationship status may interact to influence levels of jealousy. White (1981a) found that "a desire for permanence was rated as more important for females than for males" (p. 29). Also, Hatkoff and Lasswell (1979) found that within intimate relationships, women tend to experience more mania (a possessive style of love) than men. Further, Strzyzewski and Comstock (1990) found that women are more likely to discuss jealousy in cross-sex romantic relationships than are men, although this finding did not hold true for same-sex friendships. The effects of relationship status and sex on jealousy is discussed further in conjunction with the various aspects of romantic jealousy.

Emotions and Jealousy

Research has reported that several different types of emotion are connected to jealousy. White and Mullen (1989) summarized the literature in this area and posited that there are six basic affective elements in the jealousy complex: anger, fear, sadness, envy, sexual arousal, and guilt. Further, White and Mullen (1989) specified that "each element is best conceptualized as a set of related emotions, feelings, and moods" (p. 40). Thus, anger includes hate, disgust, vengefulness, contempt, annoyance, and rage. Yet, anger or any of the six primary affective components represents a distinct cluster of emotion. Other studies have isolated discomfort, insecurity, feelings of helplessness and inadequacy, desire for revenge, and being generally upset as correlates of jealousy (Bryson, 1976; Clanton & Smith, 1977; Strzyzewski & Comstock, 1990). Additionally, sex differences in the emotional expression of jealousy have been found. Women tend to report feelings of anxiety, depression, fear, and insecurity, whereas men tend to report feeling angry and competitive (Clanton & Smith, 1977; White, 1981c; White & Mullen, 1989). Thus, it is fruitful to examine sex differences across various emotions. To do so, the following hypotheses and research question are advanced:

H_1: Men report experiencing more anger in relation to jealousy than do women.

H_2: Women report experiencing more anxiety, fear, and insecurity in relation to jealousy than do men.

R_1: Are there sex differences in the experience of envy, discomfort, upset feelings, or general jealousy?

Relationship status may also affect the emotions experienced in connection with jealousy. Married individuals, for example, may feel less insecure during jealousy-invoking situations than their dating counterparts. This may be due to their perceptions of relationship permanence and stability. Emotional dependency may also play a role in determining differences due to relationship status. Therefore, a second research question is posed:

R_2: Do daters and marrieds report experiencing anger, anxiety, fear, insecurity, envy, discomfort, general jealousy, and upset feelings differently in response to jealousy-invoking situations?

Cognition and Jealousy

Cognitive jealousy may also be affected by relationship status or by the interaction of status and sex. According to several theorists, developing relationships may be marked by more uncertainty and less predictability than more stable relationships (Berger & Calabrese, 1975; Knapp, 1984). Such uncertainty could translate into suspicion and doubt, which lead to jealousy. Additionally, the higher levels of commitment and security that characterize marriage may provide protection from suspicious thoughts and worries. Thus, a third research question is posed:

R_3: Does cognitive jealousy vary as a function of relationship status and sex?

Communicative Reactions to Jealousy

Study 1 found that wives reported more behavioral jealousy than husbands. Such a finding is consistent with results from previous studies (e.g., Salovey & Rodin, 1985). However, earlier it was shown that behavioral jealousy is a broad construct that can be broken down into both communicative and non-communicative action. Therefore, the next section will examine how sex and relationship status affect communicative reactions to jealousy.

A perusal of the research on communicative responses to jealousy yields a focus on two primary types of communicative reactions: positive and negative. Positive reactions include open communication about feelings with either the spouse, the rival, or both. Francis (1977) labeled renegotiation of the rules and boundaries of the relationship as another type of constructive communicative reaction applicable to jealousy. Bryson (in press) reported strategies, such as asking the partner for an explanation and sharing feelings with the partner, as positive forms of communication. Negative communication, on the other hand, is characterized as aggressive and nonproductive. Communication focusing on partner blame, nagging, complaining, and trying to get one's own way have all been identified by Buunk and Bringle (1987) as possible negative reactions to jealousy. Francis (1977) added threats and appeals to duty to this list of negative communication strategies.

A recent study added a third type of reaction—communication avoidance. Specifically, Eloy, Guerrero, Andersen, and Spitzberg (1992) identified three clusters of communicative reactions to jealousy and labeled them *integration*, *distribution*, and *avoidance*. Integrative reactions are similar to the positive responses just explained and can be defined as constructive responses to jealousy that include disclosure of feelings, confrontation, and asking for explanations of a partner's actions. Such reactions are characterized as expressing internal thoughts and feelings without placing blame on the partner. As such, communicators are likely to perceive such reactions as either positive or neutral. Distribution, on the other hand, is likely to be negatively valenced and includes arguing, yelling and cursing, threatening the partner, and other actions that focus blame on the partner in an unproductive manner. Thus, distributive reactions encompass the negative responses discussed. Finally, avoidant reactions are those that are passive in nature or involve active avoidance of dyadic interaction. Silence and the denial of jealous feelings fall squarely within the avoidance category (Eloy et al., 1992). An examination of sex and relationship status differences in these three communicative reactions may uncover which communicative behaviors are, as Study 1 indicates, used more frequently by women than by men. The generalizability of the first study's finding on behavioral jealousy may also be extended by looking at relationship status.

R_4:   Do sex and relationship status produce differences in communicative reactions to jealousy?

METHOD

Subjects

Two hundred married individuals and 146 daters living primarily in California participated in this study (total $N = 346$). Whereas Study 1 utilized data from marital dyads, this study used individual data, with only one partner from a romantic couple participating. The majority of married subjects (nearly 70%) were in their twenties or thirties. The average married participant had been married 9.6 years and had 1.3 children. Of these married participants, 122 were female and 78 were male. Dating subjects were undergraduate students enrolled in speech communication courses at a large southwestern university (Female $N = 89$; Male $N = 57$) who were currently involved in dating relationships. The average dating subject was in his or her twenties.

Procedures

The married subjects were contacted in one of two ways. First, students in three speech communication classes and a group of graduate teaching assistants aided in data collection by having married individuals they knew complete questionnaires. Questionnaires were answered privately although the assistant was present during the entire 20-minute procedure. At the end of the procedure, the assistants enclosed the questionnaires in envelopes and sealed them in front of the subject in order to insure confidentiality. Second, students from two additional communication courses brought married individuals to a designated location to complete the questionnaire under the supervision of one of the researchers. The dating subjects completed questionnaires during class time.

Instrumentation

Cognitive and Emotional Jealousy.   A subscale of Pfeiffer and Wong's (1989) Multidimensional Jealousy Scale (MJS) was utilized in this study to measure cognitive jealousy and was found to have alpha reliability of .87. Additionally, a modified version of Pfeiffer and Wong's emotional subscale was used. This version of the emotional subscale corrects for problems outlined in Study 1 and incorporates the following affective states: envy, anxiety, discomfort, anger, jealousy, fear, insecurity, and upset feelings. Respondents rated eight questions on scales of (1) *never* to (5) *always*:

1. I feel envious when my partner comments on how attractive a member of the opposite sex is,
2. I feel anxious when my partner shows a great deal of attention to someone of the opposite sex,
3. I feel uncomfortable when my partner smiles in a very friendly manner to someone of the opposite sex,
4. It angers me when members of the opposite sex try to get close to my partner,
5. I feel jealous when my partner flirts with someone of the opposite sex,
6. I feel fearful that my partner may be going out with someone of the opposite sex,
7. I feel insecure when my partner hugs or kisses someone of the opposite sex, and
8. I get upset when my partner has to work very closely with a member of the opposite sex (in the office or at school).

This new emotion scale was found to be have .88 alpha reliability.

Communicative Reactions.   Communicative reactions to jealousy were measured using the Communicative Reactions to Jealousy Scale (CRJ) developed by Eloy et al., (1992). CRJ is a 26-item scale used to assess communicative reactions to jealousy. This scale assesses three different factors. The first factor, Distribution, consists of 11 items. Integration is measured with nine items and Avoidance with six items. This study found the *distributive, integrative,* and *avoidant* factors to have alpha reliabilities of .92, .89, and .82, respectively.

Sex and Relationship.   Sex and relationship status were indicated by responses to questionnaire items.

Social Desirability.   Hays, Hayashi, and Stewart's (1989) Socially Desirable Response Set (SDRS) was utilized. The SDRS is a five-item scale used to assess whether or not social desirability influences questionnaire responses. In the present study, the SDRS had an alpha reliability of .66. This information was collected in order for social desirability to be covaried out of the statistical design. Age also served as a covariate.

Analyses

Multivariate analyses of variance with follow-up univariate analyses of variance were conducted with alpha at .05 for all hypotheses and research questions except Research Question 3, which was tested with a 2 (dating/married)

X 2(female/male) ANOVA. Power of the ANOVAs was in excess of .99 for medium and large effects and .46 for small effects (Cohen, 1977).

RESULTS

Emotional Jealousy

Multivariate tests found main effects for both sex, $F(8, 333) = 4.81; p <$ .001; Wilks = .90 and relationship status, $F(8, 333) = 3.86; p < .001$; Wilks = .91, to be significant. The omnibus F for the interaction effect of sex and relationship status was nonsignificant, $F(8, 333) = 1.06$; Wilks = .98; $p >$ .05, rendering the main effects for sex and status interpretable. Univariate F-tests (see Table 7.2) were used to test the hypotheses and research questions. Hypothesis 1, which predicted that men would respond to jealousy with anger more often than women, was not supported, $F(1, 340) = .03; p > .05$. Hypothesis 2, which predicted that women would experience more anxiety, fear, and insecurity in jealousy-invoking situations, was only partially confirmed. Anxiety was the only variable for which a significant sex difference in the expected direction was observed, $F(1, 340) = 13.45; p < .001$; eta^2 = .04. No sex differences were found for either fear or insecurity. The first research question asked if there are sex differences in envy, discomfort, generally upset feelings, or general jealousy. Results indicate that women experience more envy of the rival, $F(1, 340) = 7.48; p < .01$; eta^2 = .02; more discomfort, $F(1, 340) = 7.67; p < .01$; eta^2 = .02; and more upset feelings, $F(1, 340) = 18.70; p < .001$; eta^2 = .05. No sex differences were found for general emotional jealousy, which may explain the lack of a sex difference finding in Study 1.

The second research question asked how emotions would differ based on relationship status. The multivariate test just reported was followed by univari-

TABLE 7.2.
Cell Means and Univariate Fs: Sex Differences in Jealousy-Related Emotions

Emotion	Males	Females	F
Envy	2.05	2.31	7.47***
Anxiety	2.10	2.47	13.45***
Discomfort	1.78	2.04	7.67**
Anger	2.35	2.32	.03
Jealousy	2.48	2.62	1.94
Fear	1.48	1.47	.01
Insecurity	1.88	1.96	.90
Upset	1.58	1.85	18.70***

*Significant at an alpha of .05. **Significant at an alpha of .01. ***Significant at an alpha of .001.

TABLE 7.3.

Cell Means and Univariate *F*s: Differences in Jealousy-Related Emotions
Due to Relationship Status

Emotion	Daters	Marrieds	Fs
Envy	2.39	2.08	4.06*
Anxiety	2.53	2.18	5.44*
Discomfort	2.09	1.82	2.35
Anger	2.57	2.15	4.46*
Jealousy	2.86	2.35	6.46*
Fear	1.78	1.25	26.08***
Insecurity	2.23	1.70	12.37***
Upset	1.90	1.60	2.37

*Significant at an alpha of .05. **Significant at an alpha of .01. ***Significant at an alpha of .001.

ate *F*-tests (see Table 7.3), which revealed that six of the eight emotions varied significantly as a function of relationship status: (1) *Envy*, $F(1, 340) = 4.06$; $p < .05$; $eta^2 = .01$; (2) *Anxiety*, $F(1, 340) = 5.44$; $p = .02$; $eta^2 = .02$; (3) *Anger*, $F(1, 340) = 4.46$; $p < .04$; $eta^2 = .01$; (4) *Jealousy*, $F(1, 340) = 6.46$; $p < .02$; $eta^2 = .02$; (5) *Fear*, $F(1, 340) = 26.18$; $p = < .05$; $eta^2 = .07$; and (6) *Insecurity*, $F(1, 340) = 12.37$; $p < .001$; $eta^2 = .04$. In all six cases, the daters reported more emotional reaction than the married couples. There were no differences in anxiety or general upset feelings based upon relationship status.

Cognition and Jealousy

The second research question asked if sex and relationship status affect cognitive jealousy. A 2 (dating/married) X 2 (female/male) ANOVA found a main effect for status, $F(1, 340) = 39.23$; $p < .001$; $eta^2 = .10$, but not for sex, $F(1, 340) = .17$; $p > .05$. Daters ($M = 16.8$) reported significantly more cognitive jealousy than marrieds ($M = 12.6$). The interaction effect between status and sex approached significance, $F(1, 340) = 3.09$; $p = .08$, two-tailed.

Communicative Reactions and Jealousy.   Intercorrelations between the distributive, integrative, and avoidant communicative reactions prompted the use of MANOVA to answer the final research question (Bartlett's sphericity test with 3 $df = 93.59$; $p < .001$). Multivariate tests found significant main effects for sex, $F(3, 338) = 7.19$; $p < .001$; Wilks = .94, and relationship status, $F(3, 338) = 2.92$; $p < .04$; Wilks = .97. The interaction effect between sex and status was nonsignificant, $F(3, 338) = 1.23$; $p > .05$. Univariate *F*-tests revealed that women report using more of all three communicative

TABLE 7.4.
Cell Means for Main Effects: Status and Sex on Communicative Reactions

Communicative Reactions	Sex		Status	
	Male	Female	Daters	Marrieds
Distribution	18.03	19.69	20.87	17.71
Integration	24.63	27.58	28.10	25.21
Avoidance	12.44	13.42	13.96	12.37

reactions to jealousy, *Distribution* $F(1, 340) = 10.02; p < .01$; eta^2 = .03, *Integration* $F(1, 340) = 15.55; p < .001$; eta^2 = .04; *Avoidance* $F(1, 340) = 6.98; p < .01$; eta^2 = .02. A second set of univariate F-tests found that daters use more *distribution*, $F(1, 340) = 7.74; p < .01$; eta^2 = .03, and more *avoidance*, $F(1, 340) = 3.87; p = .05$; eta^2 = .01 than marrieds. There was no significant difference between daters and marrieds in their use of integrative strategies, $F(1, 340) = 1.77; p > .05$ (see Table 7.4 for corresponding cell means).

DISCUSSION

Together, the preceding two studies explored the effects of sex and relationship status on various dimensions of, and reactions to, jealousy. Strikingly, all of the significant sex differences found that women possess and communicate more jealousy than men. However, no sex differences were observed for some forms of jealousy. For relationship status, all significant results indicated that daters experience and communicate jealousy more often than marrieds. These findings indicate main effects for both sex and relationship status that appear to cut across a variety of aspects of jealousy. However, the effect sizes for significant findings were small, particularly within the univariate analyses, indicating that, although sex and relationship status differences exist, they are not particularly robust. Still, a look at the possible causes of these findings will illuminate the role that jealousy plays in close relationships.

Emotion

The multivariate analysis in Study 2 found that sex had a significant effect on overall experience of emotion, with women reporting feeling more emotion than men. Univariate analyses revealed that women experience more of four specific types of jealousy-related affect: envy of the rival, anxiety, discomfort, and general upset feelings. These findings indicate that the modified version of Pfeiffer and Wong's (1989) subscale has more predictive power than the original subscale. Additionally, the modified scale's mean ($M = 16.5$) was comparable to those of the cognitive and behavioral subscales as reported in Study 1. However, despite increased validity of the instrument, women did not report feeling more fear or insecurity than men, as was predicted. One possible explanation for such findings revolves around the concept of *arousal*. Anxiety and discomfort, for example, may be indicative of high arousal levels that are attached to nervousness. Fear, on the other hand, may be connected to a different type of arousal. The role of arousal, then, should be studied in connection with jealousy, particularly since many individuals report a flush of anger (Ekman, Levenson, & Friesen, 1983) and a jealousy flash (Buunk & Bringle, 1987) indicative of subjectively experienced high arousal. Another explanation for sex differences deals with the specific situations described on the questionnaire. Although the emotion items deal with common jealousy-invoking situations, some of the situations described might provoke more emotion in females than males. For example, feeling envious when a partner comments on the attractiveness of a member of the opposite sex (a more typically male behavior) may be more threatening to women than to men. Getting upset when a partner has to work late with a member of the opposite sex may be a phenomenon that also occurs more often for women whose husbands spend more time in the office. Thus, situational aspects of jealousy also deserve more scholarly attention.

Regarding emotion and relationship status, daters reported experiencing significantly stronger reactions for six of the eight emotions than married individuals: envy, anxiety, anger, general jealousy, fear, and insecurity. Of these six, the two variables that accounted for the most variance were fear and insecurity. It is suspected that the stability and permanence of the marital relationship protects marrieds from experiencing these particular emotions. It makes sense that daters, who are likely to possess more uncertainty about the future of their relationships, would feel more insecurity and fear in jealousy-provoking situations.

Cognition

No sex effect for cognitive jealousy was observed but relationship status predicted cognitive jealousy. Just as uncertainty may evoke more emotion in dating individuals than in marrieds, so may it produce more suspicion and worry. Moreover, the lack of security in dating relationships may cause daters to be preoccupied with their relationships. These factors may help explain the second study's finding that daters are more cognitively jealous than marrieds. Although relational status explained 10% of the variance in cognitive jealousy, the interaction effect between sex and relationship status approached significance. Thus, main effects should be interpreted with caution. No main effect for sex on cognitive jealousy was found, mirroring results from Study 1.

Communicative Reactions

Two multivariate main effects were found for communicative reactions. First, women reported using more of all three reactions – distribution, integration, and avoidance – than did men. Second, daters reported using more distribution and avoidance than marrieds. No differences between daters and marrieds were found for integration. These results are not surprising, given that women and daters were two groups who also scored highest in emotional and cognitive jealousy. As the more jealous groups, one would naturally expect women and daters to use a wider array of communicative reactions to jealousy in order to try to cope with their thoughts and feelings. The sex difference in reactions may also be due to a difference in the perceived focus of the jealous threat encountered by men and women. Knapp (1984) argued that women are likely to focus on threats to the relationship, and thus, are likely to react to jealousy by trying to repair the relationship. This process of repair is likely to involve experimenting with the various types of communicative reactions to jealousy. Men, on the other hand, are likely to focus on threats to self-esteem (Knapp, 1984). Repairing esteem may not involve relational communication and may instead focus on cognitive reassessment or activities outside the primary relationship.

Last, the finding that daters report using more distribution and avoidance, but not more integration, than marrieds, has interesting implications. It may be that married couples have negotiated relationship rules and therefore refrain from the use of negative strategies. Indeed, research by Guerrero and Jorgensen (1991) found that behavioral jealousy decreased as the longevity of the relationship increased, indicating reduced manifestation of jealousy in long-term relationships. Daters may also use more distribution and avoidance because of the increased emotional jealousy they experience in comparison to marrieds. Other scholars, such as Canary and Cupach (1988), found that the use of negative communication strategies tends to increase along with emotion. Thus, daters may either avoid discussing jealousy for fear of harming the relationship and further increasing their emotional load, or they may react with distribution, focusing blame on their partner in a negative manner. Finally, despite these speculations, it seems odd that both women and daters employ more avoidance while still using more integration and distribution type reactions. This may be explained in that the need to maintain the relationship causes these individuals to actively experiment with various strategies. For daters, the strategies that work best are often uncertain. This alone should increase the use of a wide array of communicative reactions.

Implications for Relationships in Process

Relationships are canvasses on which many different emotions can be painted. When cognition, behavior, and communication are added to the picture, a relational climate is created. Jealousy is a construct that has the power to impact the climate and the continuation of relationships in process. Too much jealousy can be destructive, yet some jealousy shows that partners care for one another and value their relationships (Knapp, 1984; Salovey & Rodin, 1989). Findings of this study indicate that the experience and communication of jealousy may vary by sex and relationship status.

The finding that women tend to experience slightly more emotional jealousy and to use more communicative reactions to jealousy than men is consistent with the notion that women are primarily responsible for maintaining the intimacy level of a given relationship. Women may be more sensitive to the influence of external forces on their relationships. Communication may then be used to try to put the relationship back on course. Thus, one part of a woman's affiliative role may be to monitor and iron out problems related to jealousy by engaging in emotional expression and communication.

Despite the finding that women tend to express jealousy slightly more than men, Study 1 found jealousy to be correlated within marital dyads. This indicates that both partners are involved in the process of experiencing and coping with jealousy. Dyadic partners may work together to negotiate methods for dealing with jealousy and to try to strike a healthy balance between valuing their relationships and being compulsively possessive.

Part of the reason why daters experience more emotional jealousy than marrieds may be that they are still going through the process of negotiating the boundaries of their relationships. Furthermore, daters may be uncertain about the futures of their relationships and the level of jealousy that is acceptable. This uncertainty may prompt daters to employ a variety of communication responses in order to find the ones that work best in their relationships. Marrieds, on the other hand, are likely to feel secure due to the high level of commitment they have reached. Thus, both daters and marrieds may value their relationships, which is a prerequisite to jealousy, yet daters may see their relationships as more vulnerable to third party threats. Because no differences were found for integration, both daters and marrieds may consider such positive reactions to be instrumental in dealing successfully with jealousy.

Relationships in process, whether they involve daters or spouses, are characterized by the thoughts, emotions, and interaction experienced by dyadic partners. When jealousy occurs, these cognitive, affective, and communicative systems are activated. Sex and relationship status are only two of a host of variables that have the potential to impact these systems. Clearly, examining other individual and relational attributes will bring scholarly knowledge one stride closer to a fuller understanding of jealousy in close relationships.

REFERENCES

Balswick, J., & Avertt, C. P. (1977). Differences in expressiveness: Gender, interpersonal orientation, and perceived parental expressiveness as contributing factors. *Journal of Marriage and the Family, 39*, 121–127.

Bell, R. A., & Buerkel-Rothfuss, N. L. (1990). S(he) loves me, s(he) loves me not: Predictors of relational information-seeking in courtship and beyond. *Communication Quarterly, 38*, 64–82.

Berger, C. R., & Calabrese, R. J. (1975). Some explorations in initial interaction and beyond: Toward a developmental theory of interpersonal communication. *Human Communication Research, 1*, 99–112.

Bowers, J. W., Metts, S. M., & Duncanson, W. T. (1985). Emotion and interpersonal communication. In M. L. Knapp & G. R. Miller (Eds.), *Handbook of interpersonal communication* (pp. 500–550). Beverly Hills, CA: Sage.

Bringle, R. G., & Boebinger, K. L. G. (1990). Jealousy and the "third" person in the love triangle. *Journal of Social and Personal Relationships, 7*, 119–133.

Bringle, R. G., & Buunk, B. (1985). Jealousy and social behavior: A review of person, relationship and situational determinants. In P. Shaver (Ed.), *Self, situations, and social behavior: Review of personality and social psychology* (pp. 241–264). Beverly Hills, CA: Sage.

Bringle, R. G., & Buunk, B. (1986). Examining the causes and consequences of jealousy: Some recent findings and issues. In R. Gilmour & S. Duck (Eds.), *The emerging field of personal relationships* (pp. 225–240). Hillsdale, NJ: Lawrence Erlbaum Associates.

Bringle, R. G., Renner, P., Terry, R., & Davis, S. (1983). An analysis of situational and person components of jealousy. *Journal of Research in Personality, 17*, 354–368.

Bryson, J. B. (1976, September). *The nature of sexual jealousy: An exploratory study.* Paper presented at the annual meeting of the American Psychological Association, Washington, DC.

Bryson, J. B. (in press). Modes of responses to jealousy-evoking situations. In P. Salovey (Ed.), *The psychology of envy and jealousy.* New York: Guilford.

Buck, R. (1979). Individual differences in nonverbal sending accuracy and electrodermal responding: The externalizing-internalizing dimension. In R. Rosenthal (Ed.), *Skill and nonverbal communication: Individual differences* (pp. 140–170). Cambridge, MA: Oelgeschlager, Gunn, & Hain.

Bush, C. R., Bush, J. P., & Jennings, J. (1988). Effects of jealousy threats on relationship perceptions and emotions. *Journal of Social and Personal Relationships, 5*, 285–303.

Buunk, B. (1982). Anticipated sexual jealousy: Its relationship to self-esteem, dependency, and reciprocity. *Personality and Social Psychology Bulletin, 8*, 310–316.

Buunk, B., & Bringle, R. G. (1987). Jealousy and love relationships. In D. Perlman & S. Duck (Eds.), *Intimate relationships: development, dynamics and deterioration* (pp. 123–147). Newbury Park, CA: Sage.

Canary, D. J., & Cupach, W. R. (1988). Relational episodic characteristics associated with conflict tactics. *Journal of Social and Personal Relationships, 5*, 305–325.

Clanton, G., & Smith, L. G. (Eds.). (1977). *Jealousy.* Englewood Cliffs, NJ: Prentice Hall.

Cohen, J. (1977). *Statistical power analysis for the behavioral sciences.* New York: Academic Press.

Cozby, P. C. (1973). Self-disclosure: A literature review. *Psychological Bulletin, 79*, 73–91.

Duck, S. W. (1992). *Human relationships* (2nd ed.). Newbury Park, CA: Sage.

Ekman, P., Levenson, R. W., & Friesen, W. V. (1983). Autonomic nervous system activity distinguishes among emotions. *Science, 221*, 1208–1210.

Eloy, S. V., Guerrero, L. K., Andersen, P. A., & Spitzberg, B. H. (1992, May). *Coping with the green-eyed monster: Relational satisfaction and communicative reactions to jealousy.* Paper presented to the annual meeting of the International Communication Association, Miami, FL.

Francis, J. (1977). Toward the management of sexual jealousy. *Journal of Marriage and the Family, 39*, 61–69.

Guerrero, L. K., & Eloy, S. V. (1992). Relational satisfaction and jealousy across marital types. *Communication Reports, 5*, 23–41.

Guerrero, L. K., & Jorgensen, P. F. (1991, November). *The nature of marital jealousy: Effects of threats to permanence and interdependence.* Paper presented at the 1991 Speech Communication Association convention, Atlanta, GA.

Hatfield, E. (1984). The dangers of intimacy. In V. J. Derlega (Ed.), *Communication, intimacy, and close relationships* (pp. 207–220). New York: Academic Press.

Hatkoff, S., & Lasswell, T. E. (1979). Male-Female similarities and differences in conceptualizing love. In M. Cook & G. Wilson (Eds.), *Love and attraction: An international conference* (pp. 221–227). Oxford, England: Pergamon.

Hays, R. D., Hayashi, T., & Stewart, A. (1989). A five-item measure of social desirable response set. *Educational and Psychological Measurement, 49*, 629–636.

Knapp, M. L. (1984). *Interpersonal communication and human relationships.* Boston, MA: Allyn & Bacon.

LaFrance, M., & Mayo, C. (1978). A review of nonverbal behaviors of women and men. *Western Journal of Speech Communication, 43*, 96–107.

Mathes, E. W., & Severa, N. (1981). Jealousy, romantic love, and liking: Theoretical considerations and preliminary scale development. *Psychological Reports, 49*, 23–31.

Noller, P. (1980). Misunderstanding in marital communication: A study of couples' nonverbal behavior. *Journal of Personality and Social Psychology, 39*, 1135–1148.

Pfeiffer, S. M., & Wong, P. T. (1989). Multidimensional jealousy. *Journal of Social and Personal Relationships, 6*, 181–196.

Rubin, A., Hill, C. T., Peplau, L. A., & Dunke-Schetter, C. (1980). Self-disclosure in dating couples: Sex roles and the ethic of openness. *Journal of Marriage and the Family, 42*, 305–317.

Salovey, P., & Rodin, J. (1985). The heart of jealousy. *Psychology Today, 19*, 22–25, 28–29.

Salovey, P., & Rodin, J. (1989). Envy and jealousy in close relationships. In C. Hendrick (Ed.), *Close relationships* (pp. 221–246). Newbury Park, CA: Sage.

Shettel-Neuber, J., Bryson, J. B., & Young, L. E. (1978). Physical attractiveness of the other person and jealousy. *Personality and Social Psychology Bulletin, 4*, 612–615.

Strzyzewski, K., & Comstock, J. (1990, February). *The experience and expression of jealousy: A comparison between friends and romantics.* Paper presented at the annual convention of the Western States Communication Association, Sacramento, CA.

Teismann, M. W., & Mosher, D. L. (1978). Jealous conflict in dating couples. *Psychological Reports, 42*, 1211–1216.

White, G. L. (1980). Inducing jealousy: A power perspective. *Personality and Social Psychology Bulletin, 6*, 222–227.

White, G. L. (1981a). Jealousy and partner's perceived motives for attraction to a rival. *Social Psychology Quarterly, 44*, 24–30.

White, G. L. (1981b). Relative involvement, inadequacy, and jealousy: A test of a causal model. *Alternative Lifestyles, 4*, 291–309.

White, G. L. (1981c). Some correlates of romantic jealousy. *Journal of Personality, 49*, 129–146.

White, G. L. (1985). *Gender, power, and romantic jealousy.* Unpublished manuscript. University of Oakland, New Zealand.

White, G. L., & Mullen, P. E. (1989). *Jealousy: Theory, research, and clinical strategies.* New York: Guilford.

8

Power in Friendship and
Use of Influence Strategies

James F. Roiger[1]
University of Arizona

Emerson (1962) proposed that power is a potential that exists as a result of the interdependence of the individuals in a reciprocal relationship. This power can be manifested in a reciprocal relationship through such things as the ability to make decisions in the relationship, and the control of resources in a relationship. In fact, Blau (1964) contended that the potential for power exists as a result of an asymmetry of resources between the interactants. This resource differential could be evident in several ways such as when one relational partner has more discretionary income than another, or when one person is more socially or professionally desirable than another, or perhaps when one person simply has more knowledge and expertise than the other. Obviously these resources and others could exist in varying degrees and in innumerable combinations in these relationships.

Friendship is a reciprocal relationship in which the effect of power can be fruitfully studied. These relationships, which are voluntary in nature, are often based on social equality and private negotiation (Bell, 1981). Although individuals can "pick their friends," the opportunity to choose may be very restricted in other reciprocal relationships, such as work and family relationships. Duck (1983) proposed that friendships meet important psychological and physiological needs. Individuals who enjoy a network of good friends have fewer medical problems, rely on friends for practical advice when other relationships are in trouble, and experience less loneliness and frustration. Accord-

[1]The author wishes to thank Michael Burgoon, Deborah Newton, Paul Mongeau, and Pamela Kalbfleisch for their helpful comments on earlier drafts of this chapter.

ing to Duck (1983), friendships meet six specific needs, including (a) creating a sense of belonging, (b) providing emotional integration and stability, (c) generating opportunities for communication about ourselves, (d) providing for assistance and physical support, (e) giving reassurance of our worth and value, and (f) creating opportunities to help others. Rubin (1985) contended that friendships fulfill some needs more effectively than family and marital relationships because friendships normally have expectations that are less demanding, and friends are less judgmental than are family members and marital partners. Contarello and Volpato's (1991) review of historical literary depictions of friendships identified the core aspects of friendship as intimacy, respect, and mutual help; the same aspects that Rubin (1985) found individuals identified as necessary in an idealized friendship. Jones (1991) also found that these aspects of a friendship were major contributors to a person's sense of friendship satisfaction for both males and females. Gillies (1976) study of friendship determined that the choosing of one's friends is most like holding a mirror to oneself, but as we grow emotionally and intellectually, friends must also grow and in similar ways. Friendships exist in the present, and those friendships that are not actively maintained usually lose their importance and eventually terminate. The findings on friendship all suggest that an important aspect of a good friendship is that the friends provide support to each other and help each other, but it is also necessary that the support and help be provided equitably (Duck, 1983; Gillies, 1976; Rubin, 1985).

Equity is the key to ongoing relationships, whether the aspect is emotional support, trust, or resource exchange. Gillies (1976) noted that balance must be maintained in friendships; a dependent relationship creates a sense of imprisonment and stagnates the relationship. Although friendships do fulfill needs for both friends, that fulfillment must not be manipulative or one-sided. Rubin (1985) argued that a healthy growing friendship is a symbiotic relationship where the partners complement each other and both share in the needing and the giving. Duck (1983) believed that successful friendships are based on the fair exchange of resources, that is, the exchanges are balanced. As the friendship grows, the timespan for reciprocation may be extended and the balance may be maintained by different kinds of repayment. But, according to Duck (1983), friends do keep track of the equity issue and, if after a period of time, one of the friends believes that balance is not being maintained, the friendship will be downgraded or may be terminated. Thus, friendships represent a reciprocal relationship where an asymmetry in the exchange of resources may exist some of the time and may represent potential power for the member who is owed resources by the other member.

King (1975) argued that a favorable asymmetry of resources may serve as a power potential and may be expended in interpersonal influence attempts. In a friendship situation, the friends may not even be aware of each other's power until they attempt to influence one another. Furthermore, power gains may actually result from these influence attempts. If friendships can be seen as relationships based on social equality (Bell, 1981), a disruption in the equality through prior influence attempts, new resources acquired by either relational partner, or a perceived threat to the equality of the relationship may motivate the partners to try and restore the symmetry of the relationship. On the other hand, a temporary disruption in the implicit power in friendships may alter how friends attempt to influence their relational partners.

Prior research has studied the use of influence attempts when there is a power differential in a relationship that is based on a position in a hierarchy. For example, Baxter (1984) found that people across relationships who were in a power position used less polite (more antisocial) message strategies than those who were not in a power position. Miller (1982) and Funkhouser et al. (1985) found that, in interpersonal relationships, the number of strategies used decreased as the power of the target decreased, but the overall likelihood of strategy use increased as the power of the persuader increased. These findings suggest that power differentials between members of a relationship do have an effect on the type and use of influence strategies, such that the higher power person will use less socially acceptable strategies and use them more often.

In the study presented in this chapter, power will be operationalized not as a constant in a relationship, but as something that can vary as the relational resources vary and become asymmetrical. Although not providing direct guidance, the work of Baxter (1984), Funkhouser et al. (1985), and Miller (1982) suggests that the likelihood of using influence strategies increases as the individual's power increases. Henderson's (1981) review of limited models and general theories of social power suggested that the level of potential power and its likelihood of strategy use may be linearly related. Therefore, it follows that situational power differences may also have a linear effect on the likelihood of influence strategy usage, three hypotheses (H) are suggested:

H₁: Persuaders who have a favorable power potential will have a significantly higher overall use of influence strategies than persuaders with an unfavorable power potential.

H₂: Persuaders who have a favorable power potential will have a significantly higher overall use of influence strategies than persuaders with an equal power potential.

H₃: Persuaders who have an equal power potential will have a significantly higher overall use of influence strategies than persuaders with an unfavorable power potential.

A second situational variable that may interact with power is that of the level of self-interest on the part of the persuader. Two studies have found that high self-interest persuaders exerted more pressure on the persuadee than did low self-interest persuaders (Clark, 1979; Cody & McLaughlin, 1980), whereas one study found no effect (Boster & Stiff, 1984).

H$_4$:   Persuaders who have a high self-interest in gaining compliance will
         have a significantly higher overall use of influence strategies than will
         low self-interest persuaders.

Researchers have argued that the use of typologies of compliance-gaining
strategies in influence studies, such as Marwell and Schmitt's (1967) 16 strategies, may be an indicator of verbal aggressiveness, even if the typologies do
not represent actual strategy use (Burgoon, Dillard, Koper, & Doran, 1984;
Dillard & Burgoon, 1985; Hunter & Boster, 1987). Research has indicated
that husbands are more verbally aggressive than their wives, especially in conflict situations (Infante, Chandler, & Rudd, 1989; Infante, Sabourin, Rudd,
& Shannon, 1990). Furthermore, Infante, Rancer, and Womack's (1990) summary of previous research on argumentativeness indicates that, across situations, males are more verbally aggressive than females. If the Marwell and
Schmitt (1967) typology of influence strategies is considered an indicator of
verbal aggressiveness, males may be more willing to use more strategies and
have a higher likelihood of overall strategy use than females.

H$_5$:   Males will have significantly higher overall use of influence strate-
         gies than will females.

METHOD

Participants

The respondents ($N = 400$) were students enrolled in the basic communication course at a large western university and were randomly assigned to one
of five potential power and self-interest situations. The questionnaires were
completed during class and all solicited students volunteered to participate in
the study. Eighteen questionnaires were discarded for incomplete data and seven
questionnaires were randomly discarded to provide balanced situations. The
analyzed sample ($N = 375$) was 53% female and 47% male with a median
age of 19.

Procedure

Each participant read one of five scenarios featuring five different power situations. The situations were manipulated by varying the importance of the request to the persuader, the amount of inconvenience to the persuadee, and the
level of similar requests made or granted in the recent past. Following each
scenario, a series of strategies were listed that could be used in response. Each

strategy was described and a possible message using the strategy was provided as a referent. The respondents indicated their likelihood of using each strategy on a scale from 1 to 7.

Instrument

The five scenarios used to manipulate situational levels of power and self-interest were (a) favorable power and high self-interest, (b) favorable power and low self-interest, (c) equal power, (d) unfavorable power and high self-interest, and (e) unfavorable power and low self-interest (see Table 8.1). The three levels of power (favorable, equal, unfavorable) were chosen to create the greatest differentiation of the potential power between the requestor and requestee and are representative of an influence attempt that could be made in an ongoing friendship, that is, a request for a ride to the airport. Self-interest

TABLE 8.1.
Power and Self-Interest Situations

1. Favorable Power and High Self-Interest

   You and a friend have maintained a steady relationship in the past and expect that relationship to continue in the future. You need a ride to the airport on Friday evening for a weekend home to see your mother who is seriously ill and needs to be picked up at the airport on Sunday evening. You live close to the airport and know that your friend has no plans for the weekend. Recently you drove your friend to Los Angeles for an international flight.

2. Favorable Power and Low Self-Interest

   You and a friend have maintained a steady relationship in the past and expect that relationship to continue in the future. You need a ride to the airport on Friday evening and need to be picked up at the airport on Sunday evening. You live close to the airport and you know that your friend has no plans for the weekend. Recently you drove your friend to the airport in a similar situation.

3. Equal Power

   You and a friend have maintained a steady relationship in the past and expect that relationship to continue in the future. You need a ride to the airport on Friday evening and need to be picked up at the airport on Sunday evening.

4. Unfavorable Power and High Self-Interest

   You and a friend have maintained a steady relationship in the past and expect that relationship to continue in the future. You need a ride to the airport on Friday evening for a Utah skiing trip and need to be picked up at the airport on Sunday evening. The trip is about an hour's drive from where you live and the Friday trip will be through rush hour traffic. You know that your friend is planning an early start for a San Felipe weekend. Recently your friend drove you to Los Angeles for an international flight.

5. Unfavorable Power and Low Self-Interest

   You and a friend have maintained a steady relationship in the past and expect that relationship to continue in the future. You need a ride to the airport on Friday evening and need to be picked up at the airport on Sunday evening. You live about an hour's drive from the airport and the Friday trip will be through rush hour traffic. You know that your friend has plans for the weekend. Recently your friend drove you to the airport for a similar trip.

was manipulated by identifying the purpose of the trip, that was varied to accentuate the power differential even more, or to not identify the purpose of the trip.

Four manipulations checks for power levels were conducted on the situations. Respondents read one of the situations, rated the believability of the situation, and either rated the power of the persuader or the power of the persuadee. The situations were modified each time in response to the ratings on the believability of the situation and the perceived potential power of the requestor and the requestee. The fourth manipulation check ($N = 40$) produced a significant difference in favor of the requestor in the powerful situation, $t(16) = 2.95$, $p < .01$, a significant difference in favor of the requestee in the powerless situation, $t(12) = 2.52$, $p < .025$, and no significant difference between the requestor and the requestee in the neutral situation, $t(4) < 1$.

The influence strategies chosen for this study were Marwell and Schmitt's (1967) 16-strategy typology. The Marwell and Schmitt typology was chosen because it is well represented in the compliance-gaining literature (e.g., Burgoon et al., 1984; Cody & McLaughlin, 1980; Dillard & Burgoon, 1985; Lustig & King, 1980; Miller, Boster, Roloff, & Seibold, 1977; O'Hair & Cody, 1987; Roloff & Barnicott, 1978, 1979), and has received support as being a unidimensional scale (Burgoon et al., 1984; Dillard, 1988; Hunter & Boster, 1978, 1987) that probably represents verbal aggressiveness. As a unidimensional scale, the 16 strategies interitem reliability using Cronbach's alpha was .87.

Analysis

The unidimensionality of the 16 strategies was assessed with a principal components factor analysis and item mean correlations. The hypotheses on the perceptions of situational differences (power and self-interest) and gender differences were assessed with analysis of variance tests.

RESULTS

Scale Dimensionality

The dimensionality of the 16 influence strategies was assessed by examining the factor structure and correlations. The five power situations were combined for this dimensionality assessment. The unrotated factor structure was used to assess the initial dimensionality, followed by varimax and oblimin rotations.

In the initial examination of factor dimensionality, items were assigned to factors if their loading was at least .25 higher on that factor than on other factors, and if two or more items loaded on a single factor. An additional criteria

TABLE 8.2.
Unrotated Factor Loadings

Item	Factor 1	Factor 2	Factor 3
Altercasting, Positive	.81599*	−.06684	−.18441
Altercasting, Negative	.75869*	−.30439	.04110
Self-feeling, Positive	.75489*	.11841	−.13262
Esteem, Positive	.74939*	.01556	−.11384
Self-feeling, Negative	.74895*	−.20470	−.06468
Esteem, Negative	.74728*	−.26049	.08848
Moral Appeal	.74232*	−.04796	−.15225
Aversive Stimulation	.65240*	−.38522	.19633
Debt	.60957*	.05614	−.33105
Expertise, Negative	.55594	.15783	.49218
Threat	.50019	−.31706	.49772
Liking	.45382	.62475	.01532
Promise	.06058	.58700*	.16534
Pregiving	.47066	.53319	−.02795
Expertise, Positive	.47954	.52611	.33953
Altruism	.30897	.10879	−.69725*
Eigenvalue	6.15631	1.80823	1.36935
Percent of Variance	38.50000	11.30000	8.60000
Cumulative Percent	38.50000	49.80000	58.30000

*Denotes unambiguous items on each factor.

was that each factor should account for a similar amount of the remaining un-explained variance as the first factor (Kim & Mueller, 1978). Using these criteria nine items were loaded on Factor 1, one item on Factor 2, one item on Factor 3, and five items were unassigned. This unrotated factor solution suggests an unidimensional scale.[2]

The follow-up varimax rotation identified 10 items on three factors and the oblimin rotation indicated 13 items on three factors. These solutions, however, are not as straightforward as those yielded by the unrotated factor analysis.

Further support for an underlying unidimensional scale suggested by the unrotated factor analysis was found by examining the item mean correlations of the 16 influence strategies. This examination found 100 of the possible 120 possible correlations to be significant at the .01 level. Klingle (1991) indicated that a high degree of item mean correlation can produce spurious multiple factor solutions.

Therefore, for the subsequent analysis of variance tests in these analyses, the 16 strategies were treated as an unidimensional scale. A scale score was computed for each participant in this analysis by summing the likelihood of

---

[2]According to Michael Burgoon (personal communication, August 31, 1991), the unrotated factor structure should be used in the initial determination of whether multiple factors actually exist.

use ratings for each strategy, then dividing the total score by the constant 16 to allow easier comparisons.

Situational Power

A $2 \times 2 \times 2$ analysis of variance was conducted to test for possible interactions between power, self-interest, and sex. The cells for the ANOVA include favorable versus unfavorable power, high self-interest versus low self-interest, and males versus females. The main effect for sex was significant, $F(1, 292) = 18.2, p < .01$, Eta^2 = .05. The nonsignificant main effect for self-interest disconfirms Hypothesis 4. There were no significant higher order interactions.

In the absence of any interactions, the two high power situations and the two low power situations were combined. The equal power situation was weighted (weight = 2) to maintain a balanced design. A one-way ANOVA with contrasts was executed to test the power differential. There was a significant effect for power, $F(2, 447) = 3.99, p < .02$, Eta^2 = .02. The high power situations ($M = 3.05$) and the low power situations ($M = 2.96$) were not significantly different, $t(447) < 1$. Hypothesis 1 was not confirmed. The high power situations ($M = 3.05$) and the equal power situation ($M = 2.76$) were significantly different, $t(447) = 2.77, p < .01$. Hypothesis 2 was confirmed. The equal power situation ($M = 2.76$) and the low power situation ($M = 2.96$) approached acceptable significance but in the opposite direction, $t(447) = -1.88, p < .06$. Thus, hypothesis 3 was not confirmed. To provide protection for the familywise alpha, a Scheffe range test was conducted. The high power situations and the equal power situation were significantly different at .05 alpha. Given the findings of the contrasts, the quadratic term was tested. The quadratic term was significant, $F(1, 447) = 7.20, p < .01$. The curvilinear relationship applies to both males and females. The means by power level are listed in Table 8.3.

Although not significant, the ordering of the means for the five situations that discriminated between high and low self-interest for the powerful and powerless conditions follows the curvilinear pattern. The means are listed in Table 8.4. The pattern again holds for both men and women.

The curvilinear pattern means that individuals who are in an unfavorable power situation are as verbally aggressive as individuals who are in a favorable power situation, when compared to individuals in an equal power situation.

TABLE 8.3.
Scale Means by Gender for Power Levels

Gender	Powerful	Equal	Powerless
Male	3.249	2.947	3.227
Female	2.875	2.601	2.717

TABLE 8.4.
Scale Means for All Situations

Situation	Powerful Hi S-I	Powerful Lo S-I	Equal Power	Powerless Hi S-I	Powerless Lo S-I
Combined	3.083	3.021	2.758	2.887	3.030
Male	3.273	3.226	2.947	3.078	3.380
Female	2.917	2.832	2.601	2.710	2.723

Although male and female scale scores both follow the curvilinear pattern, male ($M = 3.18$) and female ($M = 2.76$), scale scores differ significantly, $t(373) = 5.57$, $p < .01$. Men have a higher scale score which represents a higher likelihood of use of the strategies across all situations. Hypothesis 5 was confirmed. If the rating scale represents a measure of verbal aggressiveness, the finding supports the previous research that males are more verbally aggressive than females.

DISCUSSION

The use of potential power based on an asymmetry of tangible or intangible resources within friendships was partially supported, but the use is not linear. Most models of power have suggested that more powerful persons would be more apt to make use of their power when influencing others whereas low power individuals would use fewer and less aggressive methods. In this study, that was not true; the findings indicate that the relationship of situational power and verbal aggressiveness is curvilinear. Powerful persons were more aggressive than equal power persons, but powerless persons were also more aggressive than equal power persons. Bell (1981) argued that friendships have implicit rights and obligations. The findings may be related to the perceptions of the friends as to what each other's rights and obligations are in a balanced friendship. Individuals who have a favorable power situation may be willing to use more strategies and with a higher likelihood of use because they perceive the right to do so. The other person owes them resources and has an obligation to reciprocate. On the other hand, individuals with an unfavorable power situation may also be willing to use more strategies and with a higher likelihood of use because they perceive that the friend has an obligation to provide help when required, and they have a right to ask for that help. But these individuals also perceive that, because an asymmetry of resources already exists, they will have to convince the requestee, that is, be more verbally aggressive, of the obligations that friends have toward each other. This would be consistent with Duck's (1983) argument that close friends will tolerate an increased timespan before reciprocation is required. There may be an assumption by the persuader that, because favors are already owed to the persuadee, more aggressive tactics will be required to gain an extension of the timespan and receive further favors.

The situational impact of self-interest has been inconsistent and limited (Dillard & Burgoon, 1985). Just as Boster and Stiff (1984) reported, this study found no significant effect for self-interest. However, the scale mean differences suggest that further investigation is probably warranted. Part of the problem in the present study may have been that the self-interest manipulation was inadequate and may have been perceived as an additional power factor. Alternatively, the respondents may have felt that attempting to gain compliance from a friend was inherently motivated by self-interest and did not consider the additional impact of that aspect of the situational description.

The Marwell and Schmitt (1967) typology was used as a unidimensional scale in this study. The purpose of a scale is to array people on some dimension. As Hunter and Boster (1987) and McIver and Carmines (1981) pointed out, it makes little sense to have people respond to a similar series of items and then test the items individually. Such a procedure treats each strategy as a single item scale. Single-item scale have numerous problems including: (a) poor conceptual representation, (b) questionable validity and accuracy, (c) a lack of precision, and (d) poor reliability (McIver & Carmines, 1981). Multidimensional solutions for the Marwell-Schmitt strategies have been claimed (e.g., Marwell & Schmitt, 1967; Roloff & Barnicott, 1978, 1979), yet the items were still treated singly rather than summed to produce a scale value for each of the dimensions as is normally the case with multi-item scales. Although the scale may not directly measure compliance-gaining behavior as critics have suggested (e.g., Clark, 1979; Schenck-Hamlin, Georgacarakos, & Wiseman, 1982; Wiseman & Schenck-Hamlin, 1981), it may represent a trait that is a predictor of compliance-gaining behavior (Hunter & Boster, 1987), that interacts with other situational variables, such as the situational power and the self-interest variables tested in this study.

Although single-situation and paper-pencil measures of compliance-gaining, using a priori lists, have been justly criticized, its conceptualization as a scale measuring a predictor trait rather than overt behaviors increases the reliability and the validity of the findings (Hunter & Boster, 1987), and may serve as a useful tool for teasing out subtle differences in interpersonal influence attempts. Miller, Boster, Roloff, and Seibold (1987) proposed that studies using strategy lists do answer questions about power and influence attempts and contribute to the knowledge necessary to develop theories. The finding of a curvilinear situational power pattern is evidence that the proposal is true.

It has been suggested that the underlying dimension is probably instrumental verbal aggressiveness (e.g., Burgoon et al., 1984; Dillard & Burgoon, 1985; Hunter & Boster, 1987), and the significant gender differences in the mean scale values in this study further support this contention. Because the curvilinear pattern is similar for males and females, differing only in intensity, the findings suggest the perceptions of both males and females are similar and support a verbal aggressiveness model. Three previous studies have also suggested that a perceived lack of power may lead to increased verbal aggressiveness. Winter (1973) claimed that people who have feelings of power inferiority are more apt to become more verbally aggressive and less accommodating. Cohen (1958) identified similar behavior in groups with low-status people. People may compensate for the feelings of inferiority by being willing to use more strategies. Stotland (1959) found that individuals who perceive a power differential in favor of the other person will become more verbally aggressive when pursuing their own goals. Resource exchange models have identified the problems that an asymmetry of resources may cause in any relationship, but these findings suggest that the actual conduct of the communication in the relationship is impacted. Although the findings may be an artifact of the friendship situation, Quinn's (1987) study of the cultural models that people use to identify their relationships supports a resource model. Her analysis of the metaphors that couples used to describe their relationship indicated that couples overwhelmingly used resource exchange metaphors in the descriptions. These findings may have an impact on our understanding of verbal aggressiveness in many aspects of relationships. One applicable example of possible impact might occur in conflict situations. Wilmot and Wilmot (1978) argued that a perceived disparity of resources between the parties to the conflict is one of the key factors that leads to conflict. If one person perceives an unfavorable power position, her/his responses during the conflict may become more aggressive and this reaction may actually heighten the conflict rather than alleviate it.

This study has shown that situational power based on an asymmetry of resources may be an important factor in understanding the communication patterns of all relationships and that a perceived unfavorable inequity of resources may increase the verbal aggressiveness of that partner at a time in the relationship when such behavior may be counterproductive to maintaining harmonious relations.

REFERENCES

Baxter, L. A. (1984). An investigation of compliance-gaining as politeness. *Human Communication Research, 10*, 427–456.

Bell, R. R. (1981). *Worlds of friendship.* Beverly Hills, CA: Sage.

Blau, P. M. (1964). *Exchange and power in social life.* New York: Wiley.

Boster, F. J., & Stiff, J. B. (1984). Compliance-gaining message selection behavior. *Human Communication Research, 10*, 539–556.

Burgoon, M., Dillard, J. P., Koper, R., & Doran, N. (1984). The impact of communication context and persuader gender on persuasive message selection. *Women's Studies in Communication, 7*, 1–12.

Clark, R. A. (1979). The impact of self interest and desire for liking on the selection of communicative strategies. *Communication Monographs, 46*, 257–273.

Cody, M. J., & McLaughlin, M. L. (1980). Perceptions of compliance-gaining situations: A dimensional analysis. *Communication Monographs, 47*, 132–148.

Cohen, A. R. (1958). Upward communication in experimentally created hierarchies. *Human Relations, 11*, 41–53.

Contarello, A., & Volpato, C. (1991). Images of friendship: Literary depictions through the ages. *Journal of Social and Personal Relationships, 8*, 49–75.

Dillard, J. P. (1988). Compliance-gaining message-selection: What is our dependent variable? *Communication Monographs, 55*, 162–183.

Dillard, J. P., & Burgoon, M. (1985). Situational influences on the selection of compliance-gaining messages: Two tests of the predictive utility of the Cody-McLaughlin typology. *Communication Monographs, 52*, 289–304.

Duck, S. (1983). *Friends, for life: The psychology of close relationships.* Brighton, UK: Harvester Press.

Emerson, R. M. (1962, February). Power-dependent relations. *American Sociological Review, 27*, 31–41.

Funkhouser, A., Gongah, T. B., Habermas, R., Jong-Bum, H., Hesse, M., Perez, R., & Shatzer, M. J. (1985, May). *Selection of compliance gaining strategies among four culturally diverse groups.* Paper presented at the International Communication Association convention, Honolulu, HI.

Gillies, J. (1976). *Friends: The power and potential of the company you keep.* New York: Coward, McCann & Geoghegan.

Henderson, A. H. (1981). *Social power: Social psychological models and theories.* New York: Praeger.

Hunter, J. E., & Boster, F. J. (1978, November). *An empathy model of compliance-gaining message strategy selection.* Paper presented at the Speech Communication Association convention, Minneapolis, MN.

Hunter, J. E., & Boster, F. J. (1987). A model of compliance-gaining message selection. *Communication Monographs, 54*, 63–84.

Infante, D. A., Chandler, T. A., & Rudd, J. E. (1989). Test of an argumentative skill deficiency model of interspousal violence. *Communication Monographs, 56*, 163–177.

Infante, D. A., Sabourin, T. C., Rudd, J. E., & Shannon, E. A. (1990). Verbal aggression in violent and nonviolent marital disputes. *Communication Quarterly, 38*, 361–371.

Infante, D. A., Rancer, A. S., & Womack, D. F. (1990). *Building communication theory.* Prospect Heights, IL: Waveland.

Jones, D. C. (1991). Friendship satisfaction and gender: An examination of sex differences in contributors to friendship satisfaction. *Journal of Social and Personal Relationships, 8*, 167–185.

Kim, J., & Mueller, C. W. (1978). *Introduction to factor analysis: What it is and how to do it.* Sage University paper series on quantitative applications in the social sciences (Series No. 07-013). Newbury Park, CA: Sage.

King, S. W. (1975). *Communication and social influence.* Reading, MA: Addison-Wesley.

Klingle, R. (1991, February). *Factor analysis in social influence research.* Paper presented at the Annual Meeting of the Western States Communication Association, Phoenix, AZ.

Lustig, M. W., & King, S. W. (1980). The effect of communication apprehension and situation on communication strategy choices. *Human Communication Research, 7*, 74–82.

Marwell, G., & Schmitt, D. R. (1967). Dimensions of compliance-gaining behavior: An empirical analysis. *Sociometry, 30*, 350–364.

McIver, J. P., & Carmines, E. G. (1981). *Unidimensional scaling.* Sage University paper series on quantitative applications in the social sciences (Series No. 07-001). Beverly Hills, CA: Sage.

Miller, G. R., Boster, F. J., Roloff, M. E., & Seibold, D. R. (1977). Compliance-gaining message strategies: A typology and some findings concerning effects of situational differences. *Communication Monographs, 44*, 37–51.

Miller, G. R., Boster, F. J., Roloff, M. E., & Seibold, D. R. (1987). MBRS rekindled: Some thoughts on compliance-gaining in interpersonal settings. In M. E. Roloff & G. R. Miller (Eds.), *Interpersonal processes: New directions in communication research* (pp. 89–116). Newbury Park, CA: Sage.

Miller, M. D. (1982). Friendship, power and the language of compliance-gaining. *Journal of Language and Social Psychology, 1,* 111–121.

O'Hair, D., & Cody, M. J. (1987). Machiavellian beliefs and social influence. *Western Journal of Speech Communication, 51,* 279–303.

Quinn, N. (1987). Convergent evidence for a cultural model of American marriage. In D. Holland & N. Quinn (Eds.), *Cultural models in language and thought* (pp. 173–192). Cambridge, UK: Cambridge University Press.

Roloff, M. E., & Barnicott, E. F. (1978). The situational use of pro- and antisocial compliance-gaining strategies by high and low Machiavellians. In B. D. Ruben (Ed.), *Communication yearbook 2* (pp. 193–205). New Brunswick, NJ: Transaction.

Roloff, M. E., & Barnicott, E. F. (1979). The influence of dogmatism on the situational use of pro- and anti-social compliance-gaining strategies. *Southern Speech Communication Journal, 45,* 37–54.

Rubin, L. B. (1985). *Just friends: The role of friendship in our lives.* New York: Harper & Row.

Schenck-Hamlin, W. J., Georgacarakos, G. N., & Wiseman, R. L. (1982). A formal account of interpersonal influence. *Communication Quarterly, 30,* 173–180.

Stotland, E. (1959). Peer groups and reactions to power figures. In D. Cartwright (Ed.), *Studies in social power* (pp. 53–68). Ann Arbor, MI: Institute for Social Research.

Wilmot, J. H., & Wilmot, W. W. (1978). *Interpersonal conflict.* Dubuque, IA: Wm. C. Brown.

Winter, D. G. (1973). *The power motive.* New York: Free Press.

Wiseman, R. L., & Schenck-Hamlin, W. (1981). A multidimensional scaling validation of an inductively-derived set of compliance-gaining strategies. *Communication Monographs, 48,* 251–270.

9

Who Embarrasses Whom? Relational and Sex Differences in the Use of Intentional Embarrassment

William F. Sharkey
University of Hawaii at Manoa

Relational partners develop, maintain, and terminate relationships through the use of communication. How individuals define their relationships affects the type of communication that is appropriate for their interaction. Accordingly, the type of communication used by individuals may, in turn, help to define a relationship (e.g., the difference between defining a relationship as acquaintance vs. friend). Additionaly, some researchers discovered that the sex of the interactants may have an effect on these communication behaviors as well. One such communication phenomenon is *deliberate embarrassment*. People frequently experience varying degrees of embarrassment in their daily lives (Sharkey & Stafford, 1990). Frequently, individuals experience embarrassment because of unintentional acts such as forgetting someone's name or accidentally spilling a drink. However, at times people intentionally embarrass others in order to achieve a variety of goals (Petronio & Snider, 1990, 1992; Sharkey, 1991). The present investigation is an exploratory, descriptive endeavor to discover, first, who embarrasses whom. Second, this study seeks to discover whether there are relational and sex differences in the goals attempted and the tactics employed to intentionally embarrass another person.

What is embarrassment? Embarrassment appears to have several characteristics. First, embarrassment is by necessity, social. That is, others need to be physically present, ostensibly present, or their presence is anticipated at a future time (Brown, 1968; Modigliani, 1971). Second, embarrassment is a subjective experience of anxiety or fear that one's behaviors will be negatively sanctioned or others will have a lower evaluation of the role being presented (Leary, 1982; Modigliani, 1968). Third, this fear occurs as a result of a discrepancy between a person's presented self and one's desired presentational self—an interpersonal predicament (Cupach & Metts, 1990; Goffman, 1956; Modigliani, 1968). Fourth, this fear may also revolve around the uncertainty that follows a disrupted interaction (Parrott, Sabini, & Silver, 1988; Silver, Sabini, & Parrott, 1987). Last, embarrassment is generally short-lived (Buss, 1980). However, Parrott et al. (1988) claimed that what others are thinking is of little concern. Whenever a person's social expectations are called into question, the indecisiveness about how to continue is what causes the embarrassment (Miller, in press). Nevertheless, the following definition of embarrassment is offered: *Embarrassment* is a short lived emotional/psychological response of social chagrin (i.e., a fear of negative sanctioning or lower evaluations from others) that occurs as a result of a discrepancy between one's self-presentation and desired self-presentation that may lead to uncertainty. So, for example, when an individual frequents a restaurant, he or she attempts to present personal poise. He or she understands the rules and norms of "restauranting" and expects that others will assume that he or she understands the same. When this individual spills a drink, and the spilling of the drink is in opposition with his or her desired self-presentation, this act will cause uncertainty and fear about how others will evaluate him or her. The person would probably feel embarrassed for a short time, until the drink is cleaned up and everyone has refocused their attention elsewhere. However, if a person is unaware of any discrepancy or doesn't care about what other's think, this person will probably not experience embarrassment (Miller, in press).

The previous scenario presents a situation in which the customer unintentionally created a situation in which he or she experienced embarrassment. At other times, someone may unintentionally or intentionally attempt to cause another person to experience embarrassment. Scholars have debated the definition of intention for years. This chapter will make no attempt to put this debate to rest. However, Stamp and Knapp (1990) note that scholars have reached a number of agreements in relation to intentionality that include:

(1) multiple levels or degrees of consciousness exist; (2) more than one intention can occur during the act of communicating; (3) communicative intentions can be linked to varying states of consciousness; and (4) both consciousness and intent may change during the process of communicating. (p. 283)

They also propose that three dominant perspectives on intention have emerged: (a) the message encoder perspective, (b) the message decoder perspective, and (c) the interaction perspective. Motley (1986) suggested *intention* as the motivation an individual has "*to transmit a message for eventual interpretation by a receiver*" (p. 5). This definition falls into the category of the message-encoder perspective. This perspective assumes a person is, to some degree, conscious of her or his goal(s) (Stamp & Knapp, 1990). This investigation follows this sense and concerns why and how people purposely encode messages vocally and nonvocally to elicit embarrassment in another person.

Indeed, the first question to be asked is, "Who embarrasses whom?" Research on prosocial and antisocial behaviors in interpersonal and noninterpersonal relationships may lend insight. First, conventional knowledge suggests that people must obey the rules of interaction to have successful interactions; that is, engage in prosocial behaviors. Embarrassment is generally a result of someone's violation of a rule of interaction. The disruptive and aversive nature of embarrassment restrains interactants from engaging in behaviors that would violate the interaction rules that create embarrassment for the parties involved (Edelmann, in press). Therefore, participants come to a "working consensus" of the roles to be played by each person and the rules to follow (Goffman, 1959).

People may perceive intentional embarrassment as an antisocial act because it calls into question the participant's working consensus. Although Braithwaite (1992) recently suggested that the context may actually dictate that the use of embarrassment is appropriate and expected (e.g., the embarrassment of men at coed wedding and baby showers). Nevertheless, Roloff (1976) suggested that prosocial behaviors are more evident in interpersonal relationships (e.g., friends, family) whereas antisocial behaviors are more likely to occur with noninterpersonal relationships (e.g., acquaintances, strangers). If so, we should find that people are more apt to deliberately embarrass strangers than friends. In fact, Petronio, Olson, and Dollar (1989) indicated that embarrassment may negatively affect close relationships.

On the other hand, Sharkey (1991) suggested that embarrassment may be employed as a relational maintenance strategy in that it supports relationship solidarity. If this is the case, individuals should use more intentional embarrassment with friendships and close relatives than with strangers. Further support for this premise comes from "politeness" literature. Lim (1990) found that, as individuals increase the level of intimacy toward each other, the desire to uphold each other's positive face (desire for social approval) also increases. However, this is a curvilinear association. According to Lim (1990), "When the relationship becomes so intimate that mutual acceptance is taken for granted, . . . responsibility for the partner's positive face declines" (p. 82). This indicates that as intimacy increases, violations of behavioral rules are not as face threatening for the perpetrator nor for the recipient. These violations may then become a norm of the relationship. Intentionally embarrassing one's friend or intimate partner may become an accepted behavior.

Not only could the relationship of the individual who embarrasses to the embarrassed party affect the use of embarrassment, but the sex of the individuals may indicate who embarrasses whom. Pearson, Turner, and Todd-Mancillas (1991) reviewed numerous research projects that focused on communication differences between males and females. It appears that men and women are more similar than different in their communication behaviors. The differences seem to be more evident within same sex groups (i.e., male/male, female/female). Nevertheless, it is noteworthy that, though not focused specifically on intentional embarrassment, researchers have discovered that males and females differ in the use of compliance-gaining strategies (deTurck, 1985; Falbo & Peplau, 1980) and in responses to embarrassment (Cupach, Metts, & Hazleton, 1986; Petronio, 1984; Sharkey, 1992; Sharkey & Stafford, 1989). Still others claim that there is an interaction effect between the sex of the parties involved in an encounter and communicative behaviors (see Dindia, 1987; Martin & Craig, 1983). Consequently, it may be that the use of intentional embarrassment is dependent upon the sex of the person who embarrasses in relation to the target's sex. Further studies indicate that males tend to be more aggressive and dominant overall and females tend to be submissive to males but sometimes dominant toward other females (Burgoon, Buller, & Woodall, 1989). Because intentionally embarrassing someone is a deliberate attempt to cause another person to feel uneasy, the recipient could consider this an aggressive act. Therefore, males should report embarrassing males and females with equal frequency whereas females should tend to only embarrass other females. For the present investigation, it is uncertain how the use of intentional embarrassment is affected by the relationship of the *embarrassor* (individual who perpetrates the embarrassment) to the embarrassed person and the sex of the participants. In order to address this concern, the first research (R) question presented is:

R$_1$:   Who embarrasses whom? Is there an association between the relationship of the embarrassor to the embarrassed individual, the sex of the embarrassor, and the sex of the embarrassed individual?

During communication episodes, interactants, with varying degrees of consciousness, plan the accomplishment of goals. The focus here is upon individuals who deliberately plan and devise tactics to achieve these goals. Greene (1990) defined a *tactic* as a single act utilized to achieve a goal, whereas a *strategy* is a behavioral sequence of tactics used to attain a goal. One such tactic is the use of embarrassment. Researchers are finding that, not only is embarrassment used as a tactic for achieving one's goals, but they report that it is highly successful (Sharkey, 1991). Gross and Stone (1964) and Sharkey (1991; Sharkey & Waldron, 1990) claimed that people intentionally embarrass others to achieve at least one of four goals: (a) negatively sanction inappropriate role behavior or discredit a person (i.e., to get someone to follow the rules, to teach a lesson, to punish, to discredit, to puncture false fronts), (b) establish and/or maintain power (i.e., to take control, to get ahead, to get one's way), (c) socialize persons into a culture, group or organization, or to maintain a level of solidarity (i.e., for fun, to be one of the crowd, to get a laugh from the group, to make a time memorable, to make person feel important), or (d) attain self-satisfaction (i.e., wanting to cause a reaction in another person for the soul purpose of satisfying one's self; for example, "I just like to see people's reactions").

Recent research suggests that people's goals are influenced by the relationship of the embarrassor to the embarrassed person. Sharkey and Waldron's (1990) study of superiors intentionally embarrassing subordinates indicates that 50% of superiors who reported embarrassing a subordinate stated that they used embarrassment to show solidarity. One third of the superiors claimed their goal was to negatively sanction a subordinate's inappropriate behavior. In a related study, Martin (1987) discovered that students claimed teachers attempted to retain power through the use of embarrassment. There is a link between the parties' relationship and the goals attempted.

Also, a possibility remains that the sex of the parties involved will affect the goals of the intentional embarrassor. Past research on sex differences in communicative styles (e.g., Baird & Bradley, 1979; Henley, 1977; Mulac, Studley, Wiemann, & Bradac, 1987) suggests that males are more self- and power motivated, whereas females are more relationship focused, supportive, and appear to pursue more communal types of goals and those that affect the quality of relationships (Smith, Cody, Lovette, & Canary, 1990). If this is the case, it would appear that males would tend to embarrass others to gain or retain power, whereas females would be more apt to employ embarrassment to show solidarity. However, Burgoon et al. (1989) stated that "in same-sex interactions, women are capable of displaying the same dominance behaviors as men" (p. 314). The following questions attempt to discover if differences exist between males and females in goals attempted when the relationship of the embarrassor to the embarrassed party or the sex of the embarrassed party is considered.

R_2: What is the association between the sex of the embarrassor, the relationship with the embarrassed party, and the goal attempted?

R_3: What is the association between the sex of the embarrassor, the sex of the embarrassed party, and the goal attempted?

Another avenue for analysis is the relationship of the embarrassor to the embarrassed party, the sex of the parties involved, and their affect upon tactics employed. When a goal is desired, people choose from a number of communicative tactics to achieve the goal. Sharkey (1991) uncovered a number of tactics individuals employ to embarrass others deliberately. These tactics include: (a) recognition/praise, (b) criticism/correction, (c) teasing, (d) causing one to appear unpoised, (e) violating another's privacy, and (f) associating a person with someone (or thing) who is enacting untoward behavior.

The selection of one of the aforementioned tactics is affected by the goal one is attempting (Sharkey, 1991). For example, when solidarity was attempted, teasing, recognition/praise, or violating a person's privacy was used. When a person attempted to maintain/attain power, people criticism was employed. There may also exist an association between the relationship of the embarrassor to the embarrassed person and the tactics used.

Sharkey and Waldron (1990) found that superiors tend to employ the tactics of teasing and criticism more than any other tactic. Martin (1987) found that students reported that teachers used a considerable amount of criticism that lead to embarrassment. Both studies focused on socially defined power relationships. What tactics would individuals in socially defined egalitarian relationships, such as friends, use? Would parents employ tactics when embarrassing their children that are similar to those reported by superiors and teachers?

The sex of the embarrassor and the sex of the person being embarrassed may influence the tactic used as well. When one looks to the compliance-gaining literature (e.g., deTurck & Miller, 1982), there is an indication that no differences exist between males and females in the choice of preferred message strategies. However, Burgoon, Dillard, and Doran (1983) found that the sex of the target affected the strategy choice of both males and females. And as previously stated, Pearson et al. (1991) claimed that biological sex does not appear to have an impact on communicative behavior in significant ways. Therefore, whether or not the sex of the embarrassor and the sex of the embarrassed party affect the choice of tactic is uncertain. Therefore, does the sex of the embarrassor and the embarrassed person interact to affect the tactic employed? Hence, two final research questions are addressed:

R_4: What is the association between the sex of the embarrassor, the relationship with the embarrassed party, and the tactic used to embarrass?

R_5: What is the association between the sex of the embarrassor, the sex of the embarrassed party, and the tactic used to embarrass?

METHOD

Participants

Participants consisted of students enrolled in communication classes and nonstudents over 30 years of age who were solicited by students enrolled in communication classes at a large midwestern university. Participants included 546 males and 588 females and two individuals who did not report their sex. Participants ranged in age from 18 to 77 years with a mean of 32.6 years. Participation in the study was voluntary and students received extra credit.

Procedure

The researcher delivered instructions verbally to the class and then distributed the questionnaires. One group of students completed questionnaires about themselves. A second group of students solicited persons over 30 years of age. A cover letter accompanying the questionnaires briefly explained the research to the respondents. Respondents directly returned their questionnaires to the researcher in sealed envelopes.

The Instrument

Questionnaires contained two open-ended questions and three demographic questions. All questions concerned specific instances in the participant's life as opposed to general observations, thus alleviating some of the validity problems with retrospective self-report data (Ericson & Simon, 1984). Participants were asked to (a) describe a situation in their life when they intentionally embarrassed someone, and (b) explain why they intentionally embarrassed the person (i.e., their goal).

Coding Procedure

Responses to the open-ended questions were coded for three variables of interest: (a) the embarrassor's relationship to the embarrassed party, (b) the goals of intentional embarrassment, and (c) the tactic used to embarrass. First, it was necessary to develop a coding scheme for the embarrassor's relationship to the embarrassed party. The participant's open-ended responses were used to code, inductively and intuitively, the embarrassor's relationship to the embarrassed party. The categories include: (a) intimate partner, (b) friends and extended family, (c) parents and future parental in-laws, (d) child and son/daughter in-law, (e) superior, teacher, seller/salesperson, (f) subordinate, student, buyer/customer, (g) sibling, and (h) stranger.

For the type of goal being attempted and the tactic employed, a combination of Gross and Stone's (1964) and Sharkey's (1991) typologies were employed. The four goal types used include: (a) show solidarity, (b) negative sanctioning of behaviors, (c) establish power, and (d) self-satisfaction. The categories of tactics were taken from Sharkey's (1991) research and include: (a) recognition/praise, (b) criticism/correction, (c) teasing, (d) cause to look unpoised, (e) violation of privacy, and (f) association.

After categories were established for the variables of interest, the researcher and a research assistant jointly coded 100 questionnaires. After which, the assistant independently coded another 100 questionnaires. The author checked these questionnaires for reliability of agreement. The assistant then independently coded the remaining questionnaires. Intercoder reliability was computed on 15% of the remaining data, using Scott's pi (1955), which adjusts for chance agreement. Pi values were .86 for relationship (90.3% agreement), .89 for goal (95.8% agreement), and .88 for the tactic used (94.8% agreement).

Analysis

The primary analyses consisted of log-linear model testing. A complication with models utilizing the goal of the embarrassed party as a single factor is the issue of multiple responses. Thus, the researchers chose one goal randomly when more than one goal was reported. The listing of goals by the participants appeared to be chosen from a list of alternatives and not necessarily strategically or temporally arranged (see Sharkey & Stafford, 1990). Also, the relatively small number of participants reporting multiple goals (6.1%) influenced the decision to select one goal randomly—this resulted in losing 6.6% of the total number of goals reported.

RESULTS

Of 1,136 respondents (i.e., the embarrassors), 51.8% were female, 48% were male, and .2% did not provide this information. Recipients of the embarrassing tactic included 54.3% male and 37.6% female. Additionally, 8.1% of the embarrassors reported that they embarrassed a couple. Because of the low frequency and because the question asked focused on a single person, these eleven cases were coded as unclassifiable. The relationship of the embarrassor to the embarrassed person included: (a) 65.1% were friends or extended family, (b) 9.6% were intimate partners, (c) 5.4% were superiors, teachers, or sellers, (d) 5.4% were siblings, (e) 3.7% were subordinates, students, or buyers, (f) 3.4% were parents or future parental in-laws, (g) 1.8% were children or son/daughter in-laws, (h) 1.1% were strangers, and (i) 4.5% were unclassifiable. Next, of 1,136 respondents, 85.2% attempted a single goal, 5.8% attempted two goals, 0.3% attempted three goals, and 8.5% were unclassifiable. Of 1,112 total goals reported, the most widely reported goal attempted was the goal of solidarity/socialization (approximately 50.0%), followed by the negative sanctioning of behavior (38.0%), establishing power (8.0%), and self-satisfaction (4.0%). Last, of the 1,033 tactics reported, the most frequently reported tactic employed to cause embarrassment was causing a person to look unpoised (31.5%), followed by criticism (20.8%), violations of privacy (18.6%), teasing (12.6%), association (8.4%), and recognition/praise (8.1%).

Research Question 1 addressed the relationship between the sex of the embarrassor, sex of the embarrassed person, and the relationship between the two persons. A three-way, 8 (relationship) × 2 (sex of embarrassor) × 2 (sex of embarrassed person) symmetrical-model, log-linear design was executed. Partial associations existed between each pair of variables; the saturated model

TABLE 9.1.
Conditional Proportions of Sex of Embarrassor by Sex of Embarrassed Person

	Sex of Embarrassed Person		
Sex of Embarrassor	Male	Female	n
Male	.74*	−.26*	504
Female	−.45*	.55*	539

Note. (−) denotes negative deviation from expected frequencies; all others positive deviations.
Conditional proportions rounded to nearest hundredth.
*$p < .001$.

was accepted [L^2_{7-8} (7) $=$ 251.87, $p <$ .0001].[1] Therefore, simple associations between each pair of variables change in some manner when viewed over levels of the third variable. However, when looking at symmetrical models, researchers should consider the most parsimonious model (Kennedy, 1983). Hence, further examination and comparison of more restricted models was explored. Marginal associations existed between (a) the sex of the embarrassor and the sex of the embarrassed person [L^2_{4-5} (1) $=$ 96.67, $p <$ .0001] and (b) the sex of the embarrassor and the relationship with the embarrassed person [L^2_{4-5} (7) $=$ 28.80, $p <$ .0002]. Therefore, knowledge of the sex of the embarrassor is a good predictor of both the sex of the embarrassed party and the relationship between the two parties. However, no marginal association was found between the sex of the embarrassed person and the relationship between the two parties. The results indicate that people tend to embarrass others of the same sex. Also, (a) males were more likely than females to embarrass friends and their subordinates; and (b) females intentionally embarrass their intimate partners and their children more than males. Results of significance testing on lambda parameters (the natural log of tau, which is the multiplicative counterpart to the grand mean in ANOVA models) and conditional proportions may be found in Table 9.1 and Table 9.2, respectively.

Research Question 2 addressed the relationship between the sex of the embarrassor, the relationship with the embarrassed person, and the goal attempted. A three-way, 2 (sex of embarrassor) × 8 (relationship to embarrassed party) × 4 (goal attempted) logit-model, log-linear design, with a delta value of .05 added, was constructed. (Note: Because sampling zeros were found in large tables, a delta value of .05 was added to these analyses [see Goodman, 1978;

[1]To make a decision on which model is best at explaining the data, researchers may calculate the difference between models' residual L^2 when the models are arranged in pairs. This difference is the component chi-square value. Component L^2s enable researchers to identify terms that do not contribute much to the reduction of residual chi-square. The less units of residual chi-square a model adds, the greater the goodness-of-fit. The object is to discover the model with the fewest terms that, at the same time, fits the observed data relatively well; that is, the "law of parsimony" (Kennedy, 1983. The subscript (as in, L^2_{5-6}) represents the difference between the residual chi-squares of various models (e.g., 5 and 6 in this example). The model numbers reflect the number of terms or factors included in the model (Kennedy, 1983).

TABLE 9.2.
Conditional Proportions of Sex of Embarrassor by the Embarrassor's Relationship to the Embarrassed Party

Sex of Embarrassor	Embarrassor's Relationship to the Embarrassed Party							
	Intimate	Friend	Parent	Child	Superior	Subordinate	Sibling	Stranger	n
Male	−.07*	.73*	−.02*	−.02	.07**	−.03	−.04	.02	526
Female	.13*	−.64*	.05*	.02	−.04**	.04	.07	−.01	557

Note. (−) denotes negative deviation from expected frequencies; all others positive deviations.
Conditional proportions rounded to nearest hundredth.
*p < .05. **p < .01.

Kennedy, 1983], this addition results in a more conservative procedure [Clogg & Eliason, 1987; Knoke & Burke, 1980]). No interaction effect was discovered between the sex of the embarrassor and the relationship to the embarrassed party. A main effect for the relationship to the embarrassed party after accounting for the sex of the embarrassor, however, reached significance $[L^2_{6-7} (21) = 73.01, p < .0001]$. Therefore, the relationship of the embarrassor to the embarrassed party is predictive of the goal attempted even after accounting for the sex of the embarrassor. When looking at those cells that indicate significant deviations from expected frequencies, the following combinations were found: (a) more intimate partners than expected attempted the goal of solidarity; (b) friends also tended to use embarrassment to show solidarity, but reported establishing power less than expected; (c) superiors were most likely to negatively sanction subordinate's behaviors; while, (d) subordinates attempted the goal of solidarity more than would be expected. Table 9.3 displays the trends that emerged.

Research Question 3 focused on the relationship between the sex of the em-

TABLE 9.3.
Conditional Proportions of Goal Attempted Due to the (a) Embarrassor's Relationship to the Embarrassed Party Given the Sex of the Embarrassor, (b) Sex of Embarrassor Given the Sex of the Embarrassed Party, and (c) Sex of the Embarrassed Person Given the Sex of the Embarrassor

	Goal Attempted				
	Show of Solidarity	Neg. Sanction Behavior	Establish Power	Self-Satisfaction	n
Embarrassor's Relationship to the Embarrassed Party					
Intimate	.52*	−.36	.10	−.03	101
Friends	.53***	−.35	−.06**	.05	711
Parent	−.40	−.40	.11	.09	35
Child	.48	−.43	−.05	.05	21
Superior	−.11	.75**	.14	−.00	56
Subordinate	.54*	.41	−.03	.03	39
Sibling	.40	−.43	.12	.05	60
Stranger	−.09	.64	.27	.00	11
Sex of Embarrassor					
Male	−.50	−.37**	.08**	−.05	483
Female	.49	.42**	−.05**	.04	513
Sex of Embarrassed Person					
Male	.48	.42**	−.05**	.05	592
Female	−.52	−.35**	.09**	−.04	404

Note. (−) denotes negative deviation from expected frequencies; all others positive deviations. Conditional proportions rounded to nearest hundredth.
*p < .05. **p < .01. ***p < .001.

barrassor, the sex of the embarrassed party, and the goal attempted. A three-way, 2 (sex of embarrassor) × 2 (sex of embarrassed person) × 4 (goal attempted) logit-model, log-linear design was performed. No interaction effects between the sex of the embarrassor and the sex of the embarrassed party were found. Also, no main effect due to the sex of the embarrassor existed. However, main effects for the sex of the embarrassor given the sex of the embarrassed person [L^2_{6-7} (3) = 12.35, p < .006] and main effects for the sex of embarrassed person after partialing out the sex of the embarrassor [L^2_{6-7} (3) = 14.06, p < .003] were discovered. Therefore, the sex of the embarrassor, when the sex of the embarrassed person was taken into account, and the sex of the embarrassed person when the sex of the embarrassor was considered, were good predictors of the goal attempted. Statistically (a) more males than females reported using embarrassment to gain/maintain power and less than expected used embarrassment to negatively sanction behaviors; (b) more females than males reported negatively sanctioning others' behaviors and females reported establishing/maintaining power less than expected; (c) males reported being negatively sanctioned more than females; and (d) females tended to be the recipients of more intentional embarrassment power moves than males. Conditional proportions and results of significance testing on lambda parameters may be found in Table 9.3.

Research Question 4 concerned the relationship between the sex of the embarrassor, the relationship with the embarrassed person, and the tactic used to embarrass. A three-way, 2 (sex of embarrassor) × 8 (relationship to embarrassed party) × 6 (tactic) logit-model, log-linear design, with a delta value of .05 added, was constructed. Albeit no interaction effect between the sex of the embarrassor and the relationship with the embarrassed party existed, main effects for the sex of the embarrassor (reported previously) and main effects for the relationship of the embarrassor to the embarrassed party after accounting for the sex of the embarrassor [L^2_{5-6} (35) = 81.89, p < .001] were discovered. Hence, the relationship of the embarrassor to the embarrassed party is predictive of the tactic used to cause embarrassment. Significance testing on the lambda parameters revealed that: (a) friends, parents, and siblings violated each other's privacy more than expected by chance; (b) children embarrassed their parents by employing recognition; (c) superiors overwhelmingly criticized subordinates; (d) friends were not likely to criticize one another; and (e) intimates were the least likely to cause their partners to appear unpoised. Table 9.4 shows the conditional proportions and results of significance testing on lambda scores.

Research Question 5 addressed the relationship between the sex of the embarrassor, the sex of the embarrassed party, and the tactic used to embarrass. A three-way, 2 (sex of embarrassor) × 2 (sex of embarrassed person) × 6 (tactic) logit-model, log-linear design, with a delta value of .05 added, was performed. It was found that an interaction effect between the sex of the embarrassor and the sex of the embarrassed party achieved significance [L^2_{7-8}

TABLE 9.4.
Conditional Proportions of Tactic Used Due to the Embarrassor's Relationship
to the Embarrassed Party

Embarrassor's Relationship to the Embarrassed Party	Tactic						
	Recognition	Criticism	Tease	Cause to Appear Unpoised	Violation of Privacy	Association	n
Intimate	.15	−.21	.12	−.25*	−.14	.13	100
Friends	−.07	−.18*	.14	−.33	.21*	−.09	705
Parent	.17	−.17	−.06	−.29	.26*	−.06	35
Child	.24*	−.19	−.10	−.29	−.05	.14	21
Superior	.05	.57**	−.04	.25	−.05	−.04	56
Subordinate	.13	−.15	.15	.44	−.08	−.05	39
Sibling	−.05	−.20	.15	.33	.23*	−.03	60
Stranger	−.00	.33	.08	.33	−.08	.18	12

Note. (−) denotes negative deviation from expected frequencies; all others positive deviations. Conditional proportions rounded to nearest hundredth.
*p < .05. **p < .001.

(5) = 15.26, p < .009]. Thus, the sex of the embarrassor and the sex of the person being embarrassed interact to predict the tactic employed to cause embarrassment. Follow-up testing of lambda parameters revealed that, statistically, same sex partners violated one another's privacy more than opposite sex partners. Conditional proportions and results of significance testing on lambda parameters are displayed in Table 9.5. Acceptance of the asymmetrical interaction model does not indicate whether main effects for the variables exist (Kennedy, 1983). Therefore, more restricted models were explored. It was uncovered that main effects for both the sex of the embarrassor [L^2_{5-6} (5) = 17.84, p < .003] and the sex of the embarrassed party [L^2_{5-6} (5) = 14.18, p < .015] existed. Hence, knowing the sex of the embarrassor or the sex of the embarrassed party is predictive of the tactic used by the embarrassor to embarrass. Statistically (a) more males than females employed "causing another to appear unpoised" or "association to embarrass" others while (b) females used "recognition" more than males. Table 9.6 shows the conditional proportions and results of significance testing on lambda scores.

As for the recipient of the embarrassment, (a) males were caused to look unpoised more than females, and (b) females were significantly more likely than males to be embarrassed with recognition/praise. Table 9.6 displays the trends that emerged.

DISCUSSION

This study examined how the sex of an embarrassor, the sex of the embarrassed person, and the relationship between the parties affected the use of intentional embarrassment. That is, the study asked the question "Who embar-

TABLE 9.5.

Conditional Proportions of Tactic Due to the Interaction of the Sex of Embarrassor and the Sex of the Embarrassed Party

Sex of Embarrassor	Sex of Embarrassed Party	Tactic					
		Recognition	Criticism	Tease	Cause to Appear Unpoised	Violation of Privacy	Association	n
Male	Male	-.04	-.21	-.10	.36	.22*	-.07	360
	Female	.09	.21	.13	-.28	-.12*	.18	118
Female	Male	.10	.24	.15	-.31	-.14*	.07	229
	Female	-.12	-.18	-.14	.28	.21*	-.07	283

Note. (−) denotes negative deviation from expected frequencies; all others positive deviations.
Conditional proportions rounded to nearest hundredth.
*p < .001.

TABLE 9.6.

Conditional Proportions of Tactic Due to the Sex of Embarrassor and Tactice Due to the Sex of the Embarrassed Party

		Tactic						
		Recognition	Criticism	Tease	Cause to Appear Unpoised	Violation of Privacy	Association	n
Embarrassor								
	Male	-.05***	.21	-.11	.34*	.19	.10*	478
	Female	.11***	-.20	.15	-.29*	-.18	-.07*	512
Embarrassed Party								
	Male	-.06*	.22	.12	.34**	.19	-.07	589
	Female	.11*	-.19	-.14	-.28**	-.18	.10	401

Note. (−) denotes negative deviation from expected frequencies; all others positive deviations.
Conditional proportions rounded to nearest hundredth.
*$p < .05$. **$p < .01$. ***$p < .001$.

rasses whom?" A secondary concern was to discover whether the goal of an embarrassor and the tactic employed were affected by the sex of the participants and/or the relationship of the embarrassor to the embarrassed party.

Focus on the Relationship Between Parties

The notion that intentional embarrassment is an antisocial behavior because it violates the taken-for-granted rules of interaction needs to be modified. Friends and intimate partners appear to engage in this activity more than any other relationship type, suggesting that deliberate embarrassment may be viewed as a prosocial activity in these relationships. Even though Petronio et al. (1989) claimed that "the frequency of relational embarrassment has an adverse affect [sic] on relational quality and satisfaction with relational communication" (p. 26), these results are probably an artifact of the type of situation created (i.e., a violation of privacy). Petronio et al. (1989) tentatively stated that embarrassment in a relationship "may be an early indicator of problems in [the relationship]" (p. 27). This conjecture is being called into question. If we view this phenomenon as antisocial, then we must follow Lim's (1990) claim that as relationships progress we eventually are less concerned with protecting the face of the other. Violating the rules of the relationship may become a meta-rule, which concludes that this type of behavior is acceptable (Sharkey, 1991). People may come to trust that the intent of the violation is, for example, to show solidarity, as found here, and not to establish power or negatively sanction behaviors. Still another explanation may be that violations of expectations are allowable as long as positive valued actions accompany or follow the violation, thereby compensating for the violation (Burgoon, 1983). In interpersonal relationships, this tends to be the case and hence, the violations should be expected more so than in noninterpersonal relationships. The fact that friends reported violating their friend's privacy is further support for this possibility. Sharkey and Stafford (1990) found that this type of embarrassment is perceived as the most embarrassing. It makes sense, that if employed, it would be used in a relationship where trust and positive valued actions are characteristic of the relationship to counteract the effects of the violation.

Parents play a role similar to a superior's role with their children, although there seems to be more of a balance between defining the relationship as parent (superior) and friend. This may be the reason the majority of parents report that they embarrass children to show solidarity or to negatively sanction behaviors. This claim is made cautiously, though. This is a true statement only when observing simple proportions of responses. The study does not support these findings statistically. In addition, as with friends, a majority of parents, as well as siblings, employed the tactic of violating the child's privacy. Again, this may be because it is understood that positive acts have preceded and will follow this violation.

Focus on the Sex of the Parties

First, the fact that females and males tend to embarrass same-sex partners is intriguing. Because the majority of people reported embarrassing friends, part of the explanation for the embarrassment of same-sex others may be due to males and females having more same-sex friends than opposite-sex friends (Stewart, Stewart, Friedley, & Cooper, 1990). From a ratio standpoint, this makes sense. The more we interact with people, the more chances arise to embarrass them. Gross and Stone (1964) noted that males, especially, develop games that test each other's control of poise (e.g., "drinking the other person under the table"). This may be a societal phenomenon. Many activities are sex-segregated. Hence, same-sex persons are "forced" into interaction with one another.

Males tend to embarrass friends, children, and subordinates more than females. Males embarrassing these relationship partners is not surprising. Stereotypically, males are more competitive and engage in more controlling behaviors. As for females, the fact that they reported embarrassing friends less than expected may be due to their communal orientation. They may see embarrassment as a negative emotion and hence, be more sensitive to avoid causing it. They also engage in less competitiveness. The fact that mothers reported embarrassing their children more than fathers could be traced to the time spent with the child. Typically, mothers spend more time with a child. The mere frequency of interaction would lead to more situations in which embarrassment may be employed. Also, females reported embarrassing their intimate partners more than their male counterparts.

Males and females differ in their reasons for employing embarrassment. Although proportionately, both males and females employ embarrassment to show solidarity, males use embarrassment to establish power more than females and females use embarrassment to negatively sanction behaviors more than males. Also, females are the recipients of the power plays and males are the recipients of negative sanctions. Society has traditionally viewed males as having more power in society than females. These findings lend support to the view that males are still in, or are still attempting to be in, the dominant social position whereas females are the recipients of power moves. Researchers have also claimed that males typically are more aggressive and females are more nurturing and focused on relationship maintenance (Pearson et al., 1991). The results imply that this is still the case. The fact that females negatively sanction inappropriate behaviors may, in part, be an attempt to discredit those who are trying to establish power by calling into question his or her power claim. Although females are generally stereotyped as communal/nurturing, there may be situations when this "friendliness" goal is bypassed for a goal based on self-image (Smith et al., 1990). Another possibility is that females are more attuned to emotions from an expressive and receptive mode

(Buck, Baron, & Barrette, 1982; Wagner, MacDonald, & Manstead, 1986). If females are more skilled in the display and reception of emotions, they may also be more skilled in use of tactics that elicit emotions in others. Therefore, one explanation for why females embarrass their intimate partners more than males may be that because males are still perceived as having more power than females in many intimate relationships. Females use embarrassment as a way to bring the male "down-a-notch." That is, a female may use embarrassment to negatively sanction her partner's behaviors when he steps out of line. This may be an attempt at redefining the relationship as one based on equality. Another possibility may be that in seeing male friends embarrassing each other as a show of solidarity, a male's intimate partner may engage in this type of behavior in an endeavor to achieve the same status.

As for the tactics employed, males tended to cause others to appear unpoised, or associated the target with someone engaging in an untoward act more than females. That is, males are aggressive in violating the norms of interaction. However, females reported using recognition more than any other tactic. This discovery is reflective of the claim that females are more other-oriented and communal than males. Individuals would generally consider recognition more prosocial than other tactics, and many times a show of respect. There appears to be a focus on the relationship as opposed to the individual. Both findings support gender stereotypes.

CONCLUSION

The results propose a number of implications. First, the study of intentional embarrassment enhances our understanding of emotions in general and helps us to appreciate the dynamics of relational communication specifically. The results support the notion that the type of relationship as well as the biological sex of the relational partners are variables that should continue to be actively researched. They appear to affect the goals people set and the tactics they use to attain these goals.

Second, this study assists in understanding how emotions are orchestrated during the relationship process. Bowers, Metts, and Duncanson (1985) and Sharkey and Stafford (1990) reminded us that a rational view of interactants fails to consider the important role emotional reactions play in the relationship process. Although the present investigation does not focus on the reactions to intentional embarrassment, it does inform us that relationship partners do, in fact, attempt to deliberately elicit emotional responses from one another.

Third, the notion that people embarrass others for malevolent reasons needs to be rectified. The majority of embarrassors indicated that they embarrassed others to show a degree of connectedness—solidarity. Although this could be an artifact of retrospective questionnaires and social desirability, it may well be that the use of intentional embarrassment is a way to "spice-up" a relationship, a way to add a bit of novelty to a relationship that has become or is in danger of becoming too predictable. Baxter (1988) suggests that there exists a tension between novelty and predictability in relationships. Too much predictability may lead to boredom or rigidity, whereas a relationship without expected patterns of behavior may lead to frustration and confusion. As a relationship progresses, the relational parties negotiate a balance between the novelty-predictability dialectic. So, to avoid the deadening of the emotional quality of a relationship, relational partners can employ intentional embarrassment to keep a relationship fresh. This is not to say that a constant barrage of tactics intended to cause embarrassment is in the best interest of a relationship. Sharkey (1991) discovered that the majority of people in his study reported that they deliberately embarrassed others between one and five times within the last 6 months. This seems to suggest that people generally do not employ this tactic to a great extent. However, it does cause a momentary degree of uncertainty that may prove to have a positive relational outcome—a bit of novelty.

Fourth, the results add support to Lim's (1990) claim that the protection of a relational partner's face is not as important as relationships progress. Friends and intimate partners reach a point at which the cost of momentarily putting a relational partner "on-the-spot" is outweighed by the rewards (e.g., novelty, fun). Obviously, this investigation only considered the embarrassor's perceptions. The receiver of the act may not apply the same intent to the act (Sharkey & Waldron, 1990). "The perception that one has been intentionally embarrassed may lead to undesired situational and relational ramifications" (Sharkey, 1991, p. 122). Both parties must negotiate the intention of the act.

Last, the stages or phases portrayed in models of relationship escalation, maintenance, and deterioration are differentiated by the communicative behaviors relational partners exhibit at various points in relationships (Altman & Taylor, 1973; Baxter, 1988; Knapp, 1984). One behavior that has gone unnoticed is intentional embarrassment. The results clearly indicate that deliberate embarrassment is most characteristic of friendships and more intimate relationships. This type of behavior may best be situated in, for example, Knapp's (1984) intensifying or integrating stage of relationship development. Some people, for example, males who try to outdo each other, may view intentional embarrassment as a relationship-defining behavior. In fact, one respondent stated: "If you can't embarrass your friends, who can you embarrass?"

REFERENCES

Altman, I., & Taylor, D. A. (1973). *Social penetration: The development of interpersonal relationships.* New York: Holt, Rinehart & Winston.

Baird, J., & Bradley, P. (1979). Styles of management and communication: A comparative study of men and women. *Communication Monographs, 46,* 101–111.

Baxter, L. A. (1988). A dialectical perspective on communication strategies in relationship development. In S. W. Duck (Ed.), *A handbook of personal relationships* (pp. 257–273). New York: Wiley.

Bowers, J. W., Metts, S. M., & Duncanson, W. T. (1985). Emotion and interpersonal communication. In M. L. Knapp & G. R. Miller (Eds.), *Handbook of interpersonal communication* (pp. 500–550). Beverly Hills, CA: Sage.

Braithwaite, D. O. (1992, February). *Socialization of men by intentional embarrassment at "coed" wedding and baby showers.* Paper presented at Annual Meeting of the Western States Communication Association, Boise, ID.

Brown, B. R. (1968). The effects of need to maintain face on interpersonal bargaining. *Journal of Experimental Social Psychology, 4,* 107–122.

Buck, R., Baron, R., & Barrette, D. (1982). Temporal organization of spontaneous emotional expression: A segmentation analysis. *Journal of Personality and Social Psychology, 39,* 522–529.

Burgoon, J. K. (1983). Nonverbal violations of expectations. In J. M. Wiemann and R. P. Harrison (Eds.), *Nonverbal interaction* (pp. 77–111). Beverly Hills, CA: Sage.

Burgoon, J. K., Buller, D. B., & Woodall, W. G. (1989). *Nonverbal communication: The unspoken dialogue.* New York: Harper & Row.

Burgoon, M., Dillard, J. P., & Doran, N. E. (1983). Friendly or unfriendly persuasion: The effects of violations of expectations by males and females. *Human Communication Research, 10,* 283–294.

Buss, A. H. (1980). *Self-consciousness and social anxiety.* San Francisco, CA: W. H. Freeman.

Clogg, C. C., & Eliason, S. R. (1987). Some common problems in log-linear analysis. *Sociological Methods and Research, 16,* 8–44.

Cupach, W. R., & Metts, S. (1990). Remedial processes in embarrassing predicaments. In J. A. Anderson (Ed.), *Communication yearbook 13* (pp. 323–352). Beverly Hills, CA: Sage.

Cupach, W. R., Metts, S., & Hazleton, V. (1986). Coping with embarrassing predicaments: Remedial strategies and their perceived utility. *Journal of Language and Social Psychology, 5,* 181–200.

deTurck, M. A. (1985). A transactional analysis of compliance-gaining behavior: Effects of noncompliance, relational contexts, and actors' gender. *Human Communication Research, 12,* 54–78.

deTurck, M. A., & Miller, G. R. (1982). The effect of birth order on the persuasive impact of messages and the likelihood of persuasive message selection. *Communication, 11,* 78–84.

Dindia, K. (1987). The effects of sex of subject and sex of partner in interruptions. *Human Communication Research, 13,* 345–371.

Edelmann, R. J. (in press). Embarrassment and blushing: Factors influencing face-saving strategies. In S. Ting-Toomey (Ed.), *The challenge of facework.* New York: SUNY Press.

Ericson, K. A., & Simon, H. A. (1984). *Protocol analysis.* Cambridge, MA: MIT Press.

Falbo, T., & Peplau, L. A. (1980). Power strategies in intimate relationships. *Journal of Personality and Social Psychology, 38,* 618–628.

Goffman, E. (1956). The nature of deference and demeanor. *American Anthropologist, 58,* 473–502.

Goffman, E. (1959). *The presentation of self in everyday life.* Garden City, NY: Doubleday Anchor Books.

Goodman, L. A. (1978). *Analyzing qualitative/categorical data.* Cambridge, MA: Abt Books.

Greene, J. O. (1990). Tactical social action: Toward some strategies for theory. In M. J. Cody & M. L. McLaughlin (Eds.), *The psychology of tactical communication* (pp. 31–47). Clevedon, England: Multilingual Matters.

Gross, E., & Stone, G. P. (1964). Embarrassment and the analysis of role requirements. *The American Journal of Sociology, 70,* 1–15.

Henley, N. M. (1977). *Body politics: Power, sex, and nonverbal communication.* New York: Simon & Schuster, Inc.

Kennedy, J. J. (1983). *Analyzing qualitative data: Introductory log-linear analysis for behavioral Research.* New York: Praeger.

Knapp, M. L. (1984). *Interpersonal communication and human relationships.* Boston, MA: Allyn & Bacon.

Knoke, D., & Burke, P. J. (1980). *Log-linear models.* Beverly Hills, CA: Sage.

Leary, M. R. (1982). Social Anxiety. In L. Wheeler (Ed.), *Review of personality and social psychology* (Vol. 3, pp. 97–120). Beverly Hills, CA: Sage.

Lim, T. (1990). Politeness behavior in social influence situations. In J. P. Dillard (Ed.), *Seeking compliance: The production of interpersonal influence messages* (pp.75–86). Scottsdale, AZ: Gorsuch Scarisbrick, Publishers.

Martin, J. N., & Craig, R. T. (1983). Selected linguistic sex differences during initial social interactions of same-sex and mixed-sex dyads. *Western Journal of Speech Communication, 47,* 16–28.

Martin, W. B. W. (1987). Students' perceptions of causes and consequences of embarrassment in the school. *Canadian Journal of Education, 12,* 277–293.

Miller, R. S. (in press). The nature and severity of self-reported embarrassing circumstances. *Personality and Social Psychology Bulletin.*

Modigliani, A. (1968). Embarrassment and embarrassability. *Sociometry, 31,* 313–326.

Modigliani, A. (1971). Embarrassment, facework, and eye contact: Testing a theory of embarrassment. *Journal of Personality and Social Psychology, 17,* 15–24.

Motley, M. T. (1986). Consciousness and intentionality in communication: A preliminary model and methodological approaches. *Western Journal of Speech Communication, 50,* 3–23.

Mulac, A., Studley, L. B., Wiemann, J. W., & Bradac, J. J. (1987). Male/female gaze in same-sex and mixed-sex dyads: Gender-linked differences and mutual influence. *Human Communication Research, 13,* 323–344.

Parrott, W. G., Sabini, J., & Silver, M. (1988). The roles of self-esteem and social interaction in embarrassment. *Personality and Social Psychology Bulletin, 14,* 191–202.

Pearson, J. C., Turner, L. H., & Todd-Mancillas, W. (1991). *Gender and communication* (2nd ed.). Dubuque, IA: Wm. C. Brown, Publishers.

Petronio, S. (1984). Communication strategies to reduce embarrassment differences between men and women. *Western Journal of Speech Communication, 48,* 28–38.

Petronio, S., Olson, C., & Dollar, N. (1989). Privacy issues in relational embarrassment: Impact on relational quality and communication satisfaction. *Communications Research Reports, 6,* 21–27.

Petronio, S., & Snider, E. (1990, November). *Planned strategic embarrassment.* Paper presented at the Annual Meeting of the Speech Communication Association, Chicago, IL.

Petronio, S., & Snider, E. (1992, February). *Planning strategic embarrassment: Testing a theory.* Paper presented at the Annual Meeting of the Western States Communication Association, Boise, ID.

Roloff, M. E. (1976). Communication strategies, relationships, and relational changes. In G. R. Miller (Ed.), *Explorations in interpersonal communication* (pp. 173–195). Beverly Hills, CA: Sage.

Scott, W. A. (1955). Reliability of content analysis: the case of nominal scale coding. *Public Opinion Quarterly, 19,* 321–325.

Sharkey, W. F. (1991). Intentional embarrassment: Goals, tactics and consequences. In W. R. Cupach & S. Metts (Eds.), *Advances in interpersonal communication research 1991: Proceedings of the annual conference of the Western States Communication Association* (pp. 105–128). Normal, IL: Personal Relationships Research Group.

Sharkey, W. F. (1992, February). *Sex differences in responding to intentional embarrassment.* Paper presented at the Annual Meeting of the Western States Communication Association, Boise, ID.

Sharkey, W. F., & Stafford, L. (1989, May). *So, how embarrassing was it? . . . Whadja do?: The relationship between the situation, the degree of perceived embarrassment and responses to embarrassment.* Paper presented at the Annual Meeting of the International Communication Association, San Francisco, CA.

Sharkey, W. F., & Stafford, L. (1990). Responses to Embarrassment. *Human Communication Research, 17,* 315–342.

Sharkey, W. F., & Waldron, V. (1990, November). *The intentional embarrassment of subordinates in the work place.* Paper presented at the Annual Meeting of the Speech Communication Association, Chicago, IL.

Silver, M., Sabini, J., & Parrott, W. G. (1987). Embarrassment: A dramaturgic account. *Journal for the Theory of Social Behavior, 17,* 47–61.

Smith, S. W., Cody, M. J., Lovette, S., & Canary, D. J. (1990). Self-monitoring, gender and compliance-gaining goals. In M. J. Cody & M. L. McLaughlin (Eds.), *The psychology of tactical communication* (pp. 91–135). Clevedon, England: Multilingual Matters.

Stamp, G. H., & Knapp, M. L. (1990). The construct of intent in interpersonal communication. *Quarterly Journal of Speech, 76,* 282–299.

Stewart, L. P., Stewart, A. D., Friedley, S. A., & Cooper, P. J. (1990). *Communication between the sexes: Sex differences and sex-role stereotypes* (2nd ed.). Scottsdale, AZ: Gorsuch Scarisbrick, Publishers.

Wagner, H. L., MacDonald, C. J., & Manstead, A. S. R. (1986). Communication of individual emotions by spontaneous facial expressions. *Journal of Personality and Social Psychology, 50,* 737–743.

10

What's Yours is Mine and What's Mine is Yours: Couple Friends

Lyn Bendtschneider
University of Iowa

Steve Duck
University of Iowa

"For all of us, the 'we' that is so commonly an expression of married life has both its positive side and its negative" (Rubin, 1985, p. 133). A sense of "we-ness" and feelings of connectedness are the rewards of a coupled life. Yet, of life's stages none has a greater impact on our friendships than when we move from a single life to a coupled one (Rubin, 1985). Becoming involved in a romantic relationship is a life-cycle change that exerts a major influence on an individual's friendship network (Stueve & Gerson, 1977). Partners who are in a committed dating relationship, engaged, or married tend to have less contact with their friends compared to partners who are casually dating (Milardo, Johnson, & Huston, 1983). This tendency is especially evident for women (Rose, 1984). That sense of "we-ness" within couples is competition for one-on-one friendships, and friends often take second place.

This is not to say that couples do not socialize; rather, the socializing is altered by the transition from a single life to a coupled one. Dating partners with advancing relationships tend to withdraw from their separate networks as they become more involved with each other (Johnson & Leslie, 1982; Surra, 1985) and they form a couple network of associates held in common (Milardo, 1982). Marriage partners experience similar changes in their social network of relationships as the joint network of the couple grows with the couple's involvement (Huston & Levinger, 1978). In other words, upon becoming involved in a romantic relationship, partners tend to socialize with others as a couple and, of course, they are introduced to each other's friends. Such socializing together often results in the development of shared friends or "couple friends."

Rubin (1985) noted two important roles that couple friends play in couples' lives. First, when couples share a friendship with each other, it makes the individual friendship less threatening to the couple's relationship. Second, sharing friendships with other couples is part of the social bond in a relationship because it provides support for the institutions of dating and marriage, as well as validating the choices that we make in our lives. Couple friends provide the couple with a network of contacts for socialization and companionship. They also function to socialize couples into the life they are about to share.

The increased involvement between romantic couples leads to appreciable effects on the structure of partners' friendship networks in the form of two major developments: shrinkage and overlap. Progressively shrinking friendship networks and decreased involvement with those friends who remain in the network may be the result of dyadic withdrawal that occurs due to constraints on emotion, thought, and time (Johnson & Leslie, 1982). However, Parks, Stan, and Eggert (1983) argued that the phrase "dyadic realignment" might more accurately describe this process given that romantically involved dyads experience increased contact and communication with partners' friends and family. Addressing the issue of network overlap, Milardo (1982) hypothesized that the emergence of a joint network of mutual friends could occur by a behavioral process wherein the actual network membership changes, or by a cognitive process in which the classification of friendship changes while the actual membership remains stable. He concluded that the determination whether a behavioral or a cognitive change in friendship networks would occur may depend on whether the friends identified were friends of the respondent or friends of the partner. "People might make cognitive changes regarding their own friends, and change their behavior regarding their partner's friends" (Milardo, 1982, p. 169). A more complete understanding would need to start with the origin of couple friends.

The study presented in this chapter seeks to further our understanding of the development and nature of romantically involved couples' mutual friendship networks by examining the origin and qualitative characteristics of interactions with couple friends among dating couples. To what extent do communication and gender influence the development and nature of couple friends?

The Origin of Couple Friends

Among American middle-class married couples, husbands are more instrumental in initiating couple friendships and in determining the couple's closest mutual friends (Babchuk, 1965; Babchuk & Bates, 1963). The authors explain the finding as an issue of male dominance in that men exert more influence in establishing and maintaining mutual friendships. This sex difference could be explained in terms of work and family responsibilities, given that men are more likely to be in the labor force and parenthood may restrict the networks of women more than of men. In the late 1970s, men's networks tended to show more involvement with co-workers and women's networks showed more involvement with relatives (Fischer & Oliker, 1983). However, the last decade has witnessed increasing numbers of women who now work outside the home, thereby limiting the explanatory value of this rationale.

The preceding argument suggests that couple friends develop from the male's group of friends because women do not have as many friends from which to choose. In fact, recent research has demonstrated that women tend to lose their friends more than do men at the start of a romantic relationship (Rose & Serafica, 1986). Women's friends during early marriage and parenthood are diminished relative to men's, presumably due to gender differences in work and family responsibilities (Fischer & Oliker, 1983). Apparently, husbands' close friendships established prior to marriage are more likely to survive the marriage and more likely to become close mutual friends of the couple after marriage than are the wives' friendships (Babchuk & Bates, 1963). The research seems to suggest that couple friends originate from the male's group of friends due to a differential ability for men and women to maintain friendships concurrent with a romantic relationship. However, the women's friendships may end because they do not develop into couple friends. In light of the recent relaxation of gender roles, a reexamination of this finding was deemed relevant. The following research (R) question and hypothesis (H) were proposed to illuminate the role of gender and friendship maintenance as a factor in the development of couple friends.

R_1: Do couple friends tend to originate from the male's group of friends?

H_1: Females will be more likely than males to report friendship losses and these losses will occur at a higher rate than males' friendship losses.

Definition of Couple Friends

Friends have been described as the "ideal primary group with a relationship as an end in itself" (Wiseman, 1986, p. 192). Couple friends, as defined here, represent an interesting qualification to most conceptualizations of friendship. For example, Hays (1988) defined friendship as a "voluntary interdependence between two persons over time" (p. 395). The idea that friendship is restricted to just two persons obviously does not apply to couple friends. *Couple friends* are people that the couple views as "our friends" and with whom the couple socializes. In some sense, the degree of voluntariness about the relationship for each person is reduced by the fact that he or she may have less of a choice about the ending of that relationship if their partner chooses to stay in the relationship with the other couple. Couple friends are often thought of as shared friends, even if the two partners experience differing degrees of companionship, intimacy, and affection with the friends. As Babchuk and Bates (1963) noted, when a couple interacts with others as a pair, others treat the couple as a unit or a pair. For example, couples are often invited to social events as a pair, and celebratory cards and gifts are often addressed and/or presented to the couple. Lewis (1973) argued that through their actions, the couple's social network reaffirms the couple's identity as a social unit. This means that, for the friends of the couple, the level at which the friendship occurs is not with one partner or the other, the friendship exists with the couple. By definition, if the romantically involved couple's relationship terminates and there is no couple, there can be no couple friends. In cases of relationship dissolution, where the friendship continues with one of the now-separated partners, the friendship exists once again at the level of the individual. In fact, people whose relationships deteriorated in the early stages of courtship reported they continued to interact with their same friends, but no longer considered them to be mutual friends of the ex-partner (Milardo, 1982). In cases where the relationship was terminated late in courtship, many people discontinued their interactions with former mutual friends altogether (Milardo, 1982).

Couple friends for married partners tend to be other couples rather than single individuals (Babchuk, 1965; Babchuk & Bates, 1963). However, the definition posited here includes single people, as well as other couples. As defined here, couple friends are not just other couples. They can also be individuals who socialize with the couple without their partner or they can be singles. Regardless of the coupled or uncoupled status of the friend and regardless of possible differing degrees of affection, by definition, the friendship is seen as shared. In sum, couple friends are that group of people with whom the couple socializes and labels *our friends* rather than *my friends*.

An emphasis on the friendship as shared is vital to the definition of couple friends and may be a major factor in the development of couple friends. Couple friendships often begin because of a connection between one of the partners and a friend. As the partner and the friend continue to interact, the mate begins to participate and develops a history and bondedness with the friend. Over time, the couple begins to view the friend as jointly theirs, but the probability of this occurring rests on both partners experiencing satisfactory interactions with the friend. Altman and Taylor's (1973) social penetration model of relationship development suggests that satisfactory interactions will result in relationship growth. If both partners experience satisfactory interactions with the friend, this increases the likelihood that a couple friendship will develop.

Interaction Characteristics

In *Just Friends*, Lillian Rubin (1985) noted that couples frequently remark on the difficulty of finding compatible couple friends because this essentially magnifies the task of establishing compatibility exponentially. One of the obstacles in the development of couple friendships may be due to gender differences in how friendships are developed and the nature of the talk among same-sex friends. Male friendships develop from engaging in shared activities, whereas verbal communication about oneself is more important for developing female friendships (Hays, 1985). In addition, women's conversations can be characterized differently from men's, in that women's communication is more self-disclosing and loaded with emotionally expressive messages (Caldwell & Peplau, 1982; Fox, Gibbs, & Auerbach, 1985). Diary reports of everyday conversations confirmed the findings of conversational gender differences and demonstrated that women tend to report interaction experiences of a higher quality than do men (Duck, Rutt, Hurst, & Strejc, 1991).

These differences in men's and women's friendship development and conversational styles may affect the development of couple friends. Women tend to discuss personal topics such as feelings, problems, and talking about other people (Caldwell & Peplau, 1982) and men may feel uncomfortable with these topics, because they tend to discuss task and social topics. For example, when the couple interacts with the female partner's friends and the females dominate the conversation, the male may feel left out. If he feels restless, bored, and dissatisfied with the interaction, then he will be less likely to interact with his partner's friends in the future. Of course, this is not to say all men's conversations with women follow this pattern. There are many men who experience stimulating conversations with women, but in general, "women are much more accepting of 'man talk' than men are of 'woman talk' " (Rubin, 1985, p. 125).

The influence of communication in the development of couple friends may only be relevant to the extent that couples interact as a pair with other couples or other single friends. But the important element here is to examine how interaction characteristics of men's and women's conversations are tied to the emergence of a mutual friendship network. To that end, the second research question was posited to illuminate the role of communication as a function of gender in the development of couple friends.

To examine the extent to which conversations with couple friends would reflect topics typifying men's conversations, it was hypothesized that both men and women would discuss task and social topics more frequently, in conversation with couple friends, than personal and related topics. It was anticipated that the percentages of men and women reporting topics frequently discussed with couple friends would not differ significantly given that men's conversations with couple friends are the same as women's conversations with couple friends.

R_2: To what extent are the patterns of conversation topics frequently discussed in same-sex male and same-sex female one-on-one friendships reflected in the patterns of conversational topics frequently discussed in couple friendships?

H₂: If couple friends originate from the male's group of friends, then the conversation topics will reflect patterns found in men's communication.

By definition, most friendships require ongoing interaction in order for the friendship to continue (Hays, 1988), but factors such as proximity and frequency of interaction can greatly impact the maintenance of friendships (Stueve & Gerson, 1977). The nature of the couple friendship may be affected by these factors in that they define a potential pool of friends. According to Reisman (1981), co-workers, neighbors, and classmates, the "associative friendship" network, are based on shared roles and propinquity. These friendships typically involve frequent contact, are usually casual, and not very intimate (Jackson, 1977). They require less affection than a close or best friendship, but demand more proximity to sustain them. This means they are likely to change often in some couple's lives and are fairly easily replaced when factors such as moving, marriage, raising a family, or some other change creates a new situation. Especially relevant in the lives of the educated and socially mobile middle-class, couple friends may not necessarily be lasting friendships (Rubin, 1985) and they may not be as intimate as one-on-one friendships. In same-sex, one-on-one friendships, males report lower levels of emotional intimacy than do females (Reis, Senchak, & Solomon, 1985; Williams, 1985) and females report more satisfaction when interacting with same-sex friends than do males (Hays, 1989; Wheeler, Reis, & Nezlek 1983). But these one-on-one friendship findings do little to suggest what might occur with mutually shared friends. Intimacy, whether defined as self-disclosure, emotional expressiveness, unconditional support, physical contact, or trust (cf. Monsour, 1992), may not be as important an element in the development of a couple friendship as it may be in the development of one-on-one friendships. For example, perhaps the simple fact that our children like to play together or that we are bridge partners may be enough to provide the basis for a satisfactory friendship.

Studies examining the role of the social context in the form of everyday life behaviors in the maintenance of relationships (Baxter & Dindia, 1990), loneliness and social participation (Wheeler & Nezlek, 1977), and the differentiation of relationship types through communication (Duck, et al., 1991) demonstrated an awareness that relationships develop as a natural accompaniment to ongoing activities rather than self-conscious, rational, relation-relevant decisions. Given that couple friendships are likely to be borne of role-related interactions, the third research question examines the possibility that these friendships are not as intimate as one-on-one friendships.

It was hypothesized that one-on-one friendships would be more intimate than couple friendships, but high levels of satisfaction would be reported for both friendship types. It was anticipated that the percentages of men and women rating the intimacy of conversations and relationships with couple friends would not differ significantly given that men's conversations with couple friends are the same as women's conversations with couple friends.

R_3: Is the reported intimacy and satisfaction for couple friendships significantly different from that reported for individual friendships?

H_3: Low levels of intimacy with high levels of satisfaction will be reported for couple friendships and high levels of intimacy with high levels of satisfaction will be reported for individual friendships.

METHOD

Subjects consisted of 165 first-year unmarried college students at a large midwestern university who were currently involved in a romantic relationship. The subjects were recruited by students enrolled in an introductory communication course. The students in the course received course credit for soliciting the cooperation of other students in their respective networks of acquaintances, classmates, and friends. The final sample consisted of 99 females whose mean age was 19 years and 66 males whose mean age was 19.7 years. Of the women, 54% reported they had been involved in their relationship for less than 1 year, 33% for 1 to 2 years, and 13% equal to or greater than 3 years. Of the men, 41% indicated involvement in their relationship for less than 1 year, 35% for 1 to 2 years, and 24% equal to or greater than 3 years. At the time of the study, 45% of the women's and 59% of the men's relational partners lived in the same city as the respondent.

The respondents were asked to complete a questionnaire composed of multiple-choice and Likert-scale items developed and described by the authors (alpha = .81). To determine the origin of couple friends, the respondents were instructed to: (a) note the initials of up to six couple friends, which were defined on the questionnaire as "people (nonfamily members) with whom you and your partner tend to socialize when you are together as a couple"; (b) indicate the gender of each couple friend identified; (c) specify whether they introduced that person to their partner or whether the partner introduced the person to them; and (d) indicate whether they now considered that person to be a shared friend. The associated hypothesis regarding friendship maintenance as a function of gender was addressed by two multiple-choice questions that assessed the rate and the gender composition of men's and women's friendship losses. One question asked the respondents to indicate how many friends were no longer as close as they were prior to the start of the respondent's current romantic relationship. The other question asked the respondents to indicate whether these friends were mostly males, mostly females, or an equal number of both sexes.

The second research question attempted to determine whether the typical same-sex male and same-sex female friendship conversational topics would be reflected in couple friendship conversations. The second research hypothesis stated that, if couple friends originate from the male's group of friends, the communication topics would reflect patterns found in male communication. These were both addressed by an item on the questionnaire, which asked the respondents to indicate whether they would discuss four topic choices frequently or infrequently under two conditions: (a) when they were conversing with their friends without their partner's presence; and (b) when they and their partner were together socializing with the people who by reference to their initials were identified as couple friends. The topic choices were consistent with those suggested by previous research (cf. Caldwell & Peplau, 1982) and included *task topics*, such as work, school, or organization activities; *social topics* such as politics, sports, movies, books, or religion; *personal topics* such as self, life goals, problems, or relationships; and *relationship topics* such as the friendship history or the importance of it.

The third research question and its associated hypothesis regarding the reported intimacy and satisfaction of couple friendships as different from that reported for individual friendships were both addressed with three Likert-scale questions, which asked the respondents to indicate on a scale of 1–9 (1 being very high on the scale and 9 being very low) the extent to which they perceived intimacy and satisfaction of their conversations and their relationships under the following two conditions: (a) with those couple friends identified by their initials; and (b) with their one-on-one friendships defined on the questionnaire as "friends you call your own or friends not shared with your partner." The specific questions were as follows: (a) By and large, to what extent do you think your conversations with [friendship type] are intimate?; (b) In general, to what extent do you think your relationships with [friendship type] are intimate?; and (c) On the whole, how satisfied are you with the relationships you have with [friendship type]?

RESULTS

Research Question 1 sought to verify previous findings regarding the tendency for romantically involved partners to select as couple friends those persons who originate from the male's pool of friends. The subjects identified 897 specific couple friends. The male respondents identified 430 couple friends of which 67.2% originated from their own pool of friends. The female respondents identified 467 couple friends of which 54.4% originated from their own pool of friends. The test for the difference of proportions was significant ($z = 3.96$; $p < .001$). The responses indicated a tendency for couple friends to be drawn from the male's pool of friends. In addition, the majority of couple friends were male. Of the 897 total couple friends, 54% were male.

Hypothesis 1 examined the relationship between gender and the likelihood of reporting the loss of friends from one's own network at the start of a romantic relationship. The possibility that women lose more friends than do men when involved in a romantic relationship was hypothesized as an element contributing to the development of couple friends who originate from the male's network. Table 10.1 shows the results of the Chi-square test undertaken to verify a tendency for women's friendships to end at a higher rate than men's at the onset of a romantic relationship. There were no statistically significant differences between gender and the categories of closeness [χ^2 (1 df) = .566], which suggests, contrary to prediction, that women are no more likely than men to report the loss of friends. Specifically, 71% of the women and 65% of the men reported that one or more friendships were no longer as close after the development of their romantic relationship. The Chi-square test demonstrated that both men and women reported that the friends who were no longer close tended to be same-sex friends [χ^2 (1 df) = 37.487; $p < .001$].

Research Question 2 examined the extent to which the patterns of topics of conversation frequently discussed in same-sex male and same-sex female friendships were reflected in the patterns of conversational topics frequently discussed in couple friendships. Table 10.2 shows the percentages of men and women who reported they frequently discuss task, social, personal, and relationship topics with their one-on-one friends and with their couple friends. The first step was to identify the patterns of topics frequently discussed that distinguish men's from women's conversations with their one-on-one friends. The Chi-Square test for an association between men and women reporting topics frequently discussed with their one-on-one friends demonstrated no significant difference in the percentages of male and female responses with regards to task topics [χ^2 (1 df) = 1.02; $p = .312$]. However, the percentages of male and female responses differed significantly in the frequency with which they reported they discuss social topics [χ^2 (1 df) = 8.83; $p = .003$], personal topics [χ^2 (1 df) = 7.44; $p = .006$], and relationship topics [χ^2 (1 df) = 3.79; $p = .052$] with their one-on-one friends. The second step was to identify the patterns of topics frequently discussed that distinguish men's from women's

TABLE 10.1.
Frequencies of Subjects Reporting Friends No Longer Close
After Development of a Romantic Relationship

Number of Friends	Female	Male
All friends just as close	29 (29%)	23 (35%)
One or more not as close	70 (71%)	43 (65%)
Total number of subjects	99	66

conversations with their couple friends. The Chi-Square test for an association between men and women reporting topics frequently discussed with their couple friends demonstrated no significant difference in the percentages of male and female responses with regards to any of the four topics. Specifically, men and women did not differ in the frequency with which they discuss task topics [χ^2 (1 *df*) = .196; *p* = .658], social topics [χ^2 (1 *df*) = .002; *p* = .967], personal topics [χ^2 (1 *df*) = .041; *p* = .840], or relationship topics [χ^2 (1 *df*) = .026; *p* = .872] with their couple friends.

In summary, there were significant differences between the men's and the women's conversations with their one-on-one friends, but these differences disappeared when they reported on conversations with their couple friends. The identified patterns suggest that women tend to discuss personal and relationship topics with their one-on-one friends more than do men, whereas men tend to discuss social topics with their one-on-one friends more than do women. Given the lack of significant differences in topics discussed with couple friends, the results suggest that either females or males or both change their conversational topics when conversing with couple friends.

Hypothesis 2 was in follow-up to the gender differences in changing conversational topics and posited that, if the couple friends originate from the male's network, the topics were likely to reflect the male's communication. Table 10.2 reports the result of a test to identify whether a significant difference existed between women's conversations with their one-on-one friends and women's conversations with their couple friends, as well as men's conversations with their one-on-one friends and men's conversations with their couple friends. The important aspect focuses on the change in percentages of subjects reporting topics frequently discussed when one-on-one friends are compared to couple friends. Table 10.2 shows the test for difference in proportions (Hogg & Craig, 1978) demonstrated no significant difference in the percentage of female responses with regard to task or social topics when comparing one-on-one friends to couple friends. In other words, the female respondents report no

TABLE 10.2.
Percentages of Subjects Reporting Topics Frequently Discussed
with Own Friends and Couple Friends

Topic type	Female			Male		
	Own	Couple	z	Own	Couple	z
Task topics	90%	90%	.00	85%	88%	.69
Social topics	74%	83%	1.80	92%	83%	−1.86
Personal topics	94%	71%	−2.74*	80%	69%	.06
Relationship topics	76%	51%	−4.35**	62%	52%	−1.36

*p < .01. **p < .001.

significant change in the frequency of task topics or social topics discussed with either one-on-one friends or couple friends. However, there was a significant difference in the percentages of women's responses with regard to personal and relationship topics. In other words, women seem to experience a change in topics frequently discussed when their conversations with their one-on-one friends are compared to their conversations with their couple friends. Table 10.2 shows the test for a difference in proportions (dependent samples) demonstrated no significant difference in the percentages of men's responses with regard to any of the four topics when comparing one-on-one friends to couple friends. In other words, men do *not* seem to experience a significant change in topics frequently discussed when their conversations with their one-on-one friends are compared to their conversations with their couple friends. In summary, the topics of conversations for women seems to depend on whether they are with their one-on-one friends or their couple friends, whereas for men the type of friend does not seem to dramatically affect the conversational topic.

Research Question 3 examined the intimacy of conversations, intimacy of the relationships, and satisfaction levels reported for couple friendships and compared them to those reported for one-on-one friendships to determine whether these qualitative characteristics of relationships would differentiate the two friendship types. The variables were submitted to three separate 2 (gender) $\times$ 2 (friendship type) analyses of variance with repeated measures on the second factor. The separate dependent variables in these analyses were, intimacy of conversation, intimacy of relationship, and satisfaction with the friendship.

The intimacy of conversations was examined first as a qualitative characteristic that might differentiate the friendship types. A main effect for friendship type showed that, overall, the intimacy of conversation differs when talking with one-on-one friends versus couple friends $F(1, 163 = 88.22, p < .001)$. Conversations with one-on-one friendships ($M = 2.91$) were characterized as more intimate than conversations with couple friendships ($M = 4.60$; on a scale of 1–9 with higher scores indicating lower value). A main effect for gender demonstrated that overall, men differed from women in the reported intimacy of the conversations across the two friendship types $F(1, 163 = 6.79, p < .01)$. There was a significant interaction between friendship type and gender $F(1, 163 = 12.2, p < .001)$. However, the interaction was such that the two main effects were not overturned (see Figure 10.1). Further analyses suggested that men do differ significantly from women in the reported intimacy of conversations held with one-on-one friends $F(1, 163 = 17.2, p < .001)$ a finding consistent with previous research. However, men and women do not differ significantly in the reported intimacy of conversations held with couple friends. Finally, a paired t-test was undertaken to assess the extent to which friendship type affects talk within gender. For both men ($t = 3.65, p < .001$)

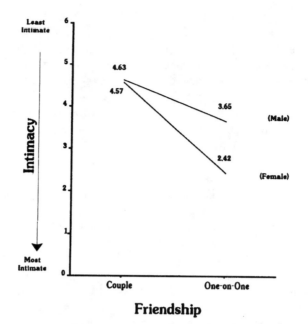

Figure 10.1.   Interaction plot of reported intimacy of conversation in couple and one-on-one friendships.

and women ($t = 10.51$, $p < .001$), the intimacy of conversations held with one-on-one friends does differ significantly from those held with couple friends, with one-on-one friends engaging in more intimate conversations.

The intimacy of relationships was examined second as an additional qualitative characteristic that might differentiate the friendship types. The main effect for the friendship type showed that, overall, the intimacy of the relationship differs when individuals report on the intimacy of their one-one-one friendships and their couple friendships $F(1, 163 = 38.6, p < .001)$. Relationships with one-on-one friends were characterized as more intimate ($M = 3.30$) than relationships with couple friends ($M = 4.48$; on a scale of 1–9 with higher scores indicating lower value). A main effect for gender demonstrated that, overall, men differed from women in the reported intimacy of the relationships across the two friendship types $F(1, 163 = 9.77, p < .01)$. A significant interaction between friendship type and gender was noted $F(1, 163 = 9.38, p < .01)$. However, the interaction was such that the two main effects were not overturned as illustrated in Figure 10.2. Further analyses suggested that men do differ significantly from women in the reported intimacy of relationships held with one-on-one friends $F(1, 163 = 17.47, p < .001)$, but men do not differ significantly from women in the reported intimacy of relationships held with couple friends $F(1, 163 = .96, p = .3287)$. Finally, a paired t-test was undertaken to assess the extent to which friendship type

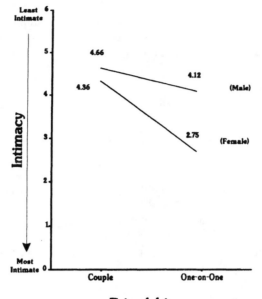

Figure 10.2.   Interaction plot of reported intimacy of relationship in couple
and one-on-one friendships.

affects the intimacy of relationships within gender. For both men ($t = 1.99$,
$p < .05$) and women ($t = 7.44, p < .001$), the intimacy of relationships held
with one-on-one friends does differ significantly from those held with couple
friends.

Finally, the reported satisfaction with the friendships was analyzed as the
third qualitative characteristic that may differentiate the friendship types. The
main effect for the friendship type showed that overall, satisfaction with the
relationship differs when individuals report on the satisfaction with their one-
one-one friendships and their couple friendships $F(1, 162 = 7.44, p < .01)$.
Relationships with one-on-one friends were characterized as more satisfactory ($M = 2.43$) than relationships with couple friends ($M = 2.86$; on a scale
of 1–9 with higher scores indicating lower value). A main effect for gender
demonstrated that overall, men do not differ from women in the reported satisfaction with the relationships across the two friendship types $F(1, 162 = 1.76$,
$p = .1869$). The friendship type by gender interaction was not significant $F(1,
162 = .0029, p = .9573$). Further analyses demonstrated that men do *not*
differ significantly from women in the reported satisfaction with relationships
held with one-on-one friends $F(1, 162 = 1.31, p = .2537$) with couple friends
$F(1, 162 = 1.2, p = .2740$). Finally, a paired t-test was undertaken to assess
the extent to which friendship type affects satisfaction with relationships with-

in gender. For men ($t = 1.68, p = .0981$) satisfaction with one-one-one friendships does not differ from satisfaction with couple relationships. However, for women ($t = 2.23, p < .05$), satisfaction with one-on-one friendships does differ significantly from satisfaction with couple friendships.

DISCUSSION

The purpose of the investigation was to further our understanding of the development of romantic couples' shared friendship networks by examining the origin of couple friends and the interaction characteristics of couple friends. In particular, the influence of communication and gender in the development and nature of couple friendships were analyzed. A tendency first documented almost 30 years ago by Babchuk & Bates (1963) and again 12 years later (Troll, 1975) still remains: Couple friends tend to originate from the male's pool of friends. The fact that this tendency persists despite a relaxation of gender roles over the past decade is intriguing, especially because it exists among 19-year-old, first-year college students. This period of "young adulthood is probably the time of life when men's and women's friendships are least constrained by sex-linked differences in status and role responsibilities" (Caldwell & Peplau, 1982, p. 730). To illuminate the reasons why the tendency exists for couple friends to develop from the male's group of friends, the role of gender and friendship maintenance was examined. It was suggested that perhaps women do not have as many friends from which to choose due to the tendency for women's friendships to end at the start of a romantic relationship. Contrary to prediction and contrary to previous findings (cf. Rose & Serafica, 1986), the women in this sample did not lose their friends at a higher rate than did men at the start of their romantic relationship. Perhaps the findings were influenced by the differences in the individuals sampled here versus those sampled by Rose and Serafica (1986). The respondents in this study were unmarried, first-year students with an average age of 19, whereas the respondents for Rose and Serafica (1986) were 2 to 6 years older and included married college graduates as well as unmarried college juniors, seniors, and graduate students. The older age and marital status of Rose & Serafica's (1986) respondents may have created more opportunities for friendship loss to occur due to life-stage changes, such as graduating, moving, marriage, raising a family, and so on. However, it is also possible that factors such as the degree of commitment to the partner and the relationship versus the commitment to the friendship play important roles in friendship maintenance, which were not assessed in this study.

More importantly, this study demonstrates the considerable impact that moving from a single life to a coupled one exerts in men's and women's friendships as evidenced by the high percentages of respondents who reported they had one or more friends who were no longer as close as they were prior to the start of the relationship. This may have occurred because those friends were not close at the start, suggesting dyadic withdrawal (Johnson & Leslie, 1982) or because the friendships were being replaced with alternative network members, suggesting dyadic realignment (Parks et al., 1983). A specific examination of the actual processes was beyond the scope of this chapter, as was an examination of the behavioral or cognitive processes by which a joint network of mutual friends occurs (Milardo, 1982). However, the fact that some friends were no longer as close suggests a cognitive process working at the level of the individuals' friendship networks, which may be the result of a behavioral process. In other words, some friendships may be classified as no longer close because the friends no longer interact as frequently due to the one friend's increased involvement with a romantic partner. In summary, this study does tend to support previous findings that an evolving romantic relationship affects the partners' degree of involvement with their individual friendship networks.

The interaction characteristics of men's and women's friendships may be another factor influencing the development of couple friendships. The tendency for couple friends to originate from the male's group of friends may be due to gender differences in how friendships are developed and the nature of the talk among same-sex friends. An analysis of conversation topics frequently discussed by men and women when communicating with their one-on-one friends versus couple friends suggests conversation topic is one reason why couple friends originate from the male's network. Research has shown that women discuss personal and relationship topics more frequently than do men. Therefore, if the women's friends were to become the couple's friends, then men would need to make this change in topics and men may not feel comfortable moving from their social oriented conversation topics to more personal topics. As a result, when a romantically involved couple develops their mutually shared network of friends, those friends tend to be ones with whom the male feels comfortable conversing. This study showed that couple friends' conversations are differentiated from conversations with one-on-one friends in that there is more discussion of task and social topics and less focus on personal and relationship topics. The study also showed that women experience a change in the frequency with which they discuss personal and relationship topics when moving from conversations with their one-on-one friends to conversations with their couple friends, whereas men do not experience a significant change in topics. The findings suggest that women are changing their conversational topic style in order to accommodate men's style of talk when socializing with their romantic partner and couple friends.

The interaction characteristics that address the quality of conversations and relationships with one-on-one friendships and couple friendships were examined in an attempt to assess the nature of romantically involved couples' mutual friendship networks and their role in the development of couple friends. The intimacy of conversations, the intimacy of the relationship, and the satisfaction with the relationship reflect significant differences in the nature of the two friendship types. Consistent with previous work on men's and women's perceptions of the intimacy of conversations and relationships with same-sex friendships, women report higher degrees of intimacy in their conversations and relationships with one-on-one friendships than do men. More importantly, however, the gender differences noted in the intimacy of conversations and relationships for one-on-one friendships were not reflected in the levels reported for couple friendships. This suggests, unlike with one-on-one friendships, both men and women perceive similar degrees of intimacy when evaluating their conversations and relationships with couple friends and both men and women reported the degree of intimacy was less than what they experience with one-on-one friendships. Similarly, there was no overall difference between men and women and the reported degrees of relational satisfaction with their one-on-one friendships and their couple friendships. Men and women perceive similar degrees of satisfaction with their one-on-one friendships and couple friendships. However, women experience differing degrees of relational satisfaction when comparing their one-on-one friendships to their couple friendships. Women perceive their couple friendships to be less satisfactory than their one-on-one friendships, whereas men perceive the two friendship types to be equally satisfying.

The lower level of satisfaction that women report for their couple friendships in combination with the findings that women experience a topic change and less intimate conversations with couple friends suggest that women may be carrying the burden of relational accommodation with respect to the development of a shared friendship network. It appears that, because the couple friends originate from the men's networks, men don't need to make the same dramatic change in conversational topics when talking with their one-on-one friends and their couple friends. And although men do perceive the intimacy of their conversations and relationships with their one-on-one friends is different from their couple friends, unlike women, men report they believe their couple friendships are just as satisfactory as their one-on-one friendships.

In summary, the results of this study indicate couple friendships do tend to originate from the male's group of friends, but this was not shown to be due to a gender difference in one's ability to maintain a friendship network. The results reveal that men and women experience differences in how their talk changes when comparing their conversations with one-on-one friends to conversations with couple friends, which suggests that women are accommodating to men's style of talk when interacting with couple friends. The findings also demonstrate gender differences in the nature of the relationships for the two friendship types, which suggest that women shoulder the conversational and relational burden for the development of couple friends.

The implications of this study for evolving romantic relationships point to the need for a closer investigation of the actual cognitive and behavioral processes that lead to the emergence of a mutual friendship network as suggested by Milardo (1982). The results suggest that both men and women reclassify some of their one-on-one friendships as "no longer close" once they start a romantic relationship. Diary-type records of conversations and interactions over time might provide a rich source of information for determining the patterns of changing cognitions as people reclassify their own friends and the patterns of changing behaviors with regards to their partner's friends. This study also suggests a need to address how couples negotiate the selection of couple friends given that this might be a source of conflict between the romantically involved partners if they experience radically different degrees of affection with the friend(s). The strategies romantically involved partners use to balance the maintenance of their one-on-one friendships concurrent with the development of their network of couple friends might also prove a fruitful avenue for further research. One might consider how each of the individuals in the pair maintain their one-on-one friendships so that they do not lose their sense of "I" concurrent with the development of friendships that give them that very important sense of "we."

REFERENCES

Altman, I., & Taylor, D. A. (1973). *Social penetration: The development of interpersonal relationships*. New York: Holt, Rinehart & Winston.

Babchuk, N. (1965). Primary friends and kin: A study of the association of middle-class couples. *Social Forces, 43*, 483–493.

Babchuk, N., & Bates, A. P. (1963). The primary relations of middle-class couples: A study in male dominance. *American Sociological Review, 28*, 377–384.

Baxter, L. A., & Dindia, K. (1990). Marital partners' perceptions of marital maintenance strategies. *Journal of Social and Personal Relationships, 7*, 197–208.

Caldwell, M. A., & Peplau, L. A. (1982). Sex differences in same-sex friendships. *Sex Roles, 8*, 721–732.

Duck, S., Rutt, D. J., Hurst, M. H., & Strejc, H. (1991). Some evident truths about conversation in everyday relationships: All communications are not created equal. *Human Communication Research, 18*, 228–267.

Fischer, C. S., & Oliker, S. J. (1983). A research note on friendship, gender, and the life cycle. *Social Forces, 62*, 124–133.

Fox, M., Gibbs, M., & Auerbach, D. (1985). Age and gender dimensions of friendship. *Psychology of Women Quarterly, 9*, 489–501.

Hays, R. B. (1985). A longitudinal study of friendship development. *Journal of Personality and Social Psychology, 48*, 909–924.

Hays, R. B. (1988). Friendship. In S. W. Duck (Ed.), *Handbook of personal relationships* (pp. 391–408). New York: Wiley.

Hays, R. B. (1989). The day-to-day functioning of close versus casual friendships. *Journal of Social and Personal Relationships, 6*, 21–37.

Hogg, R. V., & Craig, A. T. (1978). *Introduction to mathematical statistics* (4th ed). New York: Macmillan.

Huston, T. L., & Levinger, G. (1978). Interpersonal attraction and relationships. In M.R. Rosenzweig and L.W. Porter (Eds), *Annual review of psychology* (Vol. 29, pp. 115–156). Palo Alto, CA: Annual Reviews.

Jackson, R. M. (1977). Social structure and process in friendship choice. In C.S. Fischer, R. M. Jackson, L.A. Stueve, K. Gerson, L. M. Jones, & M. Baldassare (Eds.), *Networks and places: Social relations in the urban setting* (pp. 59–78). New York: Free Press.

Johnson, M. P., & Leslie, L. (1982). Couple involvement and network structure: A test of the dyadic withdrawal hypothesis. *Social Psychology Quarterly, 45,* 34–43.

Lewis, R. A. (1973). Social reaction and the formation of dyads: An interactionist approach to mate selection. *Sociometry, 36,* 409–418.

Milardo, R. M. (1982). Friendship networks in developing relationships: Converging and diverging social environments. *Social Psychology Quarterly, 45,* 162–172.

Milardo, R. M., Johnson, M. P., & Huston, T. L. (1983). Developing close relationships: Changing patterns of interaction between pair members and social networks. *Journal of Personality and Social Psychology, 44,* 964–976.

Monsour, M. (1992). Meanings of intimacy in cross and same-sex friendships. *Journal of Social and Personal Relationships, 9,* 277–296.

Parks, M. R., Stan, C. M., & Eggert, L. L. (1983). Romantic involvement and social network involvement. *Social Psychology Quarterly, 46,* 116–131.

Reis, H. T., Senchak, M., & Solomon, B. (1985). Sex differences in the intimacy of social interaction: Further examination of potential explanations. *Journal of Personality and Social Psychology, 48,* 1204–1217.

Reisman, J. M. (1981). Adult friendships. In S.W. Duck & R. Gilmour (Eds.), *Personal relationships 2: Developing personal relationships* (pp. 205–230). New York: Academic Press.

Rose, S. (1984). How friendships end: Patterns among young adults. *Journal of Social and Personal Relationship, 1,* 267–277.

Rose, S., & Serafica, F. C. (1986). Keeping and ending casual, close and best friendships. *Journal of Social and Personal Relationships, 3,* 275–288.

Rubin, L. B. (1985). *Just friends.* New York: Harper & Row.

Stueve, C. A., & Gerson, K. (1977). Personal relations across the life-cycle. In C.S. Fischer, R. M. Jackson, L.A. Stueve, K. Gerson, L. M. Jones, & M. Baldassare (Eds.), *Networks and places: Social relations in the urban setting* (pp. 79–98). New York: Free Press.

Surra, C. A. (1985). Courtship-types: Variations in interdependence between partners and social networks. *Journal of Personality and Social Psychology, 49,* 357–375.

Troll, L. (1975). *Early and middle adulthood.* Monterey, CA: Brooks/Cole.

Wheeler L., & Nezlek, J. (1977). Sex differences in social participation. *Journal of Personality and Social Psychology, 35,* 742–754.

Wheeler, L., Reis, H. T., & Nezlek, J. (1983). Loneliness, social interaction, and sex roles. *Journal of Personality and Social Psychology, 45,* 943–953.

Williams, D. G. (1985). Gender, masculinity–femininity, and emotional intimacy in same-sex friendships. *Sex Roles, 12,* 587–600.

Wiseman, J. P. (1986). Friendship: Bonds and binds in a voluntary relationship. *Journal of Social and Personal Relationships, 3,* 191–211.

IV

MATURING AND DISENGAGING RELATIONSHIPS

11

Public Portrayals of
Enduring Friendships

Pamela J. Kalbfleisch[1]
University of Kentucky

As previous chapters by Bendtscheider and Duck and Roiger discussed, on-going friendships play a valuable role in our everyday lives. Friends can provide companionship, love, and compassion (Rawlins, 1992). They can build our self-esteem (O'Connor & Brown, 1984). They can also help us deal with our life's experiences and provide social support (Cauce & Srebnik, 1990; Duck, 1973; Leatham & Duck, 1990). The importance of having friends has been well established in the research literature (cf. Adelman, Parks, & Albrecht, 1987; Duck, 1973; Rawlins, 1992; Wright, 1978).

Friendship relationships are unique from other close relationships in that they are voluntarily initiated and maintained, and they are not bound together by formal societal forces as are romantic or family relationships (Fisher, 1982; Palisi & Ransford, 1987; Wiseman, 1986). It is the voluntary nature of these friendships that enhances their significance. With few formal constraints to discourage disengagement, friendships are maintained because the relational partners want to stay in the relationship.

Friendships can vary in their closeness. They have been described as close versus casual (Hays, 1989); best, close, and casual (Rose & Serafica, 1986); superficial and developed (Wright, 1984); and best friends, close friends, average friends, specialized friends, and the pool of possible friends (Rawlins & Holl, 1987). In examining relationship terms, Knapp, Ellis, and Williams (1980)

---

[1]The author would like to thank Lynda Thomas and Jan Gierman for their assistance on this project.

found respondents rated the term *best friend* as more intimate than *close friend*, *confidant*, *buddy*, *friend*, *companion*, *chum*, or *pal*, respectively. In further analyses, Knapp et al. (1980) found that perceived personalized communication increased as more intimate terms were used to describe relationships. For their study, *personalized communication* was defined as (a) disclosure of feelings, private information, and secrets, (b) use of subtle nonverbal cues to convey information, and (c) cultivation of a personally private language.

The Best Friend

It would seem from the research examined that the type of friendship providing the most intimacy, uniqueness, and emotional support is the best friendship. Further, research has shown that best friendships are based more on affection than other types of friendships (Rose & Serafica, 1986), and best friends display significant concern for one another and appreciation of each other's uniqueness (Wright, 1984). In addition, these friendships are more self-maintaining than other forms of friendship and they are less likely to dissolve with lack of frequent contact (Rose & Serafica, 1986). Rawlins and Holl (1987) noted that best friends are often long-standing friendships. In part, it may be the very length of these intimate relationships that inspires increased confidence in the relational partners. Consequently, greater confidence and trust promote an atmosphere where relational partners should feel more comfortable with self-disclosure and mutual support (cf. Adelman et al., 1987).

Rawlins and Holl (1987) specified that the "best friendship" is exclusive in nature. It follows that emotional intimacy would be something not readily shared with many people. Not everyone would be privy to personal idioms or be able to decode subtle nonverbal cues. Additionally, special experiences would not be as unique if they were shared with everyone. In a grammatical sense, it would seem that a best friend would indicate a singular friend who would be considered the closest friend. Consequently, a *best friend* is the friend that stands out from all other friends as the one who is perceived to share: (a) the closest emotional intimacy, and (b) the most unique relationship. This friendship is likely to have endured over a period of time to have reached this level of closeness.

There are three primary issues to address when considering this definition. The first issue is whether best friends must be platonic or if they could also be romantic. Researchers studying friendship often note the classic distinction of friendship as being its voluntary nature (e.g., Bell & Healey, 1992; Wiseman, 1986). The implication is that society has norms and standards that make leaving a romantic relationship more difficult than leaving a friendship. Accordingly, a romantic friendship may not have the voluntary characteristics found in friendships existing outside of love relationships.

In chapter 6 in this volume, Baxter and her associates point out that there are different relational expectations in romantic and platonic relationships. Specifically, they reference Davis and Todd's (1985) research finding that romantic partners expected more exclusivity from their lovers than from their friends. In addition, other research by Berger, Weber, Munley, and Dixon (1977) suggested that the relationship between platonic and romantic partners may also differ in that their respondents reported feeling better understood by their friends than by their romantic partners.

Considering the research summarized, it would appear that platonic and romantic close relationships differ in terms of the obligations, expectations, and perceptions of the relational partners. Although romantic relationships may be emotionally intimate and unique, they do not share all the characteristics and expectations of the platonic best friendship. For example, one could maintain a best friendship while having a romantic relationship with another partner. In fact, a best friendship could continue through multiple romantic relationships. The self-maintaining nature of the best friendship (Rose & Serafica, 1986) may even allow the relationship to continue through lifestyle changes and moves to distant locations. On the other hand, a romantic relationship would be likely to experience difficulty enduring such dramatic changes.

In order to study best friendships as relationships distinct from romantic relationships, these relationships are best defined as *platonic relationships*. This specification does not minimize the emotional intimacy and uniqueness found in romantic relationships, it simply delineates the best friendship as a different form of relationship than the romantic relationship.

Additionally, the voluntary nature of friendship may precipitate qualitative differences in the intimate, unique relationships that exist between family members and those that exist between nonrelatives. The popular phrase "you can pick your friends, but you can't pick your relatives," reflects the perception that people are tethered to family members, but they affiliate voluntarily with their friends. Because of the apparently nonrestrictive nature of friendships, best friends are further delineated as being nonkin relationships.

The third primary issue addressed in defining best friendship is whether the perception of emotional intimacy and uniqueness of the relationship is shared by both relational partners. The definition advanced in this chapter is from the perspective of one member of the relationship. Obviously, a shared perception of this relationship would be optimal. If both members of the relationship shared similar perceptions of emotional intimacy and uniqueness, they would both be *best friends*. Reciprocal best friendships are probably what most individuals have in mind when they identify their best friend. On the other hand, it is possible that, no matter how dispassionate the relationship, a party identified as a best friend could in fact be the "best" friend that the person making this identification has ever acquired. Consequently, in the ideal case, the perception of *best friendship* should be shared by both relational partners. However, the definition presented in this chapter allows for the contingency of one relational partner perceiving greater intimacy and uniqueness than the other.

In summary, a best friend is defined as the friend that stands out from all other friends as the one perceived to share the closest emotional intimacy and the most unique relationship. The best friend is a nonfamilial, platonic friend. It is not essential that the person identified as a best friend reciprocate the perception of intimacy and uniqueness. However, it is expected that a reciprocal best friendship would evidence greater relational intimacy and exclusiveness. Prior research suggests that (a) the development of a best friendship is likely to have taken place over a period of time, and (b) the self-maintaining nature of the best friendship may allow this relationship to endure without frequent contact. Accordingly, the best friend is likely to be a member of a long-standing friendship.

Public Recognition of Close Relationships

Society has rituals and vehicles that allow participants to express the importance of their close relationships. For example, wedding ceremonies, anniversaries, Valentines' Day, Sweetest Day, and artifacts such as rings and jewelry allow romantic partners to express the importance of their relationship to one another, and to the public in general. Mothers' Day and Fathers' Day are public occasions where parents can be recognized for being a special influence and a special part of a relationship. Unfortunately, public occasions for expressing the importance of a best friend are not readily available.

Recognition of best friends has been appended to occasions such as: recognition of a friend on Mothers' or Fathers' Day for being "like a mother or father," recognition of a friend on Valentines' day for being a "real sweetie," or recognition of a best friend at a wedding as being the "best man" or the "maid or matron of honor." However, such recognition does not validate a friendship as being important in itself, but rather portrays it as an ancillary relationship or a lesser substitute for a more important relationship. In addition, the best friend is not readily observable by others. For example, in the United States, a woman wearing a corsage on Mothers' Day, or a man or woman wearing a ring on their third finger, left hand, would most likely be recognized respectively as someone's mother or someone's spouse. Yet, there is no public symbol for recognition of someone as being a person's very special friend.

It seems that the only opportunity most people have for telling others of the importance of a special friendship is after that person has died. In this sense, testimonials or eulogies serve the purpose of letting others know that a valuable person has been lost to the world, and letting others know the importance of the relationship between the deceased and the person giving the testimonial or eulogy (cf. Sternbach, 1991).

The study presented in this chapter examines how respondents publicly portray the importance of their best friend, and how they portray the intimacy and uniqueness of their relationship with their friend. In this study, a forum was provided for respondents to publicly present their best friend to others. Although the testimonial or eulogy is usually presented after a person has died, this study provided respondents with the opportunity of writing a public testimonial while their best friend was still alive.

Past research has examined descriptions of friendship through interviews (e.g., Rawlins & Holl, 1988; Wiseman, 1986), questionnaires (e.g., Palisi & Ransford, 1987), and diary logs (e.g., Hays, 1989). However, the study of public descriptions of friendship has been largely overlooked. This study examines how respondents publicly portray their very special friends. Of particular interest in this investigation is how the best friend is publicly described and how the uniqueness of a best friendship is portrayed to others. Additionally, the enduring nature of this type of relationship will be considered. Specifically, because best friends are typically friends that have had a relationship over time, this study will explore the explanations and attributions for why this relationship has continued while others have failed. Finally, there is the issue of how the respondents explain their act of acknowledging a best friend publicly. The following research (R) questions are presented:

R_1: How are best friends publicly described?

R_2: How is relational uniqueness portrayed in public descriptions of best friends?

R_3: How do respondents explain the endurance of a best friendship over time?

R_4: Why do respondents say they are using a public forum to portray their best friend, and their relationship with this friend?

The study presented in this chapter should illustrate how people publicly express the importance of their best friends. These public portrayals of best friendship should assist in understanding the characteristics of a best friendship and the factors that facilitate these relationships' endurance over time.

METHOD

Participants

Participants for this study were drawn from a metropolitan area of 256,000 in the southern United States. The local newspaper for this metropolitan area, with a Sunday readership of approximately 160,358, featured an announcement on the front page of the "Lifestyles" section of the paper requesting readers to send essays to the paper describing their best friend. Readers were told that several of the essays would appear in a future edition of the paper.

Out of this population, 72 essays were received by the newspaper. Sixty-eight of the essays were from women and four were from men. The mean age of the respondents was 31 and the mean length of the friendships was 18 years. The essays ranged from one to five typed double spaced pages in length. The average essay was two double spaced pages in length.

Because only four males responded compared to 68 females, the males were not included in the data analysis.[2] In addition, essays describing romantic partners as best friends and essays describing family members as best friends were not included in the analysis. This decision rule, for romantic partners and family members, was made in accordance with the conceptual definition of best friendship. Further, essays about entities such as Jesus or pets were also excluded from this analysis. After these types of essays were removed from consideration, 50 essays about best friends remained for analysis. All 50 of these remaining essays were written by women about other women who where their best friends. Each remaining essay referenced only one best friend.

Procedure

The announcement that was placed on the front page of the lifestyles section of the newspaper requested that the readers send in essays about their best friends. The announcement invited the readers to "tell us all about your best friend." The announcement prompted readers to mention additional aspects about their friendship such as: (a) how they met their friend, (b) what were the best and worst moments with their friend, and (c) how they have managed to stay friends when other people have drifted out of their lives. There were no length requirements listed for the essays. Respondents were free to address any aspect of their relationship with their best friend and they were not limited to the prompts listed in the announcement. Respondents were asked to type their essays and to include their name and phone number. The newspaper had not featured a similar request for essays for several years prior to this announcement.

After the essays were received by the newspaper, a reporter put together a montage about best friends using excerpts from the essays. This montage was featured in the Sunday "Lifestyle" section of the paper. The essays were then given to the author for use in a separate in-depth analysis. Respondents

---

[2]The rationale for removal of the male respondents was that there were too few males to draw meaningful comparisons with the females, and these males may have responded differently than the females in describing their best friends. Therefore, the proper approach, in this situation, was to remove the males from the analysis.

names, telephone numbers, and their best friends' full names were removed from the essays prior to this analysis.

Analysis

The information in each of the respondents' essays was categorized using Bulmer's (1979) analytic induction method. The semantic unit categorized with this procedure was the descriptive phrase. In the cases where phrases contained multiple descriptions or metaphors, these phrases were unitized as one phrase if the descriptors appeared to hold together as one thought. The essays were assessed to determine the number of descriptive phrases that fell into the domain of each of the four research questions. A count was made for the research questions to determine the base number of phrases that addressed each question.

Using the method of analytic induction, categories were developed from a subsample of the essays. These categories were then verified by adding more essays to the sample and making modifications as needed in the analytical categories. In using Bulmer's method, several verifications and modifications are made before the final analytic categories are resolved (cf. Baxter, 1991, 1992a). Four sets of analytic categories were established for: (a) characterizations of best friends, (b) descriptions of relational uniqueness, (c) explanations for relational fortitude, and (d) justification for using a public forum to describe this friendship.

Two independent coders coded the essays using each of the four category sets. Category sets were sequentially used to analyze the essays. Specifically, essays were first analyzed using one set of categories, then analyzed using the second, third, and fourth set of categories. Coder reliability was checked throughout the coding process. Disagreements concerning categorization of essay material were handled through discussion. Overall, the interrater reliability for each of the categories using Cohen's (1960) Kappa were: (a) .81 for characterizations of best friends, (b) .74 for descriptions of uniqueness and emotional intimacy, (c) .83 for explanations of relational fortitude, and (d) .91 for justifications for using a public forum to describe a best friend.

RESULTS

The results of the categorization of friendship portrayals will be presented for each research question respectively. Categories receiving the highest proportion of descriptions are presented first in each section, followed by the other categories in descending order. Table 11.1 summarizes the results of this inductive analysis.

TABLE 11.1.
Categorization of Friendship Portrayals

Portrayal Set	Category	Proportion of Descriptions Per Portrayal Set*
I. Description of Best Friend		
	1. Honest/trustworthy	.52
	2. Fun loving and humorous	.14
	3. Loyal/compassionate	.12
	4. Like a family member	.12
	5. Physically attractive	.10
II. Description of Unique Relationship		
	1. Volume of conversation	.40
	2. Private jokes, private language	.32
	3. Intuitively sensitive to friend	.14
III. Explanations for Relational Fortitude		
	1. Sharing life together	.37
	2. Challenges surmounted with best friend	.27
	3. Similarities and complementary personalities (false opposites)	.18
	4. Ritual or shared experience that sealed friendship forever	.14
IV. Reasons Respondents Wrote Portrayal		
	1. Let friends know how important they are	.41
	2. Express gratitude	.28
	3. Portray self in positive light (implicit)	.15
	4. Express deep sense of loss/grief	.10
	5. Get in touch with friend	.04

*Descriptions that could not be categorized were placed in a category of "other" for each portrayal set.

Research Question 1: Description of Best Friend

Honest/Trustworthy. The predominate description of a best friend was that of a person who was open and honest with the respondent. Descriptions of this friend either simply mentioned that the friend would always tell the respondent the truth, or they would provide examples of when the friend was not afraid to tell the truth. Samples of the descriptions are listed as follows:

- Helen has never been afraid to tell me when I was wrong, or when I have messed up royally.
- I know she will tell me the truth no matter how it hurts.
- A best friend is one who laughs at my jokes only if they are funny and tells me if I have spinach in my teeth.

In addition to portrayal of the best friend as a truth teller (at least to the respondents), the best friend was also portrayed as someone who could be trusted with the most precious secrets, and who the respondent could tell what they really were thinking, no matter how horrible the thoughts. The best friend was portrayed as a confidant. Note the following excerpts from two of the essays:

- A best friend is one with whom you can be unguarded, one with whom you can share any thought without dangers of being misunderstood.

- I may hesitate with the whole truth with someone else, but because of the trust we have built up, I am completely honest with Donna and she is with me.

The portrayals illustrated the perception, on the part of the respondents, that it was important to have a reciprocal trusting relationship with a best friend. That is, not only did the respondents portray a best friend they could say anything to, but also a best friend who would tell them private things as well. The perception of the best friendship as an environment where both participants could be truthful is particularly strong in this sample, with 52% of the descriptions of best friends focusing on the characteristics of honesty and trustworthiness.

Fun Loving and Humorous.   The next characteristic attributed to the best friend was the personality quality of being fun loving and humorous. Best friends were described as happy, funny, always there with a ready smile. The following expressions reflect this category:

- She is always ready with a smile, a kind, quick wit.
- She has a sense of humor.
- She has an intelligence and wit that is rare.
- She had a bubbly, bouncy laugh with one of those million-dollar smiles.
- She is an unpredictable character, opinionated, hilarious. . . .

Loyal/Compassionate.   The descriptions of the best friends also portrayed the best friend as one who was always loyal to the author of the essay and loyal to the relationship itself. These essays often featured the best friend as giving up some other opportunity to come help. According to these portrayals of the best friends, these friends would even put their romantic and family relationships on hold if their friend required it:

- A friend is someone who sits with you through two days of rain at your garage sale when you have a fever of 101° and she does all the bargaining because you have laryngitis and the dog is in heat.

- On more than one occasion, when called upon, my friend has left home and family to fly to my rescue.

The descriptions of the best friend's loyalty also include statements about the best friend's compassion. In some cases the compassion of the friend is blended together with the loyalty to the friend. For example, the friend gives up being home with her family, so she can help her friend (two examples of blended portrays are listed above). At other times the loyalty statements and the compassion statements are separated, as they are here:

- How would I describe my friend Helen. . . . A friend through thick or thin.
- And in those incredibly hellish times she yields compassion and love as if it were simply a part of the joy of breathing in clean air.
- Everyone who knows Charlotte will agree that the world would be so much better if more people had her compassion and philosophy of life.

Like a Family Member. Respondents also chose to reference their best friend as being like a member of the family. References to the best friend being "like a sister to me," were used more often than "like a mother to me." For example:

- Donna is the sister I always prayed for and finally found—my best friend.
- She took the place of the mother I never had.

As could be expected, the mother reference was used when the friends were further apart in age than those who employed the sister label to characterize their best friend.

The respondents who used these family terms to describe their best friend may have been trying to give the intimacy felt with a friend the legitimacy of a family member. Interestingly, Knapp et al. (1980) found in their study that although the term *mother* was perceived as being more intimate than the term *best friend*, the term *sister* was perceived as being less intimate than the term *best friend*. The differences in perceived intimacy are only slight, but it is still interesting that the terms used in the portrayals, to signify the relative importance of their best friend, are actually not perceived to differ significantly from one another.

Physically Attractive. The final category under descriptions of the best friend is that the best friend is described as being physically attractive. Originally, in this analysis other more ephemeral forms of attractiveness were included in this category (such as "pretty on the inside" and "beautiful personality"), however, when sufficient numbers of respondents were classifying their best friend as having physical beauty, it became clear that this should be a category of it's own. The coding scheme was modified (cf. Baxter, 1991) and the physical attractiveness category evolved. Examples of these statement's regarding a best friend's physical attractiveness are as follows:

- Her hair is reddish blond and hangs in her face in an endearing way. She is tall and skinny and very attractive.
- She was very beautiful. . . .
- Picture it. A girl who is 5 feet 6 inches in height. Her long thick brown hair hangs just below her waist. Her eyes are sparkling sky blue and her cheeks are lightly sprinkled with freckles. You have just met my best friend.

As can be seen with the last description of the physical attributes of a best friend, the reader is given the vision of attractiveness without the writer actually saying that her best friend is pretty. Rather, the best friend's features were described in an attractive manner giving the impression of an attractive friend. Although the friend portrayed in the last excerpt may actually not be physically attractive in a traditional sense, the essayist may have pulled out her best features for the public account. This category contains all physical descriptions of the best friend, which either state that the friend is attractive or that describe physical features of the friend, presenting them in a positive framework "sparkling sky blue [eyes]."

Research Question 2:
Description of a Unique Relationship.

The responses categorized in this section are those that portray the relationship between the best friend and the respondent as being special and unique. In portraying the uniqueness of their best friendship, the respondents also provide an indication of the level of intimacy prevalent in their relationship.

Volume of Conversation. The first and largest category concerns the sheer volume of conversation reported between the best friends. Friends are portrayed as engaging in endless conversations with the respondents. Interestingly, these conversations are more often reported as being made over the telephone than as being made face to face. The following is an example of how the respondent has made talking with her friend a regular part of her life:

- There weren't many weekends that we weren't in touch with one another. After a while it was just a natural thing for me to do in the afternoon, that is, call Jennifer and see what was going on.

Private Jokes, Private Language. The unique relationship between the best friends is probably better portrayed with these descriptions of the specific type of language the friends use. These portrayals give the reader the content of the special conversations that are only alluded to in the previous descriptions of frequent conversations. The descriptions in this category describe humor and jokes that only the friends understand or consider funny. These descriptions also contain evidence of a private language between the two friends. The next two excerpts drawn from the portrayals illustrate these "in jokes" and "private language":

- We stay up all night playing poker and telling stupid stories that always seem to be hilarious to us and us only.

- I feel secure in saying unending MUSH (o' course it's luuuv!) that she has ladled loving on to lucky me. And I feel that this sort of kindness deserves just as much in return, and that's why I can reveal her only as NIBOR THE GREAT WHITE WHALE. . . . In the time that I have known her my aquatic amour has helped me laugh when laughter was very easily furthest from my mind, and every moment is made nostalgic because of it. For example the time she and I were driving to my home and in a not at all rare fit of laughter she nearly got the chance to die for me and I her, when the car swerved onto the median. After returning to the pavement we took back every promise we made to God and Nibor exclaims "We could have hit the lamppost and died, WE DON'T EVEN HAVE OUR BATHING SUITS ON!" Heaven forbid if Dick Clark and his cast of elite Miss U.S.A. judges would show at the scene of the accident and we were unprepared.

The private language and "in jokes" are so strong in this last portrayal of best friendship that it is difficult to assess the full nature of what is going on in this story of an adventure in which the two friends were involved. For example, the nickname Nibor, could suggest that this best friend is fat, it could mean this best friend loves to swim, it could mean this friend is both fat and loves to swim, or the name could have nothing to do with whales, weight, or water.

Intuitively Sensitive to Friend. In this category are descriptions of relational language that is so private and so unique that the friends themselves do not even have to speak. This category is composed of reports of unspoken communication between the friends. For example:

- Somehow or other we can sense when one of us needs the other even though she lives in [a different city than I do].

- I can tell at a glance that Alice and I even share many unspoken thoughts.

- We know when the other is sick or feeling bad and what is hurting. We can not only finish each other's sentence, but have complete conversations in just phrases.
- We have developed a sense of knowing what the other is going to say, and often finish each other's sentences. Our husbands think we have developed a new foreign language.

Research Question 3:
Explanations for Relational Fortitude.

The relational portrayals that were placed in this set of categories were those portrayals that tried to explain why the friendship had lasted for so many years. Many of the examples provided by the participants also illustrate the perceived intimacy and uniqueness of these relationships. The examples listed in answering the third research question, are all sorted into this section because they were originally linked to statements such as "the reason our friendship has lasted so long is . . ."

Sharing Life Together. This is the category receiving the greatest proportion of descriptions explaining the relational fortitude of the best friendship. These respondents portrayed their relationship as staying together because the friends had been together for so long. Essentially, the respondents were suggesting that their relationships endure because they have always endured. For example:

- We were friends through first dances, first loves, whispered secrets in the wee morning hours during sleepovers, transition into Junior High, High School, graduation, and into adulthood.
- We experienced many stages of life together, our patterns haven't been simultaneous, but they have been remarkably similar—our teenage years, marriage, children, and middle age.
- We laughed at our different accents, cried together over silly problems, had our children and watched them grown into fine adults.
- As we grow older, our love and friendship gets stronger.
- When I asked Jenny what she though has kept us together for almost 13 years, she said, "Life has kept us together."

Challenges Surmounted with Best Friend. The descriptions in this category imply that the best friendship has often served as a conduit for overcoming grief or solving life's dilemmas. The friendships in this category were portrayed as functioning as a cooperative venture in which each friend assisted the other in the maturation process and in the performance of roles and responsibilities. Some of these portrayals described sudden traumas that the friends had gotten through, and others depicted the friends helping each other through life's transitions. These portrayals are similar to those described in the category "sharing life together," however these descriptions depict shared trauma and stress. The friendships described in these portrayals seemed to contribute a therapeutic function in helping the friends obtain perspective and healing:

- We have shared some bitter heartbreaks—the deaths of loved ones, the break-up of my marriage, job changes, new houses, broken romances, lost friendships, and major problems with children.

- Our lives were touched by divorce, mine after 25 years and she after 29 years. During those years our lives were drawn closer together.

- I think that one of the reasons our friendship has remained solid is because when things go wrong in our lives (as they so often do) our mainstay is each other.

Similarities and Complementary Personalities (False Opposites). The segments of the portrayals listed in this section feature the perceived similarities of the best friends. These similarities are more than just having had similar life experiences. These portrayals point out similarities in personalities and perspectives. Examples are provided.

- Our friendship has endured many highs and lows, but we have remained close. I think this is due in part to the fact that we have a lot of the same morals, values, and some of the same outlooks on life. We try to keep each other positive.

- We connected the very day we met because of our backgrounds and unusual sense of humor.

- Our personalities synchronize well. . . .

- It didn't take long for us to discover our philosophies of life were pretty much the same—if you are too short to reach the top of the refrigerator, you don't have to dust there; a big bowl of popcorn makes a nutritious light supper; and there is no direct correlation between intelligence and the ability to roll up hair on those tiny little pink curlers for home permanent.

Other portrayals described the best friend as an opposite from the respondent. These descriptions were not placed into a different category because with careful examination, it became clear that, although the respondents were saying they were opposites from their friends, the respondents were attributing the points that they did agree on as the glue that has held the friendship together. These portrayals were considered to be portrayals of "false opposites." Although seemingly different on many subjects, the friends were portrayed as being similar on the important aspects of their friendships:

- We were beyond opposites. The only thing we had in common was our friendship.
- Our surface difference made it seem like we would not get along. But our true selves came out and we became close friends.

Ritual or Shared Experience that Sealed Friendship Forever. Descriptions that fit in this category were those that portrayed a memorable ritual or shared experience that the respondent attributes to having kept the relationship together over the years. The following is perhaps one of the best examples of such a memorable ritual:

- She was my blood sister. We both stood by the sink in my kitchen, terrified of the needle, yet begging my mother to draw blood. We had discussed it. This was the only way we could forever secure our friendship. I still remember the sharp prick of the needle in my middle finger as I screamed out in pain. The deed had been done. We quickly mashed our fingers together and sucked the combined blood until there was no more to suck. At age ten, we didn't quite realize the impact of that moment, but we had indeed secured a friendship that would last.

After other descriptions of the friendship, this portrayal closes with this:

- One thing that is certain is that nothing can come between us. We are blood sisters.

Research Question 4:
Reasons Respondents Wrote Portrayals

This portrayal set contains the justifications given by respondents for sending their essay to the newspaper. Not all of the respondents felt it necessary to justify their portrayals; however, examining the justifications themselves sheds light on the motivations for publicly portraying a best friend. With the exception of the category "express deep sense of loss/grief," the justifications are very concise.

Let Friends Know How Important They Are. The items in this category consist of statements made directly to the best friend toward the end of the portrayal. These brief references stand out in the context of the essays, in that the standard essay is written for the general reader's consumption and these statements are somewhat jolting because they are directed right to the best friend being described:

- I can honestly say that I love my best friend and cherish what few visits we get with each other. So dear April, this is to you . . . may we make more memories in July.
- I love you, you mean everything to me. . . .
- God Bless you Sherl Lynn. . . .

Other writers expressed the importance of their best friend without breaking their writing style:

- It is hard to find a best friend like. . . .
- A friendship like this must always be cherished. In such a world like today, it is hard to find a true friend.

Gratitude.   The next category, reasons the respondents gave for writing these public portrayals, is that of expressing gratitude to the friend. These expressions were either directed toward their friend, or directed toward the general reader, as shown here:

- I just want to say thanks for being my friend.
- I just want to thank her for being my best friend for ten years.

Portray Self in Positive Light.   This category contains implicit references to the author of the essay. Specifically, these are statements such as "I just wanted to send in this song I wrote about my best friend," or "I just wanted to send in these poems in response to your announcement." Although these authors do not say "I am doing this to look good," the presence of the poems and songs in relationship to the essays is somewhat incongruous. In fact the poems and songs seem to show off the writer more than the best friend. The following is an example of one the poems:

> *Me and my sweet confidante*
> *We will always carry on*
> *I can't keep anything from you at all*
> *And confiding in you*
> *Is so easy to do*
> *'Cause you are now and will always be*
> *My sweet confidante.*

Other statements were directly in reference to self. For example, one essayist who wrote about a woman who had befriended her in the one of the city's worst housing projects wrote in her portrayal that "Not all of us in Bluegrass Aspendale are bad people." On first glance it appears that she may be taking about her friend as being one of the "good" people, but implicitly it seems as though the author is implying that she too is one of the "good people."

Express Deep Sense of Loss, Grief. The responses in this category are much more lengthy than the other justifications for writing these public portrayals. They are exclusively written by respondents who have lost their best friend, through death:

- I know I deeply regret those months when we were each, or both, too busy to get together. Jeanie died of a heart attack at 39 and I have finally grown up. My grief was so devastating at her passing, that I put it in a box and set it on the back porch of my mind.
- We cried and talked and tried to piece together what had happened to her, she remembered so little. Finally Jen told me she was getting a little tired so I leaned over, kissed her, told her that I loved her, and said good-bye. Little did I know that God had just given me a gift most people would give anything for. I got to tell my friend I loved her and to tell her good-bye. The very next day Jennifer's heart stopped and I would never see my friend alive again. Now instead of going to the movies or the mall with Jen I go to the cemetery, but I will never be without her. No longer is Jen simply my best friend, but my guardian angel as well. And I know, in my heart, that one day, when it is my turn to die, my best friend, who never made it past twenty years of age, will once again call my name and hug me for an eternity.

Get in Touch with Friend. The items in this category consisted of pleas directed toward the friend to get in touch with the authors of the essays. These admonishments were written at the conclusion of the friendship portrayal. These requests were written by respondents that had lost their friend through misunderstanding or lack of contact. The following are examples of these requests:

- Call me.
- So Mary, if you read this, please get in touch with me.

DISCUSSION

The excerpts drawn from the public portrayals of best friendship were provided as illustration of the categories derived through analytic induction, and the type of responses that best fit in each of these categories. In some cases, these excerpts also show the poignancy with which respondents portrayed their best friend and their relationship with the friend. Although no length of relationship was specified in the announcement that prompted the written responses, the mean length of these relationships was 18 years. In many cases, the respondents were writing about life-long friends that they had met as children, teens, or young adults. These enduring friendships were poignantly portrayed as friendships for life.

These images are the respondents' representations of their best friends and their relationships dressed up for the world to see. They are public proclamations of their friendships and testimonials about a special person and unique relationship. Public portrayals such as these would be difficult to obtain in the traditional research environment. Although students or members from students' networks could be encouraged to write about their best friends, the public nature of these responses would be lost. What the responses analyzed in this study demonstrate is how people would like others (the general public) to see their best friend, their relationship, and even themselves. Examining the way best friends are portrayed in these essays is a way to assess what is perceived as valuable in a friendship.

The sample of newspaper readers who sent in essays about their best friends is limited. Sitting down to type out an essay embodying the essence of a special friendship is a high-threshold activity requiring a behavioral commitment. It is indeed possible that many readers thought about describing their best friends, but simply did not have the time or the motivation to engage in this activity. Potential participants may also have been hampered by poor writing skills or the inability to type (the announcement specified the essays must be typed). Finding another person to compose an essay or to type up a hand written essay would have been another step making a response to the announcement even more difficult.

In addition to the commitment required by the task, responses may have been limited by the location of the announcement in the paper and by the public nature of the portrayals. Specifically, the announcement appeared in the "Lifestyles" section of the paper. This section features information about topics such as fashion, travel, local people, entertainment, families, and food. The announcement for essays about best friends was more appropriate for this section than the other sections of the paper such as main news, city/state news, business, or sports. However, it is likely that the location of the announcement limited the sample to the readers of this section of the paper. Although the local newspaper had no specific information about this section's readership, similar sections in other newspapers have been identified by names such as "home" and "family," and several years ago comparable sections went by the label of the "women's section" of the paper (Joan Bryant, personal communication, February 27, 1992). Although gender roles appear to be less restrictive than in previous times, it is possible that the readership of this section is predominately female. This may have accounted for, in part, the predominately female response to the announcement.

The public nature of the essays may have limited responses in that some readers may have felt uncomfortable putting their friendship on display. Just as some readers may have been motivated by seeing their names in print or calling attention to themselves and their friends, others may have shunned this attention. It is possible that the respondents may have shared some common personality attribute that influenced their decision to publicly portray their friendship.

The public nature of the essays could have also influenced the relatively large number of women, as opposed to men, who responded to the announcement. It is possible that males chose not to publicly write about their male friendships because of fear of being perceived as homosexual. Of the four men who did respond, only one wrote about a male friend. This response was written in the form of a eulogy and labeled by the respondent as a eulogy. Miller (1983) suggested that the fear of being perceived as homosexual inhibits the development of close male friendships. Further, Snell, Miller, Belk, Garcia-Falconi, and Hernandez-Sanchez (1989) indicated that, in an effort to avoid the perception of being feminine, males may adopt a masculine persona in which they limit their emotional expressiveness and openness. This fear of being perceived of as homosexual or as unmasculine could have limited male responses.

In addition, essays about cross-gender friendships may have been limited for both males and females because such public portrayals could have been viewed by the respondents or their partners as threats to the relationship. Baxter and Wilmot (1985), in their study of cross-gender close relationships, found that respondents overwhelmingly considered talking about the state of their relationships a taboo topic. Baxter and Wilmot's cross-gender platonic friends indicated that talking about the relationship might imply that they wanted the relationship to move to a closer level (perhaps romantic), when such might not be the case. Both males and females may have hesitated to write about their best friends if they were of the opposite sex for fear of readers or their friend perceiving that they wanted more out of the relationship. Additionally, if males have emotionally closer relationships with females than males, as Reisman (1990) suggested, this fear might have further limited male responses. Specifically, Reisman (1990) found that males considered their relationships and their conversations with females to be more intimate than their relationships and conversations in corresponding relationships with other males. Conversely, females were found to be more self-disclosive with other females than they were with males. Further, Duck, Rutt, Hurst, and Strejc (1991) found that both females and males rated the quality of the conversations with females as higher than the quality of the conversations they share with males. This research on gender differences combined with that on taboo topics would suggest that, if best friends are perceived to be those with whom the respondents are the most emotionally intimate, this might offer a further explanation for why females might have been more likely to respond about their female friends than their male friends, and why, for the most part, males did not respond about their friends of either gender.

It is likely that the predominately female responses and the subsequent analysis of phrases taken from only the females' essays had an influence on the categories describing best friends and these relationships. For example, the predominate references made to frequent conversations would be a characteristic of women's friendships as opposed to men's friendships. Wright (1982) and Weiss and Lowenthal (1975) characterized women's friendships as placing heavy emphasis on self-disclosure, providing emotional support, and having frequent conversations about a wide variety of topics. Male friendships would be expected to concentrate more on structured activities, specific purposes, and common ventures (Weiss & Lowenthal, 1975). Specific purposes and common ventures were not apparent themes in the essays analyzed in this study. Furthermore, although common activities were mentioned, they were discussed in terms of having similarities with the friend, or sharing life with the friend. In addition, discussion of common activities was typically made in light of other relational characteristics. Specifically, these references were not the focus of the relationship but rather a context in which conversations or fun times occurred.

On the other hand, the respondents' descriptions of private language and private jokes reflects the friendship literature that has found the emergence of private terms, idioms, and language among friends of both genders (Bell & Healey, 1992). Further, the emergence of the best friendship as a "unique mini-culture" (Baxter, 1987) is clearly illuminated by the portrayal of private jokes that no one else can understand (or think are funny if they can understand), the key ritual that sealed the friendship, and the intuitive sensitivity that the partners have for each other.

Additionally, respondents portrayed their best friends as sharing similarities with themselves and having complementary personalities. Even when respondents indicated that they and their friend were dissimilar, they indicated that the friends agreed with them on the things that were really important. Hatfield and Rapson (1992) argued that with close relationships it is important that the participants are similar. They suggested that markedly dissimilar people will run into to many conflicts over time and have to make too many compromises. Duck and Barnes (1992) and Bochner (1991) indicated that it is important for relational partners to perceive each other as having similarities. In either case, the voluntary nature of friendship may make it even more critical for the relational partners to have important similarities or at least perceive that they have important similarities. In the portrayals of best friendship, similarities and complementary personalities were often attributed as the reason why these relationships endured over time.

An interesting reference that is missing in the portrayals of best friendship is any reference to relationships as "hard work," or to "working at their relationship." In her recent study of root metaphors to describe relational development, Baxter (1992b) found that approximately 60% of her respondents used the root metaphor of "relational development as work." The closest the respondents come to mentioning work related things employed to maintain their relationship is when they talk about "carefully nurturing the relationship" and "not losing contact by frequent telephone conversation and letters." The problems that are discussed by the respondents are those problems and challenges that the two friends went through together or overcame together. These problems that both friends faced together were seen as the twine that helped bind the relationship closer and helped it to last over time. It is possible that the respondents in this study did not reference working at relationships because they were, for the most part, involved in very long-term, voluntary relationships. In contrast, the respondents in the Baxter study were involved in romantic relationships that had lasted an average of 20 months and these respondents were describing relational development, not relational maintenance.

There are several explanations for the lack of reference to "working on their relationship." One possibility is that maintaining long-term relationships may actually not be as much work as developing a relationship. Another is that romance may be more work than friendship, particularly in terms of the more voluntary nature of friendship. Although not comparing best friends to romantic partners, Rawlins and Holl (1987) indicated that best friendships were more self-maintaining than other friendships.

Gender differences in perceptions of work required to maintain a relationship do not appear to be a factor here because Baxter (1992b) did not find a significant difference in male and female usage of the work metaphors. Perhaps the difference is that, in publicly portraying a friendship, the respondents did not want to talk about the compatibility problems that the friends may have had, nor present any internal conflict that the pair may have encountered. The respondents could have been afraid that portraying the task of keeping a long-term relationship together as work would give readers the idea that the pair had multiple conflicts and disharmony. The respondents may have further wanted to avoid giving their best friends the idea that being their friend was "work." As Canary and Stafford point out in chapter 13 in this volume, the strategy of "positivity" is an effective relational maintenance behavior. In essence, Canary and Stafford suggest that positivity behaviors, such as acting cheerful and avoiding criticism of the partner, promote relational trust. They additionally suggest that the use of the strategy "positivity" fosters a rewarding climate for both relational partners. It is not clear in this case if the partners did not mention maintaining their relationship as being work because they didn't perceive this best friendship to be work, or if they were trying to present a harmonious picture of the relationship for all involved.

Although the respondents did not mention "working," they certainly mentioned "playing" with their best friend. Best friends were described by several respondents as fun loving and humorous. Totally incomprehensible private jokes were presented in the essays. In several cases, stories of shared life experiences, rituals, or similarities were presented with an underlying context of humor. Rather than "working at their relationships" the best friends appear to be "playing at their relationships."

Further, by examining the classifications of intimate play that Baxter (1992a) used in her study of intimate play, it is evident that two other aspects of the portrayals might also be considered indications of "play." These are the descriptions and use of private verbal codes and language, and the descriptions of gossip as part of the friends' frequent conversations. Baxter (1992a) indicated that these forms of intimate play, particularly the private verbal codes, are indicators of intimacy in a relationship. Perhaps the play and humor described in the portrayals of best friendship are an attempt by the respondents to capture the intimacy of their relationship. It also could be possible that the play and fun may be part of what makes these best friendships so special to the respondents.

However, the most dramatic aspect of the friendship portrayals was the strong emphasis placed on honesty and trustworthiness. Best friends were depicted as people who would always tell the truth even if the truth hurt. They were also portrayed as someone with which an individual could be truthful. This factor was so significant in these portrayals that, with the exception of the essays that began by describing the first meeting of the friends, this characteristic was consistently one of the first cited when describing a best friend.

Bauchner (as discussed in Miller, Mongeau, & Sleight, 1986) found that friends were better able to detect deception than romantic partners or strangers. Although she did not control for the type of friendship in her study, these findings do suggest that friends may be more likely to detect our lies than other people in our lives. Perhaps it may just be easier for the best friends to tell each other the truth rather than risk lying to someone who has a good likelihood of catching them in their deceit. It also could be that, in these long-term friendships, there is little to hide. For best friends who have been together since their early school days, there may be little that the friends do not already know about each other. The voluntary nature of the friendship may provide the partners the freedom to admit the truth rather than to conceal it. Deterioration of these long-term relationships does not have many of the societal complications that a deteriorating romantic relationship experiences (Palisi & Ransford, 1987; Wiseman, 1986).

In general, the portrayal of the best friend is a characterization of someone who can be implicitly trusted. This solid trust in a best friend may have been a deciding factor in the decision to publicly portray such a friendship. In terms of Baxter and Wilmot's (1985) research on taboo topics, discussing the state of the relationship could have negatively affected the preservation of these relationships. The individuals writing portrayals of their best friends risked making themselves very vulnerable in their relationships. What would happen if the best friend did not feel the same way? What if the person described in the portrayal did not consider the writer to be their best friend, or even a close friend? Obviously whatever relationship existed could be damaged by this now-apparent inequity in perspective of the friendship. However, respondents did take on a risk in publicly portraying their best friends; perhaps it is this very willingness to go out on a limb for a friend, having total trust in the friend's response, that may facilitate these relationships to endure so tenaciously over time.

REFERENCES

Adelman, M. B., Parks, M. R., & Albrecht, T. L. (1987). Supporting friends in need. In T. L. Albrecht, & M. B. Adelman (Eds.), *Communicating social support* (pp. 105–125). Newbury Park CA: Sage.

Baxter, L. A. (1987). Symbols of relationship identity in relationship cultures. *Journal of Social and Personal Relationships*, *4*, 261–280.

Baxter, L. A. (1991). Content analysis. In B. M. Montgomery, & S. Duck (Eds.), *Studying interpersonal interaction* (pp. 239–254). New York: Guilford.

Baxter, L. A. (1992a). Forms and functions of intimate play in personal relationships. *Human Communication Research*, *18*, 336–363.

Baxter, L. A. (1992b). Root metaphors in accounts of developing romantic relationships. *Journal of Social and Personal Relationships*, *9*, 253–275.

Baxter, L. A., & Wilmot, W. W. (1985). Taboo topics in close relationships. *Journal of Social and Personal Relationships*, *2*, 253–269.

Bell, R. A., & Healey, J. G. (1992). Idiomatic communication and interpersonal solidarity in friends' relational cultures. *Human Communication Research*, *18*, 307–335.

Berger, C. R., Weber, M. D., Munley, M. E., & Dixon, J. T. (1977). Interpersonal relationship levels and interpersonal attraction. In B. D. Rubin (Ed.), *Communication yearbook 1* (pp. 245–261). New Brunswick, NJ: Transaction Books.

Bochner, A. P. (1991). On the paradigm that would not die. In J. Anderson (Ed.), *Communication yearbook 14* (pp. 484–491). Newbury Park, CA: Sage.

Bulmer, M. (1979). Concepts in the analysis of qualitative data. *Sociological Review*, *27*, 651–671.

Cauce, A. M., & Srebnik, D. S. (1990). Returning to social support systems: A morphological analysis of social networks. *American Journal of Community Psychology*, *18*, 609–616.

Cohen, J. (1960). A coefficient of agreement for nominal scales. *Education and Psychological Measurement*, *20*, 37–46.

Davis, K. E., & Todd, M. (1985). Assessing friendship: Prototypes, paradigm cases and relationship description. In S. W. Duck & D. Perlman (Eds.), *Understanding personal relationships* (pp. 17–38). London: Sage.

Duck, S. W. (1973). *Personal relationships and personal constructs: A study of friendship formation.* New York: Wiley.

Duck, S., & Barnes, M. K. (1992). Disagreeing about agreement: Reconciling differences about similarity. *Communication Monographs*, *59*, 199–208.

Duck, S., Rutt, D. J., Hurst, M. H., & Strejc, H. (1991). Some evident truths about conversations in everyday relationships. *Human Communication Research*, *18*, 228–267.

Fisher, C. (1982). *To dwell among friends: Personal networks in town and city.* Chicago: University of Chicago Press.

Hatfield, E., & Rapson, R. L. (1992). Similarity and attraction in close relationships. *Communication Monographs, 59,* 209–212.

Hays, R. B. (1989). The day-to-day functioning of close versus casual friendships. *Journal of Social and Personal Relationships, 6,* 21–37.

Knapp, M. L., Ellis, D. G., & Williams, B. A. (1980). Perceptions of communication behavior associated with relationship terms. *Communication Monographs, 47,* 262–278.

Leatham, G., & Duck, S. (1990). Conversations with friends and the dynamics of social support. In S. Duck (Ed., with R.C. Silver), *Personal relationships and social support* (pp. 1–29). Newbury Park CA: Sage.

Miller, G. R., Mongeau, P. A., & Sleight, C. (1986). Fudging with friends and lying to lovers: Deceptive communication in personal relationships. *Journal of Social and Personal Relationships, 3,* 495–512.

Miller, S. (1983). *Men and friendship.* Boston: Houghton Mifflin.

O'Connor, P., & Brown, G. W. (1984). Supportive relationships: Fact or fancy? *Journal of Social and Personal Relationships, 1,* 159–175.

Palisi, B. J., & Ransford, H. E. (1987). Friendship as a voluntary relationship: Evidence from national surveys. *Journal of Social and Personal Relationships, 4,* 243–259.

Rawlins, W. K. (1992). *Friendship matters: Communication, dialectics, and the life course.* New York: Aldine De Gruyter.

Rawlins, W. K., & Holl, M. R. (1987). The communicative achievement of friendship during adolescence: Predicaments of trust and violation. *Western Journal of Speech Communication, 51,* 345–363.

Rawlins, W. K., & Holl, M. R. (1988). Adolescents' interaction with parents and friends: Dialectics of temporal perspective and evaluation. *Journal of Social and Personal Relationships, 5,* 27–46.

Reisman, J. M. (1990). Intimacy in same-sex friendships. *Sex Roles, 23,* 65–82.

Rose, S., & Serafica, F. C. (1986). Keeping and ending casual, close and best friendships. *Journal of Social and Personal Relationships, 3,* 275–288.

Snell, W. F., Miller, R. S., Belk, S. S., Garcia-Falconi, R., & Hernandez-Sanchez, J. E. (1989). Men's and women's emotional disclosures: The impact of disclosure recipient, culture, and the masculine role. *Sex Roles, 21,* 467–486.

Sternbach, N. S. (1991). Re-membering the dead: Latin American women's "testimonial" discourse. *Latin American Perspectives, 18*(3), 91–102.

Weiss, L., & Lowenthal, M. F. (1975). Life-course perspectives on friendship. In M. F. Lowenthal, M. Thurnher, & D. Chiriboga (Eds.), *Four stages of life* (pp. 48–61). San Francisco: Jossey-Bass.

Wiseman, J. P. (1986). Friendship: Bonds and binds in a voluntary relationship. *Journal of Social and Personal Relationships, 3,* 191–211.

Wright, P. H. (1978). Toward a theory of friendship based on a conception of self. *Human Communication Research, 4*(3), 196–207.

Wright, P. H (1982). Men's friendships, women's friendships, and the alleged inferiority of the latter. *Sex Roles, 8,* 1–20.

Wright, P. H. (1984). Self-referent motivation and the intrinsic quality of friendship. *Journal of Social and Personal Relationships, 1,* 115–130.

12

From Passion to Commitment: Turning Points in Romantic Relationships

Connie Bullis
University of Utah

Carolyn Clark
University of Utah

Rick Sline
University of Utah

Thirty years ago, Bolton (1961) asserted the importance of the turning point as a unit of analysis for understanding the development of romantic relationships. Since that time, relatively few studies have been conducted that examine this potentially important "window for understanding" the ups and downs of romantic associations between women and men. At the same time, relational scholars have increasingly adopted relational theories that are consistent with turning point analysis. For example, in introducing several essays, Duck (1988) cited his own earlier contention that "relational development should not be assumed to be smooth rather than jerky; steady in growth rather than marked by times of activity and inactivity; continuous rather than discontinuous; and characterized by smooth growth curves rather than steps and plateaux" (p. 363). Turning point analysis provides a means of empirically exploring a rich array of questions and issues associated with this contemporary view of relationship development. In spite of its proven value in past studies and its rich potential for the empirical study of current theories, turning point analysis has been under used to date.

Turning point analysis has been profitably used to study the rate of change in romantic relationships (Huston, Surra, Fitzgerald, & Cate, 1981); general reasons for turning points (Lloyd & Cate, 1984; Surra, 1984; Surra, Arizzi, & Asmussen, 1988); how particular events function in a variety of ways to create changes in relationships (Bullis & Baxter, 1985); commitment processes (Surra et al., 1988); organizational socialization (Bullis & Bach, 1989a; Kirk & Todd-Mancillas, 1989); and mentor relationships (Bullis & Bach,

1989b). Baxter and Bullis (1986) pointed out that studies of relationship dis-engagement (Baxter, 1986; Cody, 1982), expressing "I love you" (Nydick & Cornelius, 1984), and physical affection (Wilmot & Baxter, 1984) focused on specific turning points. These studies emphasize the complex details of relational evolution. Baxter and Bullis suggest that thorough turning point analysis can provide an in-depth view of relationship development, which includes both details and generalizations.

Baxter and Bullis (1986) investigated turning point events that people report as being significant in their evolving romantic relationships. These researchers conceptualized a turning point as "any event or occurrence that is associated with change in a relationship" (p. 470). They claimed that turning points are central to understanding relationships as processes. Moreover, turning point analysis holds potential for examining trajectories of relational development and for testing a variety of models such as Altman and Taylor's (1973) model of gradual increases in commitment, Knapp's (1984) step model, and a more recently accepted dialectic view (Altman, Vinsel, & Brown, 1981; Baxter, 1988). Turning point analysis allows for an examination of change while also linking change to a sense of continuity. The sense of continuity is fundamental to differentiating ongoing relationships from disparate momentary states of relationships (Duck & Sants, 1983). Before turning point analysis realizes this potential, a basic descriptive profile of turning point events needs to be developed.

Baxter and Bullis' (1986) exploratory study identified a descriptive base of turning point types. In their effort to increase our understanding of the descriptive nature of turning points, Baxter and Bullis (1986) identified 26 distinct phenomena that comprised turning point events for their sample. Their findings provided "tentative support for a view of relationship growth as a series of discrete events that are accompanied by positive or negative explosions of relational commitment" (p. 486). Baxter and Bullis also suggested a variety of rich directions that turning point research could take in the future. They explored several relationships between turning points and relational phenomena such as metacommunication, relational satisfaction, and partner agreement. One major problem in their study, however, is that they assumed that their descriptive base derived from their college student sample should be accepted as a basis for further work with the general population. Prior to its general use, both the set of turning point types derived from this college student sample and the validity of associations between turning points and other relational variables need to be tested with different samples.

The study reported in this chapter extends turning point analysis in two ways. It explores associations between turning point types and both intentionality (events set up by one or both partners for the specific purpose of changing commitment to the relationship) and relational turbidity (fluctuations in commitment throughout the course of the relationship).

Turning Point Types

One purpose of this examination is to test the Baxter and Bullis (1986) typology and findings using a more mature sample than their college-age (18–22) sample. The prevalent use of college student samples in the study of evolving dating relationships is a major source of concern (cf. Tolhuizen, 1989). We risk developing knowledge and theory about college students and mistakenly generalizing from such knowledge and theory to society in general. Moreover, theories may be better tested and perfected through comparative studies. Although we might expect that relational dynamics differ depending on age and life stage, comparative studies are not available. By replicating the turning point study with a more mature group of participants, we should be able both to explore the generalizability of the college-age student turning point types and associated findings and to generate comparisons between an older sample and college student sample. The present study is based on romantic partners who are 25 years of age or older. (Although we recognize that college-age students (18–22) are adults, for ease of distinction we interchangeably refer to the more mature sample in the current study as the "adult sample," the "older sample," or the "over-25 sample.")

Our first research (R) questions examined Baxter and Bullis' turning point types:

R_{1a}: What phenomena comprise relationship turning points in the perception of adult romantic relationship partners?

R_{1b}: How do adult turning points compare in content and distribution with those from the college-age sample?

Relational Communication

The value of relationship talk, or metacommunication about the relationship, has been debated for some time. Watzlawick, Beavin, and Jackson (1967) argued that the increased presence of metacommunication is a sign of an unhealthy relationship, whereas Rossiter (1974) asserted that it is a sign of healthy relationships. Fisher (1987) claimed that direct relationship talk can be helpful to some developing relationships, although harmful to others. Baxter and Wilmot (1985) found direct relationship talk to be the most avoided topic of conversation reported by people in developing relationships, presumably out of fear that such talk would have an adverse effect on the relationship. Reherman and Bullis (1989) found that certain kinds of relationship talk contribute to the growth of developing relationships more than others, and that the practice of engaging in relationship talk increases with age.

Studies of relationship talk among spouses are equally inconclusive. For example, Bernal and Baker (1979) reported that relationship talk decreases conflict between marriage partners. Acitelli (1988) reported that relationship talk engaged in by fictional characters appeared to positively affect readers' ratings of the fictional characters' feelings. However, the pleasantness of the situation and the gender of the participants appeared to relate to relationship talk in complex ways.

Contrary to the general notion that people avoid relationship talk in developing romantic relationships, Baxter and Bullis (1986) found that college-age participants reported relationship talk during or after 55% of all turning point events. By probing particular turning point types, they were able to discover that some events were more associated with relationship talk than others, proffering a more detailed basis from which to develop explanations than had been available. They pointed out that some events would be difficult to accomplish without relationship talk. Relational talk was frequently associated with *Disengagement*, and may prevent permanent dissolutions. On the other hand, they concluded that relational points during which the relationship is particularly vulnerable, such as *Get-to-Know Time* and *Physical Separation*, tend to involve less relational talk.

Given the confusion and complexities of direct relationship talk, the role that age plays in the tendency to use this talk, and the centrality of such talk to relational dynamics, the second pair of research questions in this study asks:

R_{2a}: Do partners over 25 report differences across turning point types in their proportionate use of relationship talk?

R_{2b}: How do adult patterns compare with those of the college-age sample?

Partner Agreement

Baxter and Bullis (1986) noted that, although considerable work has been conducted on the separate conceptual realities held by partners in romantic relationships (cf. Sillars & Scott, 1983), very little of this work has focused specifically on the degree of shared recollection of relationship turning points. Strong correlations (.80) between partners' relationship commitment levels have been discovered (Huston, et al., 1981) but agreement on the nature of events associated with changes in commitment may or may not be as highly correlated.

Baxter and Bullis (1986) found an overall 54.5% agreement level between partners on all turning points. They reported that their findings were comparable to researchers' reports of partner agreement in monitoring daily behavior (Christensen & Nies, 1980; Jacobson & Moore, 1981).

Baxter and Bullis (1986) simplistically interpreted their findings as supporting the assumption that partners "coexist in separate phenomenological relationship worlds" (p. 488). However, their findings may be interpreted differently by pointing out that dyadic partners agreed on more than half of their turning points. This suggests more agreement than disagreement. We suggest that, as they point out elsewhere in their discussion, certain turning point types may tend to be agreed upon, whereas others tend to be individually perceived. Rather than simplifying agreement as a crude quantitative measure, agreement should be used as a more complex index of both similarity and difference in the construction of relational experiences (Duck, 1977). By examining specific turning point types for agreement, we may explore and articulate which relational experiences tend to be jointly constructed and which relational experiences tend to be individually constructed. This provides a means of exploring the interplay of psychological and relational perspectives. Certain turning point types were more highly agreed upon than others. Specifically, those which were more readily objectively verifiable were more frequently agreed upon than were those turning point events that were subjectively and individually experienced. For example, *Reunion*, *Exclusivity*, *Serious Commitment*, and *Get-to-Know Time* were more frequently agreed upon, whereas *Positive Psychic Change*, *Quality Time*, *Sacrifice*, and *External Competition* were not. In order to test Baxter and Bullis' (1986) findings with an adult sample, our third set of research questions examines partner agreement about turning points:

R_{3a}: To what extent do relationship partners over the age of 25 agree in their identification of turning point types?

R_{3b}: How do agreement levels on turning points for adults compare with those found in the college-age sample?

R_{3c}: Do some specific kinds of events tend to be agreed upon more than others?

Relationship Satisfaction

Baxter and Bullis (1986) investigated several questions regarding the relationship between turning points and current level of relationship satisfaction. Pursuing Sillars and Scott's (1983) tentative conclusion that an association exists between partners' perceptual congruence and relational satisfaction, Baxter and Bullis (1986) found an insignificant correlation ($r = .08$; $p = .25$) between current satisfaction and proportion of identified turning points on which the partners agreed. They suggested that the lack of relationship between agreement and relational satisfaction further supports the contention that partners can not only function, but function successfully in their relationships in spite of these disparate phenomenological relational worlds.

As a further test of the frequently debated question about the value of open relationship talk (Bochner, 1982; Parks, 1982), Baxter and Bullis (1986) explored the correlation between relationship satisfaction and the proportion of turning points that involved relationship talk. However, they found no statistically significant correlation ($r = .09$; $p = .22$).

In addition, Baxter and Bullis (1986) examined the extent to which the presence or absence of particular turning point types is associated with relationship satisfaction. College-age respondents who experienced *Exclusivity* turning points were generally more satisfied with their relationships than those who had not. They also found that those who experienced *Disengagement* were less satisfied than those who did not. Some individual events, then, may have a lasting impact on relationship satisfaction, whereas others may function in either more cumulative or ephemeral ways.

In order to further test these relationships between turning points and relationship satisfaction, the fourth set of research questions probes:

R_{4a}:   To what extent do turning point type, partner agreement on the identification of turning points, and relationship talk surrounding turning points correlate with current relationship satisfaction for partners over the age of 25?

R_{4b}:   How do these correlations compare with the college-age sample?

Strategic Intentionality

Relationship researchers have often assumed that partners engage in interpersonal relationships strategically in order to accomplish personal and relational goals. For example, strategies involved in specific relational accomplishments such as disengagement (Baxter, 1982), compliance gaining (Berger, 1985), gaining information (Baxter & Wilmot, 1984), and date seeking (Berger, 1988) have been studied. However, the strategic, intentional nature of such accomplishments has typically been assumed rather than empirically questioned. Moreover, this research has focused on narrow, specific goals rather than on intentionality as a broader issue. Duck and Sants (1983, p. 28), labeling the assumption of intentionality as one of four "unwanted heirlooms," argued that people are not necessarily intentional in their relational choices. Rather, "at some times people may not really know what they are doing, even if at other times they are very much aware of their intentions, strategies, and purposes" (Duck & Sants, 1983, p. 31). Similarly, Langer's (1978) well-known research on mindlessness implies that people are not regularly intentional in their interactions. The analysis of intentionality in relationship turning points provides an opportunity to assess the presence or absence of intentionality across a wider spectrum of meaningful relational events. If turning point events are more often purposefully created by partners rather than being typically serendipitous, such findings would lend support to the contention that relational development should be studied as a function of intentional strategies. At the same time, turning point analysis encourages a more detailed analysis of this issue. We may explore the complexities of intentionality by comparing intentionality across turning point types. The fifth question in extension of Baxter and Bullis' (1986) work relates to whether specific turning point events were intentionally created by one or both of the partners as a means of intentionally changing relational commitment.

R$_5$:   To what extent are turning point events intentionally created by one or both partners in a relationship?

Relational Turbidity

Finally, we draw on uncertainty speculations to further explore the influence of turning points on relationship satisfaction. According to Duck and Sants (1983), people often sanitize their relational histories as they retrospectively create stories to tell what happened. They omit the uncertainties, complexities, and anxieties that they regularly report in daily accounts. Because turning point analysis does not assume that retrospective accounts are coherent narrative forms, turning point analysis allows for retrospective accounts that include these complexities and uncertainties. Although the focus on individual turning points provides a means for such specific uncertainties to be expressed, turning point analysis at the same time allows for exploration of broader patterns of uncertainty. Duck and Sants (1983) argued that traditional assumptions about uncertainty reduction, such as Berger and Calabrese (1975), do not hold beyond initial encounters. Once uncertainty about the other person is reduced, uncertainty about the other's true feelings toward oneself becomes "one of the great human dilemmas" (Duck & Sants, 1983, p. 37). Similarly, Bullis and Baxter (1985) argued that turning points represent shifting types of uncertainties. As uncertainty about one area, such as uncertainty about the other person, is resolved, a different area of uncertainty, such as uncertainty about the relationship, becomes salient.

One untapped potential of turning point analysis is to explore relationship uncertainty and a variety of relational variables and dynamics. Our exploration of relational turbidity or fluctuating levels of commitment provides one example of this potential. We conceptualize the total number of turning points in a relational history account as an index of turbidity. This global measure enables an exploration of the association between relational turbidity and relational satisfaction.

On the one hand, common sense suggests that high turbidity may be positively related to satisfaction. Turbidity may be associated with the dynamic life of an exciting relationship whereas certainty could engender boredom. On the other hand, uncertainty reduction theory posits that uncertainty reduction is a goal of interpersonal relationships; thus low turbidity would be positively related to satisfaction. To the extent that the number of turning points can be considered as a measure of relational turbidity, the relationship between the number of turning points and relational satisfaction should shed light on these speculations.

R_6:   To what extent does the number of turning points correlate with current relationship satisfaction in adults?

METHODS

Sample

The sample consisted of 62 individuals who were partners from 31 romantic couples ($N = 62$). A "romantic couple" was operationalized as a couple who were involved in an exclusive relationship. Following Baxter and Bullis (1986), only couples who had been in the relationship for at least 6 months were included in the sample. The length of relationships ranged from 6 to 85 months, with an average length of 28.4 months. This appears similar to the 22.1 months reported in Baxter and Bullis' study. Therefore, our confidence in the comparability of samples is strengthened. Respondents' ages ranged from 25 to 53 years, with an average age of 33.6. Because respondents came from a geographical area where there is a high concentration of membership in the Church of Jesus Christ of Latter Day Saints (LDS), religion was also included as a demographic factor in this study. Although Surra et al. (1988) reported that membership in the LDS religion did not lead to different relational patterns among spouses, it seemed reasonable to record religious preference in case it was found to be an intervening variable. The sample included 22 who indicated an LDS preference, 19 with other religious preferences, and 21 with no stated religious preference. Analyses were conducted on all of the study variables to determine whether religious differences were evident. No differences were found, so religion was not included as a variable in the final report.

Replicating Baxter and Bullis, Granovetter's (1976) "network sampling" technique was used. After a list of participants was compiled, interviewers were assigned to romantic partners whom they did not know personally. Participants from the first set of interviews were then asked to supply names of additional couples from their own social networks. These individuals were then invited to participate in the study.

Measures

This study replicated the procedures of Baxter and Bullis (1986) in their study of turning points. Huston et al.'s (1981) Retrospective Interview Technique (RIT) was used to elicit turning point data. This method is consistent with Duck and Sants' (1983, p. 33) claim that it is important to consider "thoughts, feelings, and imaginative work outside the face-to-face interactions of the relationship" because interaction approaches risk ignoring the insiders' experiences. The RIT uses descriptions of actual events as well as participants' interpretations of these events. In this methodology, respondents chronologically plot the turning points in their relationships on a graph. Monthly intervals from the date the relationship began until the date of the interview are marked on the abscissa axis. The ordinate axis represents the interviewee's sense of commitment to the relationship on a 0% to 100% scale. As each turning point is plotted, the interviewer requests detailed information about it.

Following Baxter and Bullis, an adaptation of Lloyd's (1983) interview script supplemented the graphing procedure. The interview commenced with an explanation of the purpose of the study and an assurance of confidentiality. Respondents then labeled their own graphs. They were asked to locate as the starting point on the abscissa the month when the relationship began, and to mark off monthly intervals from that point. As in the Baxter and Bullis (1986) study, the meaning of commitment was not specified, allowing respondents to formulate their own definitions of commitment because this more accurately reflects the participants' sense of commitment than does the likelihood of marriage measure.

Next the participants located anchor points on the graph by plotting their level of commitment when the relationship first began as well as their present level of commitment. They then returned to the beginning and indicated on the graph the first turning point, or change, in their level of commitment.

As respondents plotted the turning point, the interviewer elicited further information. Topics that were probed include: (a) the nature of the event that led to the change in commitment, (b) why it resulted in a change, (c) whether one or both partners intentionally planned the event as a means of affecting the commitment level, (d) whether the partners talked with each other about what the event meant in terms of their relationship (metacommunication), and (e) anything else that the respondent thought the researcher should know about the turning point. After discussing the turning point, the respondent was asked to fill in the connecting line between the previous point and the point that was currently being discussed, and to describe the relationship during that interval. This cycle was repeated until all turning points had been plotted. Respondents were then given an opportunity to look back over the graph and make adjustments.

Finally, interviewees completed Norton's (1983) six-item marital satisfaction scale. Baxter and Bullis (1986) argued that this scale is equally valid for unmarried romantic partners because it is largely based on the Dyadic Adjustment Scale (Spanier, 1976), which applies to any close romantic relationship.

Procedures

Trained interviewers contacted their respondents to schedule RIT interview times. To prevent contamination of the data, most interviews were scheduled so that partners were interviewed back-to-back in their homes or at their work places. Interviews lasted approximately 1 to 1½ hours each. After the interviews were completed, the RIT graphs, the satisfaction measure scales, the tapes of the interviews, and a written summary of each interview were retained for analysis.

Data Analysis

A team of coders reviewed a subset of the interview data and independently categorized the turning points into the 26 turning point types identified by Baxter and Bullis (1986). When turning points did not fit into the existing categories, new categories were created. The coders reached intercoder reliability of .79 using Cohen's kappa (Cohen, 1960). After establishing the level of reliability, one coder categorized the remaining turning points.

Two-category systems were used to code partner agreement in the identification of turning points, intentionality, and relational talk. For each turning point, coders used *yes* and *no* categories. Intercoder reliabilities were established as .85 for agreement. One coder then coded the remainder of the turning points into agreement. Relational talk and intentionality were coded, based on interviewees' self-reports of whether or not the turning point involved relational talk.

The overall satisfaction score for each respondent consisted of the sum of values reported for all six items. Internal reliability of the satisfaction scale, measured by Cronbach's alpha, was .93.

RESULTS

Turning Point Types

Research Questions 1a and 1b focused on the phenomena that comprise turning points in the adult sample and in the Baxter and Bullis (1986) sample of college-age students. Five hundred twenty-three (523) turning point events were identified with an average of 8.6 events per respondent and a range of 2–19 events.

The 26 categories inductively derived by Baxter and Bullis (1986) were tested by categorizing the data into them. Four new categories were added to account for additional reported types of events. One category identified previously was not used by the current sample. This resulted in a total of 29 turning point types, grouped within 17 overarching supratypes. A comparison of frequency and percentage distributions between the Baxter and Bullis study and this research is reported in Table 12.1.

The supratype *Get-To-Know Time* was the most frequently mentioned by respondents in both studies and is composed of three turning point events, all of which are common ways for people to get to know one another. *First Meeting* refers to when the partners met. *Activity Time* refers to a number of early relationship events, such as going skiing or hiking together. *First Date* is the event that the respondent identified as being the first woman–man, formal date.

The supratype *Quality Time* is also comprised of three turning point types. Each is described as a social occasion that created a forum for the couple to focus on the value of their relationship. *Quality Time* represents those occasions that the couple spent together simply enjoying each other's company without the focus of a particular external activity. The occasion of *Meeting the Family* was often particularly significant for respondents in that it served as a sign that the relationship was important enough to the couple that they wanted to bring one another into their intimate networks. *Getting Away Time* refers to a variety of routine-breaking events, ranging from going camping together to more extravagant trips to Europe. In each case, respondents identified the turning point, not so much for its value as a commodity, but rather for the opportunity it afforded to truly focus on each other and the relationship. *Meeting the Family* and *Getting Away Time* each represented approximately twice the proportion of total turning points for the older sample as it did for Baxter and Bullis' college-aged sample. However, this was clearly not the case for nonspecified *Quality Time* turning points, which represented a significantly larger proportion of the total turning point events for the younger sample than it did for the older sample.

Physical Separation is one of eight turning point types that constitutes its own supratype. It refers to events that do not result from disengagements or breaks in the relationship, but rather from events such as extended vacations or temporary job transfers. Adults reported this turning point proportionately less frequently than did college students.

Three turning point types make up the supratype, *External Competition*. *New Rival* refers to the arrival of a third person on the scene who is reported to compete for the affection of one of the partners. *Old Rival* refers to the re-emergence of a former significant other. *Competing Demands* includes other nonromantic competition for one or the other party's attention. Such demands typically included work, family, sports, and church commitments. Respondents from the two samples reported similar proportions of these turning points.

TABLE 12.1.
Distribution of Turning Point Types

Types	College-Age Sample Frequencies (N = 759)	%	Adult Sample Frequencies (N = 523)	%	χ^2
1. GET-TO-KNOW-TIME	144	19.0	89	17.0	3.08
A. First Meeting	80	10.5	49	9.4	.10
B. Activity Time	46	6.1	30	5.7	.01
C. First Date	18	2.4	10	1.9	.06
2. QUALITY TIME	117	15.4	59	11.3	2.88
A. Quality Time	85	11.2	18	3.4	20.33**
B. Meet the Family	17	2.2	21	4.0	3.23
C. Getting Away Time	15	2.0	20	3.8	3.76
3. PHYSICAL SEPARATION	76	10.0	24	4.6	9.65*
4. EXTERNAL COMPETITION	70	9.2	58	11.1	1.46
A. New Rival	39	5.1	24	4.6	.02
B. Competing Demands	16	2.1	19	3.6	2.52
C. Old Rival	15	2.0	15	2.9	3.13
5. REUNION	57	7.5	12	2.3	13.42**
6. PASSION	48	6.3	18	3.4	4.25*
A. First Sex	23	3.0	10	1.9	.86
B. First Kiss	10	1.3	2	.4	#
C. "I Love You"	9	1.2	5	1.0	#
D. Whirlwind Phenomenon	6	.8	1	.2	#
7. DISENGAGEMENT	46	6.1	24	4.6	.64
8. POSITIVE PSYCHIC CHANGE	42	5.5	7	1.3	12.17**
9. EXCLUSIVITY	34	4.5	19	3.6	.01
A. Joint Exclusivity Decision	23	3.0	2	.4	9.20*
B. Dropping All Rivals	11	1.4	17	3.2	3.75
10. NEGATIVE PSYCHIC CHANGE	29	3.8	0	0.0	17.46**
11. MAKING UP	25	3.3	5	1.0	5.72*
12. SERIOUS COMMITMENT	24	3.2	47	9.0	18.72**
A. Living Together	13	1.7	21	4.0	6.02*
B. Marital Plans	11	1.4	26	5.0	13.20**
13. SACRIFICE	23	3.0	38	7.3	10.33**
A. Crisis Help	14	1.8	17	3.2	2.37
B. Favors or Gifts	9	3.2	21	4.0	10.28**
14. COMMITMENT TENSION	-	-	39	7.4	-
15. RELATIONAL TALK	-	-	14	2.7	-
16. NEGATIVE EVALUATION	-	-	25	4.8	-
17. POSITIVE EVALUATION	-	-	21	4.0	-
18. OTHER	24	3.2	24	4.6	1.72

– Commitment Tension, Relational Talk, Negative Evaluation, and Positive Evaluation were not identified as supratype turning points in the Baxter and Bullis (1986) study.

#Insufficient expected frequencies to compute Chi Square.

*p < .05. **p < .001.

Reunion is a single-event supratype that refers to the reuniting of the partners after a *Physical Separation*. *Reunion*, like *Physical Separation*, was reported significantly less often by respondents from the over-25 sample than the college-age sample. The supratype, *Passion*, refers to turning point events that involve some sort of physical or emotional expression of affection between the partners. Included within this supratype are *First Sex*, *First Kiss*, the expression of *I Love You* and the *Whirlwind Phenomenon*, which refers to the proverbial love-at-first-sight experience. Overall, approximately half the proportion of adult respondents reported *Passion* compared to the younger sample. Proverbial love-at-first-sight *Whirlwind Experience* represented only 8% and 2% of the total turning points reported in the younger and older samples respectively.

Disengagement is a single-event supratype that refers to a reduction in relational commitment, including events such as quarrels, fights, or total breakups. Conversely, *Making Up* events are occurrences when the parties get back together after a disengagement. College-age respondents reported significantly more *Making Up* turning points than did adult respondents.

The supratypes *Positive Psychic Change* and *Negative Psychic Change* refer to intrapsychic fluctuations in a person's attitude or feeling toward the relationship, which were not reported to be triggered by an external event. *Positive Psychic Change* was reported significantly less by the adult sample and *Negative Psychic Change* was not reported at all. Instead, two new categories were identified. These categories, *Positive Evaluation* and *Negative Evaluation*, occurred when respondents observed their partners' behaviors and drew conclusions regarding the suitability or desirability of the partner. For example, when one woman observed that her partner enjoyed her children, she drew the positive conclusion that he would "fit" with her family, an important point for her. These categories differed from psychic change in that respondents specified the basis of their evaluation.

Exclusivity is a supratype consisting of two turning point events, *Joint Exclusivity Decision* and *Dropping All Rivals*. The former is a conscious, proactive decision made by a couple to engage in a single relationship, whereas the latter is the decision by one party to cease all other romances in order to maintain a monogamous relationship. Although the proportions for this supratype in each sample were nearly the same, respondents from the Baxter and Bullis (1986) study reported a significantly higher proportion of *Joint Exclusivity Decisions* than did respondents from the current study. The opposite was true for *Dropping All Rivals*, but the differences were not significant.

The supratype *Serious Commitment* includes *Living Together*, which denotes the act of moving in with one another to share households, and *Marital Plans*, which is often symbolized through formal engagement. Respondents from the over-25 sample reported a significantly higher proportion of *Serious Commitment* turning points than did respondents from the college-age sample. The adult sample reported significantly more *Living Together* turning points as well as *Marital Plans* turning points than did the college-age sample.

The supratype *Sacrifice* includes two turning point types. *Crisis Help* refers to one party's helping the other through a difficult time. *Favors and Gifts* refers to a more material sacrifice of providing gifts or favors to a partner as a means of expressing commitment to a relationship. Adults reported a significantly higher proportion of *Sacrifice* than did the college-age sample. The turning point type *Favors or Gifts* composed the majority of this difference.

Baxter and Bullis (1986) placed the remaining turning points (3.2%) into an *Other* category due to insufficient frequency of similar types. In this study, however, four additional turning point types emerged. Four and eight-tenths percent (4.8%) of the turning point types remained to be categorized as "*Other*."

Two new supratypes, *Negative Evaluation* and *Positive Evaluation*, have been described. The third new supratype category, *Commitment Tension*, involves turning points in which the partners' commitment levels were at odds. It includes a number of turning point events that respondents often described as a trepidation toward making a commitment to another person. Some referred to this as a momentary "commitment phobia" or simply a feeling of being closed-in as a result of spending too much time together. Others referred to it as a pushing for more commitment in reaction to their partners' lessening commitment. *Commitment Tension* represented 7.8% of the total turning point types in the current study.

The fourth new supratype category is *Relational Talk*. This category must be differentiated from the more general role of relationship talk in each turning point event that was examined in Research Questions 2a and 2b. For some turning points, the actual process of discussing the relationship, independent of any other particular event, constituted the reported event.

Relationship Talk

Overall, 57.3% of all turning point events involved relationship talk. This percentage is similar to the 55.1% found by Baxter and Bullis (1986).

Table 12.2 displays the proportions of each supratype of turning point that involved relationship talk for both samples. A chi-square test demonstrated that differences in the present sample were significant [$\chi^2(16, N = 523) = 67.89, p < .0001$]. The coefficient of contingency, a measure of association for categorical variables was computed ($C = .35$). *Get-To-Know-Time, Positive Psychic Change, Physical Separation*, and *Reunion* were least likely (less than the average 57.5%) to involve relationship talk for the over-25 sample. Conversely, *Making Up, Disengagement, Negative Evaluation, Serious Commitment*, and *Commitment Tension* were turning point supratypes that were most likely to involve relationship talk in the present sample.

TABLE 12.2.
Percentage of Turning Point Types that Involved Relationship Talk

Turning Point Supratype	College-Age Sample	Adult Sample
Get-To-Know Time	19.8	22.2
Quality Time	59.4	57.9
Physical Separation	37.3	50.0
External Competition	59.0	55.2
Reunion	50.0	50.0
Passion	76.7	64.7
Disengagement	79.1	83.3
Positive Psychic Change	65.2	16.7
Exclusivity	90.9	68.4
Negative Psychic Change	61.9	0.0
Making Up	86.4	100.0
Serious Commitment	77.3	72.3
Sacrifice	20.0	69.4
Commitment Tension	*	71.1
Relational Talk	*	57.1
Negative Evaluation	*	79.2
Positive Evaluation	*	55.0
Overall	55.1	57.3

*Commitment Tension, Relational Talk, Negative Evaluation, and Positive Evaluation were not identified as supratype turning points in Baxter and Bullis' (1986) study.

Differences between the percentage of each supratype involving relationship talk in the college-age sample and those in the adult sample were generally not significant, with one exception. *Sacrifice* seldom involved relationship talk in the college-age sample (20.0%) whereas it frequently involved relationship talk in the adult sample (69.4%), $\chi^2(1, N = 61) = 5.39, p < .025$.

Partner Agreement

The third research question focused on partner agreement on turning points. Table 12.3 displays the comparative data on partner agreement. Adult partners agreed on a total of 57.8% of all turning points. This is similar to the college sample agreement on 54.5% of all turning points. A chi-square test indicated that the turning point types differed in their proportions of partner agreement $\chi^2 (16, N = 523) = 57.84, p < .0001, C = .38$. Partner agreement was lower with regard to supratypes *Quality Time, Passion, Sacrifice, Positive Psychic Change*, and *Relational Talk*. Partner agreement was high with regard to supratypes *Get-to-Know Time, Reunion, Making Up, Serious Commitment, Commitment Tension*, and *Positive Evaluation*.

In the Baxter & Bullis (1986) study, agreement was higher on *Passion*,

TABLE 12.3.
Percent of Turning Point Types About Which Partners Agreed

Turning Point Supratype	College-Age Sample	Adult Sample
Get-to-Know Time	68.8	81.5
Quality Time	45.3	34.0
Physical Separation	53.9	57.1
External Competition	42.0	56.8
Reunion	63.2	87.5
Passion	50.0	28.6
Disengagement	56.5	57.9
Positive Psychic Change	38.1	42.9
Exclusivity	67.6	50.0
Negative Psychic Change	48.3	*
Making Up	56.0	75.0
Serious Commitment	75.0	80.6
Sacrifice	30.4	31.6
Commitment Tension	*	74.1
Relational Talk	*	21.4
Negative Evaluation	*	56.3
Positive Evaluation	*	75.0
Overall	54.5	57.8

Positive Psychic Change, *Exclusivity*, and *Quality Time*, whereas it was lower on *Making Up*, *Reunion*, *Get to Know Time*, and *External Competition*.

Relational Satisfaction

The fourth group of research questions examined the extent to which current satisfaction with the relationship correlates with metacommunication, agreement, and the presence or absence of particular turning point supratypes. As in the Baxter and Bullis results, there were no significant correlations between the proportion of turning points about which respondents reported metacommunicating ($r = -.1203$) or the proportion of turning points about which partners agreed ($r = -.1445$).

In t-tests of whether relational satisfaction differed depending on the presence or absence of each supratype, two supratypes showed significant differences. Respondents who reported the presence of *Negative Evaluation* reported significantly less relational satisfaction ($M = 32.2$) than did respondents who did not report the presence of *Negative Evaluation* ($M = 37.6$), $t(56) = 2.28$, $p < .03$. Respondents who reported a *Serious Commitment* turning point reported significantly higher relational satisfaction ($M = 38.6$) than those who did not ($M = 33.6$, $t(38) = 2.41$, $p = .021$).

These results were similar to those in the college-age sample in that one important positive and one important negative event were associated with relational satisfaction. They differ in that the particular turning point events involved are not the same turning point types. The particular events in the other study were *Exclusivity* and *Disengagement*.

Strategic Intentionality

Of the 523 total turning points reported by respondents in this study, 35.3% were reportedly intentionally created by one or both partners, whereas 64.7% were not. A Chi-square test indicated that there are significant differences across turning point types in their respective tendencies toward being reported as having been intentionally created by one or both partners $\chi^2(16, N = 523) = 37/94, p < .002, C = .27$. Table 12.4 indicates that *Get-to-Know Time, Disengagement, Positive Psychic Change*, and *Positive Evaluation* were the types which least frequently involved intentionality. *Quality Time, Exclusivity, Making Up, Relational Talk*, and *Commitment Tension* most frequently involved intentionality.

Relational Turbidity

The sixth research question investigated the influence that the number of turning points reported in an account has on the level of relational satisfaction.

TABLE 12.4.
Percent of Adult Turning Point Events Involving Intentionality

Get-to-Know Time	18.9
Quality Time	50.9
Physical Separation	30.4
External Competition	32.8
Reunion	41.7
Passion	29.4
Disengagement	25.0
Positive Psychic Change	00.0
Exclusivity	47.4
Negative Psychic Change	60.0
Making Up	43.5
Serious Commitment	40.5
Sacrifice	52.6
Commitment Tension	57.1
Relational Talk	33.3
Negative Evaluation	15.0
Positive Evaluation	20.0
Overall	54.5

The average number of turning points per account showed a negative correlation with satisfaction (r $-.30$, $p = .05$).

DISCUSSION

One purpose of the study reported in this chapter was to test Baxter and Bullis' (1986) turning point types and associated findings about romantic relationships with a sample that was not comprised of college-age youths. Results from the older age group in the current sample confirmed most of Baxter and Bullis' (1986) categories and findings. Four new supratypes, *Negative Evaluation*, *Positive Evaluation*, *Commitment Tension*, and *Relational Talk* emerged, whereas one of the original categories, *Negative Psychic Change*, was not mentioned by this adult sample. Otherwise, the categories were directly relevant to this adult sample, although there were some differences in the prevalence of specific turning point types.

Passion was mentioned almost twice as many times in the younger sample as compared to the over-25 sample. This suggests that the focus on passion as a turning point may lessen in the older age group. We may speculate, based on this trend and the older sample's disproportionately high reporting of *Serious Commitment*, *Sacrifice*, and *Commitment Tension*, that the focus of the relationship may shift, with age, away from the romantic, physical aspects, to more long-term considerations such as long-term commitment and willingness to sacrifice for the sake of the relationship. *Negative Evaluation*, *Positive Evaluation*, and *Relational Talk* appear to be indicative of stronger attention to monitoring the relationship's long-term potential than was indicated in the younger sample. In addition, Baxter and Bullis' (1986) observation that the large percentage of *Physical Separation* and *Reunion* turning points in their sample could have been due to vacations, overseas trips, and school breaks inherent in their college sample is supported by the relatively lower proportions of these turning point types from this older population.

These differences indicate some relational foci, which may differ as a function of life stage. This confirms Duck and Sants' (1983) contention that researchers should consider how relationships fit into the history of participants' lives.

Overall, the proportion of turning points that were reportedly accompanied by relational talk was strikingly similar between the samples. Like Baxter and Bullis' results, these results indicate that people talk about the relationship selectively, with some turning point events involving more frequent and others less frequent relationship talk.

The turning points *Get-To-Know Time*, *Positive Psychic Change*, *Physical Separation*, and *Reunion* were least likely to involve relationship talk for the over-25 sample, whereas *Making Up*, *Disengagement*, *Negative Evaluation*, *Serious Commitment*, and *Commitment Tension* were turning point supratypes that were most likely to involve relationship talk. Like the adults, college students infrequently reported relational talk during *Get-to-Know Time* and *Physical Separation* and frequently reported relational talk during *Disengagement*, *Making Up*, and *Serious Commitment*. In contrast to the adults, the college-age students tended not to discuss *Positive Psychic Change* and *Sacrifice*, whereas they did tend to discuss *Passion*. Baxter and Bullis posited that points of vulnerability in the relationship may be points when relationship talk is infrequently used. The present results contradict that supposition for adult couples. In addition to *Disengagement*, two of the most vulnerable points, *Negative Evaluation* and *Commitment Tension*, were among the most frequently discussed turning point types. This seems to further support the notion that the focus of older couples shifts from romantic, passionate, concerns that are seen in younger couples, to those of establishing more serious, long-term romantic relationships. These concerns may require relational talk during times of vulnerability, which tend to be avoided by college-age people.

We posit that, among adult couples, the lack of relationship talk surrounding some turning points could indicate that the couples did not discuss points that were probably not going to seriously affect the relationship. The turning point types which were frequently the focus of relational talk were those that were more likely to have a serious effect on the relationship. At the same time, the amount of relationship talk may vary according to the stage of the relationship. At the same time, the amount of relationship talk may vary according to the stage of the relationship. In other words, during early phases, vulnerability may inhibit relational communication. Later, especially when the long-term desirability of the relationship is being weighed, vulnerability may instigate relational talk.

Surprisingly, there was a negative, though not statistically significant, correlation between proportions of turning points involving relationship talk and relational satisfaction. This finding underscores Baxter and Bullis' (1986) criticism of the "talk-as-elixir folk myth" (p. 487). Relationship talk does not necessarily lead to better relationships.

Overall, the proportion of turning points on which partners agreed was similar in the adult and college-age samples. These results support Baxter and Bullis' results. In both samples those events that are more objectively verifiable were most often agreed on, with the exception of *Exclusivity* which was infrequently agreed upon in the adult sample. The *Exclusivity* decision may not be as salient for these adults who more frequently articulate *Serious Commitment*. Based on these two studies, turning point analysis should be used to further explore coexistent, agreed-upon, relationship histories as well as the separate phenomenological worlds participants create. Turning point analysis may be used to extend exploration of the interplay between the two.

This study has both supported and contradicted the findings from Baxter and Bullis' (1986) study. Their more general findings were confirmed. Their

turning point typology was largely confirmed by the older adult sample with
one deletion and four additions. The overall associations between turning point
types and relational satisfaction, relational talk and partner agreement, were
confirmed. Baxter and Bullis' contention that objectively verifiable events tend
to be agreed upon was confirmed. The discovery that the presence of one negative and one positive turning point type is associated with relational satisfaction was confirmed. These findings should encourage future turning point
research as Baxter and Bullis advised. Turning point research should be pur-
sued for its contribution to the growing body of research on romantic relationship development patterns from the points of view of relational participants
and their attributions (Surra, 1990).

In addition, these findings underscore the need for continued caution in ex-
trapolating generalizations from college-age samples. Discrepancies between
the adult and college-age samples need to be taken into account in further
studies. This study demonstrates that overlapping but different typologies may
be needed for different age groups. Continuing refinement of the turning point
typology will need to account for both the similarities and differences of these
studies. Moreover, the role of specific turning point types in the overall evolution of relationships may differ across age groups. The relative frequency
of these events, as well as the relationship between relational talk and relational vulnerability also merit additional attention.

These results also point out some examples of additional uses to which turning point analysis can be put in exploring contemporary relational development issues. The discovery that intentionality was reported for only 35.3%
of the turning points calls into question the common assumption that relationships are created by strategic choices made by "mindful" relational partners.
Mindlessness (cf. Langer, 1978) may be more common than often assumed.
The volume of studies on strategies may be partially an artifact of the meth-
odologies employed. The respondents in this study articulate a far less intentional pattern. Most events, according to these respondents, are not intentionally
created. These results empirically support Duck and Sants' (1983) claim and
urge care in acknowledging both intentional and unintentional relational dynamics.

Some findings, which should be further probed, are the specific turning
point types that tend to be intentionally created and those that do not. We speculate that *Get-to-Know Time* and *Positive Psychic Change* indicate relational
dynamics, which occur due to circumstances such as proximity and situational demands. Surprisingly, participants also report little intentionality regarding *Disengagement*. This, too, may represent events participants experience
that are created more by contextual pressures than strategic choices. On the
other hand, participants report actively creating relational growth through some
events such as *Quality Time*, *Exclusivity*, and *Making Up*. *Relational Talk* is
typically strategically created as people consciously decide to discuss the rela-

tionship. It is curious that *Commitment Tension* is also frequently viewed as strategic. This likely represents participants' views of their ways of dealing with the dialectical tensions articulated by Baxter (1988). These reports of *Commitment Tension* may indicate that one strategy for dealing with dialectic tensions is for relational participants to alternately and reciprocally represent differing ends of the dialectic polarities. A post hoc closer examination of these accounts suggests that this strategy entails a complex, subtle negotiation between relational parties and suggests that one strategy of handling dialectical tensions not noted by Baxter is a mutually reciprocal seesaw strategy. Partners switch roles, each embodying one end of the dialectic for a time and then shifting to opposite ends. Turning point analysis enables exploration of such complexities while not sacrificing larger patterns of issues, such as total intentionality.

The number of turning points per account was shown to have a negative correlation with relationship satisfaction. The cumulative effect of turning points, or relationship change, appears to be negative. One possible explanation for this result is that uncertainty is experienced so negatively that relationships that develop in more steady, predictable ways with less ongoing uncertainties are more satisfying than those that develop erratically, creating continuous uncertainties. Relational turbidity, then, may create more uncertainty than is comfortable in the relationship. On the other hand, the satisfaction scale is based on factors such as the stability, strength, and teamwork perceived in the relationship. If commitment levels in the relationship fluctuate frequently, respondents might report lower values for such items. These findings regarding relational turbidity appear to contradict theories espousing the virtues of conflict (Phillips & Cheston, 1979; Robbins, 1978) and rather support traditional uncertainty reduction theory (Berger & Calabrese, 1975) as well as the central importance of "reward dependability" to the existence and continuation of significant interpersonal relationships (McCall & Simmons, 1978). This raises the speculation that the virtue of change may be a theoretical construct that is not borne out in the personal relational experiences of adults. Relational turbidity, as it relates to various types of uncertainty over time, needs to be probed further through turning point analysis. This highlights the importance of continuing to use turning point analysis in ways that focus on both broad relational patterns and detailed individual turning points.

This study has underscored the value of turning point research, both by providing a comparative examination of Baxter and Bullis' (1986) earlier work and exploring intentionality and turbidity through turning point analysis. It illustrates the ability of turning point analysis to (a) work back and forth between details and broad patterns, (b) unravel complex questions, (c) understand positive and negative changes, and (d) address a variety of contemporary issues. Future work should extend turning point analysis to more fully enact its rich potential in several ways only hinted at in this work. For example, through turning point analysis, several recommendations offered by Duck and Sants (1983), but rarely followed, could be enacted. They recommend, for example, treating partner differences as data. By comparing RIT graphs, this becomes possible. They recommend examining retrospective accounts at different points in time. The RIT procedure could be used for this purpose. Turning point analysis could be used to further empirically explore the strategies identified by Baxter (1988) and extended here as partners deal with dialectical tensions. Accounts of particular turning point types should be interpreted for how they shed light on broader cultural themes. As Baxter and Bullis (1986) noted, relational trajectories should be examined. With this wealth of potential, turning point analysis needs to be treated as a serious tool for helping to close the gap between contemporary theory and empirical work in relational development.

Turning points, then, provide an alternative lens through which to understand developing, maturing, and disintegrating relationships. Through examining turning points, we may understand relational change in more concrete detail than is possible by relying on broader models. A sense of mystery or vagueness associated with general trends is reduced by the addition of these specifics. Turning points may be viewed as associated with choices relational partners make to maintain, change, or terminate relationships. Through better understanding of such specific points, more conscious choices determining relational fates may be facilitated.

REFERENCES

Acitelli, L. K. (1988). When spouses talk to each other about their relationship. *Journal of Social and Personal Relationships*, 5, 185–199.

Altman, I., & Taylor, D. A. (1973). *Social penetration: The development of interpersonal relationships.* New York: Holt, Rinehart & Winston.

Altman, I., Vinsel., A., & Brown, B. (1981). Dialectic conceptions in social psychology: An application to social penetration and privacy regulation. In L. Berkowitz (Ed.), *Understanding personal relationships: An interdisciplinary approach* (Vol. 14, pp. 107–160). New York: Academic Press.

Baxter, L. A. (1982). Strategies for ending relationships: Two studies. *Western Journal of Speech Communication*, 46, 223–241.

Baxter, L. A. (1986). Gender differences in the heterosexual relationship rules embedded in break-up accounts. *Journal of Social and Personal Relationships*, 3(3), 289–306.

Baxter, L. A. (1988). Dialectical perspective on communication strategies in relational development. In S. Duck, D. Hay, S. Hobfoll, W. Ickes, & B. Montgomery (Eds.), *Handbook of personal relationships: Theory, research, and interventions* (pp. 257–273). Chichester, England: Wiley.

Baxter, L. A., & Bullis, C. (1986). Turning points in developing romantic relationships. *Human Communication Research*, 12(4), 469–493.

Baxter, L. A., & Wilmot, W. (1984). "Secret tests": Social strategies for acquiring information about the state of the relationship. *Human Communication Research*, 11, 171–201.

Baxter, L. A., & Wilmot, W. (1985). Taboo topics in close relationships. *Journal of Social and Personal Relationships*, *2*, 253–269.

Berger, C. R. (1985). Social power and interpersonal communication. In M. L. Knapp & G. R. Miller (Eds.), *Handbook of interpersonal communication* (pp. 439–399). Beverly Hills: Sage.

Berger, C. R. (1988). Planning, affect, and social action generation. In L. Donohew, H. Sypher, & E. T. Higgins (Eds.), *Communication, social cognition, and affect* (pp. 99–116). Hillsdale, NJ: Lawrence Erlbaum Associates.

Berger, C. R., & Calabrese, R. (1975). Some explorations in initial interaction and beyond: Toward a developmental theory of interpersonal communication. *Human Communication Research*, *1*, 99–112.

Bernal, G., & Baker, J. (1979). Toward a metacommunicational framework of couple interaction. *Family Process*, *18*, 293–302.

Bochner, A. P. (1982). On the efficacy of openness in close relationships. In M. Burgoon (Ed.), *Communication Yearbook* (Vol. 5, pp. 108–124). New Brunswick, NJ: Transaction Books.

Bolton, C. D. (1961). Mate selection as the development of a relationship. *Marriage and Family Living*, *23*, 234–240.

Bullis, C., & Bach, B. W. (1989a). Socialization turning points: An examination of change in organizational identification. *Western Journal of Speech Communication*, *53*, 273–293.

Bullis, C., & Bach, B. W. (1989b). Are mentor relationships helping organizations? An exploration of developing mentee-mentor-organizational identifications using turning point analysis. *Communication Quarterly*, *37*, 199–213.

Bullis, C., & Baxter, L. A. (1985, February). *A functional typology of turning point events in the development of romantic relationships*. Paper presented at Western States Speech Communication Association meeting, Tucson, AZ.

Christensen, A., & Nies, D. C. (1980). The spouse observation checklist: Empirical analysis and critique. *American Journal of Family Therapy*, *8*, 69–70.

Cody, M. J. (1982). A topology of disengagement strategies and an examination of the role intimacy, reactions to inequity, and relational problems play in strategy selection. *Communication Monographs*, *49*, 148–170.

Cohen, J. (1960). A coefficient of agreement for nominal scales. *Educational and Psychological Measurement*, *20*, 37–48.

Duck, S. (1977). Inquiry, hypothesis and the question for validation: Personal construct systems in the development of acquaintance. In S. Duck (Ed.) *Theory and practice in interpersonal attraction* (pp. 379–404). London: Academic Press.

Duck, S. (1988). Overview. In S. Duck, D. Hay, S. Hobfoll, W. Ickes, & B. Montgomery (Eds.) *Handbook of personal relationships: Theory, research, and interventions* (pp. 363–366). Chichester, England: Wiley.

Duck, S., & Sants, H. (1983). On the origin of the specious: Are personal relationships really interpersonal states? *Journal of Social and Clinical Psychology*. *1*, 27–41.

Granovetter, M. S. (1976). Network sampling: Some first steps. *American Journal of Sociology*, *81*, 1287–1303.

Fisher, B. A. (1987). *Pragmatics of human relationships*. New York: Random House.

Huston, T. L., Surra, C., Fitzgerald, N. M., & Cate, R. (1981). From courtship to marriage: Mate selection as an interpersonal process. In S. Duck & R. Gilmour (Eds.), *Personal relationships 2: Developing personal relationships*. New York: Academic Press.

Jacobson, N. S., & Moore, D. (1981). Spouses as observers of the events in their relationship. *Journal of Consulting and Clinical Psychology*, *49*, 269–277.

Kirk, D. L., & Todd-Mancillas, W. R. (1989, February). *Turning points affecting the socialization of graduate student teachers*. Paper presented at the Western Speech Communication Association, Spokane, WA.

Knapp, M. (1984). *Interpersonal communication and human relationships*. Boston: Allyn & Bacon.

Langer, E. J. (1978). Rethinking the role of thought in social interaction. In J. H. Harvey, W. J. Ickes, & R. F. Kidd (Eds.), *New directions in attribution research* (Vol. 2, pp. 35–58). Hillsdale, NJ: Lawrence Erlbaum Associates.

Lloyd, S. (1983) A typological description of premarital relationship dissolution. Doctoral dissertation, Oregon State University. *Dissertation Abstracts International, 43,* 4057A.

Lloyd, S., & Cate, R. (1984). *Attributions associated with significant turning points in premarital relationship development and dissolution.* Paper presented at the 2nd International Conference on Personal Relationships, Madison, WI.

McCall, G., & Simmons, J. L. (1978). *Identities and interactions: An examination of human associations in everyday life.* (rev. ed.). New York: The Free Press.

Norton, R. (1983). Measuring marital quality: A critical look at the dependent variable. *Journal of Marriage and the Family, 45,* 141–151.

Nydick, A., & Cornelius, R. (1984, July). *What we talk about when we talk about love.* Paper presented at the Second International Conference on Personal Relationships, Madison, WI.

Parks, M. R. (1982). Ideology in interpersonal communication: Off the couch and into the world. In M. Burgoon (Ed.), *Communication Yearbook 5* (pp. 79–107). New Brunswick, NJ: Transaction Books.

Phillips, E., & Cheston, R. (1979). Conflict resolution: What works? *California Management Review, 21*(4), 76–83.

Reherman, T., & Bullis, C. (1989, February). *The use of metacommunication in developing romantic relationships.* Paper presented at the Western Speech Communication Association Conference, Spokane, WA.

Robbins, S. P. (1978). "Conflict management" and "conflict resolution" are not synonymous terms. *California Management Review, 21*(2), 67–75.

Rossiter, L. M., Jr. (1974). Instruction is metacommunication. *Central States Speech Journal, 25,* 36–42.

Sillars, A., & Scott, M. (1983). Interpersonal perception between intimates: An integrative review. *Human Communication Research, 11,* 593–604.

Spanier, G. B. (1976). Measuring dyadic adjustment: New scales for assessing the quality of marriage and similar dyads. *Journal of Marriage and the Family, 38,* 15–28.

Surra, C. (1984, July). *Attributions about chances in commitment: Variations by courtship style.* Paper presented at the Second International Conference on Personal Relationships. Madison, WI.

Surra, C. (1990). Research and theory on mate selection and premarital relationships in the 1980s. *Journal of Marriage and the Family, 52,* 844–865.

Surra, C., Arizzi, P., & Asmussen, L. (1988). The association between reasons for commitment and the development and outcome of marital relationships. *Journal of Social and Personal Relationships, 5,* 47–63.

Tolhuizen, J. H. (1989). Communication strategies for intensifying dating relationships: Identification, use, and structure. *Journal of Social and Personal Relationships, 6,* 413–434.

Watzlawick, P., Beavin J., & Jackson, D. (1967). *Pragmatics of human communication.* New York: Norton.

Wilmot, W., & Baxter, L. (1984, February). *Defining relationships: The interplay of cognitive schemata and communication.* Paper presented at the Western Speech Communication Association Annual Convention, Seattle, WA.

13

Preservation of Relational Characteristics: Maintenance Strategies, Equity, and Locus of Control

Daniel J. Canary[1]
Ohio University

Laura Stafford
Ohio State University

Over the last decade, communication scholars have turned their attention to the study of how people sustain their mature, personal relationships (e.g., Ayres, 1983; Dindia & Baxter, 1987). *Personal relationships* refer to involvements with others that cannot be replaced; to replace the specific person means changing the nature of the relationship (Duck, Lock, McCall, Fitzpatrick, & Cayne, 1984). *Social relationships*, on the other hand, refer to those based on stereotypic knowledge of the other person (see also Miller, 1978). Those in social involvements can be replaced without jeopardizing the nature of the relationship (see also Duck et al., 1984). The study of relational maintenance is definitionally anchored to the study of close, personal relationships.

Communication researchers have specifically focused on interaction-based approaches or strategies people use to maintain their personal relationships (see Ayres, 1983; Baxter & Dindia, 1990; Bell, Daly, & Gonzalez, 1987; Dindia & Baxter, 1987; Shea & Pearson, 1986). These research efforts share little conceptual or operational territory, however. For example, Ayres (1983) and Shea and Pearson (1986) identified relational maintenance as efforts to sustain the status quo. Baxter and Dindia (1990; cf., Dindia & Baxter, 1987) conceptualize maintenance as responses to dialectical tensions common to personal involvements (e.g., autonomy needs vs. interdependence needs). Finally, Bell et al. (1987) link maintenance to affinity seeking, where the communicator sustains his/her relationship by increasing the partner's affinity.

[1]The authors wish to thank Lynn Phelps, Claudia Hale, and Susan Yost for their assistance with data collection.

These varied approaches for examining maintenance result from the explosion of interest in the topic. At the same time, this explosion dissembles a coherent understanding of how communication functions to sustain desired relationship definitions. A coherent picture of how communication functions to maintain personal relationships will occur only in light of continued systematic research. Accordingly, this chapter continues our investigation of maintenance processes.

More specifically, in this study, we offer our theoretic commitments regarding maintenance activities. Our earlier efforts overviewed these commitments (Canary & Stafford, 1992; Stafford & Canary, 1991). They are explicated here to present a more complete picture of maintenance. Second, as will become apparent, we test interactive versus noninteractive influences on relational characteristics. To meet these objectives, we present our theoretic commitments. Following these, a study is reported that directly examines the relative contribution of maintenance strategies, equity, and locus of control in predicting fundamental relational features. Before these efforts are reported, however, we review the relational characteristics thought to be fundamental to most personal relationships. In this investigation, personal relationships include family, friends, and lovers (among other types).

RELATIONAL CHARACTERISTICS:
CONTROL MUTUALITY, TRUST, AND LIKING

One assumption of this research is that people seek to sustain desired relational definitions (see also Ayres, 1983; Dindia & Baxter, 1987). A vast array of relationally relevant phenomena are implied in the terms *relational definitions*, including survival over time (i.e., stability), *different relational types* (see, e.g., Fitzpatrick, 1988), and *different fundamental themes of relational life* (Burgoon & Hale, 1984). By relational definitions we refer to feature characteristics important to ongoing, personal relationships. More precisely, three relational features crucial to mature relationships are control mutuality, trust, and liking (for a similar taxonomy, see Millar & Rogers, 1987).

Control Mutuality

Control mutuality is defined as the extent to which relational partners agree on who has the right to determine relational goals. This concept is similar to Morton, Alexander, and Altman's (1976) mutuality of control construct. Morton et al. (1976) held that control mutuality must occur in all viable relationships, and they offered examples of such mutuality in several relational prototypes (e.g., parent–child, marital).

Research from various programs has found that disagreement concerning control or unilateral control disrupts relational stability. Negative feelings about potential friends (Bochner, Kaminski, & Fitzpatrick, 1977), misunderstanding of one's spouse (Courtright, Millar, & Rogers-Millar, 1979), coercion of one's partner (Falbo & Peplau, 1980), and reciprocation of disagreement (Canary, Weger, & Stafford, 1991) have been positively associated with unilateral control. Contrawise, mutual control orientations have been positively linked to bilateral influence strategies (Falbo & Peplau, 1980), convergence on ideas discussed between partners (Canary et al., 1991), and relational satisfaction and understanding (Courtright et al., 1979). In short, control mutuality is reflected in cooperative behaviors and goals (see also, Kelley, 1979).

Trust

Trust is a critical component of personal relationships (e.g., Rempel, Holmes, & Zanna, 1985). *Trust* refers to the degree one risks himself or herself to the partner; this risk is predicated on the belief that the partner is beneficent and dependable (Johnson-George & Swap, 1983). That is, the partner is perceived as valuing one's welfare, and the partner is seen as capable of carrying out promises. This conceptualization of trust is markedly different than the general predisposition to believe others. The conceptualization of trust adopted in this chapter is person specific (see Johnson-George & Swap, 1983; Larzelere & Huston, 1980).

It is a commonplace to note that trust is important to functional relationships. Not surprisingly, research indicates that trust is strongly associated with love (Larzelere & Huston, 1980), confidence in the partner (Johnson-George & Swap, 1982), and relational quality (Canary & Cupach, 1988). On the other hand, suspicion and lack of trust undermine various kinds of relationships (Argyle & Henderson, 1984; Larzelere & Huston, 1980; Van Yperen & Buunk, 1990). Buunk and Bringle (1987), for example, noted the varied and troublesome personal reactions to jealously arising from lack of trust. Research, as well as everyday clichés, attest to the necessity of trust in mature relationships.

Liking

Liking has been considered a fundamental feature in relationships as well. Rubin (1973) noted that *liking* connotes a preference or choice for association and is primarily composed of affection and respect. Moreover, Rubin argued that relationships have little chance without a person liking one's partner.

Maintenance and liking have been studied primarily in romantic relationships (e.g., Bell et al., 1987; Dainton, 1991). But liking (and related constructs) transcend beyond romantic relationships (e.g., Bell & Daly, 1984). Although the constructs of liking, affiliation, and affinity are not isomorphic (see Rubin, 1973), a general notion of liking permeates the literature on various relationship types. For example, the role of liking in friendship seems unquestionable, especially if liking is viewed as a choice or preference for association. Some type of liking is often thought to be a premise of ongoing friendships (Dickens & Perlman, 1981). Also, affectivity or affiliation is assumed to be part of functioning families (Beavers, 1982; Walsh, 1982).

In sum to this point, three relational features are seen as central to mature relationships. In other words, these characteristics define the nature of ongoing relationships and enable their continued existence. These features are control mutuality, trust, and liking. At issue, of course, is the means by which these relational properties are preserved.

THEORETIC COMMITMENTS

First, all mature relationships require maintenance or else they deteriorate. It is naive to assume that people continue in their developed relationships until they happen to fall apart; it appears that something more than momentum keeps dyads bonded (see also Duck, 1988). In Duck's (1988) terminology, relationships react to centrifugal forces. In other words, people expend resources and energies to keep their relationships together, otherwise they decay. More precisely, without maintenance efforts, the feature characteristics of relationships diminish, which, in turn, leads to instability and possibly termination.

Second, people are motivated to maintain equitable relationships. Equity is based on the principle of distributive justice (see Deutsch, 1985). According to the principle of distributive justice, fairness requires assessing the inputs and outcomes of each person. If the ratios are equal, the relationship is equitable; if the ratios are unequal, the relationship is inequitable (Adams, 1965). The person who claims fewer outcomes relative to inputs is underbenefited, and the person who obtains greater outcomes relative to inputs is overbenefited (Hatfield, Sprecher, Utne, & Hay, 1985).

According to theory and research, people are more content with equitable relationships than inequitable relationships (see Hatfield et al., 1985). Indeed, experiencing inequity leads to negative emotional responses and assessments of the partner (Sprecher, 1986). These negative reactions to inequity prompt people to somehow restore equity or leave the partner (Adams, 1965). In short, people are more likely to maintain those relationships characterized by equity.

Third, efforts to maintain relationships vary according to the development of the relationship. Utilizing hypothetical scenarios, Ayres (1983) assigned participants to developing, stable, or deteriorating relationship conditions. These people were then asked to rate the likelihood of using various maintenance strategies. Ayres found those in the declining condition were most likely to choose behaviors that balanced the relationship. These balance tactics involved keeping the emotional support levels constant and continuing to provide the same kinds of favors. But, those assigned to the relational escalation condition were less likely to choose balance tactics. Using survey methods, Stafford and Canary (1991) found people differed in their perceptions of partners' maintenance strategies according to relational stages. For example, married, engaged, and seriously dating people saw their partners enacting more assuring behaviors and sharing tasks than did casually dating people. Over the course of developing a mature relationship, people become more interdependent. This interdependence requires assurances about future goals and energies to perform household responsibilities (see also Kelley, 1979).

Fourth, particular maintenance behaviors operate in isolation or in combination with other types of maintenance behaviors to sustain various relational features. For example, in order to maintain the partner's current level of liking, one could show interest in the partner's activities (Bell et al., 1987), attempt to be positive and cheerful (Stafford & Canary, 1991), and/or perform one's household obligations (Stafford & Canary, 1991). In order to sustain commitment, one could offer assurances and/or include valued friends and family in joint activities (Stafford & Canary, 1991). In other words, the functional utility of maintenance behaviors depends on the relational characteristic(s) of concern. In addition, people may use one or a combination of several maintenance strategies.

Finally, both interactive and noninteractive factors function to maintain personal relationships. Interactive factors are those processes born through communication, whereas noninteractive factors are not typically born through communication. Interactive factors are separated into routine and strategic subcategories. Likewise, noninteractive factors are comprised of social and individual subcategories. Both interactive and noninteractive factors are important to maintenance processes. Thus, both factors should be represented in assessing the relative contribution of either to relational maintenance.

Routine Interaction.   Duck (1988) observed that people's routine interaction behavior and communication strategies functionally establish and preserve personal relationships. According to Duck, Rutt, Hurst, and Strejc (1991), communication "functions to assure the continuation of the relationship into the future by projecting a rhetorically forceful image of continuance not only through its language but through its very occurrence. In such a model, relationships are essentially unfinished business that needs to be perpetuated through regular mundane interaction" (p. 231). Though Duck et al. (1991) do not specifically examine maintenance, their study provides evidence that mature relationships are typified by routinized interaction. For example, Duck et al. (1991) found relatives, friends, and best friends reported less change in communication patterns compared to strangers, acquaintances, and lovers. This study indicates people experience greater interaction continuity in stable relationships.

Strategic Interaction. In addition to routine interaction, communication strategies function to maintain the relationship. In particular, maintenance strategies are communication approaches for sustaining desired relational definitions (see Ayres, 1983; Baxter & Dindia, 1987; Bell, Daly, & Gonzalez, 1987; Stafford & Canary, 1991). Because this study continues a line of research based on communication strategies, we also focus attention on maintenance strategies and not routine interaction. Elsewhere the routine kinds of interaction that serve to sustain relationships are discussed (Dainton, Stafford, & McNeilis, 1992; Duck, 1988).

Noninteractive Social Factor: Equity. Because of its centrality to relational satisfaction and stability (see Hatfield et al., 1985), equity qualifies as an important noninteractive social factor. This is a social factor because its assessment requires an evaluation of a social system (i.e., the inputs and outcomes for both self and partner). There are many bases of equity, including physical appearance, intelligence, opportunities gained or lost, finances, and so forth (e.g., Traupmann, Petersen, Utne, & Hatfield, 1981). Such noninteractive commodities function to sustain the relationship to the extent that people desire a fair distribution of these commodities. Some researchers have argued that people in mature relationships do not "count" inputs and outcomes as equity theory predicts (e.g., Mills & Clark, 1982). We believe the research indicates people are sensitive to the issue of fairness in their personal relationships and people act in accordance with equity theory predictions to achieve fairness (e.g., Sprecher, 1986).

Noninteractive Individual Factor: Locus of Control. Numerous individual differences exist, many of which are enduring (e.g., biological sex) and some of which are transitional (e.g., moods). Research over the past 20 years indicates that a person's belief that one can accomplish personal goals enables one to accomplish those goals (Bandura, 1989). In terms of relationship maintenance, it appears that people who believe their relationships are the product of their own abilities and efforts are more likely to succeed in their relational goals than those who believe their relational fates are governed by external forces (see also Lefcourt, 1981). In other words, people with an internal locus of control regarding their relationship successes (and failures) are more likely to sustain desired relational definitions than those with an external orientation (see also Steinfatt, 1987). We do not hold that locus of control is the only relevant individual factor; it is, however, a crucial one.

The aforementioned theoretical statements explicate both interactive and noninteractive factors affecting the maintenance of personal relationships. Three of these factors are reviewed in greater depth at this point.

MAINTENANCE STRATEGIES, EQUITY, AND LOCUS OF CONTROL

Maintenance Strategies

Maintenance strategies are the interactional approaches that people use to keep their relationships defined in satisfactory ways. As mentioned, communication scholars differ in their conceptualizations (and corresponding operationalizations) of maintenance strategies.

Our initial investigation of relational maintenance (Stafford & Canary, 1991) assumed that the divergent behavioral strategies reported in the literature operate separately or jointly to maintain relational properties, depending on the relational property of concern to the partners. A test of this assumption required an inclusive taxonomy of maintenance strategies. Accordingly, maintenance strategies from the published literature were synthesized with behaviors inductively derived from a sample of romantic dyads. This resulted in about 80 different behaviors, which, when factor analyzed, produced five underlying strategies. The first strategy is *positivity*, referring to one's cheerfulness, lack of personal criticism, and spontaneity. *Openness* is the second strategy and it references attempts to be direct and disclosive about the nature of the relationship. The third approach is *assurances*, which includes statements of expectations of a continuing involvement and caring. Maintenance strategy four involves the use of social *networks*, such as friends and family, that support the relationship. Finally, *sharing tasks* refers to doing one's household duties, and so forth. The results reported in Stafford and Canary (1991) indicated that positivity and assurances are strong predictors of control mutuality, commitment, and liking. Moreover, sharing tasks was a stable secondary predictor of these relational characteristics.

A second study (Canary & Stafford, 1992) examined the role of equity and maintenance strategies in preserving married couples' commitment, control mutuality, and liking. Equity and maintenance behaviors were positively associated with these relational characteristics. In addition, positivity and assurances were (again) primary predictors of the relational characteristics. One interesting finding is that one's *own* maintenance behaviors predicted one's own assessment of the relational features as accurately as the perceptions of partner strategies. Clearly, people reference their own behavior in determining their own commitment, control mutuality, and liking (of the partner).

Although this typology of maintenance strategies appears to be inclusive, it was derived and tested only within romantic associations (i.e., dating, seriously dating, engaged, or married). The present study examines the predictive power of these strategies across a variety of personal relationships: friends, family, co-worker, as well as romantic. Additionally, it is uncertain whether these relational maintenance strategies retain a primary predictive role when compared to noninteractive influences (see also Canary & Stafford, 1992).

Equity

As mentioned, equity refers to the notion that people seek distributive justice in their relationships. More specifically, equity theory (see Hatfield et al., 1985; Walster, Walster, & Berscheid, 1978) holds that partners achieve justice by balancing the amount of rewards obtained from the relationship relative to the inputs each offers to the relationship. Theoretically, the most satisfying relationships are those that are rewarding and equitable.

Research indicates that equity is positively associated with such relational properties as commitment (Sabatelli & Cecil-Pigo, 1985), contentment (Hatfield et al., 1985), dyadic adjustment (Davidson, Balswick, & Halverson, 1983), and relational satisfaction (Van Yperen & Buunk, 1990). In addition, underbenefited people, versus overbenefited people, are more emotionally distressed and less satisfied (Sprecher, in press). For example, Sprecher (1986) found that underbenefitedness (more than overbenefitedness) was strongly and inversely associated with respect, satisfaction, trust, and contentment; underbenefitedness was positively associated with sadness, frustration, depression, and anger (respectively).

Other research has challenged the particular claims equity theory holds regarding distributive justice. For example, one's reward level alone has been more strongly tied than equity of rewards to one's satisfaction (Cate, Lloyd, Henton, & Larson, 1982; see also Martin, 1985) and commitment (Michaels, Edwards, & Acock, 1984). Equity in these studies explained small amounts of variance in predicting these relational features. In addition, Van Yperen and Buunk (1990) suggested that "equity may not be equally important to everyone" (p. 290). For example, some people may have a more "communal" and less of an "exchange" orientation (Mills & Clark, 1982).

One solution to the reservation that equity is not important to all relationships is to "weight" equity by the amount of importance the person attaches to equity within a given relationship. This procedure is roughly equivalent to expected utility models (or expectancy value models), where the anticipated consequences of a particular behavior are multiplied by the social actor's subjective evaluation (positive vs. negative) of those consequences (see Ajzen & Fishbein, 1980). Accordingly, overall equity, underbenefitedness, and overbenefitedness can be adjusted by the degree to which equity is important in a particular relationship.

Locus of Control

Obviously, there are numerous individual factors that could affect relationship characteristics. Locus of control is examined due to the growing amount of research revealing that locus of control orientations are directly relevant to the ability to maintain functional relationships. *Locus of control* refers to the extent an individual believes his or her outcomes are contingent upon his or her behavior or alternative causes (Steinfatt, 1987). From a social learning perspective, people achieve a greater sense of control over their lives when they perceive that outcomes are contingent upon their own efforts (see Lefcourt, 1982; Phares, 1976). Thus, locus of control likely serves as a predictive individual orientation to relationships.

Globally, locus of control refers to the extent to which social actors perceive that their successes and failures in life are under their own personal control (Lefcourt, 1982). In addition, although early research offered a unidimensional construct (i.e., internality/externality constitute a single factor), advances in the topic have revealed that locus of control is *multidimensional* (e.g., Brenders, 1987; Bryant, 1989; Lefcourt, 1981). That is, an *internal orientation* is comprised of beliefs that successes and failures are due to self-perceived ability and effort; a *separate external orientation* refers to attributing one's outcomes to such factors as chance, the situation, or "powerful" others (Lefcourt, 1982; Levenson, 1981).

Research has indicated that internals are more successful and confident at managing relationships than are externals (Bugental, Henker, & Whalen, 1976; Dougherty & Ryder, 1979). For example, Scanzoni and Arnett (1987) reported negative correlations between an external orientation of fate to marriage and commitment (men's $r = -.25$; women's $r = -.14$), and between externality and conflict resolution (men's $r = -.26$; women's $r = -.28$).

In addition to global orientations, locus of control research reveals that people have domain-specific locus of control beliefs, some of which are directly relevant to continued functional abilities and involvements in relationships. Research comparing global locus of control to various domain-specific indices of locus of control has found such domain-specific indices to be more predictive of the particular relational variable under consideration. For example, locus of control for affiliation was more strongly associated with active listening and other social skills than was a general measure of locus of control (Lefcourt, Martin, Fick, & Saleh, 1985). Similarly, marital problem solving and subsequent relational adjustment was associated with marital locus of control to a greater degree than global measures of locus of control (Miller, Lefcourt, Holmes, Ware, & Saleh, 1986).

Affiliation locus of control appears to be the most relevant of the domain-specific orientations to maintaining various kinds of personal relationships. This construct refers to both internal and external orientations. *Internal orientations* are beliefs that successes and failures at making and keeping relationships are the result of internal properties of one's ability and effort. *External beliefs* regarding relational success and failures are composed of chance and context factors (Lefcourt, von Bayer, Ware, & Cox, 1979). It is possible that one can have an internal orientation toward relationships, an external orientation, or both.

In sum, three factors promote the stability of important relational characteristics. These factors are: (a) the relational maintenance strategies of positivity, openness, assurances, networks, and sharing tasks (an interactive strategic factor); (b) equity (a noninteractive social factor); and (c) affiliation locus of control (a noninteractive individual factor). The comparative ability of these factors to predict important relational characteristics is unclear. Accordingly, this study tests the following research (R) question:

R$_1$: Which factor best predicts the relational characteristics of control mutuality, trust, and liking: relational maintenance strategies; equity; or affiliation locus of control?

METHOD

Sample

A total of 444 undergraduate students were recruited from two midwestern universities. The sample was 60.1% female. Two questionnaires were used in this study. One questionnaire included measures of equity, maintenance behaviors, and relational characteristics, henceforth referred to as the relational questionnaire. The other questionnaire included the affiliation locus of control measure. Both questionnaires asked for demographic information, and included additional measures not germane to this study.

The participants completed the two questionnaires, referring to a specific personal relationship for the relational questionnaire. Of the 444 students, 34% completed the questionnaire in regard to a romantic relationship; 35% in regard to a friendship; 27% in regard to a family relationship; and 3% in regard to a work relationship (1% classified their relationships as *other*).

Breakdowns within these relationship types are as follows: for romantic partners, 5% were married; 10% engaged; 54% considered themselves to be seriously dating; 19% dating; and 12% indicated other. The breakdown of friendships were as follows: 87% were close friends; 7% indicated they were causal friends; 3% were acquaintances; and 3% reported other. For the family relationships: parents comprised 57%; siblings, 27%; grandparents, 3%; and other, 12%. For work relationships: 27% referenced their supervisor; 10%

thought about a subordinate; 15% referenced a colleague; 5% referenced a teacher; and 44% thought about an other category of work relationship.

Independent Factors

Maintenance Strategies. The maintenance strategies were based on those reported in Stafford and Canary (1991; see also Canary & Stafford, 1992). The maintenance strategies measure is comprised of five factors: positivity, openness, assurances, (reliance upon) networks, and sharing tasks. Participants were asked to "indicate the extent to which you perceive each of the following represents your current behavior. . . . Currently, in order to maintain this relationship, I. . . ." Example items from each scale are: "I attempt to make our interactions very enjoyable," and "I am cheerful and positive when with him/her" (positivity); "I encourage him/her to disclose thoughts and feelings to me," and "I seek to discuss the quality of our relationship" (openness); "I stress my commitment to him/her," and "I imply that our relationship has a future" (assurances); "I like to spend time with our same friends," and "I show that I am willing to do things with his/her friends and family" (social network); and "I help equally with the tasks that need to be done," and "I perform my household responsibilities" (sharing tasks).

The means and coefficient alpha reliabilities for each of the maintenance strategies were: positivity, 4.07 (alpha = .89, SD = .75); openness 3.64 (alpha = .85, SD = .95); assurances, 3.90 (alpha = .86, SD = 1.02); networks, 3.82 (alpha = .82, SD = .99); tasks, 4.04 (alpha = .88, SD = .84). (Unless indicated otherwise, the possible response range for the measures was 1 to 5, with 5 reflecting strongest agreement with the items).

Equity. Equity was measured by the same methods Sprecher (1986) used, with minor word changes to make the questions applicable to any type of personal relationship (as opposed to only romantic relationships). Sprecher employed two global measures of equity. The first was developed by Hatfield (1978; reported in Hatfield, Utne, & Traupman, 1979; Sprecher, 1986): "Considering what you put into your relationship, compared to what you get out, and what your person puts in compared to what s/he gets out of it, how does your relationship 'stack up'?" The response categories varied from 1 ("I am getting a much better deal than this person") to 5 ("This person is getting a much better deal than I"). The item midpoint reflected an equitable relationship. The second global equity measure was Sprecher's (1986) measure, which focuses on how equity is routinely achieved through increasing inputs. This measure reads, "Sometimes things get out of balance in a relationship and one person contributes more to the relationship than the other. Consider all the times when the exchange in your relationships become unbalanced, which of you is more likely to be the one who contributes more?" The responses varied from 1 ("This person is much more likely to be the one to contribute more") to 5 ("I am much more likely to be the one to contribute more"). Again, the item midpoint reflected an equitable relationship. Following each of the equity scales, a Likert-type scale asked how important it was that they were "equally rewarded" and how important it was that they "contribute equally" in the relationship, with 1 = *very important* to 5 = *very unimportant*.

Locus of Control for Affiliation (LCA).   The Locus of Control for Affiliation was measured using the affiliation portion of the Multidimensional-Multiattributional Causality Scale (MMCS; see Lefcourt et al., 1979). Lefcourt et al. (1979) reported four studies that support the convergent and discriminant validity of the affiliation locus of control internality and externality scales. An initial examination of the LCA reliability coefficients was disappointing, with all subscales under .70 and several below .50. Accordingly, a factor analysis of the LCA was undertaken. The factor analysis is reported in the Results section.

Relational Characteristics

Control Mutuality.   Control mutuality was measured using a six-item scale that assesses consensus on who has the right to make relational decisions (Canary et al., 1991). This short scale has demonstrated previous predictive validity in studies on relational maintenance (Canary & Stafford, 1992; Stafford & Canary, 1991). Example items include: "We agree on what we can expect from one another"; "Both of us are satisfied with the way we handle decisions"; and "We both have an equal 'say'." The control mutuality average was 3.99 (alpha = .90; *SD* = .97).

Trust.   Interpersonal trust was assessed using the Larzelere and Huston (1980) measure, which was designed to assess the amount of trust for specific relational partners. This eight-item scale includes such items as the following: "This person is perfectly honest and truthful with me"; "I feel that I can trust this person completely"; and "This person is primarily interested in his/her own welfare." The mean for the trust measure was 4.07 (alpha = .89, *SD* = .96).

Liking.   Interpersonal liking was measured using Rubin's (1973) nine-item scale. This scale assesses the degree of admiration (respect) and acceptance for another. Representative items are: "This person is the sort of person whom I myself would like to be"; "This person is one of the most likable people I know"; and "I think this person is one of those people who quickly wins respect." The average for the liking measure was 3.94 (alpha = .93, *SD* = .99).

Procedures

The two questionnaires were administered 2–3 weeks apart during class time. The order of the questionnaires (i.e., relational vs. locus of control measures) was counterbalanced. Prior to completion of the relational questionnaire, students were asked to write down the names of three specific people with whom they had a relationship longer than 3 months. They also indicated their relationship type (family member, romantic partner, friend, or other, e.g., co-worker). The participants were then randomly assigned to complete the relational questionnaire in regard to one of the people they had indicated. As previously mentioned, most participants indicated romantic involvements, friendships, and family relationships, and few participants nominated a work relationship. Participants were instructed to answer the locus of control scale in regard to themselves specifically (i.e., not with any particular partner in mind).

RESULTS

The research question tested in this study concerned which of the three independent factors (maintenance strategies, equity, locus of control) best predict the relational characteristics (control mutuality, trust, liking). Before the results regarding the research question are reported, computations of equity/inequity indices and the results of the affiliation locus of control factor analysis are provided.

Equity/Inequity Indices

Equity Index. Consistent with previous research, a majority of the participants rated their relationship as equitable according to the Hatfield Global measure (67.3%). But, using Sprechers' (1986) measure, a plurality saw their relationships as slightly underbenefited (29.4%) and 28.7% saw them as equitable. The Pearson correlation between the two equity scales was moderate, $r = .44$. These two measures were summed to form the equity index. The equity index average was 6.00 ($SD = 1.63$; range = 2 to 10).

Inequity Indices. Inequity is conceptualized as either being under- or overbenefited; hence, under- and overbenefitedness indices were computed. Following Sprecher (1986), participants who indicated that their relationship was equitable or overbenefited were assigned a 0 on the underbenefit index. The higher values on the equity index were then sequentially assigned to higher underbenefit scores. This resulted in an underbenefit index range of 0 to 4, with 0 = no underbenefitedness and 4 = a great deal of underbenefitedness.

The average for the underbenefit index was .62 (*SD* = .94). The overbenefit index was computed in a similar fashion. Those who reported equitable or underbenefited involvements received an overbenefit score of 0. Lower numbers on the equity index were then sequentially assigned higher values for overbenefitedness. This resulted in an overbenefit index range of 0 to 4, with 0 = no overbenefitedness and 4 = a great deal of overbenefitedness. The average overbenefit score was .62 (*SD* = .99). In short, most people did not see their relationships as either under- or overbenefited (i.e., about 60% of participants had 0 for either of these scales).

Weighted Equity. Each of the indices were used with and without participant weightings for their importance. Accordingly, the equity index was multiplied by the sum of the two equity importance items. The weighted equity index average was 7.33 (*SD* = 2.41; range = 2 to 10). The weighted underbenefit index average was 4.34 (*SD* = 7.21; range = 0 to 40; most participants had an underbenefit score of 0). The weighted overbenefit index mean was 4.33 (*SD* = 7.26; range = 0 to 32; most participants had overbenefit scores of 0).

Affiliation Locus of Control Factor Analysis

In order to derive reliable locus of control for affiliation (LCA) measures of internality and externality, a principle components factor analysis was performed, utilizing VARIMAX rotation. The criteria for factor definition were as follows: an eigenvalue greater than unity; primary loadings greater than .45, with no secondary loadings under a .20 difference; no secondary loadings above .35; and at least two items per factor. Table 13.1 reports the factor items and primary loadings, along with the alpha coefficients for each factor.

The LCA items loaded in meaningful ways, resulting in eight factors that were roughly equivalent to those reported in Lefcourt et al. (1979). In other words, the internal components of effort and ability were distinguished from the external components of luck and context. In addition, the factors were generally distinguishable in their referents of relational success or failure. But, one factor (*Ability/Success*) had a dismal reliability coefficient; and this factor also detracted from the internality scale reliability. Hence, this factor was excluded from further analyses. Internality was composed of the effort and ability subscales, and externality was composed of the luck and context subscales. The internality mean was 3.29 (alpha = .62; *SD* = .57). The average externality score was 2.94 (alpha = .60; *SD* = .57). These reliabilities are consistent with those reported in Lefcourt et al. (1979).

TABLE 13.1.
Factor Loadings of Affiliation Locus of Control

Items	Loading
Effort/Success (eigenvalue = 3.19; alpha = .66)	
Maintaining relationships requires real effort to make them work.	.75
If my relationships were to succeed, it would have to be because I worked at it.	.61
It seems to me that getting along with people is a skill.	.66
In my case, success at making friends depends on how hard I work at it.	.67
Luck/Success (eigenvalue = 2.37; alpha = .62)	
Relationships are funny business; sometimes I have to chalk up my successes to luck.	.70
In my experience, good relationships are largely a matter of having the right breaks.	.80
If my relationships were long happy ones, I'd say that I must just be very lucky.	.67
Ability/Failure (eigenvalue = 1.94; alpha = .52)	
I feel that people who are often lonely are lacking in social competence.	.75
In my experience, there is a direct connection between the absence of friendship and being socially inept.	.78
Having good relationships is simply a matter of one's social skill.	.47
Context/Failure (eigenvalue = 1.39; alpha = .55)	
No matter what I do, some people just don't like me.	.77
Some people just seem predisposed to dislike me.	.78
Luck/Failure (eigenvalue = 1.33; alpha = .65)	
Often chance events can play a large part in causing rifts between friends.	.80
Difficulties with relationships often start with chance remarks.	.84
Context/Success (eigenvalue = 1.18; alpha = .49)	
My enjoyment of a social occasion is almost entirely dependent on the personalities of the other people who are there.	.80
To enjoy myself at a party I have to be surrounded by others who know how to have a good time.	.69
Effort/Failure (eigenvalue = 1.15; alpha = .53)	
If I did not get along with others, it would tell me that I hadn't put much effort into the pursuit of social goals.	.67
When I hear of a divorce, I suspect that the couple probably did not try enough to make their marriage work.	.79
Ability/Success (eigenvalue = 1.05; alpha = .17)	
It is impossible for me to maintain close relations with people without my tact and patience.	.56
Failure to have people like me would show my ignorance in interpersonal relationships.	.48
Some people can make me have a good time even when I don't feel sociable.	.62

Regression of Relational Characteristics

Each of the relational characteristics were regressed on the following: the five maintenance strategies (positivity, assurances, openness, networks, sharing tasks); equity indices (equity, equity × equity importance, underbenefitedness, underbenefitedness × equity importance, overbenefitedness, and overbenefitedness × equity importance); and locus of control for affiliation internality and externality. Table 13.2 reports the stepwise multiple regressions for each of the relational characteristics.

As Table 13.2 reveals, the relational features were predicted by a combination of maintenance strategies and equity factors. The average amount of variance explained by the predictors was 29%.

Positivity primarily predicted control mutuality and trust, accounting for 20% and 13% of the variance, respectively. Positivity also entered on the third step in predicting liking, adding 4% explained variance. Assurances was the primary predictor of liking, explaining 18% of the variance, and it was the third predictor of trust, accounting for an additional 3% of variance.

The second predictor of all three relational features was underbenefitedness, accounting for 7%, 12%, and 7% of variance explained to the relational features of control mutuality, trust, and liking, respectively. The third predictor of control mutuality was (reliance on) social networks, which added only 2% of explained variance. The maintenance strategy of networks also added significantly, though very weakly, to the model predicting liking.

TABLE 13.2
Stepwise Regression of Relational Characteristics

Dependent Variables	Independent Variables	Beta	F-Change*	R^2**
Control				
Mutuality	1. Positivity	.37	102.10	.20
	2. Underbenefit	−.26	76.90	.27
	3. Networks	.17	56.91	.29
Trust	1. Positivity	.24	60.80	.13
	2. Underbenefit	−.36	70.86	.25
	3. Assurances	.20	52.77	.28
Liking	1. Assurances	.21	89.85	.18
	2. Underbenefit	−.13	70.16	.25
	3. Positivity	.22	55.90	.29
	4. Networks	.12	43.54	.29
	5. Equity	−.16	35.95	.30

Note. Final R^2 values are underscored.
*F-change values are significant at $p. < .001$. **R^2 are adjusted R^2s.
Underbenefit refers to underbenefitedness.

Finally, and contrary to expectations, locus of control for affiliation did not increase the predictive power of the regression models. An examination of the zero-order correlations revealed that LCA internality and externality were randomly correlated with the relational characteristics. It seemed possible that affiliation internality and externality may be associated with one's maintenance strategies, which, in turn affect the relational qualities. However, Pearson correlations between LCA internality and externality with the five maintenance strategies revealed no significant correlations, even with a sample of over 400 people. The following section interprets these results and indicates research issues for future exploration.

DISCUSSION

The purpose of this investigation was to examine the manner in which interactive and noninteractive factors predict important relational characteristics. The interactive factor was one's maintenance strategies (positivity, openness, assurances, networks, and sharing tasks). The noninteractive social factor was equity (equity, underbenefitedness, overbenefitedness, and weighted measures of each). The noninteractive individual factor was affiliation locus of control (internality and externality). The relational characteristics were control mutuality, trust, and liking.

Findings

The analyses reveal that both interactive and noninteractive factors function to preserve the relational characteristics. Importantly, the interactive factor of maintenance strategies emerged as the strongest predictors of all three relational features. This finding underscores the relative importance of communication influences on continuing, developed relationships.

The maintenance strategy of positivity was the primary predictor of control mutuality. These findings replicate three previous studies regarding romantic couples' maintenance behaviors and relational characteristics (Canary & Stafford, 1992; Dainton, 1991; Stafford & Canary, 1991). Given that this sample included a wide array of personal relationships, we are confident in inferring that positivity is an effective method for promoting the mutuality of control in relationships. Such behaviors as acting cheerful and avoiding criticism of the partner appear to do much in promoting consensus on who influences relational goals. In a similar fashion, positivity was the primary predictor of trust, a new finding.

There are several reasons why positivity emerges as the primary predictor of relational characteristics. First, interaction behaviors are likely to be reciprocated by partners. Using a microanalysis of conversational data, Burggraf and Sillars (1987) found that reciprocation of behavior was the strongest predictor of the way people communicate in marriage. This effect was stronger than relational type or interactant sex. The current study assessed perceptions of maintenance strategies; it is likely that these perceptions reflect the overall positivity in the relationship. Second, the positivity one enacts with the partner increases the reward value of the relationship. Bell et al. (1987) found that wife satisfaction was strongly predicted by affinity maintenance behaviors. Accordingly, utilizing positivity creates a social environment that is rewarding for both partners.

The maintenance strategy of assurances was the primary predictor of liking and was a significant predictor of trust. Demonstrating faithfulness and willingness to "be there" is critical to various relationships (Argyle & Henderson, 1984; Stafford & Canary, 1991). Such statements likely affect, as well as reflect, one's caring for the partner.

Including the partner in one's social networks represents an important relational decision. Especially among college students, whose social opportunities are quite salient, reliance on shared networks to maintain the relationship likely increases the amount of interdependence. As the results indicate, the maintenance strategy of (reliance on) networks significantly affected control mutuality and liking.

These data do not provide support for the relative effects of two maintenance strategies: openness and sharing tasks. Previous investigations of romantic couples revealed that, when partialling out the effects due to positivity and assurances, openness is negatively associated with relational characteristics (Stafford & Canary, 1991). Moreover, among romantic couples, sharing tasks was an important predictor of relational characteristics. This suggests that openness and sharing tasks may not be uniformly critical across relationship types. Future research is warranted to explore more completely the maintenance strategies that are reported across a number of different personal relationships.

Besides maintenance strategies, the noninteractive social factor of equity affected the relational characteristics. Specifically, underbenefitedness was the second predictor of control mutuality, trust, and liking. On the average, underbenefitedness increased the prediction of these relational features by 9%.

The effects due to underbenefitedness are consistent with Sprecher (1986), who found that both positive and negative emotions in close relationships were affected mostly by underbenefitedness rather than overbenefitedness. This finding is also consistent with other research indicating that inequity due to underbenefitedness leads to less contentment than does inequity due to overbenefitedness (Hatfield et al., 1985). In addition, in only one instance did another equity index (i.e., overall equity, which references overbenefitedness, equitable relationships, and underbenefitedness) contribute significantly to predicting a relationship characteristic. That characteristic was liking, but the added explained variance is very low, as is the partial correlation between (in)equity and liking ($r = -.10$). In combination with maintenance strategies, under-benefitedness negatively affected the relational characteristics.

It is of interest to note that the weighted equity indices did not add appreciably to the amount of variance explained in the regression models. It is possible that assessments of inequity inherently contain the importance attached to is-sues of justice in particular relationships. Or it is possible that the distributive justice rule was not as important to this college student sample as it may be among older (and, ostensibly, more experienced) friends, lovers, siblings, and co-workers. These possibilities require further examination. The null results for the effects of equity importance, however, should not dissuade continued efforts at identifying the importance of equity to relational characteristics.

Unlike maintenance strategies and underbenefitedness, locus of control for affiliation was an insignificant predictor of the relational features, contrary to our expectation. There are several explanations for this. First, affiliation locus of control may simply not be relevant to developed, personal relation-ships. Previous research using this measure has involved dyads with no previ-ous history (Lefcourt et al., 1979; Lefcourt et al., 1985). It is possible that one's control orientations to relationships in general are countermanded by ex-pectations born from interactions with specific partners. In addition, although we conceptualize locus of control as a stable predisposition, such may not be the case. Several studies have reported weak correlations between locus of control and relevant outcomes (e.g., Lefcourt et al., 1985; Scanzoni & Ar-nett, 1987). This suggests that locus of control for affiliation may not be as robust as we had believed. A third reason concerns the operations taken in this study. The locus of control scales were administered 2–3 weeks apart from the relational measures. Hence, the amount of time separating the locus of control scale from the other measures is confounded with the effects due to locus of control. Finally, given the low reliabilities, correlations with the rela-tional characteristics were attenuated. However, an examination of the zero order correlations indicated a random association with the relational features.

Limitations and Future Directions

There are limitations to this study. First, given the cross-sectional nature of the data, causal inferences must depend upon theory and previous research. Most would agree that relationships are born from interaction; and likewise, the character of relationships influences interaction behavior. In this study, we opted for examining relational outcomes as a function of interactive and noninteractive factors. Others might conceptualize these links running in the opposite direction. This chicken-and-egg issue is one that should be assessed using time series designs, a task we are now undertaking. Second, as previ-ously mentioned, strong inferences about the link between locus of control for affiliation and the relational features studied cannot be made, based only on time differences in scale administration. Still, personality factors, which are stable individual differences, should not fluctuate so much as to diminish predictions.

Future research is warranted to address some of these limitations. Moreover, longitudinal research may help reveal the dynamic interplay among these various factors, clarifying the causal processes for further theory building. In addition to examining the relevant components that predict relational characteristics over time, a closer look at the maintenance strategies is in order. Consistent with investigations of romantic partners, positivity and assurances were primary predictors of the relational features; but, unlike before, openness and sharing tasks were not significant predictors. Inductive analyses of maintenance behaviors sampled across a variety of relationships are needed before we can rest on a typology of maintenance strategies. Finally, if domain-specific locus of control orientations do affect the maintenance of particular relationships, such a measure should be constructed relevant to ongoing personal involvements. Although needless proliferation of personality measures should be avoided, previous conceptual advances and research indicate that internal and external control orientations probably affect individuals' maintenance behaviors and relational outcomes.

REFERENCES

Adams, J. (1965). Inequity in social exchange. In L. Berkowitz (Ed.), *Advances in experimental social psychology: Vol. 2* (pp. 267–299). New York: Academic Press.

Ajzen, I., & Fishbein, M. (1980). *Understanding attitudes and predicting social behavior.* Englewood Cliffs, NJ: Prentice-Hall.

Argyle, M., & Henderson, M. (1984). The rules of friendship. *Journal of Social and Personal Relationships, 1,* 211–237.

Ayres, J. (1983). Strategies to maintain relationships: Their identification and perceived usage. *Communication Quarterly, 31,* 62–67.

Bandura, A. (1989). Self-regulation of motivation and action through internal standards and goal systems. In L. A. Pervin (Ed.), *Goal concepts in personality and social psychology* (pp. 19–85). Hillsdale, NJ: Lawrence Erlbaum Associates.

Baxter, L. A., & Dindia, K. (1990). Marital partners' perceptions of marital maintenance strategies. *Journal of Social and Personal Relationships , 7,* 187–208.

Beavers, W. R. (1982). Healthy, midrange, and severely dysfunctional families. In F. Walsh (Ed.), *Normal family processes* (pp. 45–66). New York: The Guilford Press.

Bell, R. A., & Daly, J. A. (1984). The affinity-seeking function of communication. *Communication Monographs, 51,* 91–115.

Bell, R. A., Daly, J. A., & Gonzalez, C. (1987). Affinity-maintenance in marriage and its relationship to women's marital satisfaction. *Journal of Marriage and the Family, 49,* 445–454.

Bochner, A. P., Kaminski, E. P., & Fitzpatrick, M. A. (1977). The conceptual domain of interpersonal communication behavior. *Human Communication Research, 3,* 291–302.

Brenders, D. A. (1987). Perceived control: Foundations and directions for communication research. In M. L. McLaughlin (Ed.), *Communication yearbook* (Vol. 10, pp. 86–116). Newbury Park, CA: Sage.

Bryant, F. B. (1989). A four-factor model of perceived control: Avoiding, coping, obtaining and savoring. *Journal of Personality, 57,* 773–797.

Bugental, D. P., Henker, B., & Whalen, C. K. (1976). Attributional antecedents of verbal and vocal assertiveness. *Journal of Personality and Social Psychology, 34,* 405–411.

Burggraf, C. S., & Sillars, A. L. (1987). A critical examination of sex differences in marital communication. *Communication Monographs, 54,* 276–294.

Burgoon, J. K., & Hale, J. L. (1984). The fundamental topoi of relational communication. *Communication Monographs, 51,* 19–41.

Buunk, B., & Bringle, R. G. (1987). Jealousy in love relationships. In D. Perlman & S. Duck (Eds.), *Intimate relationships: Development, dynamics, and deterioration* (pp. 123–147). Newbury Park, CA: Sage.

Canary, D. J., & Cupach W. R. (1988). Relational and episodic characteristics associated with conflict tactics. *Journal of Social and Personal Relationships, 5,* 305–325.

Canary, D. J., & Stafford, L. (1992). Relational maintenance strategies and equity in marriage. *Communication Monographs, 1(59),* 243–267.

Canary, D. J., Weger, Jr., H., & Stafford, L., (1991). Couples' argument sequences and their associations with relational characteristics. *Western Journal of Speech Communication, 55,* 159–179.

Cate, R. M., Lloyd, S. A., Henton, J. M., & Larson, J. H. (1982). Fairness and reward level as predictors of relationship satisfaction. *Social Psychology Quarterly, 45,* 177–181.

Courtright, J. A., Millar, F. E., & Rogers-Millar, L. E. (1979). Domineeringness and dominance: Replication and extension. *Communication Monographs, 46,* 179–192.

Dainton, M. (1991, May). *Relational maintenance revisited: The addition of physical affection measures to a maintenance typology.* Paper presented at the annual meeting of the International Communication Association, Chicago, IL.

Dainton, M., Stafford, L., & McNeilis, K. S. (1992, November). *The maintenance of relationships through the use of routine behaviors.* Paper presented at the annual meeting of the Speech Communication Association convention, Chicago, IL.

Davidson, B., Balswick, J., & Halverson, C. (1983). Affective self-disclosure and marital adjustment: A test of equity theory. *Journal of Marriage and the Family, 45,* 93–103.

Deutsch, M. (1985). *Distributive justice: A social-psychological perspective.* New Haven: Yale University Press.

Dickens, W. J., & Perlman, D. (1981). Friendship over the life-cycle. In S. Duck & G. R. Gilmour (Eds.), *Personal relationships: Vol. 2. Developing personal relationships* (pp. 91–122). New York: Academic Press.

Dindia, K., & Baxter, L. (1987). Strategies for maintaining and repairing marital relationships. *Journal of Social and Personal Relationships, 4,* 143–158.

Dougherty, W. J., & Ryder, R. G. (1979). Locus of control, interpersonal trust, and assertive behavior among newlyweds. *Journal of Personality and Social Psychology, 37,* 2212–2239.

Duck, S. (1988). *Relating to others.* Milton Keynes, U.K.: Open University Press.

Duck, S., Lock, A., McCall, G., Fitzpatrick, M. A., & Cayne, J. C. (1984). Social and personal relationships: A joint editorial. *Journal of Social and Personal Relationships, 1,* 1–10.

Duck, S. W., Rutt, D. J., Hurst, M. H., & Strejc, H. (1991). Some evident truths about conversation in everyday relationships. *Human Communication Research, 18,* 228–267.

Falbo, T., & Peplau, L. A. (1980). Power strategies in intimate relationships. *Journal of Personality and Social Psychology, 38,* 618–628.

Fitzpatrick, M. A. (1988). *Between husbands and wives: Communication in marriage.* Newbury Park, CA: Sage.

Hatfield, E., Traupmann, J., Sprecher, S., Utne, M., & Hay, M. (1985). Equity in close relationships. In W. Ickes (Ed.), *Compatible and incompatible relationships* (pp. 91–117). New York: Springer-Verlag.

Hatfield, E., Utne, M. K., & Traupmann, J. (1979). Equity theory and intimate relationships. In R. L. Burgess & T. L. Huston (Eds.), *Social exchange in developing relationships* (p. 112). New York: Academic Press.

Johnson-George, C., & Swap, W. C. (1982). Measurement of specific interpersonal trust: Construction and validation of a scale to assess trust in a specific other. *Journal of Personality and Social Psychology, 43,* 1306–1317.

Kelley, H. (1979). *Personal relationships: Their structure and processes.* Hillsdale, NJ: Lawrence Erlbaum Associates.

Larzelere, R. E., & Huston, T. L. (1980). The dyadic trust scale: Toward understanding interpersonal trust in close relationships. *Journal of Marriage and the Family, 42,* 595–604.

Lefcourt, H. M. (1981). The construction and development of the multidimensional-multiattributional causality scales. In H. M. Lefcourt (Ed.), *Research with the locus of control construct: Vol. 1. Assessment methods* (pp. 245–277). New York: Academic Press.

Lefcourt, H. M. (1982). *Locus of control: Current trends in theory and research* (2nd ed.), Hillsdale, NJ: Lawrence Erlbaum Associates.

Lefcourt, H. M., Martin, R. A., Fick, C. M., & Saleh, W. E. (1985). Locus of control for affiliation and behavior in social interactions. *Journal of Personality and Social Psychology, 48,* 755–759.

Lefcourt, H. M., von Bayer, C. L., Ware, E. E., & Cox, D. J. (1979). The multidimensional-multiattributional causality scale: The development of a goal specific locus of control scale. *Canadian Journal of Behavioral Science, 11,* 286–304.

Levenson, H. (1981). Differentiating among internality, powerful others, and chance. In H. M. Lefcourt (Ed.), *Research with the locus of control construct: Vol. 1. Assessment methods* (pp. 245–277). New York: Academic Press.

Martin, M. W. (1985). Satisfaction with intimate exchange: Gender-role differences and the impact of equity, equality, and rewards. *Sex Roles, 13,* 597–605.

Michaels, J. W., Edwards, J. N., & Acock, A. C. (1984). Satisfaction in intimate relationships as a function of inequality, inequity, and outcomes. *Social Psychology Quarterly, 47,* 347–357.

Millar, F. E., & Rogers, L. E. (1987). Relational dimensions of interpersonal dynamics. In M. E. Roloff & G. R. Miller (Eds.), *Interpersonal processes: New directions in communication research* (pp. 117–139). Newbury Park, CA: Sage.

Miller, G. R. (1978). The current status of theory and research in interpersonal communication. *Human Communication Research, 4,* 164–178.

Miller, P. C., Lefcourt, H. M., Holmes, J. G., Ware, E. E., & Saleh, W. E. (1986). Marital locus of control and marital problem solving. *Journal of Personality and Social Psychology, 51,* 161–169.

Mills, J., & Clark, M. S. (1982). Exchange and communal relationships. In L. Wheeler (Ed.), *Review of personality and social psychology* (pp. 121–144). Beverly Hills, CA: Sage.

Morton, T. C., Alexander, J. F., & Altman, I. (1976). Communication and relationship definition. In G.R. Miller (Ed)., *Explorations in interpersonal communication* (pp. 105–126). Beverly Hills: Sage.

Phares, E. J. (1976). *Locus of control in personality.* Morriston, NJ: General Learning.

Rempel, J. J., Holmes, J. G., & Zanna, M. P. (1985). Trust in close relationships. *Journal of personality and social psychology, 49,* 95–112.

Rubin, Z. (1973). *Liking and loving.* New York: Holt, Rinehart & Winston.

Sabatelli, R. M., & Cecil-Pigo, E. F. (1985). Relational interdependence and commitment in marriage. *Journal of Marriage and the Family, 47,* 931–937.

Scanzoni, J., & Arnett, C. (1987). Enlarging the understanding of marital commitment via religious devoutness, gender role preferences, and locus of marital control. *Journal of Family Issues, 8,* 136–156.

Shea, B. C., & Pearson, J. C. (1986). The effects of relationship type, partner intent, and gender on the selection of relationship maintenance strategies. *Communication Monographs, 53*, 354–364.

Sprecher, S. (1986). The relation between inequity and emotions in close relationships. *Social Psychology Quarterly, 49*, 309–321.

Sprecher, S. (in press). Social exchange perspectives to the dissolution of close relationships. In T. L. Orbuch (Ed.), *Close relationship loss: Theoretical approaches*. New York: Springer-Verlag.

Stafford, L., & Canary, D. J. (1991). Maintenance strategies and romantic relationship type, gender, and relational characteristics. *Journal of Social and Personal Relationships, 8*, 217–242.

Steinfatt, T. M. (1987). Personality and communication: Classical approaches. In J. C. McCroskey, & J. A. Daly (Eds.), *Personality and interpersonal communication* (pp. 42–126). Newbury Park: CA: Sage.

Traupmann, J., Petersen, R., Utne, M., & Hatfield, E. (1981). Measuring equity in intimate relations. *Applied Psychology Measurement, 5*, 467–480.

Van Yperen, N. W., & Buunk, B. P. (1990). A longitudinal study of equity and satisfaction in intimate relationships. *European Journal of Social Psychology, 20*, 287–309.

Walsh, F. (1982). Conceptualizations of normal family functioning. In F. Walsh (Ed.), *Normal family processes* (pp. 3–42). New York: The Guilford Press.

Walster, E., Walster, G. W., & Berscheid, E. (1978). *Equity: Theory and research*. Boston: Allyn & Bacon.

14

Metaphors in Accounts of Romantic Relationship Terminations

William Foster Owen
California State University, Sacramento

The past decade has witnessed considerable scholarly attention in two research domains brought together in the study presented in this chapter. Both romantic relationship termination (e.g., Baxter & Wilmot, 1985; Duck, 1982) and metaphor analysis of personal relationships (e.g., Owen, 1985a, 1990; Quinn, 1987) have received extensive research focus. Relationship termination has been examined, for example, as an event or as a gradual process (e.g., Baxter, 1984), as one of many relational turning points (Baxter & Bullis, 1986) and as a state comparable to divorce (e.g., Kressel, Jaffee, Tuchman, Watson, & Deutsch, 1980). Metaphor analysis of personal relationships has focused on, for example, the role metaphor plays in constituting the changing nature of relationships (e.g., Owen, 1990) and on the metaphorical images of self and partner in relationships (e.g., Owen, 1989). Moreover, some researchers have addressed such important relational concepts as *love* and *happiness* (e.g., Kovecses, 1988, 1991; Quinn, 1987).

Research on relationship termination generally has focused on three approaches. First, the chronology or process of termination, patterned after a relational penetration focus (e.g., Altman & Taylor, 1973; Miller & Sunnafrank, 1982), has been examined. For example, Duck (1982) proposed four phases of relational dissolution: intrapsychic, dyadic, social, and "grave dressing." Perhaps the key feature of Duck's phases was the idea that relational partners alternated within given phases, between decisions to separate or to remain in the relationship, until critical thresholds were reached. Similar to Duck's phases were Lee's (1984) five stages of dissolution: discovery of dissatisfaction, exposure, negotiation, resolution, and transformation.

Second, how couples strategically accomplish relational disengagement has supplemented our understanding of the process nature of termination (e.g., Baxter, 1982, 1985; Wilmot, Carbaugh, & Baxter, 1985). Early efforts studied issues such as how self-disclosure is used to terminate relationships (Baxter, 1979), whereas more recent attention has shifted to the step-by-step sequencing of disengagement strategies. For example, Baxter (1984) had college students record the stages or "turning points" encountered in recollected disengagements within the students' past 12 months. Although the resulting research yielded numerous disengagement strategies in eight "trajectories" (e.g., "fading away," "cost escalation," "negotiated farewell"), Baxter (1984) concluded that "a single set of stages or steps does not generalize to all, or even most, relationship dissolutions" (p. 43).

Third, the analysis of relational "break-up accounts" has emerged from the first two approaches to relationship termination. This type of inquiry assesses how participants perceive, describe, and interpret their relationships (e.g., Baxter, 1986). Research on relational accounts or sense making has taken several forms, using diverse perspectives and methods. For example, Hopper, Knapp, and Scott (1981) identified idiomatic restricted codes employed by partners as forms of relational cohesiveness. Baxter (1987) examined the types and functions of symbols used to understand romantic and friendship relationships. Owen (1984, 1985a) identified relational themes and metaphors partners embedded in talk about their relationships. Still others have examined larger units of discourse, such as stories, as organized narratives to account for and to explain their relationships (e.g., Burnett, McGhee, & Clarke, 1987; Harvey, Agostinelli, & Weber, 1989). Regarding relational termination, Baxter and Philpott (1982) had respondents write stories about hypothetical relationships thought to be near a break-up. Among other findings, these researchers found that the stories indicated a cycling oscillation between approach and avoidance strategies. Other research reports the reasons participants gave for terminations. Hill, Rubin, and Peplau (1976) found that college dating couples cited different interests, boredom with the relationship and conflicting attitudes about marriage as reasons for break-ups. However, they also found that such external factors as summer vacation or the end of the semester assisted terminations. Cody (1982) examined accounts of relationship problems leading to disengagement strategies, finding that perceived personality faults in the partner, failure to compromise by the partner, and the perception that the relationship was constraining were the most frequent problems leading to break-ups. Finally, only two studies have assessed respondents' own accounts for the break-up of relationships. Cupach and Metts (1986) had divorcees and nonmarried individuals write open-ended stories of problems leading to break-ups, finding that the most frequent problems leading to break-ups were partner or self-attributes. Baxter (1986) collected almost 300 reasons for break-ups embedded in student essays on "Why We Broke Up." She found that the need for autonomy, dissimilar attitudes, beliefs and values, and lack of supportiveness were the most frequent reasons given for terminations.

Metaphors have been used to study personal relationships as researchers increasingly have recognized the fact that metaphors go beyond their traditional linguistic function as figures of speech or poetic expressions (e.g., Black, 1962; Bowers, 1990; Ortony, 1979). As "figures of thought" (Lakoff, 1986a), metaphors also "structure how we perceive, how we think, and what we do" (Lakoff & Johnson, 1980, p. 4). Moreover, it has been argued that metaphors are not merely "nice," but instead are "necessary" (Ortony, 1975), as metaphors allow people to express meanings that are difficult or impossible to express literally (cf. Lakoff, 1986b). Numerous theoretical advancements in philosophy and linguistics have advanced our understanding of conventionalized metaphorical concepts used by the "*idealized* native speaker" (Lakoff, 1986a, p. 223; see also Johnson, 1987; Lakoff, 1987a, 1987b). However, empirical metaphor use in diverse contexts has illustrated how people use metaphor to organize, shape, and change their realities. For example, researchers have studied metaphors use in such contexts as organizations (Berg, 1985; Koch & Deetz, 1981; Pacanowsky & O'Donnell-Trujillo, 1983; Smith & Eisenberg, 1987), small groups (Ettin, 1986; Owen, 1985b), counseling and psychology (Amundson, 1988; Davis & Sandoval, 1978; Moore, 1988; Papp, 1982) and the creative writing process (Tomlinson, 1986). Because metaphor analysis in each of these contexts has revealed new conceptual understandings, it is likely that the study of metaphorical accounts of romantic relationship terminations also will reveal new insights.

Metaphor analysis already has increased our understanding of personal relationships and concepts intrinsic to relational functioning. For the most part, studies have used the analysis when two domains of meaning are linked in the sense that an understanding is attempted of a target or tenor domain in terms of an already understood source or vehicle domain (i.e., the often cited, "A IS B" form credited to Lakoff & Johnson, 1980). For example, Quinn (1987) explored how married couples described their marriages using such metaphors as, MARRIAGE AS AN INVESTMENT, A MANUFACTURED PRODUCT, and A JOURNEY. Kovecses (1988) explained hundreds of conventionalized metaphorical expressions of love, including: LOVE AS MACHINE, HEAT, FORCE, NUTRIENT, JOURNEY, and GAME. More recently, Kovecses (1991) collected numerous metaphorical expressions for the concept of happiness, some of which center on the metaphor, BEING HAPPY IS BEING OFF THE GROUND (e.g., "*I was flying high,*" "*She was on cloud nine,*" "*We were on top of the world*" (p. 31).

Using case study materials, Owen (1985a, 1990) showed how developing romantic relationships can be understood metaphorically. In Owen's first study, not only were such metaphors as RELATIONSHIP IS CAPTIVATION (e.g., "Sometimes I feel like *I'm* walking into a *trap*"), RELATIONSHIP IS

WORSHIP (e.g., "She says: 'You're my *faithful servant*'") and RELATION-
SHIP IS MACHINE (e.g., "It's like when you see a movie where the *sound-
track* is ahead of the *picture*") illustrated, but an argument was made for
the interrelationship or external coherence of seemingly separate metaphors
(1985a, pp. 6–8). In Owen's second study, an analysis of participant discourse
explained how an individual's previous metaphor (e.g., RELATIONSHIP IS
JOURNEY: "It's like you're on a trip and just *sitting in your car*") foreshadowed
a subsequent one RELATIONSHIP IS A CONTAINER: "it was like you *walk*,
you *walk*, you *walk*—you *stopped* and then *walk into the circle*") (1990, pp.
41–43).

Although the studies just cited have advanced our knowledge of the conceptualization and methods of metaphor analysis, they also have been limited
in various ways. Much linguistic research continues to extend our understanding
of conventionalized metaphorical expressions (e.g., Johnson, 1987; Kovecses,
1988, 1991). However, we do not know the actual empirical occurrences of
these expressions, nor their relational significance. Moreover, the few empirical metaphor analyses of relationships we have are limited to dating relationships (Owen, 1985a, 1989, 1990) or marital couples (Quinn, 1987), without
reference to any developmental points in these relationships and also with very
limited sample sizes. In addition, researchers have unsystematically used such
metaphors as *dissolution* (Edwards & Saunders, 1981; Miller & Parks, 1982),
disengagement (e.g., Baxter, 1979, 1984), *break-up* (Baxter, 1986; Hill et
al. 1976) and *sudden death*, or *fading away* (Davis, 1973) to define and describe
the end of relationships. We do not know, however, whether these or other
terms accurately represent the actual metaphors people use as they attempt
to make sense of their romantic relationship terminations. This chapter describes
the metaphors used by romantic partners in accounts of their relationship terminations. Previous research has not described these metaphors in detail nor
the general metaphorical themes subsuming the images used by romantic partners in describing their relationship terminations.

METHOD

Procedures

Given that research has shown that metaphors are used in a wide range of
contexts, including personal relationships, it was inferred that people experiencing romantic terminations also would utilize, at least in part, metaphorical concepts to describe and understand the process. Thus, metaphors were solicited
directly in an attempt to gather a large number of metaphorical expressions.

Participants were 110 volunteer undergraduate students (60 females, 50
males) enrolled in a communication theory course at a large southern univer-

sity. The mean age of participants was 21.8 years and the mean duration of their most recently ended relationships was 17.5 months. The elapsed time since the relationships terminated ranged from 24 hours to 7 years, with a mean elapsed time of 3.3 months. The participants were asked to focus on their most recent relationship that ended and to record written responses in an independent, open-ended classroom task lasting approximately 30 minutes. Specifically, they were asked to describe the metaphors that best represented their relationships as they ended. Also, they were asked not only to give the metaphor(s) but also to explain why the metaphor(s) captured the nature of the relationship during the time it was ending. To stimulate their responses, the author gave a 20-minute lecture before the written task. In the lecture, the conceptual nature of metaphor was given based exclusively upon the first two chapters of Lakoff and Johnson's work (1980). Such metaphors as AR-GUMENT IS WAR were given, complete with quoted examples (e.g., "He *shot down* all of my arguments," "Your claims are *indefensible*," Lakoff & Johnson, 1980, p. 4). No relational metaphors were given throughout the lecture to the research participants.

Participants also were asked to provide all communication, psychology, and related course work so the author could determine if they may have received instruction in relational metaphors previously. Twenty-three participants' written reports were discarded because such course designations as Interpersonal Communication, Marriage and the Family, and Relational Development were reported.

ANALYSIS

Metaphors and similes were coded based on Owen's (1985a) conceptual framework. Briefly, key verbs, nouns, adjectives, and adverbs were noted as indicators of similar terminology argued to systematically manifest a main metaphor. These indicators are noted throughout this chapter by italics. For example, as part of a broad metaphorical theme of RELATIONSHIP TERMINATION IS ORGANIC GROWTH/DETERIORATION, there was the SELF IS INJURED metaphor constructed of such discourse as, "It's like having a *rock in your shoe*; you know it's there and you keep *shaking it out*, but it doesn't seem to ever leave," "My heart was *broken in half*." "It was like a *headache*," and "I was a *stupid lamb falling into a trap*." In some cases, one or two metaphorical expressions, such as the examples just given, were counted as one coded metaphor. Scores of reports, however, gave metaphors as part of over one page of narrative per report. Still, although a person may have utilized more than one metaphor, the counting of main metaphors (e.g., SELF IS INJURED) was not based on the number of metaphorical terms per report.

The author coded all reports in several iterations or readings until all metaphors from all reports were coded. Each metaphor per report was recorded on a separate card, along with additional participants' comments that shed light on the intent of the metaphor. As individual main metaphors were coded, they were grouped into broader metaphorical themes that unified the subsumed main metaphors. A random sample of approximately 25% of the report data and metaphor categories were coded by two independent undergraduate coders unfamiliar with the project. Coder agreement with the author was .74 and .81 respectively. These reliabilities were assessed by dividing the number of agreements by the sum of agreements and disagreements.

RESULTS

There were 167 metaphors coded (107 provided by females, 60 provided by males). There was a mean of 1.52 metaphors coded per person (1.78 from females, 1.20 from males). As Table 14.1 indicates, there were seven main metaphors depicting the participants' subjective experience of relationship termination subsumed under three metaphorical themes. These broad metaphorical themes, UP/DOWN, ORGANIC GROWTH/DETERIORATION, and PRESENCE/ABSENCE, each comprised approximately one-third of the total metaphors and will organize the results given. Prior to a discussion of these metaphors and themes, however, a brief discussion of the dialectical or bipolar nature of the themes is offered.

A general finding in this study involves the claim that reports indicated the dialectical or bipolar quality of the three metaphorical themes. Termination, regardless of the circumstances or type of relationship, involves change. Such relational change may be in terms of reflecting on past relational episodes, or relationships, or perhaps of projecting into a plausible relational future. It is argued that participants in this study understood termination through paired concepts. One view of paired concepts involves dialectical thinking. As Baxter (1990) noted, "to a dialectical thinker, the presence of paired opposites, or contradictions, is essential to change and growth" (p. 70). Indeed, relational "growth," as Baxter put it, may precede and/or follow "death" or "deterioration." From a dialectical perspective, growth and death negate or contradict each other. A second view of paired concepts—the view adopted in this study—may be derived from Derrida's deconstructive grammatology (Derrida, 1976). In this perspective, growth and death mutually depend on each other for a conceptual definition. That is, growth (or "life") is understood in terms of death, death in terms of growth, and so on. Thus, although not every supporting example indicates its polar opposite, because each pole defines its complementary opposite, such bipolar interdependence does exist.

TABLE 14.1
Summary of Termination Metaphors

| Metaphors/Themes | Number by Gender | | Total Number/ Percentage[a] |
	Male	Female	
UP/DOWN			53 (31.70)
PARTNER IS UP/DOWN	3	5	8 (4.80)
SELF IS UP/DOWN	12	10	22 (13.20)
RELATIONSHIP IS UP/DOWN	7	16	23 (13.70)
ORGANIC GROWTH/DETERIORATION			64 (38.30)
SELF IS INJURED	10	22	32 (19.15)
RELATIONSHIP IS LIVING/DYING	12	20	32 (19.15)
PRESENCE/ABSENCE			50 (30.00)
SELF IS LACKING OR MISSING	6	15	21 (12.60)
RELATIONSHIP IS EXISTING/NONEXISTING	10	19	29 (17.40)
Totals	60	107	167 (100.00)

[a]Figures in parentheses represent percentages of the total metaphors coded.

ROMANTIC RELATIONSHIP TERMINATION METAPHORS

Relationship Termination Is Up/Down

As the main metaphors constituting this theme are explained, it is important to point to common characteristics of UP/DOWN. Metaphors and similes comprising this theme (31.7% of the total metaphors given) were defined by any description of a relational state of or movement between *up/down, top/bottom, high/low, over/under,* or *above/below.* Consistent with Lakoff and Johnson's (1980) orientation metaphors, in terminations UP was generally favorable, good, or positive, whereas DOWN was generally unfavorable, bad, or negative. See, for example, Lakoff and Johnson's (1980) "GOOD IS UP/BAD IS DOWN" metaphor (e.g., "Things are looking *up*," "Things are at an all-time *low*") (p. 16). However, the claim here is that UP/DOWN is not contradictory; each takes meaning from the other (cf. Baxter, 1988, 1990). By contrast, one's DOWN experience constitutes prior or future UP experience. Furthermore, some good and bad experience can be expressed by UP or DOWN or both. For instance, one female wrote that the relationship "was *bumpy*. It had it's *peaks* and its *lows*. It was like a *bottle of soda*. If we shook it up, feelings would *bubble up* inside and then, if you *opened the bottle*, all those feelings would *spill* out and there would be a loud discussion." Here, the "bubbling up" was dreaded and, therefore, negative. Thus, not all UP IS GOOD. UNKNOWN or OUT OF CONTROL IS UP (e.g., "I guess that's still *up in the air*," "Costs are *out of sight*") and KNOWN or IN CONTROL IS DOWN (e.g., "Let's *nail this down*," "This manuscript is *under* control").

In the PARTNER IS UP/DOWN metaphor, comprising less than 5% of all metaphors, individuals characterized their partners as bad or even evil. For example, one female labeled her male partner a "*snake* in the *grass*," whereas another woman echoed, "he was *lower* than a *snake's belly*." Also, a male described his relationship as an "*ugly sludge* at the *bottom of the barrel*," and that she was a "*pig rooting around in the mud*." Interestingly, some of these partners reached these unflattering, negative, LOWER positions after having been viewed in positive UPPER positions. For example, the female who described her partner as "*lower* than a *snake's belly*," saw him before termination as "someone I could *look up to*—sort of admire." And, a woman who wrote glowingly about her male as "having an intellect *over* all guys I've ever met," later changed her view when they terminated. She wrote, "he turned out to be so *shallow*; I told him, 'I've *stepped* in *deeper puddles* than your heart.'" Moreover, another female noted that "he was really *heavy* into Pat (a rival female) and I had trouble staying second." Here, a heavy object, say a rock thrown into a pond, typically results in a low, bottom, under, or down location. In sum, it is curious to note that not only do some accounts place partners DOWN, where previously they had been UP (e.g., admired), but also that the person giving the account sometimes was UP or a "better person" than the partner. Note, for example, how the woman above had "moved" from admiring her partner's intellect "*over* all guys I've met" (he was UP, she was DOWN), to disrespect brought on by termination. Then, she felt she had "*stepped* into *deeper puddles*" than his heart (she was UP, he was DOWN). It is clear that the UP/DOWN theme forms a bipolar concept affording movement between its poles.

The SELF IS UP/DOWN metaphor comprised just over 13% of all metaphors. As foreshadowed, participants gave accounts that sometimes placed themselves in a superior UP position as a concomitant of viewing their partners as DOWN, in an evil, inferior, or "bad" position. Most accounts involving this metaphor, however, personalized self in terms of the positive and negative consequences of the termination. For example, a man facing an inevitable termination strained under the burden, feeling as if a *"heavy burden* had been *lifted from my back,* like a *pack horse unloaded"* once the relationship ended. A strikingly similar account also was offered by a female: "I was so worried when we were having trouble, like a *burden"* and "It was like a huge *weight* had been *lifted from my shoulders."* The process of going through termination burdened participants, resulting in a DOWN orientation. After participants recovered emotionally from the termination, at least partially, interpretations switched from DOWN to UP (i.e., the relief of unburdening). Of the 12 accounts given by males, 10 expressed this kind of transition from DOWN to UP, whereas only 1 female of 10 illustrated such a shift. It may be that these results depended on which particular part of the termination an account focused on to determine if the DOWN position would ultimately convert to UP. However, it may be that males are more likely to recover quickly than females as evidenced in the males' movement from DOWN to UP. This contrasts with the Hill et al. (1976) study, which found that males apparently took longer to recover emotionally from break-ups. Moreover, some participants in fact sensed the impending recovery of post-termination in such expressions as: "When we were really fighting and trying to talk things out, it was fighting an *uphill* battle" (female) and "It was like *running uphill;* the more energy and effort required to maintain the relationship, the more *bogged down* in *deep* discussions we became" (male).

It is important to point out, however, that 11 of the 22 accounts (nine females, two males) expressing this metaphor constituted SELF IS DOWN characterizations. For example, female reports included: "As *rocky* as a *mountain slide,* I felt *lower* than a *well-digger's ass";* "It was like having the *floor drop out from under me";* "The split made me feel *dropped* like a hot potato"; "We broke up twice. Both times I felt like he was taking me for granted. I felt like *dirt,* really *depressed";* "First I was *head over heels* in love, then I *slid downhill."* A male, too, illustrated the metaphor similarly: "At first, it was like skating on a beautiful *iced over* lake, then *I fell through the ice."*

Almost 14% of all reports expressed the RELATIONSHIP IS UP/DOWN metaphor. This metaphor differs from the two preceding ones in that the relationship as an entity is described. Also, all reports were characterized by metaphors with inherent, simultaneous UP/DOWN processes. For example, 17 of the 23 reports labeled the relationship as a "roller coaster" (e.g., "It's like a *roller coaster,* without the excitement"; "We were both on *cloud nine,* then things went bad and started going *downhill,* an emotional *roller coaster"*). Two dominant meanings were expressed in the UP/DOWN metaphor: inevitability and hope of saving the relationship. The general cycle of UP/DOWN was perceived as an inevitable *"ride* that I couldn't control or stop," but more microscopically each *"low point"* offered hope of the next *"peak,"* or good time. As one female noted, "We had times when we were at the *top,* but I knew that the only place to go was *down;* still, when we rode the *roller coaster* to the *bottom*, I knew we would soon make up and head back to greater *heights*." There were other images beyond the *roller coaster*, however, that also expressed inevitability and hope of reconciliation. For example, one male described an impending termination as, "things got out of hand like a *popcorn machine*, problems *popping up* one by one." "It became a *domino reaction*," he continued, "just as sure as we would try to deal with one problem—putting it *to rest*—another would pop *up*." But, he concluded, "with each solving of a problem, I felt we still had a chance to still be together." Still others, such as two females, depicted terminations similarly, "I was ready *to take a hike*, but it was like the relationship became an endless succession of *peaks* and *valleys*—the *peaks* were so good that I almost forgot how bad the *valleys* were;" "We were a *boat in a storm*, rocking *up and down* and back and forth at the mercy of the storm—we just had to *ride it out*." "It could've gone either way," she added, "either we would *sink* or be happy and *ride it out*." Importantly, then, by focusing on the rhythmic, oscillating ups and downs of the relationship, unlike focusing on either partner, the relationship was perceived to have hope of survival and continuance.

Relationship Termination is Organic Growth/Deterioration

Metaphors of this theme (comprising 38.3% of the total metaphors) were defined through such concepts as *growth/decay*, *life/death*, and *health/injury* or *illness*. Rather than focusing on orientation, such as UP/DOWN, these metaphors drew on organic, living (and dying) processes for understanding the termination process. The metaphors in this theme focused on self or relationship; no partner attributions were found.

It should come as no surprise to find that about 19% of all metaphors coded were the SELF IS INJURED metaphor. Termination for most is a painful, injurious process. It is perhaps more interesting to note that 22 of the 32 descriptions were given by females. Indeed, this represents the most frequent singular metaphor given individually by males or females found in the study. Examples of the metaphor given by females include heart injuries: "My heart was *broken in half*"; "He *bored a hole* in my heart"; "He left a *huge hole* in my heart"; "My heart felt like a *dart board* always being *poked*"; "It (the termination) was a *knife stabbed into my heart*"; and "Our *break-up* was a total *heart by-pass*." In fact, 19 of the 22 female descriptions of SELF IS INJURED were heart "injuries," suggesting the conventionalized nature of this metaphor. Curiously, many of these females also had described their relationships during happier times as physically enhancing: "He *filled* my heart with love"; "My heart *fluttered* when we were together." The remaining three female characterizations were less personal (e.g., "It [the relationship] was an *uncomfortable car seat*, everything seemed in the wrong place, not *adjusted* quite right"; "It was like having a *rock in your shoe*").

Males gave exclusively less intimate self-injured attributions. For example, males explained termination as, "Like a *headache*, with the *break-up* being the *cure*"; "I was *torn to shreds*" and "Living close together is *a twin razor* with a *double edge*—we can enjoy each other and *grow*, but I can also get *hurt* or *cut*"; "It [the termination] was like a *wisdom tooth*, it starts *hurting*, but if you get it *pulled* you have great relief." We do not know from these accounts, however, if males were less "injured" than females, if they were more guarded in their accounts, or if females have more vivid personal accounts than males. It is interesting that, with the exception of one male who was "*torn to shreds*," females essentially were "mortally wounded" (i.e., heart "injuries" are life or relationally threatening). That is, to say that a termination was a "*knife stabbed into my heart*" is to illustrate SELF (and RELATIONSHIP) IS DEAD or DYING, not merely INJURED. This specific expression of SELF IS INJURED, then, offers little hope of relational continuance.

About 19% of all metaphors coded focused on the RELATIONSHIP IS LIVING/DYING, comprised of alive/dead or more creative expressions of *flourishing/decomposing*, *growth/decay*, and so on. As was mentioned when discussing the RELATIONSHIP IS UP/DOWN metaphor, LIVING/DYING included a dominant meaning of hope of survival, or minimally, a recognition of progressive DYING. For example, there were 12 expressions of *growth/death*, organismic metaphors (nine females, three males): "It was like a *flower that blossomed then withered*—now it's *extinct*;" "The relationship went *dry*, but now it's starting to *blossom* again"; "It (the relationship) was *dead*, but he tried to *resurrect* it"; "The relationship has *growth spurts*"; and "The relationship most resembles *cactus and water*, the *cactus* does not want or require *water*, but it enjoys the *water* it gets—the problem, however, is that too much could *kill* it." The point here is that all organisms are in an ongoing, entropic process of living/dying/regeneration until life ceases. Thus, relationships viewed as LIVING/DYING need not terminate and may, given sufficient care, "*resurrect*," or "*blossom*" anew.

Interestingly, another 12 expressions of this metaphor (six from females, six from males) illustrated creative, progressive DECAY, DETERIORATION or SPOILAGE: "Over a two-week period, I began to notice problems—it was becoming as *old* as *mold* on food—I could see the relationship *rot* each day;" "The relationship was a *dirty diaper* that *smelled* as it got worse;" "It [the relationship] went *sour* and *dropped off* like *rotten fruit*"; and "When we first started, we were like a *VW* and *beer*, then as things got rough, we became more like an *Edsel* and *near beer*, with the end of it, we're a *rusty tin can* and *piss*." Just as the organismic metaphors engendered hope of renewed "growth," the recognition by participants of the progressive decay or worsening of their relationships also provides some possibility that the process could be reversed.

For example, the female who noticed her relationship becoming "*old* as *mold on food*" noted how she "tried extra hard to keep the relationship from becoming completely *rotten*." Again, an oscillating focus on the relationship continuum of LIVING/DYING, like UP/DOWN, enabled a kind of movement that included reversal of the termination process. Nonetheless, again just as UP/DOWN might terminate in DOWN, LIVING/DYING for the remaining eight expressions (five from females, three from males) illustrated the RELATIONSHIP IS DEAD metaphor: "The relationship is *dead* as a *doornail*"; "What we had is *dead*—I mean, I could *smell a rat*"; "Our relationship is *dead*, it's *history*." In sum, it appears that some metaphors, perhaps those focusing on the relationship as an entity on a continuum, enable possible avoidance of termination.

Relationship Termination is Presence/Absence

Metaphors of this theme (comprising 30% of all coded metaphors) were defined by such concepts as: *possessing/lacking, full/empty, existing/nonexisting, on/off, together/alone,* and *appearing/disappearing.* With each concept, the absence of some individual or relational quality or condition preceded and/or followed an interpretation of the presence or existence of such a quality. In general, polar terms, such as *lacking, empty, nonexisting,* and *disappearing,* constituted the termination proper. In addition, each term's complement denoted extra-termination meanings. As found previously, these metaphors were about self or relationship.

The SELF IS LACKING or MISSING metaphor comprised about 12% of all metaphors reported (6 by males, 15 by females). Two males and 10 females reported they lacked, missed, or felt incomplete as a result of the termination. These metaphorical expressions, although varying, were interpretations indicating internal states of the self: "I felt I was *missing a piece* after we broke-up"; "I felt *less than whole*"; "I felt *empty* and anxious"; "I feel *nothing*, like being *shot with novocaine*"; and "There's just a *blank space* where she used to be before." Both males indicated feeling "*nothing*" or a "*blank space.*" Eight of the ten females who used this aspect of the metaphor utilized a FULL/EMPTY scheme to describe themselves before and after termination: "I never knew how full of life and love I was until I felt the *empty loss* of not being with him"; "After we stopped seeing each other, I kept waiting to be *filled up* by his love—I was *empty*" and "he left a *huge hole* in me that will probably never be *filled up.*" These descriptions of FULL/EMPTY closely relate to the well known CONTAINER metaphor explained in the literature (see Johnson, 1987; Owen, 1990).

A second major characterization of metaphors listed by the remaining four males and five females extends this lacking or emptiness to a perception of the disappearance of self, loss, or aloneness of self: "I felt *sweet as candy*, but now I'm a *sucker* which *disappears*"; "It [the effects of the termination] was like being *lost* in a giant airport"; "I felt alone, a *tumbleweed* alone in the desert *blowing with no direction*." One female gave a particularly poignant account: "The end of our relationship was especially lonely for me. It was a *closing door*, an anticipation of return, like being *left in a department store*, wondering if someone's gonna *come back* to get you, but knowing he won't." These accounts indicate that males described their termination experience in terms of being "*lost*," whereas females emphasized feelings of being "*left*" by their partners.

The RELATIONSHIP IS EXISTING/NONEXISTING metaphor comprised about 17% of all coded metaphors (10 from males, 19 from females) through such terms as *dissolving, fading, melting,* and *disappearing*. An interesting aspect of this metaphor, like the UP/DOWN and LIVING/DYING relational metaphors already explained, is the process nature in the descriptions. That is, the focus on the *relationship*, coupled with the bipolar, oscillating nature of concepts used, revealed a possibility of reversing terminations already completed or preventing them from occurring. Fifteen of the 19 females using this metaphor, and only 1 of the 10 males, used the metaphor in ways that indicated possible recovery and continuance of the relationship. Some female reports include: "We just *faded into the sunset*, but like every *sunset* with each day there's a new *sun* and maybe we'll *walk back out* and start over"; "It's like we just *stopped* or *disappeared into nothingness*, but then we'd *reappear* or be a relationship again—this kind of *now you have it-now you don't* kind of relationship is hard to take." The sole male using this metaphor gave a similar image: "It [the relationship] was a *lingering ghost*, sometimes it was *there*, then it was *gone*, then it was *back in view* again; I wish we could get a *sharp, solid* relationship."

The remaining four females gave metaphors that appeared less likely to indicate such hope for relational continuance: "Our relationship was like a *sweet dissolving piece of candy*, at first it was *very sweet* and good, but it didn't *last*"; "Our relationship is *nothing*"; "We are *nonexistent*." Perhaps more interesting, however, is the fact that 9 of the 19 males using this metaphor illustrated complete, unrecoverable terminations: "It's a *black hole*, once we ended it, *nothing* could return"; "Now it's a *vacuum*—no air or anything—we have no relationship"; "It's a *void*"; "The relationship is *zero, null* and *void*."

DISCUSSION

The seven specific metaphors found in this study and the three themes that subsume them show that relationship termination is explained, described, and understood in physical terms. They resemble, therefore, what Johnson (1987) calls "embodied schemata," or "structures that are constantly operating in our perception, bodily movement through space, and physical manipulation of objects" (p. 23). Johnson has explained such schemata as: FROM-TO, NEAR-FAR and IN-OUT. The FROM-TO schema, for example, is built on such primitive recurrent bodily actions as: walking from one location to another, giving an object to another person, throwing an object (e.g., a rock) to another place (e.g., at or toward a metal can), "punching your brother" and "the melting of ice into water" (Johnson, 1987, p. 28). These physical bases underlie such metaphorical expressions as: "Will you get *to the point*?!" "Let me tell you where I'm *coming from*."

In terms of the findings in this study, termination as UP/DOWN, GROWTH/DETERIORATION, and PRESENCE/ABSENCE is built on non-metaphorical physical bases. For example, UP/DOWN likely is constructed of such familiar movements as: (a) getting up and sitting down in a chair, (b) holding an arm up to ask a question, and (c) losing the grip on an object, resulting in it falling down to the ground. Here, too, these actual up–down movements and orientations may become metaphors we draw on in social circumstances: "If you want to know what 'metaphor' means, look it *up*!" "What are you *up* to?" and "Get *down* and boogie!" Because actual movement and other physical interactions are inherent to life for all humans, it is argued that the schemata from which they come are fertile concepts for understanding social, relational phenomena. Apart from the recent linguistic explorations of such physical metaphors or schemata (e.g., Johnson, 1987; Kovecses, 1991; Lakoff, 1987a), and the limited case analyses (e.g., Owen, 1990), the study reported in this chapter is one of the first to show which metaphorical themes form broad concepts for specific phenomena. This study gives evidence that UP/DOWN,GROWTH/DETERIORATION, and PRESENCE/ABSENCE are physical, metaphorical themes that are appropriate concepts for relational termination sense-making. Because these three themes pertain specifically to termination, a logical next step is to identify other metaphorical themes participants might use to make sense of relationships not threatened by the prospect of termination.

Not only is it interesting to note that participants characterized termination (the nonphysical) in terms of physical experience, it is interesting to explore further the patterns of metaphors across these themes. First, as was argued, the metaphors in this study were paired, bipolar concepts. However, one's thinking at a particular time may center on one pole. This, too, was evident when discussing the schemata. For instance, "Will you get *to* the point!?" accents the TO more than the FROM. In this study, in the UP/DOWN theme, both PARTNER IS UP/DOWN and SELF IS UP/DOWN particularly focused on DOWN or UP (especially the DOWN of termination). An interesting finding, however, was the notion that in each of the three themes, a focus on the oscillatory, intermittent movement *between* polar concepts engendered a perception of greater likelihood of relationship continuation (cf. Altman, Vinsel, & Brown, 1981). For example, in the RELATIONSHIP IS UP/DOWN metaphor, the *roller coaster* and *peaks and valleys* interpretations offered hope of relational continuation. Additionally, RELATIONSHIP IS LIVING/DYING ("The relationship went *dry*, but now it's starting to *blossom* again"), and RELATIONSHIP IS EXISTING/NONEXISTING ("We just *stopped* or *disappeared* into *nothingness*, but then we'd *reappear* or be a relationship again") also illustrated points of recovery or termination avoidance. These three oscillating metaphors account for 84 of the 167 or just over half of all metaphors coded (55 females, 29 males). This may mean that, apart from the four females and nine males who used the EXISTING/NONEXISTING metaphor and gave no direct expression of termination recovery or avoidance, an oscillatory focus is a common experience deserving further research attention (see Baxter, 1988, 1990). This finding is in partial agreement with Baxter's (1984) study which found that, of a set of 97 respondents, "one-third of the relationships in this data set oscillated at least once between termination and repair" (p. 45). It is possible that future studies of couples who have reconciled, compared with those who have not, may be explained at least in part by different language usage.

Second, there were some gender-specific patterns of metaphor usage across themes. As previously discussed, there were three oscillating metaphors that afforded termination avoidance or recovery. Of the 84 oscillating metaphors, 55 were given by females and 29 by males. These numbers represent just over 51% of all female metaphors and just over 48% of all male metaphors coded. Because these metaphors focused on the relationship and not on self or partner (e.g., RELATIONSHIP IS LIVING/DYING), they present an interesting contrast to a commonly held belief in relationship research. Namely, it is said often that females are more relationship oriented than the individually oriented males (see Baxter, 1986; Gilligan, 1982; Wood, 1986). This finding may be an artifact of data collection as participants were asked to write about their failed relationships. However, the data may show that males and females may focus about equally on self- and relational concerns when understanding terminations.

Females, more so than males, described their termination experience in the SELF IS UP/DOWN metaphor by accenting DOWN or negative images (e.g., "I felt *lower* than a *well-digger's ass*"). Males explained a transition from DOWN to UP (e.g., "a *heavy burden* had been *lifted from my back*"). Females, too, used the SELF IS INJURED and SELF IS LACKING or MISSING metaphors in greater number than males. Thus, by summing these three SELF metaphors, we find that females utilized 47 expressions to 28 male expressions of the same three metaphors. Apart from these numbers, though, female descriptions were more personalized, hurtful, and dramatic than those given by males. Recall that females reported "heart injuries" (e.g., "My heart was *broken in half*") and SELF IS LACKING in terms of "emptiness" (e.g., "I was *empty*"), whereas males reported terminations as "like a *headache*," "being *lost*," and "feeling *nothing*." As mentioned earlier, this finding contrasts with the Hill et al. (1976) study, which reported that males were more distraught emotionally than females as a result of break-ups. It may be that, in addition to giving slightly more metaphors than males overall, females may give more vivid, and therefore personalized and dramatic, metaphors than males. Nonetheless, more research is needed to understand more fully the subjective experience of termination.

This study introduced new concepts for understanding the romantic relationship termination process. There are justifications for using some of the metaphors that have appeared in the literature on termination. For example, "sudden death" and "fading away" (e.g., Davis, 1973) are found in the ORGANIC GROWTH/DETERIORATION and PRESENCE/ABSENCE metaphorical themes, respectively. "Dissolution," too, is part of the latter theme (e.g., Edwards & Saunders, 1981; Miller & Parks, 1982). Even "break-up" (e.g., Baxter, 1986; Hill et al., 1976) may be part of the UP/DOWN theme. As a result of this study, however, we now know more about what is meant when participants use such metaphors to describe their romantic relationships that are "on the rocks."

REFERENCES

Altman, I., & Taylor, D. (1973). *Social penetration: The development of interpersonal relationships.* New York: Holt, Rinehart & Winston.

Altman, I., Vinsel, A., & Brown, B. B. (1981). Dialectic conceptions in social psychology. In L. Berkowitz (Ed.), *Advances in experimental social psychology* (Vol. 14, pp. 107–160). New York: Academic Press.

Amundson, N. E. (1988). The use of metaphor and drawings in case conceptualizations. *Journal of Counseling and Development, 66,* 391–393.

Baxter, L. A. (1979). Self-disclosure as a relationship disengagement strategy: An exploratory investigation. *Human Communication Research, 5,* 215–222.

Baxter, L. A. (1982). Strategies for ending relationships: Two studies. *Western Journal of Speech Communication, 46,* 223–241.

Baxter, L. A. (1984). Trajectories of relationship dissolution. *Journal of Social and Personal Relationships, 1,* 29–48.

Baxter, L. A. (1985). Accomplishing relationship disengagement. In S. W. Duck & D. Perlman (Eds.), *Understanding personal relationships: An interdisciplinary approach* (pp. 243–265). Beverly Hills, CA: Sage.

Baxter, L. A. (1986). Gender differences in the heterosexual relationship rules embedded in break-up accounts. *Journal of Social and Personal Relationships, 3,* 289–306.

Baxter, L. A. (1987). Symbols of relationship identity in relationship cultures. *Journal of Social and Personal Relationships, 4,* 261–280.

Baxter, L. A. (1988). A dialectical perspective on communication strategies in relationship development. In S. W. Duck, D. F. Hay, S. E. Hobfoll, W. Iches, & B. Montgomery (Eds.), *Handbook of personal relationships* (pp. 257–273). Chichester, England: Wiley.

Baxter, L. A. (1990). Dialectical contradictions in relationship development. *Journal of Social and Personal Relationships*, *3*, 69–88.

Baxter, L. A., & Bullis, C. (1986). Turning points in developing romantic relationships. *Human Communication Research*, *12*, 469–493.

Baxter, L. A., & Philpott, J. (1982). Attribution-based strategies for initiating and terminating relationships: A process view. *Communication Quarterly*, *30*, 217–224.

Baxter, L. A., & Wilmot, W. W. (1985). Interaction characteristics of disengaging, stable, and growing relationships. In R. Gilmour & S. W. Duck (Eds.), *The emerging field of personal relationships* (pp. 145–160). Hillsdale, NJ: Lawrence Erlbaum Associates.

Berg, P. (1985). Organization change as a symbolic transformation process. In P. Frost, L. Moore, M. Louis, C. Lundberg, & J. Martin (Eds.), *Organizational culture* (pp. 281–300). Beverly Hills, CA: Sage.

Black, M. (1962). *Models and metaphors: Studies in language and philosophy.* Ithaca: Cornell University Press.

Bowers, J. W. (1990). Dating "a figure of thought." *Metaphor and Symbolic Activity*, *5*, 249–250.

Burnett, R., McGhee, P., & Clarke, D. (1987). *Accounting for relationships.* London: Methuen.

Cody, M. J. (1982). A typology of disengagement strategies and an examination of the role intimacy, reactions to inequity, and relational problems play in strategy selection. *Communication Monographs*, *49*, 148–170.

Cupach, W. R., & Metts, S. (1986). Accounts of relational dissolution: A comparison of marital and non-marital relationships. *Communication Monographs*, *53*, 311–334.

Davis, M. S. (1973). *Intimate relations.* New York: The Free Press.

Davis, J. M., & Sandoval, J. (1978). Metaphor in group mental health consultation. *Journal of Community Psychology*, *6*, 374–382.

Derrida, J. (1976). *Of grammatology.* Translated by G. C. Spivak. Baltimore: Johns Hopkins Press.

Duck, S. W. (1982). A topography of relationship disengagement and dissolution. In S. W. Duck (Ed.), *Personal relationships 4: Dissolving personal relationships* (pp. 1–30). New York: Academic Press.

Edwards, J., & Saunders, J. (1981). Coming apart: A model of the marital dissolution decision. *Journal of Marriage and the Family*, *43*, 379–389.

Ettin, M. F. (1986). Within the group's view. *Small Group Behavior*, *17*, 407–426.

Gilligan, C. (1982). *In a different voice.* Cambridge: Harvard University Press.

Harvey, J. H., Agostinelli, G., & Weber, A. L. (1989). Account-making and the formation of expectations about close relationships. In C. Hendrick (Ed.), *Close relationships* (pp. 39–62). Newbury Park: Sage.

Hill, C. T., Rubin, Z., & Peplau, L. A. (1976). Breakups before marriage: The end of 103 affairs. *Journal of Social Issues*, *32*, 147–168.

Hopper, R., Knapp, M. L., & Scott, L. (1981). Couples' personal idioms: Exploring intimate talk. *Journal of Communication*, *31*, 23–33.

Johnson, M. (1987). *The body in the mind: The bodily basis of reason and imagination.* Chicago: University of Chicago Press.

Koch, S., & Deetz, S. (1981). Metaphor analysis of social reality in organizations. *Journal of Applied Communication Research*, *9*, 1–15.

Kovecses, Z. (1988). *The language of love: The semantics of passion in conversational English.* Lewisburg, PA: Bucknell University Press.

Kovecses, Z. (1991). Happiness: A definitional effort. *Metaphor and Symbolic Activity*, *6*, 29–46.

Kressel, K., Jaffee, N., Tuchman, B., Watson, C., & Deutsch, M. (1980). A typology of divorcing couples: Implications for mediation and the divorce process. *Family Process*, *19*, 101–116.

Lakoff, G. (1986a). A figure of thought. *Metaphor and Symbolic Activity*, *1*, 215–225.

Lakoff, G. (1986b). The meanings of literal. *Metaphor and Symbolic Activity*, *1*, 291–296.

Lakoff, G. (1987a). *Women, fire, and dangerous things.* Chicago: University of Chicago Press.

Lakoff, G. (1987b). Image metaphors. *Metaphor and Symbolic Activity*, *1*, 219–222.

Lakoff, G., & Johnson, M. (1980). *Metaphors we live by*. Chicago: University of Chicago Press.

Lee, L. (1984). Sequences in separation: Framework for investigating endings of the personal (romantic) relationship. *Journal of Social and Personal Relationships*, *1*, 49–73.

Miller, G. R., & Parks, M. (1982). Communication in dissolving relationships. In S. W. Duck (Ed.), *Personal relationships 4: Dissolving personal relationships* (pp. 127–154). New York: Academic Press.

Miller, G. R., & Sunnafrank, M. J. (1982). All is for one but one is not for all: A conceptual perspective of interpersonal communication. In F. E. X. Dance (Ed.), *Human communication theory: Comparative essays* (pp. 220–242). New York: Harper & Row.

Moore, B. (1988). A young child's use of a physical-psychological metaphor. *Metaphor and Symbolic Activity*, *3*, 223–232.

Ortony, A. (1975). Why metaphors are necessary and not just nice. *Educational Theory*, *25*, 45–53.

Ortony, A. (1979). *Metaphor and thought*. New York: Cambridge University Press.

Owen, W. F. (1984). Interpretive themes in relational communication. *Quarterly Journal of Speech*, *70*, 274–287.

Owen, W. F. (1985a). Thematic metaphors in relational communication: A conceptual framework. *Western Journal of Speech Communication*, *49*, 1–13.

Owen, W. F. (1985b). Metaphor analysis of cohesiveness in small discussion groups. *Small Group Behavior*, *16*, 415–424.

Owen, W. F. (1989). Image metaphors of women and men in personal relationships. *Women's Studies in Communication*, *12*, 37–57.

Owen, W. F. (1990). Delimiting relational metaphors. *Communication Studies*, *41*, 35–53.

Pacanowsky, M. E., & O'Donnell-Trujillo, N. (1983). Organizational communication as cultural performance. *Communication Monographs*, *50*, 126–147.

Papp, P. (1982). Staging reciprocal metaphors in a couples group. *Family Process*, *21*, 453–467.

Quinn, N. (1987). Convergent evidence for a cultural model of American marriage. In D. Holland & N. Quinn (Eds.), *Cultural models in language and thought* (pp. 173–192). New York: Cambridge University Press.

Smith, R. C., & Eisenberg, E. (1987). Conflict at Disneyland: A root-metaphor analysis. *Communication Monographs*, *54*, 367–380.

Tomlinson, B. (1986). Cooking, mining, gardening, hunting: Metaphorical stories writers tell about their composing processes. *Metaphor and Symbolic Activity*, *1*, 57–79.

Wilmot, W. W., Carbaugh, D. A., & Baxter, L. A. (1985). Communicative strategies used to terminate romantic relationships. *Western Journal of Speech Communication*, *49*, 204–216.

Wood, J. T. (1986). Different voices in relationship crises: An extension of Gilligan's theory. *American Behavioral Scientist*, *29*, 273–301.

V

SUMMARY AND PERSPECTIVE

15

Communication and Interpersonal Relationships: Lust, Rust, and Dust

Mary Anne Fitzpatrick
University of Wisconsin

This book presents a coherent set of chapters examining communication in interpersonal relationships at various points in time. I have been interested in the study of communication in social and personal relationships for the past 20 years. I am pleased that Pamela Kalbfleisch has asked me to write this epilogue because it gives me the opportunity to consider these excellent chapters in making general commentary on the state of the research and theory in the area.

The agreement across these authors on a variety of issues can be credited to the editor of this volume who has a clear and consistent picture of the work she wants to highlight. These chapters share two important background assumptions made by these authors that form the core rationale for their studies of communication in evolving relationships. First, each chapter starts with the assumption that communication processes are central to the initiation, development, maintenance, and ending of interpersonal relationships. All of our interpersonal relationships are accomplished through communication. Interaction is significantly affected by the relationship between communicators and vice versa. This assumption is one that I share with the authors but one on which we need to keep a skeptical eye. As long as we say communication in relationships is central and not proscribe the kind of communication we are talking about, I think we are on firm ground.

The second working assumption of researchers in the study of communication in relationships is not only that communication is central to relational processes but also that any key relational process will be displayed in a linguistic and/or nonverbal form. A researcher in this tradition who wants to study violence in couples, for example, would assume that, in a laboratory interaction, the violence between the pair would be displayed symbolically. How couples talk provides a window on their relationships.

I think we can consider the connection between interpersonal communication and interpersonal relationships as the core of relational communication. Interpersonal communication is not merely the talk that occurs among partners. Instead, this communication is a transactional process among individuals who share ties of loyalty and identity (cf. Fitzpatrick & Wamboldt, 1990; Noller & Fitzpatrick, in press). The points of consensus across the chapters in this volume represent major shifts and trends in the study of interpersonal communication in relationships. It is conceptualizations such as these that will change the nature and shape of the relational research enterprise and make a lasting contribution to the multiple disciplines that study these relationships.

In addition to these points of consensus, the authors of these chapters are clearly open to the acceptance of a multiplicity of methods for studying interpersonal relationships. Poole and McPhee (1985) argued that there is no necessary inherent connection between the type of explanation (i.e., causal, conventional, or dialectical) one is attempting to offer and the method of data collection chosen (i.e., hypodeductive, modeling, or grounded). For example, laboratory studies can be employed to uncover the rules people have for relationships and grounded data collection methods can be used to offer causal explanations. Such methodological flexibility is evident in this book.

In today's intellectual climate, it is cosmopolitan to be open to employing a diversity of methods for studying interpersonal relationships. I support this openness for a variety of reasons, not the least of which is the inherent difficulty of studying social and personal relationships. Methodological innovation is necessary if we are to get anywhere. The Bullis, Clark, and Sline chapter in this volume is a wonderful example of using a methodological innovation to study romantic relationships. Kalbfleisch in her chapter on enduring friendships also employed a resourceful technique for gaining insight into these relationships. In my own work, I have employed a variety of different methods and approaches and have even recently been examining in-depth interviews with individuals about their earliest memories of their families (cf. Fitzpatrick, 1988, 1991; Fitzpatrick, Fey, & Segrin, in press).

Although I support catholicity of method in acquiring information, I am more orthodox about the nature of the explanations we ultimately should be striving for in the study of communication in social and personal relationships. I believe that whatever method we employ, we should be striving toward causal explanations of relational phenomena. Following Greenwood (1991), I have a realist philosophy of social science. This view asserts that a scientific approach to the study of communication in social and personal relationships must be anchored in three important premises for the ultimate goals of empirical social science.

First, empirical social science is objective. The explanations and descriptions it advances are true or false according to whether or not reality does have the properties attributed to it.

Second, social science advances causal explanations. The job of science is to explain how certain regularities, events, or structures are produced or generated. To argue for the primacy of causal explanation does not necessarily support much of the "baggage" that went along with causal explanations in the received view of the philosophy of science (Suppe, 1977).

A realist conception of causality does not require acceptance of the principle of singularity of causation. In other words, every relational event does not necessarily have one and only one causal explanation. Such a view also does not require a principle of invariance in space and time for our explanations of relational phenomena. We can set boundaries in our casual explanations and that is vital for studies of communication in relationships. Finally, to advance a causal explanation for relational phenomena does not require acceptance of a principle of causal determinism. Clearly, some human powers referenced in causal explanations of human action may be under the control of human agents.

Third, science employs observational methods in order to discriminate casual factors and eliminate competing causal explanations. To focus on observational methods does not necessarily mean that only laboratory experiments are helpful in understanding social and personal relationships. Although laboratory experiments have many fine features (e.g., ruling out competing explanations, control, etc.), they may be less useful for understanding human relationships and communication. And, the really interesting explanations that might tell us something powerful about the nature of communication in human relationships are probably not ethically testable in a laboratory setting.

Consider Planalp's work on uncertainty in interpersonal relationships (Planalp & Honeycutt, 1985; Planalp, Rutherford, & Honeycutt, 1988). Planalp and her associates examined events that caused uncertainty in relationships. The premise in Planalp's research program is that when new information that violates established knowledge is presented in a relationship, the very basis of the relationship is undermined. All of us can think of a number of ways to test existing knowledge bases, create a laboratory condition in which some participants have this knowledge undermined, and then, ways to assess the damage done. But can any of us think of ways to do this ethically? If we do not want to change the relationships we study in either a positive or a negative direction (perhaps a naive view), we probably have to abandon the laboratory.

The study of communication in interpersonal relationships has clearly moved beyond a rudimentary positivist philosophy and now endeavors to consider relationships in contexts. Much of the research presented in this volume clearly reflects this shift to a study of interpersonal relationships in context. For example, Bendtschneider and Duck, in their chapter, even tackle the complexity of "couple friends."

Finally, this entire book is based on the metaphor of interpersonal relationships as evolving entities. This is an interesting variation from the traditional growth metaphor that has been used so powerfully in the study of communication in interpersonal relationships. Instead of conceptualizing relationships as moving from lust, to rust, to dust, this book presents a more encouraging perspective of relationships as moving along phases of evolution. With this perspective, the growth of relationships is not a given—neither is their eventual deterioration. Relationships may slide backward and decelerate or they may evolve into highly intimate, long-term relationships. It is also possible that the relational partners never evolve beyond any particular maturation phase.

This is a useful perspective because it suggests interesting directions for future research in interpersonal relationships that have previously been overlooked. Owen's chapter in this volume and his previous work (e.g., Owen, 1985, 1989) illustrates the power of metaphors in conceptualizing our interpersonal relationships. As researchers studying personal and social relationships, we need to develop more sensitivity to the metaphors we use to illuminate and constrain our thinking about relationships. The combined strength and danger of our scientific metaphors is that although they can light the way for research progress, they can also blind us to other processes. Scientific metaphors are like the gestalt picture of the young lady and the old hag. When you see the young lady, you can't see the old hag. Conversely, focusing on the old hag obscures the young lady from view.

The perspective advanced in this book considers the anomalies in the traditional growth metaphor and brings another distinct relational process into view. As scholars, let us use such metaphors to guide us in advancing knowledge and not allow conventional metaphors to obscure our view. Further, let us remind ourselves not to stop the process of seeking out key pieces to the puzzle of communicating in interpersonal relationships. Today's illumination may well become tomorrow's dogma. We should be forever vigilant in the process of understanding human behavior.

REFERENCES

Fitzpatrick, M. A. (1988). *Between husbands and wives: Communication in marriage.* Newbury Park, CA: Sage.

Fitzpatrick, M. A. (1991). Understanding personal relationships through media portrayals. *Communication Education, 40,* 213–218.

Fitzpatrick, M. A., Fey, J., & Segrin, C. (in press). Attachment in various types of marriages. *Journal of Language and Social Psychology.*

Fitzpatrick, M. A., & Wamboldt, F. (1990). Where is all said and done: Merging intrapersonal and interpersonal models of family communication. *Communication Research, 17,* 421–432.

Greenwood, J. D. (1991). *Relations and representations: An introduction to the philosophy of social psychological science.* London: Routledge.

Noller, P., & Fitzpatrick, M. A. (in press). *Communication in family relationships.* Englewood Cliffs, NJ: Prentice Hall.

Owen, W. F. (1985). Thematic metaphors in relational communication: A conceptual framework. *Western Journal of Speech Communication, 49,* 1–13.

Owen, W. F. (1989). Image metaphors of women and men in personal relationships. *Women's Studies in Communication, 12,* 37–57.

Planalp, S., & Honeycutt, J. (1985). Events that increase uncertainty in personal relationships. *Human Communication Research, 11,* 593–604.

Planalp, S., Rutherford, D. K., & Honeycutt, J. (1988). Events that increase uncertainty in relationships: Replication and extension. *Human Communication Research, 14,* 516–547.

Poole, S., & McPhee, R. (1985). Methodology in interpersonal communication research. In M. Knapp & G. R. Miller (Eds.), *Handbook of interpersonal communication research* (pp. 100–171). Beverly Hills, CA: Sage.

Suppe, F. (1977). *The structure of scientific theories.* Urbana IL: University of Illinois Press.

Author Index

Subject Index